THE INDEPENDENCE OF SPANIS

This book provides a new interpretation of the process of Spanish American independence (1808–1826), one that emphasizes political processes and cultural continuities instead of the break with Spain. It is the first book to examine the representative government and popular elections introduced by the Spanish Constitution of 1812. Rodríguez argues that independence did not constitute an anticolonial movement, as many scholars assert, but rather formed part of the revolution within the Spanish world.

The collapse of the Spanish Monarchy following Napoleon's invasion led to the creation of a parliament, the Cortes, and the Constitution of 1812, which established a representative government for the worldwide Spanish Nation in which all free men, regardless of their race or status, became Spaniards. In America, a struggle over who would govern accompanied the political revolution of the Spanish world.

The Independence of Spanish America is a revised and expanded version of the Spanish-language work *La independencia de la América española* (1996). The English version explains the nature of Hispanic political culture in greater depth than the original Spanish version. It also includes new material, based on additional research in Mexican, Spanish, and Ecuadorian archives, on the popular elections of 1812–1814 and 1820–1822.

Jaime E. Rodríguez O. is Professor of History at the University of California at Irvine. The recipient of Rockefeller, Fulbright, Mellon, and Organization of American States fellowships, and the Hubert Herring prize, Rodríguez is a Corresponding Member of the National Academy of History of Ecuador and of the Centro de Estudios Históricos del Guayas. Previous works include *The Emergence of Spanish America* (1975), *The Forging of the Cosmic Race: A Reinterpretation of Colonial Mexico* (1980–90) with Colin MacLachlan, *Down from Colonialism* (1983), and *El Proceso de la Indepencia de México* (1992). Rodríguez has also edited a dozen volumes, among the most recent, *The Origins of Mexican National Politics, 1808–1847* (1997) and, with Kathryn Vincent, *Myths, Misdeeds, and Misunderstandings: The Roots of Conflict in U.S.–Mexican Relations* (1997).

CAMBRIDGE LATIN AMERICAN STUDIES

84

THE INDEPENDENCE OF SPANISH AMERICA

THE INDEPENDENCE OF
SPANISH AMERICA

JAIME E. RODRÍGUEZ O.

CAMBRIDGE
UNIVERSITY PRESS

PUBLISHED BY THE PRESS SYNDICATE OF THE UNIVERSITY OF CAMBRIDGE

The Pitt Building, Trumpington Street, Cambridge CB2 1RP, United Kingdom

CAMBRIDGE UNIVERSITY PRESS

The Edinburgh Building, Cambridge CB2 2RU, UK   http://www.cup.cam.ac.uk
40 West 20th Street, New York, NY 10011-4211, USA   http://www.cup.org
10 Stamford Road, Oakleigh, Melbourne 3166, Australia

© Fideicomiso Historia de las Américas 1998

Originally published as *La indepencia de la América española,*
© 1996 by Fondo de Cultura Económica

First published 1998

Printed in the United States of America

Typeset in Garamond 3 11/12 pt, in QuarkXPress™ [BB]

Library of Congress Cataloging-in-Publication Data
Rodríguez O., Jaime E., 1940–
[Independencia de la América española. English]
The Independence of Spanish America / Jaime E. Rodríguez O.
p.   cm. – (Cambridge Latin American studies : 84)
Includes bibliographical references and index.
ISBN 0-521-62298-0 (hc). – ISBN 0-521-62673-0 (pbk.)
1. Latin America – History – Wars of Independence, 1806–1830.
2. Spain – Colonies – America – Administration.   I. Title.
II. Series.
F1412.R68213   1998   97-36310
980'.02 – dc21   CIP

A catalog record for this book is available from the British Library.

ISBN 0 521 62298 0 hardback
ISBN 0 521 62673 0 paperback

In Memory of
Luis A. Rodríguez S.

Contents

ix

Preface

Although the Spanish language version of this work, *La independencia de la América española,* was written between 1993 and 1995, in one way or another I have been working on the subject for nearly a quarter of a century. My first book, *The Emergence of Spanish America: Vicente Rocafuerte and Spanish Americanism, 1808–1832* (Berkeley: University of California Press, 1975), examined some aspects of the period. Chapter 1, entitled "The Spanish Heritage," considered the Bourbon reforms and the first constitutional period (1810–14), and chapter 2 dealt with "The Spanish Constitution Restored." In that work, I first advanced the notions that a revolution had occurred within the Spanish world and that Spanish American leaders initially "had favored the creation of a constitutional Hispanic commonwealth. But the subsequent failure of the Spanish Cortes (1810–1814 and 1820–1823) forced" them to seek independence.

Since the time of that work, I have become intrigued by the process of nation building. In particular, I was perplexed by the question of why one former colony, the United States, established a stable government and developed economically, whereas the other former colonies, the Spanish American countries, endured political chaos and economic decline during the nineteenth century. I therefore began two separate studies, one of Ecuador – the former Kingdom of Quito – and the other of Mexico – the former Viceroyalty of New Spain – in an effort to understand how those two very different regions made the transition from kingdoms of the Spanish Monarchy to independent nations.

Other concerns, among them a six-year stint as dean of graduate studies and research at the University of California, Irvine, subsequently intervened. In 1986, upon completing my administrative duties, I returned to work on a volume on the First Federal Republic of Mexico. But conversations with colleagues from Mexico, Canada, and the United States convinced me that I, as well as other scholars, lacked a genuine understanding of the causes, the process, and the consequences of the independence movement. I therefore returned to the archives in Mexico, Ecuador, and Spain to reexamine the period. Also, I decided to engage other colleagues concerned with similar or related inquiries. Between 1987 and 1992 I organized a series of symposia dedicated to various aspects of the question. The first considered *The Independence of Mexico and the Creation of the New Nation* (Los Angeles: UCLA Latin American Center, 1989); the second, *The Revolutionary Process in Mexico* (Los Angeles: UCLA Latin American Center, 1990); the third, *Patterns of Contention in Mexican History* (Wilmington: Scholarly Resources, 1992); the fourth, *The Evolution of the Mexican Political System* (Wilmington: Scholarly Resources, 1993); and the fifth, *Mexico in the Age of the Democratic Revolutions, 1750–1850* (Boulder: Lynne Rienner, 1994). The symposia raised more questions than they answered, but they proved extremely useful in opening new avenues of inquiry.

As a result of my work on the period, Clara Lida, then editor of the journal *Historia Mexicana,* invited me to contribute a historiographical essay on Spanish American independence for a special issue she was preparing on the occasion of the Quincentenary. In the resulting article, entitled "La independencia de la América española," I surveyed the literature, concluding that independence had not constituted an anticolonial movement but was part of a political revolution in the Spanish world and the dissolution of the Spanish Monarchy. The essay merited the praise of a number of colleagues, among them Manuel Miño Grijalva, who recommended to Alicia Hernández Chávez, president of the Fideicomiso Historia de las Américas, that I be invited to write a volume on the subject. Professor Hernández Chávez kindly agreed and proved to be patient and supportive as I worked on the book. I am most grateful to her for granting permission to publish an English language edition.

This work is a revised and expanded version of the earlier volume. I have corrected errors that unfortunately crept into the Spanish language edition. Since it is my contention that Spanish America was not a colony of Spain but an integral part of the Spanish Monarchy, a heterogeneous confederation, in this edition I have taken the opportunity to eliminate words that might suggest colonial status, such as *colony, colonial, empire,* or *imperial,* that appeared in the first. Instead, I have introduced terms such as *Spanish Monarchy, Crown,* and, after the Monarchy collapsed in 1808, *government in Spain* to refer to the various entities that administered the Spanish Monarchy during the period. As a result of questions from colleagues who kindly read the original manuscript, I have provided additional explanations in several parts of the work, among them the reasons why the rural masses supported the Crown and the changing nature of the autonomous juntas in America. Finally, I have incorporated additional research that I conducted in Spain, Mexico, and Ecuador after the Spanish language edition went to press.

The intellectual debts I have incurred in preparing this book are numerous. First, I should like to acknowledge the influence of *mi maestra,* Nettie Lee Benson. Her pioneering research of Spanish and Mexican politics has illuminated my path. My work also has been influenced by Virginia Guedea's studies reinterpreting Mexican politics during the 1808–21 period. In addition, I am grateful to her for encouragement, support, and advice over the years, as well as for having read the manuscript in both its English and Spanish versions with great care, having saved me from errors, and having suggested improvements. Also, I thank William F. Sater, Kathryn Vincent, Colin M. MacLachlan, Hugh M. Hamill, Jr., Paul Vanderwood, Christon I. Archer, Manuel Chust Calero, John Tutino, Peter Guardino, Mark Burkholder, Rebecca Earle, and Alan Knight, who read various versions of the work and offered valuable suggestions for its improvement. My greatest debt is to Linda Alexander Rodríguez, who has encouraged, supported, and advised me for more than three decades, and who read the present work in all its versions and whose suggestions for improvement helped clarify and enrich my analysis of independence. Of course, these generous academics are not responsible for any errors of fact or interpretation that I might have made.

The present volume is part of my effort to understand the process by which the American kingdoms of the Spanish Monarchy transformed themselves into independent nations. During the years that I have worked on this subject, I have been fortunate in receiving financial aid from the Academic Senate Committee on Research of the University of California, Irvine, the University of California Institute for Mexico and the United States (UC MEXUS), the Fulbright Foundation, and the president of the University of California in the form of a President's Humanities Fellowship. I am also grateful to the Rockefeller Foundation for its invitation to reside for five weeks in its Study and Conference Center in Bellagio, Italy, which afforded me the opportunity to read, think, and discuss my ideas about the process of independence with other colleagues.

I am grateful to Leonor Ortiz Monasterio, director of the Archivo General de la Nación de México from 1983 to 1994, and to her staff for many courtesies during those years. I also express my gratitude to the directors and staffs of the Biblioteca Nacional de México, the Centro de Estudios de Historia de México of the Fundación Cultural de Condumex (Mexico, D. F.), the Archivo del Ayuntamiento de Jalapa, the Archivo Histórico del Banco Central del Ecuador (Quito), the Archivo Municipal de Quito, the Archivo Nacional de Historia (Quito), the Archivo del Congreso de Diputados (Madrid), the Archivo Histórico Nacional (Madrid), the Archivo General de Indias (Seville), the Benson Latin American Collection (Austin), the New York Public Library, the Bancroft Library (Berkeley), the UCLA Research Library, and the UCI Library. Finally, I am grateful to Louise Calabro who navigated this volume through the dangers of the production process with great care and skill.

This work is lovingly dedicated to the memory of my father, a distinguished Ecuadorian nationalist, who would not agree with my interpretation but who, as always, would defend my right to make it.

Jaime E. Rodríguez O.

Our kings, far from having considered establishing in our Americas the modern system of colonies of other nations, not only made our [kingdoms] the equals of Spain but also granted us the best [institutions] she possessed. . . . It is evident that under the constitution granted by the kings of Spain to the Americas, these lands are kingdoms independent of her [Spain] without any other link but the king. . . . When I refer to the social pact of the Americans, I do not refer to Rousseau's implicit pact. Rather, it consists of a pact between the Kingdom of New Spain and the sovereign of Castilla. The rupture or suspension of that pact . . . results, as an inevitable consequence, in the reassumption of sovereignty by the Nation. . . . When that occurs, sovereignty reverts to its original owner.

Sevando Teresa de Mier
Madrid, ca. 1800

How different are the Spaniards and the French . . . ! How false, how perfidious, how arrogant, how cruel, how devilish the latter! . . . In contrast, the Spaniards how sincere, how loyal, how human, how kind, how religious, and how brave! I speak principally of the lower and middle classes for among the higher classes there are many who are selfish, ignorant, haughty, and bad citizens.

José Mexía Llequerica
Madrid, May 1808

We are among the first to sacrifice our meager personal and common belongings, our repose and tranquillity, our children and our families . . . in order not to submit to [Napoleon] who only merits the just anger of our Nation. . . . And . . . we are determined to shed the last drop of our blood rather than abandon the defense of God's law and our Catholic monarch [Fernando VII] (May God protect him).

Declaration of Indian Officials
Mexico City, July 1808

Since the French nation has subjugated through conquest nearly all Spain, since José Bonaparte has crowned himself king in Madrid, and, therefore, since the Junta Central, which represented our legitimate sovereign, has been extinguished, the people of this capital – faithful to God, the *patria,* and the

king – have created another [junta] equally supreme and
interim . . . until H. M. recovers the Peninsula or comes to
America to govern.

Marqués de Selva Alegre
Quito, August 1809

Equality! The sacred right of equality. Justice is founded upon
that principle and upon granting every one that which is
his. . . . The true fraternal union between European Spaniards
and Americans . . . can never exist except upon the bases of
justice and equality. America and Spain are two integral and
constituent parts of the Spanish Monarchy. . . . Anyone who
believes otherwise, does not love his *patria*.

Camilo Torres
Santa Fé de Bogotá
November 1809

Q. What is the Spanish Nation?
A. The union of all Spaniards of both hemispheres.
Q. Who are Spaniards?
A. According to the Constitution [of 1812], Spaniards are: (1) all free
   men born and residing in the Spanish dominions and their children;
   (2) foreigners who have obtained naturalization papers from the
   Cortes; (3) those, who without them, legally reside ten years in any
   town of the Monarchy; and (4) freedmen who acquire their freedom
   in the Spains.
Q. What is a constitution?
A. An organized collection of fundamental or political laws of a nation.
Q. Do we possess a constitution?
A. We have such an excellent one that it will make us happy if we
   observe it and contribute to its observance.
Q. Is the Constitution a novelty recently introduced among us?
A. No. Its principal rules had been in use earlier; but since they neither
   constituted a single body of law nor was their application
   guaranteed, those interested in violating the Constitution had caused
   it to fall into disuse. The Cortes have made the Constitution live
   again.
Q. What are the Cortes?
A. The gathering of all the deputies who represent the Nation, freely
   elected by the citizens to make the laws.
Q. What is a king?
A. The person in whose name everything is carried out in a monarchical
   government.

Q. From whom does he receive his authority?

A. From the very Nation he governs.

Q. Is the king not sovereign?

A. The king is a citizen, just like everyone else, who obtains his authority from the Nation.

Q. What are the rights [of Spaniards]?

A. Life, security, property, and equality.

Q. Could these rights be abused or abrogated?

A. Spaniards regained their rights after despotism had usurped them. The heroic efforts they made and are making to maintain their independence are convincing proof that they will not permit anyone to despoil them of their liberty, which is assured by the exact observance of the wise Constitution they have sworn [to uphold].

Q. What are the individual obligations of Spaniards?

A. Every Spaniard must love his *patria,* be just and kind, obey the Constitution, obey the laws, respect the established authorities, contribute, without any distinction, in proportion to his wealth, to the expenses of the state, and defend the *patria* with arms when called upon by the law. That is, there can be no privilege whatsoever with regards either to taxation or to military service.

Catecismo político
[Primary school text]
Cádiz, 1813

In 1810 we did what we had to. We only aspired to remain free of foreign domination and not to follow Spain's misfortune if she were lost. . . . No one knew what would be the result of Spain's struggle for her liberty, or if King Fernando would return or not to the throne of Spain. At that time we still looked to that king with expectation and hoped that some day he would end our ills. . . . But suddenly these expectations were destroyed. In Spain, [upon his return in 1814, the king] punished those who had obeyed the Cortes, and he waged a bloody war against the natives of America who, not recognizing [those Cortes] as legitimate, just as that king did, had disobeyed them. Thus, . . . we began to detest so unjust a king who without a hearing sought to destroy men, more faithful than many of those who surround him [at court].

El Censor
Buenos Aires 1816

It was for their king and lord that they were going to die, and
not as rebels nor for the *patria;* they did not know what this
patria was, nor who it was, nor what form the *patria* had; no
one knew if the *patria* was a man or a woman; as for the king,
he was well known, his government well established, his laws
respected and faithfully observed.

> Declaration of royalist Indians in Upper Peru
> prior to execution by pro-independence forces
> December 31, 1816

[Men of goodwill should be] seeking the happy pacification
of America. Animated by the spirit of the great Spanish
family and electrified by the effects of the Sacred Constitution,
we will form institutions which have as their foundation
the understanding of our reciprocal interests, fortified by the
powerful ties of a common tongue and a common
religion.

> Vicente Rocafuerte
> Havana, 1820

Madrid and the entire Peninsula constitute a glorious
spectacle. It is an entirely free theater where the most
important questions of practical politics relative to the future
of Spain's America are treated.

> José Miguel Ramos
> Arizpe
> Madrid, 1821

I love the Spanish nation like my grandmother and America
like my mother. I weep to see these beloved persons destroyed.

> Manuel Lorenzo de
> Vidaurre
> Philadelphia, 1823

Introduction

The independence of Spanish America can best be understood as part of the larger process of change that occurred in the Atlantic world in the second half of the eighteenth and the early nineteenth centuries. This period has been called the *Age of Democratic Revolutions* because during that time some monarchical societies were transformed into democratic ones. That is, subjects of monarchies became citizens of nation-states. Although scholars have studied that process for the United States and France, the Spanish world has not been examined from that perspective. Most historians end the period of democratic revolutions in 1799, when Napoleon Bonaparte seized control of France.[1] The political revolutions of the Spanish world, or *Spanish Monarchy*, as it was called, however, occurred after 1808. Moreover, the independence of Spanish America did not constitute an anticolonial movement, as many assert, but formed part of both the *revolution* within the Spanish world and the *dissolution* of the Spanish Monarchy. Indeed, Spain was one of the new nations that emerged from the breakup of that worldwide polity.

The American continent underwent significant transformations in the wake of the Seven Years' War (1756–1763) when both the Spanish and British crowns reordered their possessions in America, a process known in the Spanish world as the *Bourbon reforms*. Although both Spanish and Anglo Americans objected to many of these changes, the Spanish kingdoms in the New World did not imitate their northern brethren in rebelling against the Crown. On the contrary, the Spanish Monarchy was sufficiently certain of its American subjects that it fought Great Britain during the Anglo American struggle and signed the Treaty of Paris of 1783, which granted independence to the United States. Although the Spanish Americans opposed certain aspects of the Bourbon reforms, sometimes violently, they did not

---

1 See, for example, the classic works of Jacques Godechot, *La Grande Nation: L'expansion révolutionnaire de la France dans le monde de 1789 à 1799*, 2 vols. (Paris: Aubier, 1956); and Robert R. Palmer, *The Age of Democratic Revolutions: Political History of Europe and America, 1760–1800*, 2 vols. (Princeton: Princeton University Press, 1959–1964).

seek separation from the Spanish Crown. Only when the Spanish Monarchy collapsed in 1808, as a result of the French invasion of the Iberian Peninsula – thirty-two years after the Anglo Americans rebelled – did the Spanish Americans insist upon home rule.

The disintegration of the Spanish Monarchy in 1808 triggered a series of events that culminated in the establishment of representative government in the Spanish world. The initial step in that process was the formation in Spain and America of local governing *juntas* (committees) that invoked the *Hispanic* legal principle that in the absence of the king, sovereignty reverted to the people. Ultimately, this process resulted in the creation of a parliament, the Cortes, and the Constitution of 1812, which established a representative government for a worldwide *Spanish Nation* in which all free men, regardless of their race or status, became Spaniards.

In America, a struggle over who should govern accompanied the political revolution of the Spanish world. The first phase of that conflict pitted European Spaniards, formerly a privileged group, against the American Spaniards (*criollos*), the New World bourgeoisie. There were divisions within as well as between these groups: Some European Spaniards supported the new order, whereas many criollos favored the old regime. The upper- and middle-class struggle for power provided an opportunity for politically discontented popular rural and urban groups to press their demands. Regional strife further complicated the political conflict within the American kingdoms. These tensions precipitated violence, civil war, and terror, offering military leaders opportunities for power, wealth, and status. Despite the significant participation of the rural and urban masses in the conflict, the American struggle for independence was fundamentally a political process that resulted in the triumph of the criollos, the New World bourgeoisie.

American efforts to obtain home rule within the Spanish Monarchy form a critical aspect of the process of independence. The New World discourse was based on the belief that the American realms were not colonies but equal and integral parts of the Spanish Crown. Law, theory, and practice all confirmed the Americans' belief that their kingdoms were coequal with the Iberian Peninsula. It was a principle the leaders of the New World insisted upon during the period following the 1808 crisis of the Spanish Monarchy. Indeed, the majority of these leaders demanded *equality* rather than *independence:* They sought *home rule,* not *separation* from the Spanish Crown. This distinction is crucial because when the documents of the epoch use the word *independence,* they generally mean *autonomy.* Only when the government in Spain refused to grant their demand for *autonomy* did most Americans opt for *emancipation.*

Perhaps the biggest obstacle to understanding the process of independence is the belief in its inevitability. The assumption that what occurred had to happen permeates virtually every work on independence. Yet, at the time, many prominent American political leaders frequently discussed the possibility of establishing a system of federated monarchies along the lines of the early British commonwealth. Royal officials began to discuss proposals for some form of New World autonomy in 1781, and American deputies to the Spanish Cortes proposed it as a solution to the conflict as late as 1821.

The political process that resulted in Spanish American independence, part of the larger political revolution in the Spanish world, began in the latter part of the eighteenth century when the urban upper and middle classes of Spain and America sought to form a modern polity. Although the political transformation of the worldwide Spanish Monarchy also constituted part of the larger process of political change in the Atlantic world, the Hispanic movement was unique in its scope. The development of modern political thought in the Spanish world occurred throughout the vast Monarchy.

The generation of Spaniards and Americans who directed the political revolution after 1808 had been educated in the reformed institutions of the Spanish Monarchy. Although influenced by the new ideas of the Enlightenment, their views were grounded on Hispanic thought, which included the important concepts of popular sovereignty and representative government. Spain and Spanish America, a major segment of Occidental civilization, drew upon a shared Western European culture that originated in the ancient classical world. The independence of the United States and the French Revolution provided exciting examples of political change, but they did not present models radically different from those already common within Hispanic culture. The political revolution in the Spanish world, therefore, evolved within the boundaries of an idealized political legitimacy and developed a unique political culture and institutions that derived not from alien models but from the traditions and the experience of the Spanish world itself.

This work concentrates on politics and political processes. It seeks to understand Spanish American independence within the context of the broader political revolution for representative government within the Spanish world. Although it focuses on what is called *high politics,* it does not assume that *low politics* did not exist. The urban and rural lower classes possessed their own interests and concerns. Some of these, primarily those of the rural groups, have been studied. But scholars generally assume that the *campesinos* (peasants), as well as the urban poor, either did not know, understand, or care about the pressing political issues of the day. That is incorrect. Urban and rural popular groups not only knew and understood the advantages and disadvantages of what has been called the *social compact* of the Monarchy but were also keenly aware of the political revolution carried out by the Spanish Cortes. The evidence indicates that poor people, whether urban or rural, were not only affected by high politics but also understood their interests and took action to defend them; that is, they engaged in politics.[2]

Some participated in autonomist and insurgent movements. Others took advantage of the upheavals to pursue their own concerns. Many others joined members of the urban upper and middle classes who remained loyal to the Crown. Indian communities from the highlands of southern Peru and Upper Peru, the region that experienced the great Túpac Amaru Revolt in 1780, for example, remained the Monarchy's most devoted adherents.[3] Their staunch defense of the Spanish Crown continued until

2 On the nature of mass political participation in Mexico, see Virginia Guedea, "El pueblo de México y la política capitalina, 1808 y 1812," *Mexican Studies/Estudios Mexicanos* [hereafter cited as *MS/EM*], 10:1 (Winter 1994), 27–61; my "The Constitution of 1824 and the Formation of the Mexican State" in *The Evolution of the Mexican Political System*, ed. Jaime E. Rodríguez O. (Wilmington: Scholarly Resources, 1993), 79–82; Peter Guardino, *Peasants, Politics, and the Formation of Mexico's National State: Guerrero, 1800–1857* (Stanford: Stanford University Press, 1996); Richard A. Warren, "Vagrants and Citizens: Politics and the Poor in Mexico City, 1808–1836" (Ph.D. diss., University of Chicago, 1994). As Terry Rugeley notes: "peasant communities were receiving regular news regarding the decisions of the Cortes." *Yucatán's Maya Peasantry & the Origins of the Caste War* (Austin: University of Texas Press, 1996), 39.

3 José Santos Vargas, a commander of one of the pro-independence groups in Upper Peru, described an encounter with pro-royalist Indians is his diary as follows: "[Our men] surprised the royalist Indians about 2 or 3 in the morning . . .; they tied up the 11, that was all there was, none escaped; they took them to the bluff of Calayasa where they were all killed with cudgels, stones, and lances. Some, with great heroism, declared that their death mattered little. Others said that it was for their king and lord that they were going to die, and not as rebels nor for the *patria;* they did not know what this *patria* was, nor who it was, nor what form the *patria* had; no one knew if the *patria* was a man or a woman; as for the king, he was well known, his government well established, his laws respected and faithfully observed. That is how the 11 died." *Diario de un comandante de la independencia americana, 1814–1825,* ed. Gunnar Mendoza I. (Mexico: Siglo XXI, 1982), 118.

For some scholars, such a quote confirms their belief that the Indians, or the *campesinos,* did not understand the political, economic, or social implications of the struggle for independence. Jean Piel, for example, has argued that "At Junín and Ayacucho, the Peruvian soldiers on the two sides, that of the Crown and that of Independence, killed each other without a thought. To the majority the idea of an independent Peru meant nothing." Jean Piel, "The Place of the Peasantry in the National Life of Peru in the Nineteenth Century," *Past and Present*, 46 (February 1970), 116. Although Piel argues that the independence leaders did not offer the Indians socioeconomic reasons to support them to explain why the *campesinos* would "kill each other without a thought," he nonetheless considers the natives merely "cannon fodder." Such views, however, demonstrate only the lack of understanding expressed by their authors. They appear unable to ask the question of why anyone, however untutored, would be willing to die for no reason.

In discussing why some *campesinos* in Peru rebelled in the name of King Fernando VII in 1825–1828, *after* royalist forces had been defeated, Cecilia Méndez offers another, more realistic explanation: "If the Indians of Iquicha rose against Bolívar's republic, it was not because they had been 'deceived' nor because they wished to perpetuate . . . the colonial system. On the contrary. They rebelled to defend the rights and *status* which, *as Indians,* they had received from the colonial system and which the Creole republic threatened to eliminate" [emphasis in the original]. Cecilia

independence finally was achieved in 1826, eighteen years after the crisis unleashed by the collapse of the Monarchy in 1808.

This book consists of two parts. The first examines the interplay of relations between Spain and America. Chapter 1 focuses on the late-eighteenth-century cultural, institutional, and political transformations that set the stage for revolutionary changes after 1808. Chapter 2 considers the impact of the new intellectual and cultural attitudes of the eighteenth century, as well as the political crisis caused by the French invasion of the Peninsula and the destruction of the Spanish Monarchy. It also analyzes the similar responses of Spain and America to the crisis and the search for an alternative regime. Chapter 3 concentrates on the formation of a representative government, the Cortes, and its profound impact upon the Spanish world.

The second half of the book emphasizes primarily the American response to the collapse of the Spanish Crown. Chapter 4 examines the disparate reactions of those regions of the New World that did not accept the parliamentary solution to the crisis of the Monarchy. Geographic, economic, and social differences affected those responses. The chapter also demonstrates that the experiences of the American autonomist regions, although different from those of Spain and large sectors of the New World, were nevertheless influenced by the Hispanic experiment in representative government. Chapter 5 considers the failure of both Fernando VII, after his return in 1814, and the reestablished Cortes, after 1820, to restore unity in the Spanish world, as well as the vastly different experiences of *América Septentrional* (North America) and *América Meridional* (South America) in the final process of emancipation.

Although America ultimately severed its ties with the Spanish Monarchy, the leaders of the new countries remained ambivalent about their recently achieved freedom. Independence produced new and difficult challenges. The once powerful worldwide Spanish Monarchy shattered into many weak nations; the war against the French in the Peninsula and the wars of independence in America destroyed local economies and divided society. The reconsolidation of the state and the restructuring of the economy would constitute long and difficult processes both in America and in Spain.

Méndez, "Los campesinos, la independencia y la iniciación de la República. El caso de los iquichanos realistas: Ayacucho 1825–1828," in, *Poder y violencia en los Andes,* ed. Henrique Urbano (Cusco: Centro de Estudios Regionales Andinos Bartolomé de Las Casas, 1991), 184. See also her "Rebellion without Resistance: Huanta's Monarchist Peasants in the Making of the Peruvian State, Ayacucho 1825–1850" (Ph.D. diss., State University of New York at Stony Brook, 1996).

The available evidence indicates that the urban and rural masses did not serve merely as cannon fodder for their elite leaders. Clearly, they acted for their own very good reasons, some of which happened to coincide with those of the elites.

Two opposing political traditions emerged between 1808 and 1826 during the struggle for independence. One, forged in the crucible of war, emphasized executive power, and the other, based on civilian parliamentary experience, insisted upon legislative dominance. Proponents of the two traditions struggled to control the new American nations. Although military strongmen – *caudillos,* not a modern institutional military – frequently came to dominate their countries, they could not eliminate the liberal tradition of constitutional, representative government that had emerged in the Cortes of Cádiz. That tradition, together with the achievement of nationhood, remains the most significant heritage of Spanish American independence.

1

Spanish America

At the end of the eighteenth century, the Spanish Monarchy's possessions in America constituted one of the world's most imposing political structures. Its territory, which included most of the Western Hemisphere, stretched along the entire Pacific coast from Cape Horn in the south to Alaska in the north. On the east coast, it shared South America with Brazil and the Guianas, Central America with British Honduras, and North America with the United States and Canada, both of which were limited to strips of land along the Atlantic. In the Caribbean, the Spanish Crown possessed the principal islands. The Spanish Indies – generally called *America* in the eighteenth century – also included the Philippines and other islands in the Pacific.

Spanish America originally consisted of two viceroyalties, New Spain and Peru; the Crown further subdivided South America when it established the viceroyalties of New Granada and the Río de la Plata in 1739 and 1776. But the most enduring territorial units were those areas administered by the *audiencias* (high courts), often referred to as *reinos* (kingdoms). With the exception of the *audiencias* of New Spain, these were the areas that became the new nations of Spanish America. New Spain possessed two *audiencias*, Mexico and Guadalajara. The Philippines, a dependency of New Spain, enjoyed its own *audiencia*, Manila. The other *audiencias* of Spanish America consisted of Guatemala (Central America), Santa Fé de Bogotá (New Granada), Caracas (Venezuela), Quito, Charcas (Alto Peru), Lima (Peru), Santiago (Chile), Buenos Aires (Río de la Plata), and Santo Domingo (the Caribbean). Although Cuzco obtained an *audiencia* in 1787, that high court had not existed long enough when independence was achieved to consolidate the region's separate identity. The area subsequently formed part of the Republic of Peru.

In 1800 Spanish America had a population of approximately 13.6 million people, nearly half of them residing in New Spain. Although the population of Spanish America was multiracial, class rather than ethnicity became important in the most developed areas toward the end of the eighteenth century.

7

Population of Spanish America ca. 1800

New Spain	5,900,000
Philippines	1,000,000
Guatemala (Central America)	1,100,000
Caribbean islands	550,000
New Granada	1,000,000
Venezuela	500,000
Quito	700,000
Charcas	650,000
Peru	1,200,000
Chile	500,000
Río de la Plata	500,000
Total	13,600,000

Spanish America was a diverse and complex region. Not only were some areas, like the Viceroyalty of New Spain, more populated, developed, and prosperous than other realms, but even within kingdoms, some regions were more advanced than others.

The Spanish Crown's possessions in America may be divided for purposes of analysis into four general areas. First were the core areas of central New Spain, Guatemala, New Granada, Quito, Peru, and Upper Peru, which possessed complex economies, including commercial agriculture, manufacturing [i.e., textile *obrajes* (workshops) and other artisanal production], and some important mining regions. Second were the mainly agricultural and pastoral areas that supplied the more developed core regions, including portions of New Galicia and some parts of Central America, Chile, and the Río de la Plata. Third were the tropical areas, primarily Cuba, Puerto Rico, Venezuela, parts of coastal New Granada, Guayaquil, and some coastal regions of Peru, which were characterized by plantation agriculture, generally oriented to an export market either in Europe or in Spanish America. (Guayaquil and Venezuela, for example, found their principal market for cacao in New Spain.) New Spain also possessed important tropical regions, Veracruz and the *tierra caliente* (hot lands) on the Pacific. But these locations were integrated into the larger economy of the viceroyalty. The Philippines, although also a tropical region dependent upon New Spain, possessed a special place in that kingdom's economy because it served as an entrepôt of trade with Asia. Finally, there were the frontier regions, the Provincias Internas (interior provinces) of northern New Spain, the southern portions of Chile and the Río de la Plata, the Banda Oriental (eastern bank of the Uruguay River), and Paraguay, which served as buffers

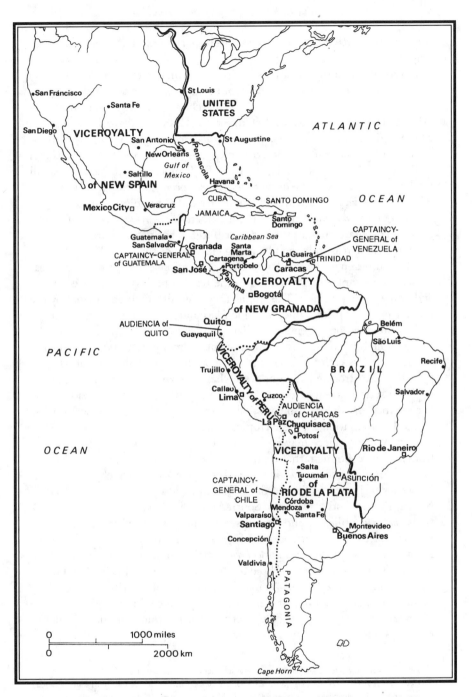

Map 1. Spanish America, c. 1800. (From *Cambridge History of Latin America,* Vol. III,
Cambridge: Cambridge University Press, 1985, p. 6. Reprinted with permission.)

between the settled areas and nomadic Indians as well as other European empires.

Regional economic variations in Spanish America fostered social diversity. The core areas included significant urban groups – a varied elite of government officials, clergy, professionals, merchants, landowners, miners, and other entrepreneurs – as well as diverse artisanal and working sectors. Those regions also possessed a complex *campesinado* (peasantry) – predominantly Indian but also composed of mestizos (a mixture of Europeans and Indians), criollos, blacks, and *castas* (people of color) – which included small landowners, renters, resident workers, day laborers, and corporate villagers. Although Indians constituted the majority of the population in core areas, many were not *juridical* Indians, the members of the *repúblicas de indios* who lived in corporate villages subject to tribute. In the urban centers, the population was increasingly defined along class rather than racial lines.

Although generally similar to the core regions, the agricultural areas possessed a simpler social structure, the result of a less complex economy and a smaller population. The tropical regions, although dominated by the plantation labor force, which included large groups of blacks and *castas,* as well as smaller contingents of Indians, mestizos, and criollos, contained a comparable but smaller urban component. In many respects, tropical rural society was less differentiated than its counterpart in the core areas. The peripheral, or frontier, regions were characterized by a sharp distinction between settled groups, mostly mestizo, and the generally nomadic "barbarous Indians." They also contained a much smaller population and less social differentiation than the tropical areas.

New World society may be best understood if we analyze its structure from a socioeconomic rather than a caste perspective. The traditional static view of American society as one of estates and races, a hierarchy in descending order of European Spaniards (*peninsulares,* also known as *gachupines* in North America and *chapetones* in South America), American Spaniards, mestizos, *mulatos,* blacks, and Indians, or some variation thereof, fails to account for the dramatic social changes resulting from economic development. Rather than the *feudal* and *premodern* hierarchical structure espoused by some scholars, the late eighteenth century was, as Felipe Castro Gutiérrez has noted, an epoch of "transition from the older society ordered by socioracial estates to a new society of classes, where ethnic origin would be of little importance."[1] Thus, a modern socioeconomic structure, similar to that of Western Europe, was emerging.

1 Felipe Castro Gutiérrez, "Orígenes sociales de la rebelión de San Luis Potosí, 1767," in *Patterns of Contention in Mexican History,* ed. Jaime E. Rodríguez O. (Wilmington: Scholarly Resources, 1992), 47. Others who advance similar views include José Luis Mirafuentes Galván, "Identidad india, legitimidad y emancipación política en el noroeste de México (Copala, 1771)," and Virginia Guedea, "De la fidelidad a la infidencia: Los gobernadores de la parcialidad de San Juan," in *Patterns of Con-*

As I recently argued when comparing the French Revolution and Mexican independence, the Kingdom of France and the Viceroyalty of New Spain possessed similar social structures on the eve of the Revolution and independence. With certain reservations, a similar comparison can be made with the rest of Spanish America:

> The European Spaniards in New Spain may be compared to the French aristocracy since both represented a special privileged group. Although they included a few immensely wealthy families, the majority were moderate and, sometimes, even poor individuals. . . . The criollos of colonial Mexico were comparable to the French bourgeoisie. The upper echelons resembled the rich aristocrats in wealth, power, and influence. And like the nobility, they engaged in a variety of lucrative enterprises. . . . [Many], however, consisted of urban professionals, particularly lawyers, many of whom worked for the state. [Some criollos, of course, were poor.] The French bourgeoisie and the criollos of New Spain shared a sense of nationalism – they considered themselves less subjects of the Crown and more Frenchmen and Americans –, and believed that they represented the true interests of the nation.[2]

Like the aristocracy and the bourgeoisie in France, the European Spaniards and the criollos in America possessed interests that both united and divided them. Members of both groups were usually found in the same families and tended to act in unison where family interests were concerned. Class also often united them. Upper-class *peninsulares* and Americans usually were linked by their wealth as well as by marriage. Likewise, middling and poor Spaniards and criollos belonged to their respective classes. In that regard, socioeconomic factors rather than place of origin determined their position in society. But most *peninsulares* were united in their belief that they were both racially and culturally superior to New World natives, and even the poorest and least educated European Spaniard expected favored treatment from royal officials.[3] Differences, particularly among upper- and middle-class *peninsulares* and Americans became intense when competing for business opportunities, civil and clerical appointments, and honors. But perhaps the greatest hostility erupted between lower-class Spaniards, who often engaged in petty trades, and the urban and rural poor, who considered them their exploiters.[4] Thus, despite the emerging society

---

tention, Rodríguez O., ed., 49–67, 95–123; Dennis N. Valdés, "The Decline of the Sociedad de Castas in Mexico City" (Ph.D. diss., University of Michigan, Ann Arbor, 1978).

2 Jaime E. Rodríguez O., "Two Revolutions: France 1789 and Mexico 1810," *The Americas* 47:2 (October 1990), 164–5.

3 As Alexander von Humboldt observed: "The lowest, least educated and uncultivated European believes himself superior to the white born in the New World." *Political Essay on the Kingdom of New Spain,* 4 vols. (London: Longman, Hurst, Rees, and Brown, 1811), 1:205. See also Cheryl English Martin, *Governance and Society in Colonial Mexico: Chihuahua in the Eighteenth Century* (Stanford: Stanford University Press, 1996), 129–39, for an interesting account of the role of Spaniards in a frontier region of New Spain in the late eighteenth century.

4 On this point see Peter Guardino, "Identity and Nationalism in Mexico: Guerrero, 1780–1840," *Journal of Historical Sociology* 7:3 (September 1994), 314–42.

of classes, place of birth remained significant in late-eighteenth- and early-nineteenth-century America.

The cities and towns of France and New Spain contained similar social groups. Artisans and workers of various sorts constituted a prosperous urban class. But late eighteenth-century France and New Spain were characterized by a large and growing urban lumpen proletariat which existed at the margins of society. . . . Rural society was also similar. Absentee landlords, many of whom resided near the seat of government or in the major provincial cities, generally owned the great estates. A small, but important, group of owners of middle sized lands, *rancheros* in New Spain and wealthy peasants in France, operated as "linking agents" in the countryside. Tenants and sharecroppers also constituted the middling group of rural society. Although the corporate Indian villages of colonial Mexico [the *repúblicas de indios*] represented a large and unique group with its own interests, they may be compared, albeit with qualifications, to the peasant villages of France. [It is worth noting that, as I have indicated on various occasions, I find little difference between late-eighteenth- and early-nineteenth-century American Indians and Spanish campesinos. Both groups led a relatively primitive rural life, ordinarily were members of "corporate" villages, often practiced syncretic forms of Christianity, and frequently did not speak Castilian. The principal difference, it appears, tended to be skin color.] Finally, the two countries possessed a large and growing landless, or almost landless, rural proletariat who had become increasingly marginalized.[5]

The comparison I made between the clergy of France and that of New Spain also seems appropriate to the rest of America:

As a group, the clergy in France and New Spain shared many characteristics. The hierarchy, particularly the episcopate, consisted mainly of nobles in France and Spaniards in Mexico, while in both countries the majority of priests, the *curas,* were relatively poor and from other social groups. The interests of the higher clergy not only differed from those of the lower, but closely resembled that of the French nobility and its colonial Mexican counterpart.[6]

The Spanish Monarchy in America had proven to be flexible and able to accommodate social tensions and conflicting interests for nearly 300 years. In many respects, such discord may be considered a normal aspect of life that was continually changing as the contending groups achieved accommodation. Although at the end of the eighteenth century there was evidence of discontent among some groups, it would have been difficult to predict in 1800 that a great cataclysmic upheaval was about to occur. Indeed, so astute an observer as the Prussian scientist Alexander von Humboldt, who traveled throughout northern South America and New Spain for several years, noted the discontent and opined that it would not lead to

5 Rodríguez O., "Two Revolutions: France 1789 and Mexico 1810," 164–5.
6 Ibid., 164.

a break with the mother country. He stated: "The Creoles prefer to be called Americans. Since the Peace of Versailles, and in particular since the year 1789, they are frequently heard to declare with pride, 'I am not a Spaniard, I am an American,' words which reveal the symptoms of a long resentment."[7] But he also noted: "They would no doubt prefer a national government and complete liberty to commerce . . . , but this desire does not sufficiently . . . impel them to long and painful sacrifices."[8] Von Humbolt's observations highlight two contradictory tendencies that emerged during the second half of the eighteenth century: the American assertion of a *conciencia de sí* (sense of identity) and the drive of the Bourbon kings to transform America into a profitable colony.

The Rise of an American Identity

Some residents of the New World developed a sense of their unique identity within the Spanish Monarchy. Like their counterparts in the Peninsula, these Spanish Americans identified with their locality and its history. A number of educated criollos and mestizos claimed a form of cultural *mestizaje* (miscegenation). They not only wrote about the conquest and the spread of Christianity, but they also embraced the Indian past. One of the first to do so was Garcilazo de la Vega, son of a *conquistador* and an Inca princess. He challenged the school of imperial historians in his *Comentarios reales de los Incas* (1609), which argued that the South American Indians had achieved high culture and possessed a government that followed the dictates of natural law. In New Spain another mestizo, Fernando de Alva Ixtlilxóchitl, descendant of the *conquistadores* and the royalty of Texcoco, wrote a series of works exalting the natives of central Mexico, particularly Texcoco and its great philosopher, King Nezahualcoyotl. As Alva Ixtlilxóchitl explained in his dedication: "From my adolescence, I always had a great desire to learn about the things which occurred in the New World, which were of no less importance than those of the Romans, Greeks, Medes and other gentiles who enjoy fame in the universe."[9]

In a few instances, Spaniards also contributed to the developing sense of an American consciousness. Fray Juan de Torquemada, a Spaniard who had been taken to Mexico City as a child, published in 1615 his massive *Monarquía indiana,* a multivolume work that chronicled the rise of the *Mexica* (the

---

7 Humboldt, *Political Essay on the Kingdom of New Spain,* I, 205.

8 Alexander von Humboldt, *Personal Narrative of Travels to the Equinoctial Regions of the New Continent during the Years 1799–1804,* 4 vols., 3d ed. (London: Longman, Hurst, Rees, and Brown, 1822), 3:329.

9 Fernando de Alva Ixtlilxóchitl, *Obras históricas,* 2 vols., ed. Edmundo O'Gorman (Mexico: Universidad Nacional Autónoma de México [hereafter cited as UNAM], 1975–7), 1:525.

people now called Aztecs).[10] In the years and decades that followed, many American scholars wrote treatises about their *patrias* (local areas) that helped to form the history of their regions.[11]

Novohispanos (the people of New Spain) created a unique religious interpretation of their history. Beginning with Alva Ixtlilxóchitl, scholars of the northern viceroyalty identified the pre-Hispanic Indian culture hero Quetzalcoatl with the apostle St. Thomas. That approach culminated in the late eighteenth century with Fray Servando Teresa de Mier's assertion that St. Thomas-Quetzalcoatl had converted the natives to the True Faith, that the ancient Mexicans had been Christians, that the Europeans had not introduced Christianity to America, and that therefore the Spanish Crown possessed neither a legal nor a moral right to the New World.[12]

The most powerful symbol of American Christianity was the Virgin of Guadalupe, who, it was alleged, appeared to an Indian, Juan Diego, at Tepeyac near Mexico City in 1531. The first account of the apparition of the Virgin of Guadalupe was published in 1648. Although *novohispanos* became particularly possessive of Nuestra Señora de Guadalupe, by the middle of the eighteenth century she had become the patron of America. Criollos, Indians, mestizos, and *castas* were united in their devotion to the Virgin of Guadalupe.[13] Ultimately, the pope recognized her as the queen and patron of America.

It was the Enlightenment, however, that engendered a determined American *conciencia de sí*. A number of European scholars, *philosophes* who embodied the Enlightenment, asserted that the New World and its inhabitants were inherently inferior to the Old. The anti-American prejudices of Enlightened authors in the Old World undermined the authority of European thought, causing some New World intellectuals to reexamine the assumptions of Old World supremacy that they had taken for granted. The

10 Juan de Torquemada, *Monarquía indiana,* 7 vols., ed. Miguel León-Portilla (Mexico: UNAM, 1975–83). Torquemada's text is found in the first six volumes; the seventh consists of critical analyses of the work.

11 See, for example, David Brading, *The First America: The Spanish Monarchy, Creole Patriots, and the Liberal State, 1492–1867* (Cambridge: Cambridge University Press, 1991), 255–92; and Enrique Florescano, *Memoria mexicana. Ensayo sobre la reconstrucción del pasado: Epoca prehispanica–1821* (Mexico: Joaquín Mortiz, 1987), 143–246.

12 Servando Teresa de Mier, "Carta de despedida a los mexicanos," in *Obras completas de Servando Teresa de Mier,* vol. 4, *La formación de un republicano,* ed. Jaime E. Rodríguez O. (México: UNAM, 1988), 107–14.

13 Perhaps the best works from a vast literature on the Virgin of Guadalupe are Edmundo O'Gorman, *Destierro de Sombras. Luz en el origen de la imagen y culto de Nuestra Señora de Guadalupe del Tepeyac* (México: UNAM, 1986); Richard Nebel, *Santa María Tonantzin, Virgen de Guadalupe: Continuidad y transformación religiosa en México* (Mexico: Fondo de Cultura Económica, 1995); and Stafford Poole, *Our Lady of Guadalupe: The Origins and Sources of a Mexican National Symbol, 1531–1797* (Tucson: University of Arizona Press; 1995).

French savant George-Louis Leclerc Buffon argued in his *Histoire natural* (1747) that America was a new land full of lakes, rivers, and swamps, colder and damper than Europe. As a result, its animals were smaller and less numerous than those in the Old World. The humans of that continent, like its plants and animals, were degenerate. The men were small, weak, and hairless; they lacked sexual passion; and they possessed little intelligence or spirit. Moreover, European men, animals, and plants degenerated in America.

Buffon's arguments were expanded in Corneille de Pauw's *Recherches philosophiques sur les Américains* (1768). De Pauw carried the notion of degeneracy to absurdity when he maintained that New World dogs could not bark and that the inhabitants of the American continent were impotent and cowardly. The Abbé Guillaume-Thomas Raynal's *Histoire philosophique et politique des établissements et du commerce des Européens dans les deux Indes,* which appeared in over fifty editions between 1770 and the end of the century, each more radical than its predecessor, expanded on the degeneracy of America and Americans. Raynal's *Histoire,* composed by perhaps a dozen philosophes, including such prominent individuals as Denis Diderot, was a distillation of Enlightenment thought on the topic. "The men there," the *Histoire* asserted, "are less strong, less courageous, without beard or hair: degenerate in all signs of manhood. . . . The indifference of the males toward that other sex to which Nature has entrusted the place of reproduction suggests an organic imperfection, a sort of infancy of the people of America similar to that of the individuals in our continent who have not reached the age of puberty."

The most successful and popular account of the New World was William Robertson's *History of America,* which appeared in 1777 and was rapidly translated into a number of languages. The Scottish historian's work was widely accepted in Europe because it contained an extensive scholarly apparatus and because it supported the "philosophic" notions of American degeneracy. Since it also praised the regime of Carlos III, Robertson's work was well received in the Peninsula. The Spanish Royal Academy of History elected him to its ranks and sponsored the translation of his history into Castilian. Although less hostile to the New World than other Enlightened European authors, Robertson also noted the degenerative affects of that continent. "Nature was not only less prolific in the New World, but she appears likewise to have been less vigorous in her productions. The animals originally belonging to this quarter of the globe appear to be of an inferior race, neither so robust, nor so fierce, as those of the other continent." Sadly, in his view, nature in America proved no less damaging to humans and their society.

These attacks on the New World did not go unchallenged. Although many Spaniards eagerly accepted the condemnation of their American brethren, some defended them. The clearest voice belonged to Fray Benito Jerónimo Feijóo, who not only praised the Americans but also argued that some of their achievements surpassed those of the Europeans.[14]

Novohispanos quickly rose in defense of their *patria* and their culture. In response to the renowned *savio* Manuel Martí, dean of Alicante, who advised a friend not to visit America because it was an "intellectual desert" without books and libraries, a land fit only for Indians, not for "civilized" people, Juan José de Eguiara y Eguren, rector of the University of Mexico and canon of the cathedral, responded with the vast *Bibliotheca mexicana* (1755), a work that demonstrated the extensive scholarly achievements of his countrymen. In Berlin, Juan Vicente de Güemes Pacheco y Padilla, the criollo son of the former viceroy of New Spain, the first count of Revillagigedo, and later a viceroy himself, publicly defended America from De Pauw's attacks. The younger Revillagigedo declared De Pauw mistaken in nearly all cases. He pronounced the men of the New World "extremely inclined to engage in sex" and not at all effeminate. Similarly, he argued that the fruits and animals of America were superior to those of Europe.[15]

Exiled American Jesuits, however, were the most vehement defenders of the New World. Far from home, in a hostile Europe, they wrote histories of their *patrias*. The Jesuits contributed substantially to the growth of New World patriotism because their works, while defending America as a whole, concentrated on their individual lands, such as New Spain, Quito, or Chile.

The *novohispano* Francisco Javier Clavijero published the four-volume *Storia antica del Messico* (1780–1), the most erudite expression of American patriotism, as well as a direct refutation of De Pauw and other European critics of the New World. Clavijero declared his intention in writing the work: "To serve my *patria* in the best possible manner, [and] to restore to its splendor the truth so obfuscated by an incredible mob of modern writers." An enlightened scholar, Clavijero presented a coherent and *modern* account of the history of the ancient Mexicans, comparing them with the classical world. "Texcoco was, so to say, the Athens of Anáhuac and Nezahualcóyotl the Solon of those peoples." In the process of likening the Mexica to the ancient Romans, Clavijero demonstrated that they were not an inferior people; that their culture, although not Christian, was not the work of the devil, as some earlier Spanish chroniclers had maintained; and that eighteenth-century *novohispanos* were the heirs of the ancient Mexicans. The fourth volume of *Storia antica* consisted of nine dissertations on the land,

---

14 The classic work on the conflict between the Old World and the New is Antonello Gerbi, *The Dispute of the New World: The History of a Polemic, 1750–1900,* revised and enlarged ed. (Pittsburgh: University of Pittsburgh Press, 1973).

15 Ibid., 194–5.

plants, animals, and inhabitants of New Spain; the work carefully, criti-
cally, and systematically refuted De Pauw, Buffon, Raynal, and Robertson.[16]

Clavijero's *Storia antica del Messico* became an immediate success and was
translated into several languages. The work stimulated European interest
in Mexican antiquities. Its greatest impact, however, was in New Spain
because, by reading it, educated criollos and mestizos discovered a glorious
past that they could appropriate as their own. The fact that Clavijero's book
was "a history of Mexico written by a Mexican" and that it was "a testimony
of my most sincere love of the *patria*" only strengthened the desire of many
novohispanos to claim equal rights in the Spanish world.

The publication of *Storia antica* coincided with the discovery of two
ancient monoliths in Mexico City. The criollo scholar Antonio de León y
Gama wrote a notable study, *Descripción histórica y cronológica de dos piedras*,
which applied the new scientific methods to his country's Indian past,
thereby integrating pre-Hispanic history into the universal strands of the
Enlightenment. Fellow *novohispanos*, the exiled Jesuits Andrés Cavo and
Francisco Javier Alegre, contributed to American patriotism with histories
of the viceroyalty and of the Jesuit order in New Spain. Such works allowed
the educated urban groups of New Spain to ground their patriotism in their
Indian as well as their Spanish heritage.[17]

Juan de Velasco, an exiled Jesuit from Riobamba, was as zealous and as
unfettered by the facts in his defense of America as the European detractors
he sought to discredit. In his *Historia del Reino de Quito* (1789), he invented
a distinct and glorious pre-Hispanic history for his *patria*. Like his fellow
Jesuits from the north, Velasco was determined to demolish De Pauw, Buffon, Raynal, Robertson, and other critics of the New World. He divided his
Historia into three volumes. The first, which attempted to refute directly
the European critics, examined the geography, climate, mineral resources,
flora, and fauna of Quito, concluding with an analysis of the moral, civic,
spiritual, and intellectual abilities of the Indians. Throughout the volume,
Velasco demonstrated that the detractors were wrong in their assessments
of the New World. Volume two was dedicated to the "Ancient History" of
Quito and volume three to the "Modern History." Whereas the latter
recounted postconquest events until the early eighteenth century, the former endowed his *patria* with a prehistory as brilliant as that of Peru and
New Spain.[18]

16 Ibid., 196–208; Brading, *The First America*, 450–62.

17 Florescano, *Memoria mexicana*, 261–2.

18 Juan de Velasco, *Historia del Reino de Quito en la América meridional*, in Biblioteca Ecuadoriana Mínima, *Padre Juan de Velasco S. I.*, 2 vols. (Puebla: Editorial Cajica, 1961). Although Father Velasco
   submitted his history for publication to Spain in 1789, the work did not appear until 1839, when

Although no exiled Jesuits from New Granada or Peru entered the debate, a Chilean did. In his *Historia geográfica, natural y civil del Reino de Chile,* Juan Ignacio Molina dismissed De Pauw's writings as flights of fancy, noting that he had never been to America, distorted his sources, and made as much sense as if he were writing about the moon. Chile had fertile soil and a mild climate, which made it a most desirable land. Although the area was a frontier region with no highly developed Indian societies, Molina praised the Araucanians as much as the land. The Chilean Jesuit argued that his compatriots possessed talent but lacked opportunity. If they had the resources found in Europe, he declared, Chileans would advance dramatically in the sciences. Molina's work, which was widely read, contributed to a sense of regional identity.[19]

Ironically, the expulsion of the Jesuits from America in 1767 also contributed to the formation of a *conciencia de sí* in the New World by providing opportunities for a new generation of intellectuals. The Jesuits, who controlled many academic institutions, had been engaged in a process of introducing *modern* thought to the American kingdoms. When they were exiled, their disciples and collaborators frequently gained control of former Jesuit institutions. In Quito, for example, the Indian-*mulato* scholar Francisco Javier Eugenio de Santa Cruz y Espejo formed the first public library in Spanish America from the former Jesuit collections in that city. Others became professors in former Jesuit colleges and assumed important posts previously held by members of the order. Thus, a younger and somewhat more secular generation of Americans asserted control over the continent's cultural institutions. They used their new positions and opportunities to study the special characteristics of their *patrias.* Scholars such as the *novo-hispanos* José Antonio Alzate and Juan Ignacio Bartolache published important periodicals, such as the *Gaceta de literatura de México* and *Mercurio Volante,* to demonstrate that New Spain was not only wealthy but also cultured. Espejo published *Primicias de la cultura de Quito* for the same purpose. Other periodicals, such as the *Mercurio Peruano* or the *Telegráfo Mercantil* of Buenos Aires, also chronicled the achievements of Americans. The knowledge imparted by such publications contributed to patriotism. But in addition, American writers openly fostered nationalism when they referred to the "*patria,*" the "nation," or "our America."

Increasingly the *patria,* the nation, or the America that they discussed was their individual *patria.* Indeed, the locality often became the *patria* as regions within *reinos* were in contention with one another, particularly with

a partial French edition was published. Other partial and distorted editions were published over the years. The first complete and accurate edition is the one in the Biblioteca Ecuatoriana Mínima sponsored by the Ecuadorian government.

19 Gerbi, *The Dispute of the New World,* 212–17.

their capital cities. Although part of the same Monarchy, the American kingdoms had little contact with one another unless they were neighbors, in which case they experienced considerable interaction. Often, however, their interests conflicted. That reality weakened their ability to act collectively vis-à-vis the Crown. As the *Gazeta de Buenos Ayres* noted with regard to New Spain, "we have no more relations with that people than with Russia or Tartary. . . . How could we reconcile our interests with those of the Kingdom of Mexico? That realm would be content with nothing less than to reduce these provinces to the condition of colonies."[20]

The Bourbon Reforms

The growing sense of American identity conflicted with the determination of Spain's eighteenth-century rulers to reduce the New World to the status of a colony. The process began with the advent of a new dynasty. Felipe V's victory in the War of the Spanish Succession allowed the new Bourbon monarch to initiate a series of changes designed to centralize government in Spain, restore finances, and reorganize the armed forces. French advisers and Spanish reformers such as José Patiño and José del Campillo revived the Spanish economy by applying mercantilist policies. Among the most important transformations was the establishment of the intendant system of administration in the Peninsula. The intendant was a provincial administrator with military, financial, economic, and judicial authority. Directly responsible to the king, the new official was instructed to reduce regionalism and strengthen the national government.[21]

During the reign of Carlos III (1759–1788), zealous officials, bent on creating a more efficient and a more rational society, restructured administration, education, agriculture, industry, trade, and transportation. These men of the Enlightenment wanted a better and more effective government. They rejected the Habsburg concept of *federated* kingdoms, insisting instead upon a united and centralized Spain ruling over its overseas possessions. Indicative of their attitude was the change in the monarch's title. In Habsburg times it had been *King of the Spains and of the Indies;* under the Bourbons it became *King of Spain and Emperor of America.* Carlos III's officials were the first to refer to the American possessions as *colonias* (colonies), a term borrowed from England and France, instead of the traditional *reinos.*[22]

---

20 *Gazeta de Buenos Ayres,* I, Núm. 27 (6 de diciembre de 1810), 423–4.

21 Jaime E. Rodríguez O., *The Emergence of Spanish America: Vicente Rocafuerte and Spanish Americanism, 1808–1832* (Berkeley: University of California Press, 1975), 2.

22 Colin M. MacLachlan, *Spain's Empire in the New World: The Role of Ideas in Institutional and Social Change* (Berkeley: University of California Press, 1988).

Although the Bourbon program of regeneration began with Spain, in 1743 José del Campillo turned his attention overseas in a study entitled *Nuevo sistema de gobierno económico para la América* (*New System of Economic Government for America*). He proposed that the Crown conduct a general inspection of the New World to gather precise data. Then, on the basis of that information, it could institute reforms. He also suggested that the introduction of intendancies and the establishment of free trade within the Monarchy become the cornerstone of American reform. Little was accomplished, however, until the advent of the Seven Years' War. Shocked by Britain's capture of Havana in 1762 and dismayed by the trading boom that resulted, the Spanish Crown moved to initiate changes upon the cessation of hostilities.[23]

Although the war clearly demonstrated that the Spanish Monarchy needed to control its American possessions if it were to reclaim its place as a major world power, conditions in the New World also contributed a sense of urgency. As John Lynch observes: "There were features of American government which disturbed the Bourbons. Institutions did not function automatically by issuing laws and receiving obedience. The normal instinct of colonial subjects was to question, evade or modify laws, and only as a last resort obey them. . . . [T]he colonial bureaucracy came to adopt a mediating role between the crown and subjects which may be called a colonial consensus."[24]

To the Bourbon reformers, perhaps the most disturbing aspect of the situation in the New World was the fact that Americans exerted considerable control over their own affairs. Local elites in the different kingdoms or regions of the Western Hemisphere possessed economic power. They owned haciendas, mines, *obrajes,* and other enterprises. Although European-born Spaniards dominated the large-scale monopoly trade between Spain and America, criollos and mestizos often engaged in extensive internal and inter-American trade. Similarly, Americans exercised significant political influence.

In theory, royal officials – who were expected not to establish ties with local groups – governed the area. But the royal administration in America was weak, and its representatives often were forced to collaborate with regional elites to govern effectively. Local notables coopted royal bureaucrats through friendship, marriage, business activities, and bribes.[25]

---

23 Miguel Artola, "Campillo y las reformas de Carlos III," *Revista de Indias,* XII (October–December 1952), 687–90. Although Campillo's study was not published until 1762 as part of Bernardo Ward's *Proyecto económico* and independently in 1787, it had circulated widely in manuscript form.
24 John Lynch, *Bourbon Spain, 1700–1808* (Oxford: Basil Blackwell, 1989), 329, 333.
25 See, for example, John L. Phelan, *The Kingdom of Quito in the Seventeenth Century: Bureaucratic Politics in the Spanish Empire* (Madison: University of Wisconsin Press, 1967).

Alcaldes mayores and *corregidores,* mid-level officials who operated locally, were thought to be particularly prone to cooptation and corruption since they derived their income not from salaries but from trade. They obtained funds from local merchants and entrepreneurs and then advanced cash, equipment, and supplies to small farmers and Indians in their jurisdiction through the *repartimiento de comercio* (a system of distribution of merchandise on credit). Although it served as an effective system of credit in many areas, and although campesinos and Indians often used it to serve their own interests, the *repartimiento* was abused in other cases as many rural people were forced to produce for the export market and to buy goods they did not need.[26] In Peru the *repartimiento* was the cause of innumerable complaints. Nevertheless, it served entrenched local groups well.

Americans also sought office in their *patrias.* They wished to govern themselves in the same fashion that Peninsular kingdoms, such as Cataluña, had done in the seventeenth century. They not only desired the majority of appointments in the New World, they wanted them in their own *patrias.* In that sense, criollos from other regions were perceived as only slightly different from *peninsulares.* It became possible to obtain positions at home in the mid-seventeenth century when the Crown, desperate for funds, began selling offices. As a result, Americans obtained appointments to *corregimientos* (provincial governments), *ayuntamientos* (city councils), *audiencias,* and on occasion the office of viceroy.[27] Thus, the New World kingdoms became relatively autonomous.

Americans gained control of *audiencias* in their regions during the period 1687 to 1750. Although the Habsburgs initiated the practice, the first Bourbon kings, Felipe V and Fernando VI, accelerated the process. During the first half of the eighteenth century, they appointed 108 criollos to 136 *audiencia* posts. The financial demands of the European wars led to the increased sale of *oidor* (*audiencia* judge) positions. The Monarchy sold most *audiencia* judgeships in less threatened regions, such as Guadalajara, Quito, Lima, Charcas, and Santiago de Chile, and sold the fewest *oidor* positions in those *audiencias* subject to British attack, like Santo Domingo, Santa Fé de Bogotá, and Mexico. Concerned by the growing power of Americans, the

---

26 A recent evaluation of the significance of the repatimiento is Jeremy Baskes, "Coerced or Voluntary? The *Repartimiento* and Market Participation of Peasants in Late Colonial Oaxaca," *Journal of Latin American Studies* 28:1 (February 1996), 1–28.

27 John H. Parry, *The Sale of Public Office in the Spanish Indies under the Habsburgs* (Berkeley: University of California Press, 1963); Fernando Muro, "El 'beneficio' de oficios públicos en Indias," *Anuario de Estudios Americanos,* 35 (1978), 1–67; Alfredo Moreno Cebrián, "Venta y beneficios de los corregimientos peruanos," *Revista de Indias,* 36:143–4 (January–June 1976), 213–46; Kenneth J. Andrien, "The Sale of Fiscal Offices and the Decline of Royal Authority in the Viceroyalty of Peru, 1633–1700," *Hispanic American Historical Review* (hereafter cited as *HAHR*), 62:1 (February 1982), 49–71.

Crown ceased selling *audiencia* posts in 1750. But so many Americans had gained office that they retained their majority in the *audiencias* of Mexico, Lima, and Santiago until the 1770s.[28]

Americans eagerly sought government posts because they believed they could determine their own destiny through control of local government. that was possible because, as John L. Phelan has indicated:

> The Spanish monarchy was absolute only in the original medieval sense. The king recognized no superior inside or outside his kingdoms. He was the ultimate source of all justice and all legislation. The late medieval phrase was, "The king is emperor in his realm." The laws that bore the royal signature, however, were not the arbitrary expression of the king's personal wishes. Legislation, and the extent to which it was enforced, reflected the complex and diverse aspirations of all or, at least, several groups in that corporate, multiethnic society. The monarchy was representative and decentralized to a degree seldom suspected. Although there were no formal representative assemblies or cortes in the Indies, each of the major corporations, such as the cabildos, the various ecclesiastical groups, the universities, and the craft guilds, all of which enjoyed a large measure of self-government, could and did speak for their respective constituents. Their views reached the king and the council of the Indies, transmitted directly by their accredited representatives or indirectly through the viceroys and the audiencias, and their aspirations profoundly shaped the character of the ultimate decisions.[29]

Americans considered their *patrias* to be kingdoms in the worldwide Spanish Monarchy, not colonies, like those of Britain and France. They were convinced that an "unwritten constitution" required "that basic decisions were reached by informal consultation between the royal bureaucracy and the king's . . . [New World] subjects. Usually there emerged a workable compromise between what the central authorities ideally wanted and what local conditions and pressures would realistically tolerate."[30]

The Bourbon reformers, however, believed in an absolutist state, not one based on consensus. Moreover, they rejected the Habsburg reliance on the Church in favor of a secular administration of civil and military bureaucrats. Like twentieth-century liberals, the men of the eighteenth-century

---

28 Mark A. Burkholder and D. S. Chandler, *From Impotence to Authority: The Spanish Crown and the American Audiencias, 1687–1808* (Columbia: University of Missouri Press, 1977). Three important articles on the subject appeared in the *HAHR*, 52 (1972): Leon G. Campbell, "A Colonial Establishment: Creole Domination of the Audiencia of Lima during the Late Eighteenth Century," 1–25; Mark A. Burkholder, "From Creole to Peninsular: The Transformation of the Audiencia of Lima," 395–415; and Jacques A. Barbier, "Elites and Cadres in Bourbon Chile," 416–35. See also John L. Phelan, "El auge y caída de los criollos en la audiencia de Nueva Granada," *Boletín de Historia y Antiguedades,* 59 (1972), 597–618; and David A. Brading, *Miners and Merchants in Bourbon Mexico, 1763–1810* (Cambridge: Cambridge University Press, 1971), 40–4.

29 John L. Phelan, *The People and the King: The Comunero Revolution in Colombia, 1781* (Madison: University of Wisconsin Press, 1978), 82.

30 Ibid., xviii.

Enlightenment believed that the state was the institution best suited to promote the Monarchy's prosperity and well-being. Although they faced enormous local opposition, the reformers nonetheless proceeded with determination because they enjoyed the king's support.

Following the Seven Years' War, Cuba became the location for an experiment in reform. The Bourbons first instituted a *visita*, or inspection, during the years 1763 and 1764. Then they established an intendancy, a new standing army, and introduced freer trade within the Monarchy. The outcome was positive from the reformers' perspective – Americans were slowly eliminated from office, tax collections increased, and the new army appeared to function relatively well. The Bourbons did not wait to learn the results of the changes in Cuba before deciding to institute the reforms throughout America.

New Spain experienced the first large-scale attempt to introduce the transformation with the *visita general* of José de Gálvez from 1765 to 1771. The extremely anti-American Visitador General Gálvez set the pattern for royal reform. He boldly assaulted the old order, questioning the concept of viceroyalty that formed the core of the Habsburg structure of government. Gálvez's aggressive approach, and his decisive action to remedy the problems he perceived, offended *novohispanos* who viewed his acts as unrestrained use of authority. Accustomed to consensus politics, they found it difficult to accept his transformations. José de Gálvez hoped to replace the viceroyalty with a system of commandancies-general and powerful secondary-level intendancies, which he believed would increase tax collection and maintain order more effectively. He proposed to eliminate the *repartimiento de comercio* and replace the *alcaldes mayores* and *corregidores* with paid officials. The audiencia, as an important element in the traditional structure, also came under attack. Gálvez reduced the jurisdiction of the *oidores* by conceding *fueros*, the right to try their own dependents, to many agencies, such as the postal service; the gunpowder, tobacco, and playing card monopolies; and fiscal bodies.

The reform gained momentum in 1776 when Gálvez became minister of the Indies. Despite the opposition he had encountered in New Spain, he was determined to introduce the reforms throughout America. The same year Antonio de Areche, one of Gálvez's most trusted lieutenants in New Spain, began a *visita general* of Peru that would last until 1784. Areche had already demonstrated a virulent anti-American attitude in New Spain, which he characterized as almost a desert with only four or five poorly formed cities. His most stinging condemnations, however, were for the process of miscegenation and the moral character of *novohispanos*.[31] Given

31 Areche's views are discussed in Christon I. Archer, "What Goes Around Comes Around: Political Change and Continuity in Mexico, 1750–1850," in *Mexico in the Age of Democratic Revolutions, 1750–1850*, ed. Jaime E. Rodríguez O. (Boulder: Lynne Rienner, 1994), 264–6.

such an outlook, Areche's *visita* of Peru only succeeded in provoking great discord. Juan Francisco Gutiérrez de Piñeres, another of Gálvez's deputies, proved equally hostile to Americans during his *visita general* of New Granada in the years 1778 to 1781.

The reformers' efforts to transform administration, abolish long-established arrangements, and increase taxes encountered massive opposition in America. Throughout the region, those harmed by the changes used all legal remedies to stymie or modify the new system. In some areas the population turned to armed resistance to redress their grievances. The first upheaval occurred in Quito, a center of textile production whose *obrajes* had suffered substantially at the hands of European competition. The increase in taxes, particularly those on *aguardiente* (spirits), led to protests and, in 1765, to violent riots.[32] Sporadic uprisings occurred in numerous highland areas of the Audiencia of Quito in the following years.[33] In 1766 *tumultos* (riots) erupted in various regions of New Spain – San Luis Potosí, Guanajuato, Michoacán, and other areas in the north. The revolts in New Spain, aggravated by the expulsion of the Jesuits, most of whom were American born, expanded, the following year. The masses attacked the tobacco and powder monopolies, sacked shops and the offices of the royal treasury, freed prisoners from jail, assaulted those charged with expelling the Jesuits, and put the military and royal officials to flight.[34] During the years 1777 to 1780, the cities of Alto Peru also endured similar unrest.

The greatest upheavals, however, transpired in Peru and New Granada. The Túpac Amaru Revolt threatened to engulf the entire Viceroyalty of Peru. Begun by the *cacique* (Indian leader) José Gabriel Túpac Amaru, who claimed to be a descendant of the Incas, the revolt initially sought to correct the abuses of the *corregidores* and the *repartimiento* system, as well as end the *mita* (Indian forced labor), improve working conditions in the mines and *obrajes,* and establish an *audiencia* in Cuzco. Although directed to the Indian masses, the movement attempted to win the support of mestizos, criollos, and black slaves, whom it emancipated. As large areas of the highlands joined the rebels, other groups in Peru, fearing the results of a race

32 The best studies of this event are Anthony McFarlane, "The 'Rebellion of the Barrios': Urban Insurrection in Bourbon Quito," *HAHR,* 69:2 (May 1989), 283–330; and Kenneth J. Andrien, "Economic Crisis, Taxes and the Quito Insurrection of 1765," *Past and Present,* 129 (November 1990), 104–31.

33 Segundo E. Moreno Yánes, *Sublevaciones indigenas en la Audiencia de Quito,* 3d ed. (Quito: Universidad Católica del Ecuador, 1985), 103–332.

34 See, for example, Felipe Castro Gutiérrez, *Movimientos populares en Nueva España: Michoacán, 1766–1767* (Mexico: UNAM, 1990), and his *Nueva ley y nuevo rey; Reformas bórbonicas y rebelión popular en Nueva España* (Zamora and Mexico: El Colegio de Michoacán and UNAM, 1996).

and class conflict, distanced themselves from it and, indeed, backed the military forces that suppressed the revolt in 1783.[35]

Although the other great rebellion of the period, the *Comunero* Revolt in New Granada (named after the members of the communes or towns), arose from similar grievances, it took a much different form. Substantial tax increases and the enforcement of the tobacco monopoly precipitated widespread protests in the tobacco-producing regions of Socorro and San Gil. When Visitador General Gutiérrez de Piñeres refused to consider their grievances, the local people, led by Francisco Berbeo, a *vecino* (citizen) of Socorro, formed a "supreme council of war." The rebels demanded the abolition of the monopoly, the end to many taxes, the expulsion of the *visitador,* and greater local autonomy. When nearly 20,000 persons marched toward the capital, the authorities compromised, accepting many of their demands. The *comuneros* (the participants in the Comunero Revolt), as Phelan indicates, compelled "the authorities to act within the spirit of the 'unwritten constitution' whose guiding principles were consultation, cogovernment, and compromise."[36] Despite their achievements, the *comuneros* only retarded, but did not halt, the Bourbon drive for control of America.

The centerpiece of American reform, the intendancy, prompted considerable local opposition. Initially introduced in Cuba in 1764, the reform had improved administration, particularly tax collection, but so outraged the island's elite that the captain general requested that the ordinance be revoked. Although the Crown refused, the Cuban reaction delayed implementation of intendancies elsewhere in America. Visitador General Gálvez proposed establishing intendancies in New Spain in his *Plan de intendencias* of 1768. But the reform languished until 1776, when he became minister of the Indies. Because of the opposition of the American elite and the obstruction of royal bureaucrats, Gálvez began introducing reforms in peripheral areas of the Monarchy. In 1776 the Commandancy General of the Provincias Internas was established in northern New Spain as a way of providing cohesion for the region and protection for the settlers there. The same year, Venezuela was reorganized into a captaincy general and an intendancy was headquartered in Caracas. The Viceroyalty of the Río de la Plata was created in 1776, but it did not receive intendancies until 1782. Two years later the system was introduced into Peru and in 1786 into New Spain. Although Visitador General Gutiérrez de Piñeres proposed estab-

---

35 There is a vast literature on the Túpac Amaru Revolt, much of which attempts to interpret it as an early independence movement. The best study is Scarlett O'Phelan Godoy, *Rebellions and Revolts in Eighteenth-Century Peru and Upper Peru* (Cologne: Böhlau Verlag, 1985), 209–56. See also Leon G. Campbell, "Ideology and Federalism during the Great Rebellion, 1780–1782," in *Resistance, Rebellion, and Consciousness in the Andean World, 18th to 20th Centuries,* ed. Steve J. Stern (Madison: University of Wisconsin Press, 1989), 110–39.

36 Phelan, *The People and the King,* 239–40.

lishing intendancies in New Granada in 1782, the viceroy's opposition and the aftermath of the Comunero Revolt prevented the introduction of the system there. The Audiencia of Quito experienced only partial change when the southern province of Cuenca became an intendancy. The Crown established other intendancies in Puerto Rico, Chiapas, Nicaragua, San Salvador (present-day El Salvador), and Chile.[37]

Although the intendancy system succeeded in improving provincial government, increasing tax collections, and promoting regional economic development, its ultimate legacy was regionalism. The powerful new officials disrupted existing political and economic networks, which linked local elites to their counterparts in the viceregal capitals, but they also provided opportunities for economic and social mobility at the provincial level. Improved roads, public works, better sanitation and water supplies, and other public services also contributed to civic pride. Since the introduction of strong, prestigious, and well-paid officials enhanced the status of provincial capitals, the intendants and the local elites often cooperated to achieve greater influence and authority in their areas. As a result, the new officials not only inadvertently contributed to the growth of regionalism but also found themselves becoming enmeshed in local politics.

The second-level officials, the *subdelegados* who replaced the *corregidores* and *alcaldes mayores,* fared less well. Without the income and prestige of the intendants, the *subdelegados* found themselves unable to provide good administration and justice in the countryside. Many soon succumbed to demands for the restoration of the *repartimiento de comercio.* In some instances, local elites believed the *repartimiento* was necessary to force Indian communities to participate in trade. But in others, people wished to restore it because the *repartimiento de comercio* was the only viable system of credit available for small farmers and Indian communities.[38]

The Bourbon reformers viewed the Church as an obstacle to their plan to

37 Lillian E. Fisher, *The Intendant System in Spanish America* (Berkeley: University of California Press, 1929); Luis Navarro García, *Intendencias en Indias* (Seville: Escuela de Estudios Hispanoamericanos, 1956); John Lynch, *Spanish Colonial Administration, 1772–1810* (London: Athlone Press, 1958); John R. Fisher, *Government and Society in Colonial Peru: The Intendant System, 1784–1814* (London: Athlone Press, 1970); Herbert Priestley, *José de Gálvez, Visitor-General of New Spain, 1765–1771* (Berkeley: University of California Press, 1916); Ricardo Rees Jones, *El despotismo ilustrado y los intendentes de la Nueva España* (Mexico: UNAM, 1979); Horst Pietschmann, *Las reformas borbónicas y el sistema de intendentes en Nueva España* (Mexico: Fondo de Cultura Económica, 1996); Ignacio del Río, *La aplicación regional de las reformas borbónicas en Nueva España: Sonora y Sinaloa, 1768–1787* (Mexico: UNAM, 1995); Douglas A. Washburn, "The Bourbon Reforms: A Social and Economic History of the Audiencia of Quito, 1760–1810" (Ph.D. diss., University of Texas at Austin, 1984), 117–22.

38 Margarita Menegus Bornemann, "Economía y comunidades indígenas. El efecto de la supresión del sistema de reparto de mercancías en la intendencia de México, 1786–1810," *MS/EM* (Summer 1989), 201–19. For a recent careful assessment of the repartimiento in New Spain, see Arij Ouweneel, *Shadows over Anáhuac: An Econological Interpretation of Crisis and Development in Central Mexico,*

modernize Spain. The Church not only wielded great influence, it possessed enormous wealth. Reformers considered the numerous clergy as unproductive parasites burdening society. By holding land in mortmain, the Church deprived the state of revenues and removed productive wealth from society. The Conde de Campomanes, for example, suggested that expropriation might be required to remedy the imbalance between a wealthy Church and a needy state.

The reformers sought to increase the power of the state at the expense of the Church. In Spain, the Church, and particularly the Society of Jesus, controlled higher education in a variety of ways. One was through the *colegios mayores,* residences originally intended for poorer students but taken over by the sons of wealthy landholding families. Because of their advantages, the *colegiales,* the products of the *colegios mayores,* dominated the clergy and possessed great influence in the royal administration. The sons of the lower nobility, excluded from the *colegios mayores* and disdainfully known as *manteistas* because of the long capes, *mantas,* they were required to wear, struggled to obtain an education. Their relative deprivation helped to forge an anticlerical bias that would assert itself during the reign of Carlos III; many of his reform-minded officials were *manteistas.* Since they opposed the power of the Church, they were also considered Jansenists by their opponents. Thus two groups formed with regard to the status of the Church: the ultramontanists – the *colegiales* – identified with the Jesuits, who favored the traditional order, and the reformers – *manteistas* – who wished to end the Jesuits' power over Hispanic society. The opportunity to force change came in March 1766 when a *motín* (riot) occurred in Madrid opposing the reforms of Carlos III's Italian-born minister, the Marqués de Esquilache.

Although the *motín de Esquilache* arose from a complex series of factors, such as bad harvests, increased taxes, and Spain's failures in the Seven Years' War, royal officials blamed the riot on the machinations of the Jesuits, the *colegiales,* and other opponents of reform. When order had been restored, a commission of inquiry determined after a secret investigation that the Jesuits had fomented the riot. Consequently, on February 27, 1767, the king ordered the Jesuits expelled from Spain and all its dominions.[39]

The expulsion of perhaps 2,500 Jesuits from the Spanish Monarchy profoundly affected America. Many were natives of the New World, where the

1730–1800 (Albuquerque: University of New Mexico Press, 1996), 159–209. See also Stanley J. Stein, "Bureaucracy and Business in the Spanish Empire, 1759–1804: Failure of a Bourbon Reform in Mexico and Peru," *HAHR,* 61:1 (February 1981), 2–28; Jacques A. Barbier and Mark A. Burkholder, "Critique of Stanley J. Stein's 'Bureaucracy. . . . , ' " and Stanley J. Stein's "Reply," *HAHR,* 62:3 (August 1982), 460–9, 469–77.

39 Constancio Eguía Ruiz, *Los jesuitas y el motín de Esquilache* (Madrid: Consejo Superior de Investigaciones Científicas, 1947); Vicente Rodríguez Casado, *La política y los políticos en el reinado de Carlos III* (Madrid: Ediciones Rialp, 1962); Laura Rodríguez, "The Riots of 1766 in Madrid," *European*

Society of Jesus played a major role. Jesuits were the teachers and advisors of the local elite. They dominated the continent's colleges and universities; they possessed many haciendas and *obrajes;* they ran hospitals, orphanages, and other charities; they manned the missions in the extreme north and south; and in Paraguay, the Jesuits operated largely autonomous enclaves. The Bourbon reformers viewed the Society of Jesus as the extreme example of quasi-independent Church power in Spanish America.[40]

Initially, Americans reacted with great anger at the expulsion, which they viewed as an inexplicable act. In some areas, particularly in New Spain, the population rioted. Throughout the New World the elite criticized the royal action that expelled their relatives, teachers, and advisors. In time, however, they were mollified because valuable expropriated Jesuit property was sold to those with credit and status. Others, including other regular orders, assumed control of Jesuit colleges, missions, and charities. Although the transfer of Jesuit properties, institutions, and influence found ready takers in America, the Jesuits took with them a powerful asset, American patriotism, which – as we have seen – would subsequently inform their writings and influence the attitudes of the leaders of the New World.

The redefinition of the state's legal jurisdiction over clerical affairs became the most important point of contention between the reformers and the Church. Ecclesiastical *fueros* permitted diocesan courts to claim exclusive jurisdiction over certain offenses committed by the clergy. Although churchmen enjoyed personal immunity from civil authorities, they also claimed the right to interfere in secular society. In the case of asylum, the Church stood between the people and the king's justice. The Crown attempted to exclude certain criminal categories and declared some churches *iglesias frías* that could not offer asylum. By declaring all property to be temporal, the reformers transferred to secular courts jurisdiction over

Studies Review, 3:3 (May 1973), 223–42; and her "The Spanish Riots of 1766," *Past and Present,* 59 (May 1973), 117–46.

40 On the Jesuits, see Ignacio Osorio Romero, *Colegios y profesores Jesuitas que enseñaron latín en Nueva España, 1572–1767* (Mexico: UNAM, 1979); Magnus Mörner, *The Political and Economic Activities of the Jesuits in the La Plata Region* (Stockholm: Victor Pettersons Bokindustri Aktiebolag, 1953) and his *The Expulsion of the Jesuits from Latin America* (New York: Knopf, 1965); Alberto Francisco Pradeau, *La expulsión de los Jesuitas de las Provincias de Sonora, Ostimuri y Sinaloa en 1767* (Mexico: Antigua Librería Robredo de Porrúa, 1959). The best studies of Jesuit estates are Herman W. Konrad, *A Jesuit Hacienda in Colonial Mexico: Santa Lucía, 1576–1767* (Stanford: Stanford University Press, 1980); Germán Colmenares, *Las haciendas de los Jesuitas en el Nuevo Reino de Granada* (Bogotá: Universidad Nacional de Colombia, 1969); and Nicolas P. Cushner's three volumes: *Lords of the Land: Sugar, Wine, and Jesuit States of Coastal Peru, 1600–1767,* (Albany: State University of New York Press, 1980); *Jesuit Ranches and the Agrarian Development of Colonial Argentina, 1650–1767* (Albany: State University of New York Press, 1983); and *Farm and Factory: The Jesuits and the Development of Agrarian Capitalism in Colonial Quito, 1600–1767* (Albany: State University of New York Press, 1982).

land titles and other types of Church property. They also restricted personal clerical immunity from prosecution or arrest by secular officials. By the end of the eighteenth century, criminal courts of the *audiencias* were trying clerical offenders. Although some in the hierarchy accepted many of the reforms as necessary, the majority of churchmen, particularly the lower clergy, bitterly opposed and resented the loss of ecclesiastical immunity. It was an issue that influenced many *curas* during the later struggle for independence.[41]

The army, in contrast to the Church, gained new power and influence in America. After the Seven Years' War, Britain and Spain became the principal competitors for control of the New World. Both militarized the continent by establishing standing armies. The Crown decided to defend America with an army built around a core of regular Spanish troops and a trained local militia as a reserve. Americans would pay for the new armed forces with an increase in the *alcabala* tax from 2 to 6 percent. The process, which began in Cuba in 1763, later spread to New Spain, New Granada, Quito, and Peru. The army of America rapidly became an American army; by the end of the century, Americans constituted 60 percent of the officer corps and 80 percent of the troops. The militias were almost entirely American. To encourage enlistment, the new army and the militia received a *fuero militar,* a privilege extended to some degree even to *castas* and *pardos* (Afro-Indians who lived in coastal regions), which provided the protection of military courts and a degree of fiscal exemption.[42]

The *fuero militar* and other distinctions appealed to the Americans' desire for recognition. In some regions, especially those with substantial African-origin populations, such as Cuba, Venezuela, New Granada, and Peru, the army and the militia provided an avenue for social mobility. The South American elites also benefited from the new structure. There, possessing an officer's commission increasingly enhanced one's socioeconomic status. Many Americans, however, lacked enthusiasm for military service since it took them from their homes. For militia officers, maneuvers meant disrup-

---

41 The best work on clerical reform is Nancy M. Farriss, *Crown and Clergy in Colonial Mexico, 1759–1821: The Crisis of Ecclesiastical Privilege* (London: Athlone Press, 1968). See also David A. Brading, *Church and State in Bourbon Mexico: The Diocese of Michoacán, 1749–1810* (Cambridge: Cambridge University Press, 1994); and William Taylor, *Magistrates of the Sacred: Priests and parishioners in Eighteenth-Century Mexico* (Stanford: Stanford University Press, 1996).

42 The military reform is the most thoroughly studied of all the Bourbon transformations. See, for example, Allan J. Kuethe, *Cuba, 1753–1815: Crown, Military, and Society* (Knoxville: University of Tennessee Press, 1986), and his *Military Reform and Society in New Granada, 1773–1808* (Gainesville: University of Florida Press, 1978); Christon I. Archer, *The Army in Bourbon Mexico, 1760–1810* (Albuquerque: University of New Mexico Press, 1977); Leon G. Campbell, *Military and Society in Colonial Peru, 1750–1810* (Philadelphia: American Philosophical Society, 1978); and Juan Marchena Fernández, *Oficiales y soldados en el ejército de América* (Seville: Escuela de Estudios Hispanoamericanos, 1983).

tion of their business activities, and for soldiers, army duty often resulted in extreme hardship for themselves and their families.

The new military structure in America achieved varied results. Although the army of America strengthened the continent's defenses, the militia often proved ineffective. It failed to quell the Túpac Amaru revolt in Peru, where a combination of civil, clerical, and regular army action was necessary to quash the upheaval. The militia was most effective in frontier regions, where it helped maintain internal peace and defend the area against the assaults of nomadic Indians and foreign invaders. Its most spectacular success occurred in Buenos Aires, where the militia repelled two British invasions in 1806 and 1807. In addition, army officers were often agents of change and modernization, as they engaged in bridge and road construction, mapping and charting regions, conducting resource surveys, and studying volcanoes and other natural phenomena. Although the military reform was necessary, Spanish authorities in the New World worried about the Americanization of the armed forces. Their fears proved to be well founded. Later, many militia officers led insurgent units during the struggle for independence.

Economic reform, another major plank of the Bourbon program, like political transformation, sought to increase Crown control. As the enlightened Viceroy of New Spain, Juan Vicente Güemes de Pacheco, the second Conde de Revillagigedo, explained to his successor:

It must not be forgotten that this is a colony which ought to depend on its matrix, Spain, and yield to it some profit in return for the benefits of protection. And, thus, great care is required to coordinate the dependency and to make the interest mutual and reciprocal, for it [the relation] would cease the moment European manufactures and products are no longer needed.[43]

In an effort to dominate New World trade, the Bourbon reformers issued regulations in 1778 which called for *comercio libre y protegido* (free and protected trade), designed to reduce Americans to the role of colonial suppliers of bullion and raw materials and consumers of finished products from Spain. Starting in 1765, Spanish authorities abolished the Cádiz monopoly by opening trade in the Caribbean first, to eight other ports in the Peninsula and then to Louisiana in 1768, Campeche and Mérida in 1770, and Peru, Chile, and the Río de la Plata in 1778. Although later that year the Crown issued the *Reglamento de comercio libre y protegido,* Venezuela and New Spain were excluded for another decade because the former was under the control of the Caracas Company and because the authorities feared that the latter's vast economy would displace the poorer regions in America. Venezuela was included in the system in 1788 and New Spain the follow-

43 Quoted in Catalina Sierra, *El nacimiento de México,* 2d ed. (Mexico: Miguel Angel Porrúa, 1984), 177.

ing year. While ending the Cádiz monopoly, *comercio libre* still limited American trade to Spanish and Spanish American ports. Commerce with foreigners remained forbidden since the intention was to reduce the New World to the status of a colony. Because Spanish industry could not satisfy all the needs of the Monarchy, foreigners continued to participate in Spanish American trade by transshipping their goods through the Peninsula and by smuggling.[44]

Free trade expanded commerce with Spain as Basque, Catalan, and Galician ports began to trade openly with America. Between 1778 and 1796, the period when *comercio libre* functioned before it collapsed in 1797 as a result of Spain's alliance with revolutionary France, Peninsular shipments to the New World grew fourfold and American exports to Spain increased ten times. Although Barcelona, the center of Spain's industry, shipped manufactured goods, most Spanish exports to America were agricultural products. Reshipment of foreign goods also expanded. Although silver remained the most important American commodity, agricultural products, such as tobacco, cacao, sugar, cochineal, indigo, and hides constituted 44 percent of total exports from 1778 to 1796. New Spain remained the largest importer and exporter, not only because it was the greatest silver producer but also because it was the wealthiest, most developed, and most populous region in America.[45]

Comercio libre did not benefit the New World uniformly. The manufacturing sectors of the core regions suffered a decline. In some cases, such as the textile industry of the Bajío in New Spain, internal factors also contributed, but in others, such as Quito, the decline was a direct result of administrative and commercial changes within Spanish America.[46] The creation of the Viceroyalty of the Río de la Plata damaged the economies of Peru and Quito. Similarly, the end of the Caracas Company and the creation of the Intendancy of Venezuela harmed Guayaquil's cacao industry.[47] On the other hand, the agriculture-producing regions of South America, particularly the Río de la Plata and Chile, benefited from the changed conditions.[48] In the north, the vast, populous, and wealthy Viceroyalty of New Spain readjusted internally as its agricultural and plantation regions, such

44 John Fisher, *Commercial Relations between Spain and Spanish America in the Era of Free Trade, 1778–1796* (Liverpool: University of Liverpool, 1985).

45 Javier Ortiz de la Tabla, *Comercio exterior de Veracruz, 1778–1821* (Seville: Escuela de Estudios Hispanoamericanos, 1978).

46 John Super, *La vida en Querétaro durante la colonia, 1531–1810* (Mexico: Fondo de Cultura Económica, 1983); Robson Tyrer, *Historia demográfica y económica de la Audiencia de Quito* (Quito: Banco Central del Ecuador, 1988).

47 Michael T. Hamerly, *Historia social y económica de antigua provincia de Guayaquil, 1763–1842* (Guayaquil: Archivo Histórico del Guayas, 1973), 57–85.

48 Guillermo Céspedes del Castillo, *Lima y Buenos Aires: Repercusiones económicas y políticas de la creación del virreynato del Río de la Plata* (Seville: Escuela de Estudios Hispanoamericanos, 1949); Sergio Villa-

as New Galicia, the Bajío, Veracruz, Oaxaca, and Yucatán, took advantage of the opportunities presented by *comercio libre*.

The gradual adjustment of the kingdoms of America to the new conditions was disrupted by wars in Europe that profoundly affected commerce. In 1793 Bourbon Spain joined other European monarchies in war against the regicide French Republic. When hostilities began, royal finances were sound and the economy was prosperous. By the end of the year, however, the situation had changed drastically. The war forced the Crown to raise taxes and impose the first direct levies on the nobility. To meet the emergency, the government also issued *vales reales* (royal bonds) and ordered the expropriation of Church property in the Peninsula. These measures, which failed to halt the deterioration of the economy, eroded popular support for the government. Worse, drastic military defeats forced Madrid to accept a humiliating treaty that bound the Peninsula to France, thus making Spain an enemy of Britain.

The new international alignment forced the Spanish Monarchy into a series of wars with Great Britain and its allies, further straining the Spanish economy. In 1796 the British fleet blockaded Spanish ports, cutting off the Peninsula from its overseas possessions. Spanish trade with America was virtually ended. In March 1797, the Cuban authorities opened the port of Havana to neutral shipping. In 1799, in a belated effort to retain some measure of control over American trade, Madrid authorized neutral shipping to carry goods to the New World, particularly mercury and powder to the silver mines. The measures benefited the United States, the only neutral maritime nation. The Peace of Amiens (1802) ended hostilities, allowing Spain's distressed economy to revive. Trade with America increased and production in the Peninsula recovered, reaching a peak in 1804; the government even began withdrawing the *vales reales* from circulation. But by then, France and Spain were once again at war with Britain. The defeat at Trafalgar the following year destroyed much of the Spanish navy; America was cut off from Spain. In 1807 not a single Spanish ship reached Havana, and the Peninsula received not one shipment of silver. Again, the only possible solution was to turn to neutral shipping.[49]

The disruptive effects of the new international alignments were not the only grievance Americans held against the Crown. Massive tax increases constituted the New World's greatest complaint. Carlos III and all his advisers were convinced that America should yield greater "profit" to the

---

lobos, *El comercio y contrabando en el Río de la Plata y Chile* (Buenos Aires: Universidad de Buenos Aires, 1965).

49 Antonio García-Baquero, *Comercio colonial y las guerras revolucionarias* (Seville: Escuela de Estudios Hispanoamericanos, 1972); John Fisher, *Trade, War, and Revolution: Exports from Spain to Spanish America, 1797–1820* (Liverpool: University of Liverpool, 1992). For a recent reinterpretation of these changes, consult David Ringrose, *Spain, Europe and the "Spanish Miracle" 1700–1900* (Cambridge: Cambridge University Press, 1996), 106–32.

Monarchy. Indeed, nearly all the Bourbon reforms were designed to raise revenues to their "proper level." The royal government increased the *alcabala* tax from 2 to 4 percent and finally to 6 percent in the last years of the eighteenth century. It introduced a variety of taxes on *aguardiente,* grains, cattle, and other commodities and created a number of state monopolies, such as cards, gunpowder, and tobacco. Despite protests and even violent revolts in Quito, Peru, New Granada, and New Spain, royal officials insisted on tax collection. The tobacco monopoly earned vast sums; for example, in New Spain the tobacco monopoly earned 69.4 million pesos in the period from 1765 to 1795, 44.7 million of which were remitted to Spain.[50] Tax collection in New Spain expanded enormously; from 1780 until 1810 the *alcabala* grew by 155 percent over the previous thirty years. The expansion was due, in part, to more efficient tax collection – extortion in the view of *novohispanos.*[51]

Increased tax collection was not limited to wealthy New Spain. The depressed Reino de Quito also provided the Crown with growing revenues. The treasuries of Quito, Guayaquil, and Cuenca averaged 5.4, 3.8, and 4.7 percent annual increases in public revenues during the period from 1777 to 1804.[52] As Kenneth Andrien has noted: "The dramatic rise in per capita tax rates in the late colonial period provides graphic evidence of the growing fiscal control of the Bourbon state. . . . Although a great economic and military power, England was never able to levy taxes so effectively in its relatively prosperous North American colonies. Despite the decline of textile manufacturing in the north-central highlands, taxpayers in the Quito district paid twice as much in per capita taxes as the English colonists in North America."[53]

Spain's incessant and growing demands for money to sustain the wars in Europe undermined the finances of America. Although revenues increased substantially, they could not match expenditures, particularly for the military, which expanded at an even faster rate. Deficits grew. In New Spain, for example, the government debt rose from 3 million pesos in 1780 to 31 million pesos in 1810. The financial disintegration of the royal government in America, as John TePaske has noted, "was a gradual, inexorable process beginning in the early 1780s and, in fact, the financial collapse of the state

---

50 W. Kendall Brown, *Bourbons and Brandy: Imperial Reform in Eighteenth-Century Arequipa* (Albuquerque: University of New Mexico Press, 1986); Susan Deans-Smith, *Bureaucrats, Planters, and Workers: The Making of the Tobacco Monopoly in Bourbon Mexico* (Austin: University of Texas Press, 1992).

51 Juan Carlos Garavaglia and Juan Carlos Grosso, "Estado borbónico y presión fiscal en la Nueva España, 1750–1821," in *América Latina: Dallo Stato coloniale allo Stato nazionalle (1750–1940),* 2 vols. (Milan: Franco Angeli, 1987), 1:78–97.

52 Kenneth J. Andrien, *The Kingdom of Quito, 1690–1830: The State and Regional Development* (Cambridge: Cambridge University Press, 1995), 200–2.

53 Ibid., 200, 202.

was almost an accomplished fact by . . . 1810."[54] Moreover, periodic demands for loans to meet extraordinary expenses in the Iberian Peninsula adversely affected the economy because they drained specie from the New World. In 1783, for example, the mining guilds of New Spain and Peru were forced to lend millions to Spain. Subsequently, the craft guilds were ordered to transfer their funds from Church-affiliated sodalities and to place them under government control. Merchant financiers and silver bankers also were directed to make their capital available to the state.[55]

Perhaps the greatest single disruption of the New World's economy occurred when the king extended the Royal Law of Consolidation to America in 1804. First enacted in Spain in 1798 to redeem *vales reales* and liquidate other war debts, the law authorized officials to seize and auction Church real estate. In return, clerical institutions would receive 3 percent on their "loans" to the government. The Crown believed that the measure would be beneficial because the auction would provide small farmers and other entrepreneurs the opportunity to acquire land. Because the Church in New Spain served as the country's principal banker, the measure could ruin the viceroyalty. Despite desperate and even threatening protests, the authorities enforced the consolidation decree. By 1808, royal officials in New Spain had raised more than 12 million pesos, approximately one-fourth of the total debt owed to the Church. It appears that members of the middle class – primarily Americans – were most seriously affected by the enforcement of the consolidation decree. Similar measures were taken in some other regions of the continent.[56] For many Americans, the Law of Consolidation came to symbolize the Crown's – and especially Minister Manuel Godoy's – utter lack of concern for the interests of the New World.

As if these exactions were not enough, during the second half of the eighteenth century Americans felt inundated by a new wave of Spanish immigrants. Government officials, merchants, and simple immigrants came to the New World to "*hacer la América*" (to get rich in America). At a time

54 John J. TePaske, "The Financial Disintegration of the Royal Government in Mexico during the Epoch of Independence," in *The Independence of Mexico and the Creation of the New Nation*, ed. Jaime E. Rodríguez O. (Los Angeles: UCLA Latin American Center, 1989), 63.

55 Carlos Marichal, "Las guerras imperiales y los préstamos novohispanos, 1781–1804," and Josefa Vega, "Los primeros préstamos de la guerra de independencia," *Historia Mexicana* 39:4 (April–June 1990), 881–907, 909–31. Luis Antonio Jáuregui Frías, "La anatomía del fisco colonial: La estructura administrativa de la real hacienda novohispana, 1786–1821" (Ph.D. diss., El Colegio de México, 1994), chapters V and VI, provide a detailed analysis of the impact of the crisis of the Spanish Monarchy on the finances of New Spain.

56 Romeo Flores Caballero, *La contrarrevolución en la independencia: Los españoles en la vida política, social y económica de México, 1804–1838* (Mexico: El Colegio de México, 1969), 33–65; Asunción Lavrin, "The Execution of the Law of Consolidation in New Spain," *HAHR*, 53 (February 1973), 27–49; Anthony McFarlane, *Colombia before Independence: Economy, Society, and Politics under Bourbon Rule* (Cambridge: Cambridge University Press, 1993), 306.

when the regime favored *peninsulares,* Spanish officials and entrepreneurs preferred to employ their compatriots and kinsmen rather than Americans. Canary Islanders, Galicians, Asturians, and Basques sought fortunes in the New World. Although these immigrants rapidly integrated into American society through marriage, they generally did not lose their Spanish ties. Naturally, many criollos resented the newcomers. Despite the constant struggle between American elites and upper- and mid-level Europeans for government jobs and business opportunities, the greatest conflict arose at lower levels of society. Spanish retail merchants, itinerant traders, and petty bureaucrats rapidly earned the hostility of the masses. Although their numbers were never large – perhaps 40,000 throughout the New World in 1800 – Americans perceived the newly arrived, highly visible Spaniards as predators who deprived them of their rightful opportunities.[57] It was a hostility that increased over the years as the government in Spain and European Spaniards in the New World demanded that Americans subordinate their needs to those of an imperiled metropolis.

The Bourbon reforms were not a carefully orchestrated, determined, and well-executed plan of action. Although the New World's armed forces were rapidly overhauled after 1763, they were subject to substantial change over the years. The commercial reforms, the administrative transformations, and even the attempts to prevent Americans from holding office in their *patrias* were uncertain, halting, and inconsistent. The intendant system was introduced piecemeal in some areas over the years, whereas others, such as New Granada, never experienced the transformation. Similarly, New Spain, the richest, most developed, and most productive American kingdom, waited decades before it enjoyed the benefits of *comercio libre.*

Americans everywhere either objected to or opposed those innovations that injured them and managed to modify many to suit their interests. Although the Bourbon reforms initially harmed some areas and groups even as they benefited others, the Spanish Crown doubtless would have eventually reached acceptable accommodations with all concerned. Events in Europe at the end of the eighteenth century, however, prevented an orderly readjustment. The onset of the French Revolution unleashed twenty years of war in which Spain became an unwilling participant. Thus, in the early nineteenth century, the Spanish Monarchy faced the greatest crisis of its history.

---

57 Flores Caballero, *La contrarrevolución,* 15–23; Brading, *Merchants and Miners,* 14–15, 105–6; Alberto Flores Galindo, *Aristocracia y plebe: Lima, 1760–1830* (Lima: Instituto Nacional de Cultura, 1984), 78–96; P. Michael McKinley, *Pre-Revolutionary Caracas: Politics, Economy, and Society 1777–1811* (Cambridge: Cambridge University Press, 1985), 13–18.

2

Revolution in the Spanish World

During the second half of the eighteenth and the early nineteenth centuries, the Atlantic world underwent a major transformation. That process included a number of interrelated changes: a demographic expansion; the emergence of the bourgeoisie, or middle class; the growth of the region's economies; the restructuring of the British, French, and Iberian empires; the emergence of Britain as the first great industrial and commercial power; the triumph of a modern system of thought known as the Enlightenment; and the transformation of Western political systems, including the expansion of representative government in Britain, the independence of the United States, the French Revolution, the new French imperialism, and the European wars it engendered. These events culminated in a profound political revolution in the Spanish world.

The Intellectual Revolution

The great enlightened king Carlos III (1759–1788) presided over a major intellectual transformation in Spain and America. During his reign, the Enlightenment won adherents in the Spanish world. The Hispanic variant was neither radical nor anti-Christian, as in France. But like the Enlightenment everywhere, the Hispanic movement admired classical antiquity, preferring science and reason to authority and useful knowledge to theory.[1] As José Miranda indicated, "The Enlightenment was neither a theory nor a doctrine, but a new way of looking at things and interpreting life. . . . The Enlightenment possessed, however, a principle common to the multitude

---

1 There is an extensive debate about the nature of the Enlightenment. Peter Gay's *The Enlightenment: An Interpretation*, 2 vols. (New York: Knopf, 1966–1969), favors the anti-Christian view. Alfred Cobban, on the other hand, emphasizes its diversity and pragmatism, as well as the key role of English writers in *In Search of Humanity: The Role of the Enlightenment in Modern History* (London: Cape, 1960). On Spanish America, see Arthur P. Whitaker, "Changing and Unchanging Interpretations of the Enlightenment in Spanish America," in *The Ibero-American Enlightenment*, ed. A. Owen Aldridge (Urbana: University of Illinois Press, 1971), 21–57.

of ideas that sprouted in its bosom: the liberty or autonomy of reason."[2] Although the Hispanic Enlightenment did not challenge the authority either of the Church or of the Crown, its emphasis on science and reason created the intellectual climate that would ultimately incline some to consider new political ideas. Although a few, particularly in the Church, opposed aspects of the new system of thought, their concerns were muted by the support that the monarch lent the movement.

Enlightenment ideas did not suddenly transform the Neoscholastic intellectual climate of Habsburg Spain and America. Instead change began in the 1670s and 1680s when some scholars started questioning aspects of Scholasticism. These individuals, who are known as *eclectics,* introduced *modern philosophy* to the Spanish world at the end of the seventeenth century and the early decades of the eighteenth.[3] The new critical approach was widely disseminated through the writings of Benito Gerónimo Feijóo, who sought to introduce and popularize the scholarly and scientific achievements of the age. Declaring that Spain needed no more works on theology, since it already possessed the best, he insisted that the country required modern science that did not clash with religion. Starting in 1739 with the nine-volume *Teatro crítico universal,* Feijóo discussed art, literature, philosophy, theology, mathematics, natural science, geography, and history. Subsequently, he published five additional volumes of essays entitled *Cartas eruditas.* His approach was critical, exposing the fallibility of physicians, false saints and miracles, and in all cases advancing the cause of modern analytical thought. Although Feijóo's publications aroused great controversy, his works became extremely popular, appearing in countless editions in subsequent decades. In 1750 King Fernando VI issued a decree prohibiting criticism of Feijóo because his writings merited "the royal pleasure."[4] The monarch's approval did not mean that the new ideas were accepted everywhere. It did, however, provide an incentive for change that reformers used to transform Spanish governmental, educational, and clerical institutions.

Periodical publications played a central role in disseminating "the new way of looking at things and interpreting life" in the Spanish world. Called

2 José Miranda, *Humboldt y México* (Mexico: UNAM, 1962), 11.

3 Olga Victoria Quiroz-Martínez, *La introducción de la filosofía moderna en España* (Mexico: El Colegio de México, 1949).

4 Quoted in Richard Herr, *The Eighteenth-Century Revolution in Spain* (Princeton: Princeton University Press, 1958), 39. Feijóo's work was widely read in America. His writings, for example, have been found in Nueva Granada in the libraries of the leading *próceres* of independence, such as Camilo Torres, Joaquín Camacho, and Antonio Nariño. Rafael Gómez Hoyos, *La independencia de Colombia* (Madrid: Editorial Mapfre, 1992), 80–1. Ekkehard Keeding emphasizes Feijóo's influence in eighteenth-century Quito in his *Das Zeitalter der Aufklärung in der Provinz Quito* (Cologne: Böhlau Verlag, 1983), 161–83.

gazetas, they were originally few in number and published in Madrid, Mexico City, and Lima. The *Gazeta de Madrid,* which appeared in 1701, the *Gazeta de México* (1722, 1728–39, 1784–1809), and the *Gazeta de Lima* (1745–1800) sought to record important political and cultural occurrences, other events of interest, and significant medical and scientific discoveries. The *Diario de Madrid,* founded in 1758, became the first daily newspaper in Europe. The pace of publication accelerated in the 1780s when large numbers of periodicals, which addressed a variety of issues, appeared in Spain and in America. Madrid and Mexico City became the principal centers of publication. Among the important Madrid periodicals were the *Semanario erudito* (1781–1791), *El Observador* (1781–1877), *El Correo literario de Europa* (1781–1787), *El Censor* (1781–1787), the *Mercurio de España* (1784–1830), the *Correo de Madrid* (1786–1791), *El gabinete de la lectura española* (1787–1793), *El Observador* (1787), the *Memorial literario* (1787–1791), and the *Espíritu de los mejores diarios* (1787–1791), a digest of leading European publications that circulated widely in America as well as in Spain. Influential Mexico City publications included the *Diario literario de México* (1768), the *Mercurio volante* (1772–1773), and the *Gazeta de literatura de México* (1788–1795). By the turn of the century, the press flourished both in the capital of New Spain and in important provincial cities like Veracruz.[5]

Unlike the Peninsula, where Madrid's publications were distributed throughout the country, America was too large for any great city to dominate the press. Although Mexican imprints circulated widely in the Viceroyalty of New Spain and in the Kingdom of Guatemala, they were only sporadically distributed in South America. Lima publications had a more restricted circulation. Toward the end of the century, other periodicals appeared in various regions of America, most sponsored by local *sociedades amigos del país* (societies of friends of the country); *El Mercurio peruano de historia, literatura y noticias públicas* (1791–1795), *El Papel periódico de la ciudad de Santa Fé de Bogotá* (1791–1796), *Las Primicias de la cultura de Quito* (1792), the *Gazeta de Guatemala* (1797–1816), *El Correo curioso, erudito, económico y mercantil de la ciudad de Santa Fé de Bogotá* (1801), *El Telégrafo mercantil, rural, político-económico e historiográfico del Río de la Plata* (1801–1802), and the *Lonja mercantil de La Habana* (1801), to mention only the most prominent.[6] As some of their titles indicate, the publications of

5 Herr, *The Eighteenth-Century Revolution,* 183–200; Virginia Guedea, "La medicina en las gacetas de México," *MS/EM,* 5:2 (Summer 1989), 175–99; Ruth Wold, *Diario de México: Primer cotidiado de Nueva España* (Madrid: Editorial Gredos, 1970); José Ignacio Bartolache, *Mercurio Volante,* ed. Roberto Moreno (Mexico: UNAM, 1979); José Antonio de Alzate, *Obras,* vol. I, *Periódicos,* ed. Roberto Moreno (Mexico: UNAM, 1980).

6 Robert J. Shafer, *The Economic Societies in the Spanish World, 1763–1821* (Syracuse: Syracuse University Press, 1958).

the Spanish world continued the practice of disseminating the new "scientific" knowledge, particularly information to improve health, education, technology, manufacturing, and agriculture.

Periodicals also informed their readers about history, art, literature, philosophy, and major events. The works of the principal writers of the age, including the English and the French *philosophes,* were either translated or presented in summary form. Although the press was not free, censorship was sporadic and inconsistent, in part because it was a relatively new and poorly understood medium. Statements hostile to the Catholic religion or the Spanish Monarchy were excluded. In some cases, the periodicals merely reported that certain works, such as Edward Gibbon's *Decline and Fall of the Roman Empire,* had been prohibited "because . . . [they] contained false, heretical, and impious doctrines, inimical to the Catholic religion."[7] But other writers, such as Thomas Paine, were translated or paraphrased without comment. Moreover, events that might have had revolutionary implications were openly reported; for example, Madrid newspapers carried accounts of the U.S. struggle for independence. Subsequently, they published a Spanish edition of the U.S. Constitution of 1787.[8] Similarly, periodicals such as *La Gazeta de México, El Mercurio Peruano,* and *El Papel periódico de la ciudad de Santa Fé de Bogotá* discussed aspects of the French Revolution while defending the Catholic faith and the Spanish Monarchy.[9]

Periodicals and pamphlets, which became increasingly popular after the French Revolution, reached an important but limited audience in Spain and America. Although the major publications from Madrid, Mexico, and Lima circulated in the provinces by means of subscriptions, they directly reached only a few thousand people. Oral communication played a greater role in disseminating modern ideas to a broader public. *Tertulias,* originally informal family occasions on which men and women were joined by friends and acquaintances, expanded at the end of the seventeenth and the beginning of the eighteenth centuries to become social gatherings to discuss lit-

---

7 *Diario de México,* II, Núm. 1454 (September 24, 1809).

8 The *Gazeta de Madrid* (May 7, 1776) and the *Mercurio histórico y político* (July 1776), for example, note the appearance of Thomas Paine's *Common Sense.* With regard to the independence of the United States, see José de Covarruvias, *Memorias históricas de la última guerra con la Gran Bretaña, desde el año de 1774: Estados Unidos de América, año 1774 y 1775* (Madrid: Imprenta de Antonio Ramírez, 1783). See also Luis Angel García Melero, *La independencia de los Estados Unidos de Norteamérica a través de la prensa española* (Madrid: Ministerio de Asuntos Exteriores, 1977); and Mario Rodríguez, *La revolución americana de 1776 y el mundo hispánico: ensayos y documentos* (Madrid: Editorial Tecnos, 1976).

9 See the following articles, which discuss the reporting of the French Revolution in American periodicals: Carlos Herrejón Peredo, "México: Luces de Hidalgo y de Abad y Queipo"; Jean Pierre Clément, "La Révolution française dans le *Mercurio Peruano*"; and Renan Silva, "La Revolución Francesa en el 'Papel Periódico de Santafé de Bogotá'," *CARAVELLE: Cahiers du Monde Hispanique et Luso-Brasilien,* 54 (1990), 107–35, 137–51, 165–78.

erature, philosophy, science, and current events. In Spain and America *tertulias* brought elites – noble and nonnoble – merchants, government officials, clergymen, professionals, and other educated people together to discuss a variety of topics. At the turn of the century, distinguished noblewomen of the large capital cities, such as Madrid and Mexico, held fashionable *tertulias* in their homes that attracted the leading personages of the region.[10] *Tertulias* held in private houses remained a popular form of discourse and sociability for educated and higher socioeconomic groups in Spain and America until the nineteenth century because of their familiar, informal, and private nature. Other *tertulias* were composed of special groups, such as university professors and students, lawyers, and clerics.

Although *tertulias* were extremely successful in disseminating ideas, particularly the new useful knowledge, among like-minded and socially prominent groups, members of the emerging middle class sought other venues. In the 1760s it became common for some *tertulias* to be held in private rooms in inns. Although initially limited to a special group, within a short time such *tertulias* became public affairs, incorporating a more diverse group of participants. By the end of the next decade, cafes and taverns became new arenas for social discourse.

Cafes evolved from places where one went to *merendar* (to eat something light in the late afternoon) to locations where society engaged in animated discussion. It became common for subscribers of periodicals to read them aloud in cafes and for patrons to talk for hours about important issues. In Madrid, merchants complained that cafe discussions spread to the streets and shops, preventing business from being conducted. Some forbade discussions in their establishments, claiming that *"tertulias* are harmful." By the end of the century it was alleged that

everyone has become a politician. All anyone talks about is the news, the reforms, the taxes, etc. Even the boys on the corner buy the *Gazeta*. In the taverns and in upper class estab-

---

10 On the role of women, see Alfonso E. Pérez Sánchez and Eleanor A. Sayre, *Goya and the Spirit of the Enlightenment* (Boston: Little, Brown, 1989). Subsequently, during the period of the Cortes at Cádiz, for example, several distinguished women held *tertulias:* Margarita López de Morla's *tertulia* was frequented by the *liberales,* whereas the *serviles* attended the one at doña Frasquita Larrea's house. Mariana de Pontejos, on the other hand, devoted her *tertulia* to the arts. Ramón Solís, *El Cádiz de las Cortes. Vida en la ciudad en los años 1810 a 1813* (Madrid: Editorial Alianza, 1969), 322–30. In Mexico City, for example, María Ignacia Rodríguez de Velasco, popularly known as *la Güera Rodríguez,* hosted one of the most prominent *tertulias* during the independence period. Jaime E. Rodríguez O., "The Transition from Colony to Nation: New Spain, 1820–1821," in *Mexico in the Age of Democratic Revolutions, 1750–1850,* ed. Jaime E. Rodríguez O. (Boulder: Lynne Rienner, 1994), 116. On popular *tertulias* and gatherings, see Virginia Guedea, *En busca de un gobierno alterno: Los Guadalupes de México* (Mexico: UNAM, 1992); and her "The Conspiracies of 1811 or How the Criollos Learned to Organize in Secret," paper presented at the conference: Mexican Wars of Independence, the Empire, and Early Republic, University of Calgary, April 4–5, 1991.

lishments next to Mariblanca, and in the cafe, one hears nothing but talk about revolution, the convention, national representation, liberty, equality. Even whores ask you about Robespierre and Barrère, and it is necessary to have a good stock of newspaper stories to please the girl one is courting.[11]

Similar locations for public discourse also appeared in the New World. According to the *Mercurio peruano,* the first "cafée [sic] público" in America was established in Lima in 1771. Yearning for simpler times, the periodical complained that twenty years later everyone talked only about the great European philosophers and about the events of the day.[12] Mexico City also possessed cafes that by the 1780s had become places where individuals read *gazetas* and discussed current events, history, art, and philosophy. As one writer commented: "The public frequents the cafes. And although science may not be cultivated there, everyone can enrich his command of our Spanish language and exercise reason while developing the ideas that occur to him."[13] Similarly, provincial capitals also became centers of an active public life.[14]

Whereas *tertulias* and cafes catered to the wealthier segments of society, taverns, avenues, parks, and other public places became centers of discussion for a broader public. There the "popular" segments of society – craftsmen, muleteers, small shopkeepers, lower-level employees, and often the unemployed – gathered to talk about the events of the day. As the *Diario de México* noted in 1806, "Even though the rude and coarse people do not read the dailies and other public papers, perhaps even ignoring their very existence, the useful information which they contain is transmitted imperceptibly by enlightened persons. Thus, little by little knowledge is spread."[15] With such open and widespread interest in the ideas and events of the day, it was only natural that the authorities in Spain and America should become concerned lest unrest occur. Taverns particularly worried officials because they perceived them as places where popular discontent might explode. In 1791, when fear of French revolutionary ideas became

---

11 Quoted in Javier Varela Tortajada, "La élite ilustrada ante las nuevas ideas: Actitudes y contradicciones," in *España y la Revolución francesa,* ed. Enrique Moral Saldoval (Madrid: Editorial Pablo Iglesias, 1989), note 18, pp. 63–4.

12 *Mercurio peruano,* No 12 (February 10, 1791).

13 *Diario de México,* XII, Núm. 1616 (March 5, 1810).

14 Isabel Olmos Sánchez, *La sociedad mexicana en vísperas de la independencia (1787–1821)* (Murcia: Universidad de Murcia, 1989), 277–8.

15 *Diario de México,* II, Núm. 105 (January 13, 1806). A decade and a half later, Joel R. Poinsett remarked that in Mexico "Most of the people in the cities can read and write. I would not be understood as including the *leperos;* but I have frequently remarked men, clothed in the garb of extreme poverty, reading the Gazettes in the streets." *Notes on Mexico made in the Autumn of 1822* (Philadelphia: H. C. Carey and Lea, 1824), 83.

paramount, the authorities restricted for a time the nature of activities in many public places.[16]

The success of *tertulias* encouraged some individuals to establish more formal organizations. Inspired by the Royal Society of London, the Society of Dublin, and the royal academies of Paris, Berlin, and St. Petersburg, a group in the provincial city of Vergara, Spain, transformed the *tertulia* of the Conde de Peñaflorida into a formal organization known as the *Sociedad Vazcongada de Amigos del País* (Basque Society of Friends of the Country) in 1764. The society initially attracted the most important men from the Basque provinces as its members. Soon it admitted other prominent Spaniards and a few distinguished foreigners. The Sociedad Vazcongada supported education in Vergara. After the Jesuits were expelled, its members founded the Real Seminario Patriótico Vazcongado in 1776, an institution that became a distinguished academy for scientific and technological education, focusing on useful sciences. Subsequently, the curriculum was expanded to include the humanities. The society and the seminary became major centers for discussion of all sorts of useful knowledge. Members and prominent visitors often presented papers on a wide variety of subjects, many of which appeared in the society's *Extractos* or in the *Espírito de los mejores diarios*. As the Sociedad Vazcongada gained influence, its membership expanded to include Americans; by 1773 it had admitted numerous overseas members, the vast majority in New Spain: 120 in Mexico City, 5 each in Querétaro and San Luis Potosí, 4 in Oaxaca, 3 in Valladolid, 2 in Zacatecas, 1 each in Guadalajara and Veracruz, 14 in Havana, 6 in Cartagena, 4 in Lima, 3 in Quito, 2 in Manila, and 1 in Buenos Aires. Others joined in later years.

Subsequently, other *sociedades de amigos del país* were established in Spain: Tudela (1770) and Baeza (1774). The following year Pedro Rodríguez, Conde de Campomanes, founded the Sociedad Económica Madrileña (Madrid Economic Society). He also prevailed upon the Council of Castilla to issue a circular encouraging other cities to establish such organizations. By 1820, seventy *sociedades amigos del país* existed in the Peninsula. After 1775 all were modeled on the Madrid society. Although these groups tailored their activities to local circumstances, most addressed social and economic problems; they emphasized agriculture, health, education, and what today is called *economic development*. Although most societies consisted only of men, the Sociedad Madrileña admitted several women, among them the

---

16 *Diario de México,* II, Núm. 105 (January 13, 1806). On taverns, see also Virginia Guedea, "México en 1812: Control político y bebidas prohibidas," *Estudios de Historia Moderna y Contemporánea de México,* Núm. 8 (1980), 23–65, and her "The Conspiracies of 1811 or How the Criollos Learned to Organize in Secret"; as well as Luis González Obregón, *La vida en México en 1810* (Mexico: Viuda de C. Bouret, 1911).

enlightened noblewoman and patron of the arts the Condesa-Duquesa de Benavente. In 1787 she founded the Junta de Damas Matritense (Junta of Madrid Ladies), which devoted itself to addressing problems of social justice, such as prisons and orphanages, as well as education and hygiene.[17]

Several *sociedades de amigos del país* were established overseas after 1780: Manila in 1781, Santiago de Cuba in 1783, Mompox, New Granada, in 1784, Lima in 1787, Quito and Havana in 1791, Guatemala in 1794, and Santa Fé de Bogotá and Buenos Aires in 1801. Most were founded to support the publication of periodicals, such as the *Mercurio peruano,* the *Primicias de la cultura de Quito,* the *Gazeta de Guatemala,* the *Papel periódico de Santa Fé de Bogotá,* and the *Telégrafo mercantil del Río de la Plata.* The American societies, unlike those in Spain, faced opposition from the royal authorities, who objected to their criticism of existing institutions and, often, of government officials.

Although most American societies existed for only a short time, they nonetheless contributed substantially to the well-being of their areas. Like the societies in Spain, the American associations disseminated new knowledge, addressed local issues, and concerned themselves with practical improvements. Also, like their Peninsular counterparts, they organized literary *tertulias,* dramas, plays, and other functions.[18] It is striking that the populous and wealthy Viceroyalty of New Spain did not develop economic societies, even though some were proposed for Veracruz and Mérida. Apparently, *novohispanos* did not require such associations to disseminate modern philosophy and to discuss local questions. The area possessed many institutions of higher education, professional associations, and other bodies that supported newspapers and contributed to public discourse. Nonetheless, the absence of the societies remains puzzling.

The numerous universities and colleges in Spain and America also became centers of intellectual change in the latter part of the eighteenth century. Although the Jesuits and the Franciscans had been active in introducing modern philosophy, the major impetus occurred in 1771 with the reform that modernized the curriculum of the University of Salamanca, the premier institution in Spain and the model for American universities.[19] Thereafter, although not without struggle, modern scientific views were taught at all the institutions of higher learning in the Spanish world. The transformation had a profound effect because university graduates of the

---

17 Paula de Demerson, *María Francisca de Sales Portocarrero, Condesa de Montijo: Una figura de la Ilustración* (Madrid: Editora Nacional, 1975), 132.

18 Shafer, *The Economic Societies,* is the most detailed account of these organizations.

19 George M. Addy, *The Enlightenment in the University of Salamanca* (Durham: Duke University Press, 1966). See also Batia B. Siebzehner, *La universidad americana y la Ilustración: Autoridad y conocimiento en Nueva España y el Río de la Plata* (Madrid: Mapfre, 1992).

1780s and 1790s, both from Spain and from America, led the great political revolution of the Spanish world after 1808.[20]

John Tate Lanning, who devoted his life to studying academic culture in Spanish America, concluded as follows:

[Spanish American] students in 1785 had an infinitely more varied and adequate grasp of the problems of the learned world than any scientist . . . would expect of undergraduates today. From the methodical doubt of Descartes, or the gravitation of Sir Isaac Newton, to Franklin's experiments in electricity, or the latest developments in hydraulics, there was scarcely a problem not defended or reviewed in some examination . . . in the last half of the eighteenth century. The colonial professor made thoroughgoing moderns of at least 95 percent of his students without dependence on prohibited books. . . .

Indeed, the intellectual revolution in the Spanish colonies depended very little upon the exuberant radicalism of the *philosophes*. What boots it that an Olavide [from Peru] moved in the salons of Paris? He was educated in America and what counts is that the whole creole element revised its ideas at home, openly, and above board.[21]

Educated Americans, like their Spanish counterparts, were modern, enlightened individuals who were well prepared to address the many complex problems of their age. Indeed, when a military and political crisis ensued in 1808, Americans proved to be as able to assume political responsibility during that emergency as their Peninsular colleagues.[22]

In its effort to promote modern science, the Crown also created a number of institutes, academies, and seminaries in America. During the 1780s, it sent a distinguished group of Spanish scientists and scholars to the New World to staff the new Enlightenment institutions in New Spain, such as the College of Mines — the first technological institute established on the Continent — the Botanical Gardens, and the Academy of San Carlos. Many of these Spaniards, including Martín de Sessé, Vicente Cervantes, Andrés Manuel del Río, and Fausto de Elhuyar, had studied in Germany and already had established reputations as scientists. The Crown also sponsored scientific research; especially noteworthy were the great botanical expedi-

---

20 On the transformation in America, see "The Last Stand of the Schoolmen," chapter 3 of John Tate Lanning, *Academic Culture in the Spanish Colonies* (London: Oxford University Press, 1940), 61–89; and Siebzehner, *La universidad americana y la Ilustración*, 125–230. On Spain, see Juan Marichal, "From Pistoia to Cádiz: A Generation's Itinerary, 1786–1812," in Aldridge, *The Ibero-American Enlightenment*, 97–110.

21 John Tate Lanning, *The Eighteenth-Century Enlightenment in the University of San Carlos de Guatemala* (Ithaca: Cornell University Press, 1956), 115.

22 The American deputies to the Cortes of Cádiz — for example, men educated at the universities of Guadalajara, Guatemala, Quito, Chuquisaca, and Caracas, as well as those of Mexico and Lima – distinguished themselves in that parliament. As María Teresa Berruezo noted, "The American deputies possessed a high level of knowledge, indeed, even greater than that of the *peninsulares*." *La participación americana en las Cortes de Cádiz (1810–1814)* (Madrid: Centro de Estudios Constitucionales, 1986), 303.

tions of José Celestino Mutis to New Granada, Hipólito Ruiz and José Antonio Pavón to Peru, and Vicente Rodríguez Olmedo to Quito. To their surprise, if not always to their delight, the European scientists found distinguished Americans, such as José Antonio Alzate in Mexico City, Pedro Fermín Vargas in Bogotá, José Mexía Llequerica in Quito, and Hipólito Unanue in Lima, already practicing modern science.

The arrival of the Europeans not only brought the latest scientific methods to the New World, it also stimulated intellectual interchange between Americans and Spanish scholars. Scientific expeditions, such as those of Alejandro Malespina and José Mariano Moziño to the Pacific coast, provided Americans the opportunity to participate. But relations between Peninsular and New World scientists did not always prove to be harmonious. To their dismay, Americans discovered that enlightened Spaniards possessed many prejudices about the New World. The scientific exchange, therefore, impressed upon Americans the need to maintain an independent and critical attitude. Further, it underscored the fact that they were the intellectual equals of the Europeans. Such realizations not only filled them with pride in their accomplishments but also contributed to their growing belief that they should obtain political equality.[23]

Although there were a number of other institutions that contributed to public discourse in the latter part of the eighteenth century, two were particularly important in America: the *consulados* (merchants' guilds) and the *colegios de abogados* (colleges of lawyers or bar associations). *Consulados* had existed in the New World since the late sixteenth century. After the introduction of the system of *comercio libre,* new *consulados* were established in Spain and America. In the New World, these institutions sought to stimulate regional development. From Veracruz to Buenos Aires, the new *consulados* devoted themselves to studying local social and economic conditions. On the basis of these researches, they issued reports suggesting how to improve their economies. These activities naturally contributed to the heightening of a *conciencia de sí.*[24]

23 José Joaquín Izquierdo, *Montaña y los orígenes del movimiento social y científico de México* (Mexico: Ediciones Ciencia, 1955); José Luis Peset, *Ciencia y libertad: El papel del científico ante la Independencia americana* (Madrid: Consejo Superior de Investigaciones Científicas, 1987); Thomas F. Glick, "Science and Independence in Latin America (with Special Reference to New Granada)," *Hispanic American Historical Review,* 71:2 (May 1991), 307–34; Arthur R. Steele, *Flowers for the King: The Expeditions of Ruiz and Pavón and the Flora of Peru* (Durham: Duke University Press, 1964); Iris H. W. Engstrand, *Spanish Scientists in the New World: The Eighteenth-Century Expeditions* (Seattle: University of Washington Press, 1981).

24 See, for example, the reports of José María Quirós, *Guía de negociantes. Compendio de la legislación mercantil de España e Indias* (Mexico: UNAM, 1986); and Germán O. E. Tjarks, *El Consulado de Buenos Aires y sus proyecciones en la historia del Río de la Plata,* 2 vols. (Buenos Aires: Universidad de Buenos Aires, 1962).

Like the merchants, those who possessed knowledge of *el derecho* (the law) contributed to the creation of a modern climate of opinion in the Spanish world. Initially, not all such individuals were lawyers in the formal sense; many were members of other professions, such as notaries, clergymen, writers, and academics. What mattered was that they understood the law. Formal institutions of the legal profession, such as law faculties at leading universities, the college of lawyers, and the academy of jurisprudence, had long existed in Spain. These bodies, which were also introduced into America, became the vehicles for analysis and commentary of the legal system and its relationship to society. In the Spanish world, the law provided the basis for significant political concepts, such as the relationship between individuals and the state, the responsibility of the ruler to the people, and, most important of all, the nature of sovereignty. Among the concepts legal commentators, such as the seventeenth-century scholar Francisco Suárez, advanced, two would become significant in the early nineteenth century – the notion of a compact between the people and the king and the idea of popular sovereignty.[25] In the New World, the study of *derecho indiano,* the laws of the Indies, strengthened the growing belief that America possessed a special body of constitutional law. That notion also contributed to the growing *conciencia de sí* in the New World.[26]

The intellectual transformation of the Spanish world in the late eighteenth century coincided with the emergence of new political ideas. In Spain nationalists reinterpreted history to create a new national myth. Enlightened Spaniards argued that the early Visigoths had enjoyed a form of tribal democracy. Supposedly, these Germanic ancestors forged the first Spanish constitution. Later, in the thirteenth century, Spain developed the

25 Francisco Suárez, *Tratado de las leyes y de Dios legislador,* trans. Jaime Torrubiano Ripoll (Madrid: Reus, 1918).

26 On the nature of juridical concepts and the state, see Colin M. MacLachlan, *Spain's Empire in the New World: The Role of Ideas in Institutional and Social Change* (Berkeley: University of California Press, 1988). On law and lawyers in Spain, consult Richard L. Kagan, *Lawsuits and Litigants in Castile, 1500–1700* (Chapel Hill: University of North Carolina Press, 1981). See also María del Refugio González, "El Real e Ilustre Colegio de Abogados de México durante la transición al México independiente," in *Five Centuries of Mexican History/Cinco siglos de historia de México,* 2 vols., eds. Virginia Guedea and Jaime E. Rodríguez O. (Mexico and Irvine: Instituto Mora and University of California, 1992), 1:267–84; and her "El Ilustre y Real Colegio de Abogados de México frente a la Revolución francesa (1808–1827)," in *La Revolución francesa en México* eds. Solange Alberro, Alicia Hernández Chávez, and Elías Trabulse (Mexico: El Colegio de México, 1992), 111–35; Charles R. Cutter, *The Legal Culture of Northern New Spain, 1700–1810* (Albuquerque: University of New Mexico Press, 1995); Margarita Garrido, *Reclamos y representaciones. Variaciones sobre la política en el Nuevo Reino de Granada, 1770–1815* (Bogotá: Banco de la República, 1993), 71–6; and Victor Manuel Uribe Uran, "Rebellion of the Young Mandarins: Lawyers, Political Parties and the State in Colombia, 1780–1850" (Ph.D. diss., University of Pittsburgh, 1993), 68–186, and his "Kill All the Lawyers!: Lawyers and the Independence Movement in New Granada, 1809–1820," *The Americas,* 52:2 (October 1995), 175–210.

first parliament of Europe, the *cortes*. According to this interpretation of history, medieval Spain had enjoyed democracy but the despotic Habsburg kings destroyed it. Although earlier *cortes* had represented individual kingdoms, such as Aragón and Castilla, not the entire nation, reformers had a unified body in mind when they spoke of reconvening a *cortes*. Their ideas culminated in the works of Spain's foremost legal historian, Francisco Martínez Marina, whose massive *Teoría de las cortes* implied that the restoration of a national representative body was necessary to revitalize the country.[27] Subsequently, these historical and legal interpretations would have a profound effect on the Spanish political system. They would provide the basis for notions of popular sovereignty and representative government.

Educated groups in America were familiar with Spanish legal and political concepts. During the late eighteenth and early nineteenth centuries, New World legal scholars – especially professors in the law faculties of the continent's universities – reinterpreted Suárez's compact theory to further their own interests. Like the Peninsulars, Americans looked to their past to forge a national myth that suited their needs. As in the mother country, a new interpretation of history contributed to the formation of a new ideology. The study of preconquest history, particularly the work of the exiled Jesuits, provided the basis for the belief that pre-Hispanic states formed the core of the New World kingdoms.

Many Americans, like the nationalist Spaniards, also based their own national myths on a historic constitution. According to this interpretation, Americans were mestizos who derived their rights from two sources: their Indian progenitors, who originally possessed the land, and their Spanish ancestors, who in conquering the New World obtained privileges from the Crown, including the right to convene their own *cortes*. The agreement, however, was not between America and Spain, but between each New World kingdom and the king. The pact with the monarch seemed to be further confirmed by the existence of the special laws of the Indies. Since the sixteenth century, European as well as New World legal scholars had commented on the unique nature of *derecho indiano*. The publication of the great *Recopilación de leyes de los Reynos de las Indias* in 1680 provided the impetus for extensive new interpretations. In the second half of the eighteenth century, a number of jurists published new collections of laws issued in America.[28]

27 Herr, *The Eighteenth Century Revolution*, 337–47; Francisco Martínez Marina, *Teoría de las cortes*, 2 vols., Biblioteca de Autores Españoles (Madrid: Ediciones Atlas, 1968–1969). His critical introduction to the *Siete Partidas* has been reissued together with an excellent study of his thought as Volume 194 of Biblioteca de Autores Españoles (Madrid: Ediciones Atlas, 1966).

28 Collections of laws, such as Eusebio Ventura Beleño's *Recopilación sumaria de los autos acordados de la Real Audiencia y Sala del Crimen de esta Nueva España*, 2 vols., ed. María del Refugio González (Mexico: UNAM, 1981), and legal manuals like José María Alvarez's *Instituciones de derecho real de Castilla*

Such works contributed to the notion that the New World possessed its own unwritten constitution. As Father Servando Teresa de Mier, one of the most distinguished advocates of the thesis of American rights, declared: "Our kings, far from having considered establishing in our Americas the modern system of colonies of other nations, not only made our [kingdoms] the equals of Spain but also granted us the best [institutions] she possessed." And he maintained, "in conclusion it is evident: that under the constitution granted by the kings of Spain to the Americas, these lands are kingdoms independent of her [Spain] without any other link but the king, . . . who, according to political theorists, must govern us as though he were the king of each one of them [the American realms]."[29] The *Gazeta de Buenos Ayres* echoed his view on December 6, 1810, when it asserted: "once the links that tied these peoples to the monarch were dissolved, each province became the master of its destiny since the social compact did not directly establish relations between them [Spain and America], but between the king and these peoples."[30] So widespread was that view that Henry M. Brackenridge, a U.S. agent in South America, reported in 1818: "The Spanish Americans, as the descendants of the first conquerors and settlers, ground their political rights on the provisions of the code of the Indies. They contend that their constitution is of a higher nature than that of Spain; inasmuch as it rests on a compact, between the monarch and their ancestors."[31] Thus, historical and legal interpretations would also provide the intellectual basis of American notions of popular sovereignty, local rights, and equality within the Spanish Monarchy.

By the beginning of the nineteenth century, the educated people of the New World had developed a strong sense of regional identity. They were *novohispanos,* Guatemalans, *quiteños,* Peruvians, and Chileans, as well as Americans. They also had developed a modern critical perspective. Although it took approximately two to four months for news to travel from Europe to America, the people of the Western Hemisphere were not isolated. They were up-to-date in their views and knowledge of current events. Moreover, they possessed a strong sense of their rights, and they

---

y de Indias, 2 vols., eds. Jorge Mario García Laguardia and María del Refugio González (Mexico: UNAM, 1982) provided Americans with a sense of their own unique identity. As Gómez Hoyos noted, many of the independence leaders were lawyers with a "solid classical education in the humanities, especially in the branches of law . . . [; they did not have to rely on] French sources." *La independencia de Colombia,* 83.

29 Servando Teresa de Mier, "Idea de la Constitución dada a las Américas por los reyes de España antes de la invasión del antiguo despotismo," in *Obras completas de Servando Teresa de Mier,* vol. 4, *La formación de un republicano,* ed. Jaime E. Rodríguez O. (Mexico: UNAM, 1988), 57.

30 *Gazeta de Buenos Ayres,* Núm. 27 (December 6, 1810), 423.

31 Henry M. Brackenridge, *Voyage to South America Performed by Order of the American Government in the Years 1817 and 1818,* 2 vols. (London: J. Miller, 1820), 1:34–5.

resented the restrictions imposed by royal authorities. Although a tiny minority of extremists talked about revolution, most Americans preferred to utilize the political processes to obtain local autonomy and equal status within the Monarchy. Given the historic flexibility of the Spanish Monarchy, it is likely that in time Americans would have achieved recognition of those rights and an acceptable measure of home rule, possibly a commonwealth arrangement similar to the one that Canada obtained. Events in Europe, however, prevented an orderly restructuring of the relationship between the Crown and America.

The Crisis of the Monarchy

The French Revolution of 1789, which plunged Europe into twenty years of war, and the upheavals it unleashed precipitated a political crisis in the Spanish world. Precisely when the Monarchy required strong, farsighted, and experienced government, it lost the great reformer King Carlos III in December 1788. His successor, Carlos IV, was weak, vacillating, and ineffectual. Initially, the new king continued his father's policies by retaining the Conde de Floridablanca as chief minister. But the radicalism of the French Revolution frightened Floridablanca, who imposed press censorship in an attempt to insulate the Spanish world from the French revolutionary virus. When this tactic failed, he instituted more repressive measures, including suspending the press in 1791 and reactivating the Inquisition to search out dangerous books and potential subversives.[32]

These actions provoked strong opposition in Spain and threatened Carlos's cousin, Louis XVI of France, who had sworn to uphold the French constitution. To calm the country and to reduce the tensions between Spain and France, Carlos IV replaced Floridablanca with the Francophile Conde de Aranda in February 1792. The change in ministry permitted news from France and revolutionary propaganda to pour into Spain because Aranda relaxed censorship. The policy reversal concerned many Spaniards. As radicalism increased in France, palace intrigues against Spain's first minister gained support. As a result, the elderly Aranda was ousted and replaced by a favorite of the royal family, the twenty-five-year-old guards' officer Manuel Godoy.

The new minister governed Spain from 1793 to 1808, a period that would have taxed the talents of a more experienced and respected statesman. Godoy, unfortunately, possessed neither the education nor the experience for such a formidable task. He gained unprecedented power because he enjoyed the confidence of the king and queen. The people, both in Spain and in America, resented Godoy's influence and his unmerited rise to

32 Herr, *The Eighteenth-Century Revolution*, 239–314; Shafer, *The Economic Societies*, 22–3.

power, resentment that increased when the king bestowed titles and favors upon his minister. Godoy's lack of credentials and his relationship with the royal family made the minister a ready target for detractors. Rumors circulated that he was the queen's lover and that anyone could buy his favor. These stories tarnished the reputation of the royal family and the Crown at a time when the tensions resulting from the grave international situation were creating discontent with the government. The concentration of power in the hands of one man concerned many who believed that what came to be known as *ministerial despotism* nullified the traditional checks and balances of the Spanish Monarchy.

Godoy, who considered himself a man of the Enlightenment, attempted to continue the policies and reforms of Carlos III. This tactic won him little support from either the bureaucracy or the intellectual community, who considered him an upstart. At the same time, his policies alienated traditionalists who feared that religion and society were threatened by the excesses of the French Revolution. Because Godoy's administration became the symbol of the abuse of power and extreme corruption, many individuals appointed to office both in Spain and in America during his long tenure were discredited.[33]

The Jacobin reign of terror and Louis XVI's execution shocked the Spanish world and drove the nation into conflict with France. Thus, in 1793 Carlos IV joined other European monarchs in a war against the regicide French Republic, only to see his country defeated. The struggle strained the Spanish political system and caused severe economic dislocations. When hostilities began, royal finances in Spain were sound and the economy was prosperous. The war, however, forced the Crown to raise taxes and to impose the first direct levies on the nobility. To meet the emergency, the government began to issue *vales reales* and ordered the expropriation of Church property. These measures, which failed to halt the deterioration of the economy, further eroded the government's popular support. Worse yet, in the treaties of 1795 and 1796, Paris imposed a humiliating peace that bound Spain to France, thus converting the country into an enemy of Britain.

The new international alignment forced Spain into a series of wars with Britain and its allies, further damaging the Spanish economy. The Peace of Amiens (1802) briefly ended hostilities between Britain and France, allowing the Peninsula's distressed economy to revive. But by 1804 France and Spain were once again at war with Great Britain. The British defeated the Spanish navy at Trafalgar, and the French blockade of 1806, Napoleon's *continental system,* devastated Spain's economy. These disasters not only dis-

33 Herr, *The Eighteenth-Century Revolution,* 239–375; Miguel Artola, *Los orígenes de la España contemporánea,* 2 vols. (Madrid: Instituto de Estudios Políticos, 1959), 1:103–46; Gabriel Lovett, *Napoleon and the Birth of Modern Spain,* 2 vols. (New York: New York University Press, 1965), 1:86–132.

rupted commerce with Spanish America but also caused massive unemployment and severe inflation, eventually bankrupting the government. The country's economic and political misfortunes were popularly attributed to Godoy's malign influence.[34]

Those who hoped to restore the nation to its former prosperity looked to Crown Prince Fernando as their champion because he opposed Godoy and resented his parents' dependence upon the favorite. In March 1808 the prince's followers forced Carlos IV to abdicate in favor of his son, who became Fernando VII. The quarrel within the royal family coincided with the entry of French troops into the Iberian Peninsula. In 1807 Napoleon had obtained permission to cross Spain in order to occupy Portugal to enforce his continental system. Once his troops entered the country, the emperor of the French decided to replace the Spanish Bourbons. Using the dispute over the Spanish Crown as an excuse, Bonaparte lured the royal family into France, where he compelled them to abdicate in his favor. Then he granted the Spanish Monarchy to his brother Joseph.

Although the Spanish authorities, the royal bureaucracy, the nobility, the clergy, and the army at first accepted José Bonaparte as king of Spain, the people did not. Even before the abdications, on May 2, 1808, the population of Madrid rose against the French, an initiative emulated throughout Spain. Their actions triggered a series of political and military events that transformed the Spanish world. In ways no political theorist ever contemplated, a worldwide monarchy was cast adrift. As Lord Byron aptly observed, now they were "a Kingless people for a nerveless state."[35]

The Political Revolution

The vast majority of Spaniards and virtually all Americans opposed the French. After two centuries, we have come to accept the results of the French Revolution as beneficial. But at the time, the Hispanic people associated the French movement with the revolutionary excesses: the terror, atheism, anticlericalism (particularly the civil constitution of the clergy), and a new and virulent imperialism that had brutally subjugated other European peoples. Far from offering opportunities for democracy and progress, the French epitomized all that the people of Spain and America dreaded. Indeed, French domination implied more centralization and even greater economic exactions.

The people of the Peninsula and the New World, therefore, were virtu-

---

34 Richard Herr, "Hacia el derrumbe del antiguo régimen: Crisis fiscal y desamortización bajo Carlos VI," *Moneda y Crédito,* Núm. 118 (September 1971), 37–100; Brian R. Hamnett, *La política española en una época revolucionaria, 1790–1820* (Mexico: Fondo de Cultura Económica, 1985), 47–58.
35 Lord Byron, *Childe Harold's Prilgrimage* (London: Murray, 1859), canto I, stanza 86, p. 63.

ally unanimous in their opposition to the French. The external threat
heightened the factors that united them: one monarchy, one faith, one culture, one society in crisis. They constituted what soon came to be known as
la Nación Española, a nation consisting of the Peninsula and the overseas
kingdoms. As Simón Bolívar later recalled, "the habit of obedience; a community of interests, of understanding, of religion; mutual goodwill; a tender regard for the birthplace and good name of our forefathers; ultimately,
all that fulfilled our expectations came from Spain. From these arose a principle of fidelity that seemed eternal."[36]

While sharing the belief that they belonged to one Spanish Nation, the
people of Spain and America differed on a number of issues. Neither the
Bourbon reforms nor the rise of American patriotism, however, had shattered the legitimacy of the system or created an unbridgeable chasm
between Spaniards and Americans. Although those processes engendered
contention, the Spanish Monarchy still retained the flexibility required to
achieve a new equilibrium. It is likely that, had not European events prevented it, in time the two parties would have reached an acceptable accommodation. Thus in 1808, Spain and Spanish America responded in the
same way to the collapse of the Monarchy. The people of both areas drew
upon common concepts and sought similar solutions to the evolving crisis.
Inspired by the intellectual revolution of the late eighteenth century and
the legal foundations of the Monarchy, most agreed that in the absence of
the king, sovereignty reverted to the people, who now possessed the
authority and the responsibility to defend the nation.

News of four events – Carlos IV's abdication in favor of his son Fernando
VII, the abdication of the royal family in Bayonne, the rising of the people
of Madrid against the French on May 2, and the creation of local juntas in
Spain – first reached the Atlantic ports of America in May, June, and July
and then spread to other areas of the continent. The situation mystified
both the royal authorities and the people. Who ruled Spain? Who, if anyone, should be obeyed? What should be done? Americans of all races and
classes were unanimous in expressing their fidelity to Fernando VII, their
opposition to Napoleon, and their determination to defend their *patrias*
against the French.

As the startling events in Europe unfolded, it became evident that,
depending on their interests, groups favored differing responses. The royal
authorities in the New World found themselves in a delicate position.

36 Simón Bolívar, "Carta de Jamaica," in *Pensamiento político de la emancipación, 1790–1825,* 2 vols. eds.
José Luis Romero and Luis Alberto Romero (Caracas: Biblioteca de Ayacucho, 1977), 2:84. Carole
Leal Curiel provides a detailed account of the nature of "American loyalty" in Venezuela during the
last years of the eighteenth century in *El discurso de la fidelidad: Construcción social del espacio como símbolo del poder regio* (Caracas: Biblioteca de la Academia Nacional de la Historia, 1990), especially
101–69.

Many had been appointed by Godoy, who was now discredited and suspected of treason by most Americans. Papers that arrived from Spain and Britain depicted a complex and evolving situation that pitted the Spanish people against the royal officials. The constituted authorities in the Peninsula had recognized the abdication of the royal family in favor of Napoleon, but the people of Spain refused to accept the change in dynasty. Since they had received their mandate from the king, the royal officials in America possessed no authority unless they recognized a new government in Spain, either that of Joseph Bonaparte or of some still unknown entity. Many, however, argued that inasmuch as they had been legitimately appointed, they could legitimately retain their posts until Fernando was restored to the throne. A few officials in the New World, like some of their counterparts in the Peninsula, favored the French, but most preferred waiting in the hope that new information would help them reach the correct decision.

Initially, the political uncertainty generated by the collapse of the Monarchy provided Americans favoring greater local control, generally but not exclusively the urban elite, an opportunity to press for home rule. That tendency emerged with great clarity in New Spain. News of events in the Peninsula reached Mexico City in June and July 1808. Throughout the viceroyalty, people expressed their support for Fernando VII and their opposition to Napoleon. The capital and the leading provincial cities held festivities in honor of the king that, according to Hira de Gortari Rabiela, constituted "a brief collective catharsis which immediately alleviated the insecurity and concern. Thus, the festivities allowed the people temporarily to forget the uncertainty and fear provoked by the French occupation of Spain."[37]

Despite the show of unity, the new situation divided the upper classes. Most European Spaniards wanted either to temporize or to recognize an authority in Spain. In Mexico City, many criollos, such as the *regidores* (city councilmen) Juan Francisco de Azacárate, Francisco Primo de Verdad, and the Marqués de Uluapa; the *alcalde de crimen* (magistrate of the criminal chamber) of the *audiencia,* Jacobo Villaurrutia; and prominent citizens such as the Conde de Medina, the Conde de Regla, and the Marqués de San Juan de Rayas, on the other hand, favored autonomy. On July 19 the American-dominated Ayuntamiento of Mexico submitted a resolution to Viceroy José de Iturrigaray asking him to continue *provisionally* in charge of the government. The *ayuntamiento* justified its position on the basis of traditional Spanish political theory, reminding Iturrigaray that "in the absence or during the impediment [of the king], sovereignty lies represented in all the kingdom and the classes that form it; and more particularly in those supe-

---

37 Hira de Gortari Rabiela, "Julio–agosto de 1808: 'La lealtad mexicana,'" *Historia Mexicana,* 39:1 (July–September 1989), 201.

rior tribunals that govern it and administer justice and in those corporations that represent the public voice."[38] According to the *ayuntamiento,* the representatives of the nation were those groups and entities that traditionally possessed the right to representation in the *cortes* of Spain. As soon as they learned of the proposal of the Ayuntamiento of Mexico, other cities such as Querétaro and Valladolid requested the convocation of a congress of municipalities.

Viceroy Iturrigaray appeared to accede to the arguments of the American Spaniards. On September 1, 1808, he requested that the *ayuntamientos* of New Spain appoint representatives to a meeting in the capital. The Real Acuerdo (royal council), composed primarily of European Spaniards, objected to the summoning of a congress of cities. Instead, Viceroy Iturrigaray convened four meetings of the principal corporations of Mexico City – the *audiencia,* the *ayuntamiento,* the *consulado,* the mining guild, the military, the *fuero* courts, the university, the monasteries of Guadalupe, Santo Domingo, and Carmen, the nobility, and the Indian governors of the city's *parcialidades* (Indian communities) – on August 9 and 31 and on September 1 and 9 to advise him: in short, a body very similar to that recommended by the *ayuntamiento* but limited to the capital.

The meetings were tempestuous. Recently arrived representatives of the juntas of Sevilla and Oviedo competed with one another for recognition as the legitimate authorities in Spain. The viceroy rejected their claims, declaring that "Spain is now in a state of anarchy. There are supreme juntas everywhere, and we should not obey any of them." Although the meetings resolved nothing, they convinced the *gachupines* that Iturrigaray's apparent support for the American autonomists threatened their position in the viceroyalty. News from Spain that mobs in Cádiz had removed Godoy's appointees, calling them French collaborators, only added to the Spaniards' apprehension. Unwilling to permit the American elite to indulge in their desire for home rule, shortly after midnight on September 16, 1808, a small group of Spaniards led by Gabriel Yermo arrested the viceroy. At two o'clock in the morning, immediately after the *golpe de estado,* the archbishop and the audiencia approved the viceroy's removal from office and appointed the eighty-year-old Field Marshal Pedro Garibay acting viceroy. The conspirators subsequently arrested the leaders of the autonomy movement.[39]

38 "Testimonio de la sesión celebrada por el Ayuntamiento de México, el 19 de julio de 1808," in *Documentos históricos mexicanos,* 7 vols., ed. Genaro García (Mexico: Museo Nacional de Arqueología, Historia y Etnología, 1910), I, 27.

39 Virginia Guedea, "Criollos y peninsulares en 1808: Dos puntos de vista sobre lo español" (Licenciatura thesis: Universidad Iberoamericana, 1964); Enrique Lafuente Ferrari, *El Virrey Iturrigaray y los orígenes de la independencia de México* (Madrid: Instituto Gonzalo Fernández de Oviedo, 1941).

The following morning, they informed the inhabitants of Mexico that "The people, which has taken the person of the . . . viceroy, has imperiously demanded his separation [from office] for reasons of utility and general convenience." As Virginia Guedea notes, the conspirators appealed to the authority of *the people* in an effort to legitimate their actions because by that time the concept of popular sovereignty had gained considerable authority; in Spain popular movements had removed officials whom the people distrusted.[40] Although the European Spaniards dominated the viceroyalty, their *golpe de estado* shattered legitimacy in New Spain. Their actions convinced some Americans that force would be necessary to secure their rights as citizens of the Spanish Monarchy.

The Peninsular crisis also created divisions in Venezuela, which had been characterized by relatively harmonious relations among elite groups. Earlier, in 1806, Francisco de Miranda, an inveterate revolutionary, convinced the British government that the time was ripe for an invasion of Caracas. With British support, Miranda twice attempted to take Venezuela, once in April with three ships and 150 men and the second time in August with ten vessels and 500 men. The local militias repelled the invaders on both occasions. In neither instance did the people of the area express any support either for Miranda or the British.[41] The residents of the Captaincy General of Venezuela, however, feared that these attacks and the subsequent assault on the Río de la Plata indicated that a larger invasion of the region was likely. Indeed, the British government was preparing a 10,000-man invasion of South America when the French occupation of Spain changed its plans.

News of events in the Peninsula heightened feelings of uncertainty in Venezuela. The Ayuntamiento of Caracas eagerly recognized the accession of Fernando VII on May 9, 1808. Then, on July 15, the French vessel *Serpent* brought documents from the Council of the Indies informing Captain General and Governor Juan de Casas that the Spanish monarchs had abdicated and that the new king was José I, and requiring all officials to swear obedience to the new monarch. Casas, a Francophile, would have recognized José, but popular sentiment was so hostile to the French and so loyal to Fernando VII that he instead convened a junta of notables on July 17 to discuss what ought to be done.

The meeting highlighted the divisions within the elite. The *audiencia,* controlled by *peninsulares,* favored maintaining the status quo, whereas the American-dominated *ayuntamiento* wished to establish a local governing

---

40 Virginia Guedea, "El pueblo de México y la política capitalina, 1808–1812," MS/EM, 10:1 (Winter 1994) 36–7.
41 Caracciolo Parra Pérez, *Historia de la Primera República de Venezuela,* 2 vols. (Madrid: Ediciones Guadarrama, 1959), 1:231–64.

body. After much debate, it was decided to await further news from Spain before taking action. Ten days later, upon learning of the formation of provincial juntas in Spain, Captain General Casas proposed establishing "a junta, following the example of Sevilla." The *ayuntamiento* responded by recommending a junta of eighteen persons that included civil, clerical, and military authorities and representatives of the merchants, planters, the clergy, the university, the college of lawyers, and the people. Fear of a possible republican conspiracy, however, convinced Casas to reject the proposal early in August. Instead, he hoped to maintain the status quo. Nevertheless, leading individuals, both Peninsular and criollo, continued to favor the establishment of a junta. On November 24, they submitted a petition with forty-eight signatures requesting such a body. Although the petitioners represented the elite of Caracas, including many Spaniards, Casas responded by arresting all the signatories. Although some were released shortly, others remained under house arrest until May 1809. Casas's actions prevented the formation of a moderate local junta, but they also caused much discontent that would subsequently emerge in a more radical form.[42]

Events in Europe also profoundly affected the once-isolated Viceroyalty of the Río de la Plata. Buenos Aires, like Caracas, had been the object of an invasion. During the recent war between Britain and France and Spain, a British expeditionary force commanded by Sir Home Popham crossed the Atlantic from the Cape of Good Hope and captured Buenos Aires on June 27, 1806. The viceroy, the Marqués de Sobremonte, fled to the interior, but the *vecinos,* both Europeans and Americans, enrolled in the militias to defend the realm. Led by Santiago Liniers, a French officer in the service of Spain, the Buenos Aires militias defeated the British on August 12, capturing 1,200 men, including the commander. With the backing of the nearly 8,000-strong American militia, Liniers became the military commander of Buenos Aires.

The euphoria of the *porteños* (the people of the port city of Buenos Aires) was short-lived. A second, larger British force captured the fortified city of Montevideo across the estuary from Buenos Aires on February 3, 1807. Once again, Viceroy Sobremonte had failed. In response to popular demands, the *audiencia* ordered Sobremonte deposed and arrested and named Liniers acting captain-general. Although unusual, the action was not contrary to Spanish practice. The Duque de Escalona, a *grande* of Spain, for example, had been similarly removed in New Spain in 1642. Like Sobremonte, Escalona had been accused of incompetence. In that regard, the removal of the viceroy of the Río de la Plata was not a revolutionary act. Indeed, it was less of a threat to legitimacy than the removal of Viceroy Iturrigary in New Spain the following year. In Buenos Aires the other

42 Ibid., 1:329–46.

authorities had agreed on the need to remove the viceroy, whereas in Mexico City they were deeply divided. In all cases, the government in Spain restored normality by appointing new viceroys.

The British force of 9,000, under the command of General John Whitelocke, subsequently crossed the Río de la Plata, outflanked Liniers's troops, and entered Buenos Aires. But the *porteños* led by the senior *alcalde* (city magistrate) of the *ayuntamiento* Martín de Alzaga, a Peninsular merchant, trapped the British in the narrow streets of the city, forcing General Whitelocke to surrender and withdraw from the region.[43] The second and definitive victory over the British, together with the earlier removal of the viceroy, increased *porteño* pride and contributed to a sense that the people of Buenos Aires possessed not only the right but also the ability to function as full-fledged citizens of the Spanish Monarchy.

A potential threat from the neighbor to the north, Brazil, complicated the situation in the Río de la Plata. In 1807, the Portuguese monarch escaped from invading French forces and fled to Rio de Janeiro. Since Portugal was allied with Britain and therefore an enemy of Spain, the possibility of conflict in South America increased with the arrival of the Portuguese Crown. The Ayuntamiento of Buenos Aires, with the support of the *audiencia,* sought to negotiate an agreement with the Portuguese that would ensure peaceful trade throughout the region. As those discussions proceeded, in July 1808 news arrived of the events in Spain. The Ayuntamiento of Buenos Aires, like those of other cities in the viceroyalty, proposed to reject Napoleon and govern in the name of Fernando VII. But Acting Viceroy Liniers hesitated, insisting on waiting for further news. In mid-August a representative of Napoleon arrived, only to be rebuffed. Later that month, Princess Carlota, sister of Fernando VII and wife of the prince regent of Portugal, proclaimed in Rio de Janeiro that she was regent of Spain and the Indies and would rule in the name of her imprisoned brother. If she were recognized as her brother's regent, however, the Río de la Plata would be subordinated to the Portuguese Crown.

The new international situation divided the people of the Río de la Plata. Most Americans backed Liniers, but many Spaniards feared that the acting viceroy favored French rule. Also, they were apprehensive about the growing influence of the Americans. In September, Governor Francisco Javier Elío of Montevideo repudiated the acting viceroy, charged him with treason, and convened a *cabildo abierto* (open town meeting) that established a junta, composed of *peninsulares,* that would govern in the name of Fernando VII. Like the Spaniards of Mexico City, the Europeans of Montevideo had

---

43 Bartolomé Mitre, *Historia de Belgrano y de la independencia argentina,* 4 vols., 6th ed. (Buenos Aires: J. Roldán, 1927), 1:132–55; Tulio Halperín-Donghi, *Politics, Economics, and Society in Argentina in the Revolutionary Period* (Cambridge: Cambridge University Press, 1975), 111–34.

violated the legitimate order in their efforts to retain power. In Buenos Aires, the Spaniards decided to emulate their compatriots in Montevideo. Because of the power of the American militia, they organized a conspiracy to take control of the *ayuntamiento* during that body's elections on January 1, 1809. The Europeans arrived in large numbers. Surprising Liniers and the Americans, they dominated the *ayuntamiento* meeting and established a governing junta composed entirely of Spaniards. The criollos of Buenos Aires, however, responded with force. American troops overwhelmed the *peninsulares*. Alzaga and other Spanish conspirators were exiled to Patagonia. The Europeans had not only failed to take control of the government, they had succeeded in concentrating power in the hands of the Americans. For all intents and purposes, Buenos Aires had achieved autonomy. The city's leaders exercised power in the name of Fernando VII and insisted upon the obedience of the rest of the viceroyalty.[44]

The other parts of the Spanish Monarchy also rejected the French. Juntas of notables in Manila, Havana, Guatemala, Santa Fé de Bogotá, Quito, Lima, Chuquisaca, and Santiago de Chile, for example, expressed their support for Fernando VII. The capitals and many provincial cities also held formal ceremonies to demonstrate their loyalty and the continuity of the established order.[45] Nevertheless, many royal officials and other Spaniards feared that the criollos might insist upon full autonomy unless the Peninsula reasserted its authority.

Although many Americans desired greater local control, most reacted with great patriotism to the French invasion of Spain. While insisting upon their unique Americanness, the people of the New World also reaffirmed their rights as Spaniards. The Ayuntamiento of Santiago de Chile, for example, made its position clear in September 1808 when it declared: "The loyalty of the inhabitants of Chile has in no way degenerated from that of their forefathers. . . . All we want is to be Spaniards; all we want is the rule of our incomparable king."[46] Later, even the insurgents asserted that claim. The first insurgent paper published in New Spain, *El Despertador Americano,* declared on December 20, 1810: "We are now the true Spaniards, the sworn enemies of Napoleon and his lackeys, the legitimate successors to all the

44 Halperín-Donghi, *Politics, Economics, and Society,* 111–34. On the significance of the militia in Buenos Aires, see Lyman L. Johnson, "The Military as Catalyst of Change in Late Colonial Buenos Aires," in *Revolution and Restoration: The Arrangement of Power in Argentina, 1776–1860,* eds. Mark D. Szuchman and Jonathon C. Brown (Lincoln: University of Nebraska Press, 1994), 27–53; and Tulio Halperín Donghi, "Revolutionary Militarization in Buenos Aires, 1806–1815," *Past and Present* 40 (July 1968), 84–107.

45 Xiamara del Carmen Avendaño Rojas, "Procesos electorales y clase política en la Federación de Centroamérica (1810–1840)" (Ph.D. diss., El Colegio de México, 1995), 39–42.

46 Quoted in Simon Collier, *Ideas and Politics of Chilean Independence, 1808–1833* (Cambridge: Cambridge University Press, 1967), 50.

rights of the subjugated [Spaniards in the Peninsula] who neither won [the war] nor died for Fernando [VII]."[47]

The Elections of 1809 in America

In Spain the first impulse after May 1808 was centrifugal – that is, regional juntas were formed to govern individual provinces. Each provincial junta acted as though it were an independent nation. As Miguel Artola has observed, "The overwhelming desire to reassert the sovereignty of the people, clearly seen in all the writings of the time, is the most far reaching result of those events which occurred throughout Spain and in which all Spaniards participated."[48]

Although the Spanish juntas achieved a great victory at Bailén in the summer of 1808, forcing the surrender of a Napoleonic army for the first time, and although the heroic defense of Zaragoza electrified the oppressed peoples of Europe, it was evident that the country could not survive if its government remained splintered. The need for a unified defense led to the organization of a national governing committee, the Junta Suprema Central y Gubernativa de España e Indias (Supreme Central Governing Committee of Spain and the Indies), which first met in Aranjuez on September 25, 1808. Although some provincial bodies initially refused to recognize the Junta Central, most agreed that it should act as a government of national defense in order to wage a war of liberation.[49]

The Spanish reformers were deeply divided. To some, José Bonaparte represented an opportunity to continue the modernization of the Spanish world. He could become the social engineer for whom the *philosophes* had yearned. After all, such a man was remolding the world from Paris. Those few who chose to follow the intruder king came to be known as *afrancesados*.[50] Others rejected the French as foreign invaders who threatened Spain. But nationalist reformers refused to postpone their quest for a modern secular state. Indeed, some, disenchanted with enlightened despotism, saw the invasion, the king's absence, and the revival of the concept of popular sovereignty as an opportunity to introduce modern constitutional government to Spain. Moderate Spaniards, however, believed the Junta Central should convoke a *cortes* in order to unify the country and establish legitimacy until Fernando VII returned. But the majority in the Junta Central favored con-

47 *El Despertador Americano* (December 20, 1810), in Juan E. Hernández y Dávalos, *Colección de documentos para la historia de la guerra de independencia de México de 1808 a 1821*, 6 vols. (Mexico: José María Sandobal Impresor, 1877–1882), 2:312.

48 Miguel Artola, *La España de Fernando VII* (Madrid: Espasa-Calpe, 1968), 68.

49 Artola, *Los orígenes*, 1:145–226; Lovett, *Napoleon and the Birth of Modern Spain*, 1:85–298.

50 Miguel Artola, *Los afrancesados* (Madrid: Instituto de Estudios Políticos, 1953).

solidating the national government and defending the nation without convening a *cortes*.

The Junta Central was particularly concerned about countering French overtures to America. In July 1808, José I invited the New World kingdoms to send six representatives – one for each viceroyalty and one each for Guatemala and Cuba – to a constitutional convention in Bayonne, France. Although the Americans rejected the overture, the Junta Central believed action was necessary to appease the New World's desire for representation.[51] It dispatched royal commissioners, often natives of the region, to serve as liaison agents between local authorities and the government in the Peninsula. In addition, because Spain desperately needed the support of its overseas possessions to continue the struggle, the members of the Junta Central decided to expand the body to include representatives from the New World. On January 22, 1809, it decreed:

Considering that the vast and precious dominions which Spain possesses in the Indies are not properly colonies or factories, such as those of other nations, but an essential and integral part of the Spanish Monarchy . . . , H. M. has chosen to declare . . . that the kingdoms, provinces, and isles which constitute the said dominions should have immediate national representation before his royal person and form part of the Junta Central . . . through their respective deputies. In order for this royal resolution to take effect, the viceroyalties of New Spain, Peru, New Kingdom of Granada, and Buenos Aires, and the independent captaincies general of the island of Cuba, Puerto Rico, Guatemala, Chile, Province of Venezuela, and Philippines are to each name an individual to represent his respective district.[52]

Thus, the Junta Central recognized the Americans' claims that their lands were not colonies but kingdoms, that they constituted integral parts of the Spanish Monarchy, and that they possessed the right of representation in the national government. The decree indicated that the *ayuntamientos* of the provincial capitals were to elect three individuals "of well known probity, talent and learning" and select one by lot. Then the *real acuerdo* would elect three from that group and choose the final representative by lot. In addition, the *ayuntamientos* of the provincial capitals were to provide their delegates with credentials and instructions.[53]

The electoral process – the use of *terna* (selection from among three candidates), for example – clearly relied upon existing election procedures to corporate bodies. Furthermore, the process implicitly recognized the

51 Jorge Castel, *La Junta Central Suprema y Gubernativa de España e Indias* (Madrid: Imprenta Marte, 1950), 71–6.

52 "Real Orden de la Junta Central expedida el 22 de enero de 1809," in Julio V. González, *Filiación histórica del gobierno representativo argentino,* 2 vols. (Buenos Aires: Editorial "La Vanguardia," 1937–1938), 1:267.

53 Virginia Guedea, "The First Popular Elections in Mexico City, 1812–1813," in *The Evolution of the Mexican Political System,* ed. Jaime E. Rodríguez O. (Wilmington: Scholarly Resources, 1993), 45–7.

ancient putative right of the provincial capitals of America – the *ciudades cabezas de partido* – to representation in congresses of cities. The major difference was that traditional electoral processes were being adapted for new political purposes.

The 1809 elections constituted a profound step forward in the formation of modern representative government for the entire Spanish Nation. For the first time, elections were held in the New World to choose representatives for a unified government for Spain and America. Even more startling, only the New World held elections. In Spain, the existing provincial juntas had selected their representatives to the Junta Central. The Americans, however, objected to the fact that they would not have *equal* representation. Each province of Spain possessed two deputies to the Junta Central, whereas the nine American kingdoms were allocated one apiece. As Camilo Torres complained, "the provincial juntas of Spain would not agree on the formation of the [Junta] Central except on the basis of strict equality. . . . Thirty six or more deputies are necessary for Spain, and for the vast provinces of America, only nine are sufficient."[54] Nevertheless, as Virginia Guedea indicates, "as a consequence of these elections, the *ayuntamientos* . . . [of America] began to regain the role which some of them, especially the Ayuntamiento of Mexico, so strenuously had sought in 1808: that those corporations obtain the right to represent the provinces . . . [of the kingdoms of America]."[55]

Although they were pleased that the government in Spain had recognized their right to direct representation, the small number of delegates allotted to the New World disturbed most Americans. The *audiencias* of Guadalajara, Quito, and Charcas had not been granted independent representation because they were not also independent captaincies general; therefore, they were included in the representation of the Viceroyalties of New Spain, New Granada, and the Río de la Plata. Quito and Charcas, however, considered themselves essentially independent kingdoms. Quito bitterly complained that "isolated in a corner of the earth, it had no one to sustain its hopes, to dissipate its fears, or to take any measure whatsoever in its defense."[56]

New World authorities implemented the election decree in various ways. New Spain, controlled by the *peninsulares golpistas,* interpreted the decree in its narrowest form, granting only the capitals of the intendancies and two other cities, which managed to convince the authorities of their

---

54 Camilo Torres, "Memorial de agravios," in Romero and Romero, *Pensamiento político de la emancipación,* 1:34–5.

55 Guedea, "The First Popular Elections," 46–8.

56 "Manifiesto del Pueblo de Quito," in *Boletín de la Sociedad Ecuatoriana de Estudios Históricos Americanos,* II, Núm. 6 (May–June 1919), 430.

rights, the privilege of holding elections. Officials in other kingdoms understood the decree to mean that those cities and towns possessing *ayuntamientos* could hold elections. Thus, New Spain, with nearly half the population of Spanish America, granted only fourteen cities the right to hold elections, whereas in the much smaller Guatemala, an equal number of cities enjoyed that privilege. The situation varied widely in South America: Twenty cities held elections in New Granada, seventeen in Peru, sixteen in tiny Chile, twelve in the Río de la Plata before the process was suspended, and six in Venezuela.[57]

Many cities that did not qualify as provincial capitals – because they were not the capitals of intendancies or of recognized provinces – nonetheless claimed the right to vote. Some, like Tlaxcala in New Spain, argued that they deserved the privilege because of their historic contributions to the Crown, others because they claimed to be *ciudades cabeceras de provincia* (provincial capitals). The royal authorities in America extended the franchise only to a few cities.[58]

The elections were complicated and lengthy. In most cases, months passed before a kingdom selected its representative. In some instances, such as in Valladolid, New Spain, charges of fraud had to be resolved. In others, such as Córdoba, Río de la Plata, the viceroy had to intervene before the city finally chose its representative. The city of Loja, in the southernmost highland region of the Kingdom of Quito, was forced to send its instructions indirectly to Santa Fé, the capital of the Viceroyalty of New Granada, because an autonomist junta had assumed power in Quito while Loja had been electing its representative.[59] Several kingdoms, among them Guatemala, Chile, and Río de la Plata, proved unable to complete the process before the Junta Central dissolved in January 1810. In most cases, the representatives were persons of great prestige who held either civil, clerical, or military positions. In Quito, for example, the men selected for the *terna,* although Americans, were members of the oligarchy: the Conde de Puñonrrostro, a *grande* of Spain, and two young officers, sons of *quiteño* nobles, Carlos Montúfar y Larrea and José Larrea y Jijón.[60] Many represen-

---

57 Guedea, "The First Popular Elections," 46–7; Mario Rodríguez, *The Cádiz Experiment in Central America, 1808 to 1826* (Berkeley: University of California Press, 1978), note 37, p. 245; González, *Filiación histórica,* 1:215; François-Xavier Guerra, *Modernidad en independencias: Ensayos sobre las revoluciones hispánicas* (Madrid: Editorial Mapfre, 1992), 221–2.

58 See, for example, "Sobre derecho de las Provincias Internas para elegir en cada una Diputado que sea comprendido entre los demas del Reyno donde se ha de sortear el que baya a la Suprema Junta," AGN: Historia, vol. 416, Guerra, *Modernidad e independencias,* 192–4.

59 "Ynstrucción que forma el Ylustre Cavildo de Loxa para que se dirija al Diputado Representante del Virreynato, en que se comprende esta Provincia . . . ," Archivo Histórico del Banco Central del Ecuador: Fondo Jijón y Caamaño (hereafter cited as AHBCE:FJC) 5/4, ff. 32–4.

60 The election in Quito was typical: First, the members of the *ayuntamiento* voted. Then the names of

tatives were *peninsulares*. Whereas Americans outnumbered Europeans in Chile and Peru, in New Spain, according to Guedea, "the majority – eight of fourteen – had been born in the Peninsula and were closely aligned with its interests . . . and had distinguished themselves, or would distinguish themselves, as ardent defenders of the colonial system and the status quo."[61] Although family, regional, business, and professional interests influenced the elections, in many cases the conflict pitted the "European party" against the "American party." The predominance of *peninsulares* in the elections of New Spain undoubtedly reflected the control that Europeans had exercised over that kingdom since their *golpe de estado* of 1808. The defeat of prominent Americans, such as Isidro Huarte in Valladolid, New Spain, and Camilo Torres in Santa Fé, New Granada, contributed to subsequent autonomist activities in those cities.[62]

The *ayuntamientos* of America provided their representatives to the Junta Central with very detailed instructions. All declared their loyalty to Fernando VII, and most insisted upon equality for America. Thus, the inhabitants of the New World reaffirmed their support of the Monarchy while simultaneously asserting their rights within the Nación Española. As Guanajuato declared: "This America should not be considered a colony, but a very essential part of the Spanish Monarchy. . . . Under this fundamental and invariable constitutional concept, New Spain shall be considered equal to Old Spain, without any difference whatsoever, in all provisional actions, deliberations, and even variations of the laws and the national government."[63] Zacatecas voiced its desire for reform most clearly. It demanded "that legislative power be restored to the nation represented in the Cortes, that the abuses introduced by the executive branch be reformed, and that the king's ministers be held responsible for any future wrongdoings. . . ." That was a clear reference to the abuses of the Godoy administration. Zacatecas also insisted "that the most perfect, just, and inviolable equilibrium be established not only between the two powers [the executive and the legislative], but also in national representation in a future *cortes* by means of increased representation [for the New World] resulting from the

the three individuals with the largest number of votes were placed in a bowl. Finally, a child, Antonio Albufa, selected one, which turned out to be José de Larrea y Jijón. Archivo Municipal de Quito (hereafter cited as AMQ), Actas del Consejo, 1809 a 1814 (June 9, 1809), ff. 23–4v.

61 Guedea, "The First Popular Elections," 46–7.

62 Guerra, *Modernidad e independencias,* 190–206; Nettie Lee Benson, "The Election of 1809 in New Spain," unpublished manuscript (June 1989), Benson Latin American Collection, University of Texas, Austin; Carlos Juárez Nieto, *La oligarquía y el poder político en Valladolid de Michoacán, 1785–1810* (Morelia: Congreso del Estado, CNCA–INAH, Instituto Michoacano de Cultura, 1994), 243–70; Rodríguez, *The Cádiz Experiment,* 38–43.

63 Cited in José Miranda, *Las ideas y las instituciones políticas mexicanas, primera parte, 1521–1820,* 2d ed. (Mexico: UNAM, 1978), 227–8.

sovereign declaration that the Americas are an integral and essential part of the Monarchy. . . ."[64]

The *ayuntamientos* of America interpreted the elections of 1809 as an opportunity not only to obtain greater representation in the government of the Monarchy but also to seek long-desired improvements. Many *ayuntamientos* instructed their representatives to obtain support for their agricultural and manufactured products; better roads, granaries, and other facilities; the establishment of courts, bishoprics, schools, and universities; civil and ecclesiastic reforms; and legal recognition of frontier areas by the creation of new provinces, particularly the establishment of new intendancies.[65]

In a brief period, a little more than a year and a half, the people of America, like their counterparts in Spain, had undergone a profound political transformation. They had begun by rejecting Napoleon and reaffirming their loyalty to the Spanish Monarch, Fernando VII. But they had moved rapidly to insisting upon equal representation in the new government of the worldwide Spanish Nation. Some even proposed a radical restructuring of government: the convocation of a representative, constitutional parliament – the *cortes*. Although couched in the guise of maintaining traditional institutions, the entire process was a drastic departure from earlier experience. The people of America were embarking upon a political transformation whose ultimate outcome was unforeseen. One detects, in addition, a concern in most instructions that the authorities in Spain not surrender America to the French.[66] It was a fear that profoundly influenced New World actions.

In Search of Autonomy

Before the newly elected delegates from America could join the Junta Central, the French renewed their drive to conquer the Peninsula. In early December 1808, French armies reoccupied Madrid; later that month, Catalan forces suffered a crushing defeat; in Castilla, Marshal Victor smashed

---

64 Quoted in Guerra, *Modernidad e independencias*, 212–13.

65 Loja's instruction is a good example of the varied needs expressed by the *ayuntamientos*. The city made seven requests: (1) support for its cascarilla and cochinilla production, (2) clerical reform, (3) the establishment of a pious fund for a college, (4) the establishment of an intendancy in the province, (5) military reform, (6) the development of quina production, and (7) a home for abandoned children. "Ynstrucción que forma el Ylustre Cavildo de Loxa," AHBCE:FJC, 5/4, ff. 27–31. The instructions from the *ayuntamientos* of New Spain are located in AGN:Historia, vol. 417.

66 Roger L. Cunniff, "Mexican Municipal Electoral Reform, 1810–1822," in *Mexico and the Spanish Cortes, 1810–1822*, ed. Nettie Lee Benson (Austin: University of Texas Press, 1966), 62–3; Rodríguez, *The Cádiz Experiment*, 245; Guerra, *Modernidad e independencias*, 206–19. John Fisher, "Royalism, Regionalism, and Rebellion in Colonial Peru," *HAHR*, 59:2 (May 1979), 242–3.

the Spanish Army of the Center in January 1809; Zaragoza capitulated on February 20; and in the battle of Medellín on March 28, the French destroyed a Peninsular army of 20,000. Although Spanish forces continued to resist large French armies throughout most of 1809, on October 19 they suffered a disastrous defeat – 10,000 dead and 26,000 men captured – at Ocaña in the valley of the Tajo. Thereafter, French troops poured into Andalucía, occupying Sevilla at the end of January 1810. The Junta Central retreated first to Cádiz and then to the Isle of León, the last corner of Spain free from French control, thanks to the guns of the British navy. On January 29, 1810, the beleaguered body appointed a Council of Regency to govern the nation and two days later dissolved itself.[67]

News of these calamities frightened Americans, many of whom believed that Spain would not survive as an independent nation. It is not surprising, therefore, that in 1809, even as they were electing their representatives to the Junta Central, a series of movements for autonomy, led by the elite and professional groups, erupted throughout the continent. The first two movements occurred in the two South American kingdoms that had not been granted individual representation to the Junta Central: Upper Peru and Quito.

Isolated in Chuquisaca – present-day Sucre – the capital of the Audiencia of Charcas, the authorities of Upper Peru were dismayed when they learned of events in Spain. The region had experienced economic disruptions during the latter part of the eighteenth century, particularly after 1776, when it was incorporated into the new Viceroyalty of the Río de la Plata. Although Charcas reoriented its activities toward Buenos Aires, it nonetheless retained many ties with Peru. The European crisis brought into the open enmities that had festered among the royal authorities. Initially, the intendant and president of the *audiencia,* Ramón García León de Pizarro, and the archbishop, Benito María de Moxó y de Francoli, favored recognizing the Junta of Sevilla. But the *oidores* of the *audiencia* insisted upon waiting to discover the true circumstances in the Peninsula. In November 1808, José Manuel de Goyeneche, a native of Peru, arrived as commissioner of the Junta of Sevilla. But in addition, Goyeneche brought letters from Princess Carlota asserting her right to act as regent for her imprisoned brother. President García León and Archbishop Moxó favored recognizing Carlota, but the *audiencia* opposed that action. For months the two sides sought support among prominent individuals at the university and the *ayuntamiento.* In May 1809 the president-intendant decided to arrest the judges for obstructing order. Instead, appealing to the people, the *audiencia* arrested President García León on the evening of May 25, 1809. The following day the *oidores* organized a junta to govern in the name of

67 Lovett, *Napoleon and the Birth of Modern Spain,* I, 181–359.

Fernando VII. Although the dissension in Chuquisaca consisted primarily of a dispute among the royal authorities, the conflict affected other parts of Upper Peru.

On July 16, 1809, the Ayuntamiento of La Paz deposed the intendant and the bishop, accusing them of disloyalty to Fernando, and established a Junta Tuitiva to govern in the name of the imprisoned monarch. The Junta selected as its president Pedro Domingo Murillo, a military officer of mestizo background. The La Paz Junta, directed by middle-class Americans, many of them urban professionals, declared that they were acting "for the king, religion and the *patria.*" The leaders of the Junta voiced beliefs similar to those of many Americans throughout the continent; they declared their loyalty to the king, but they did not acknowledge their allegiance to some unknown body in Spain. Although they appealed to the *peninsulares* to support them, they obtained little backing from that quarter. The leaders of the Junta Tuitiva sought to strengthen their position vis-à-vis the viceroys of Peru and the Río de la Plata by winning over the mestizo and Indian masses with promised reforms. They also sought, without success, the support of other cities in Upper Peru. Both the new viceroy of the Río de la Plata, Baltasar Hidalgo de Cisneros, and José Fernando de Abascal of Peru sent armies to subdue the rebels. The Junta of La Paz was brutally crushed on October 25; Chuquisaca fell shortly thereafter.[68]

The creation of juntas in Chuquisaca and La Paz was indicative of both a sense of insecurity in light of events in Europe and a desire for local autonomy. Isolated in the highlands, the Audiencia or Kingdom of Charcas believed itself to be at the mercy of decisions made by distant officials with other priorities. News of the earlier upheavals in Buenos Aires and Montevideo heightened the awareness of the residents of Chuquisaca and La Paz that their political fate was not in their hands. Dominated first by the authorities in Lima and later in Buenos Aires, Upper Peru desired to assert its own identity. It is not an accident that the Junta of Chuquisaca corresponded with Montevideo in an effort to obtain allies against Buenos Aires. Nor is it surprising that the viceroys of the Río de la Plata and Peru, despite their very different concerns, insisted on crushing a pretentious interior province. Although the viceregal capitals of Lima and Buenos Aires demanded autonomy for themselves, they refused to permit such liberties for their interior provinces.

68 Jorge Siles Salinas, *La independencia de Bolivia* (Madrid: Editorial Mapfre, 1992), 139–95; Manuel M. Pinto, *La revolución de la Intendencia de La Paz en el virreinato del Río de la Plata* (La Paz: Alcaldía Municipal, 1953); Charles W. Arnade, *The Emergence of the Republic of Bolivia* (Gainesville: University of Florida Press, 1957), 1–31; Scarlett O'Phelan Godoy, "Por el Rey, religión y la patria: Las juntas de gobierno de 1809 en La Paz y Quito," *Bulletin de L'Institut Français D'Etudes Andines,* 17:2 (1988); 61–80.

Quito, another proud but dependent highland *audiencia,* also resented its secondary status. Like Charcas, Quito struggled for autonomy from two viceregal capitals, Lima and Santa Fé de Bogotá. Although Quito was the oldest of the South American capital cities and although its economy gained importance from the early years, the region failed to obtain the coveted status of an independent captaincy-general. While formerly peripheral areas such as Buenos Aires and Caracas won greater autonomy by becoming the seats of a new viceroyalty and a new captaincy-general, Quito lost ecclesiastic, juridical, and financial control over some of its provinces during the latter part of the eighteenth century.[69] At the same time, the Kingdom of Quito entered a period of substantial economic decline. In part, the downturn was the result of the imperial reorganization and the creation of the Viceroyalty of the Río de la Plata, which oriented trade away from Quito. In addition, Bourbon reformers increased taxes drastically, further damaging the economy. Even the booming plantation economy of Guayaquil suffered from massive tax increases. But the decline was also the result of increased competition from Europe that nearly drove Quito textiles from the South American market.[70] The economic depression, as well as the loss of authority and status, engendered considerable discontent among the kingdom's elite.

In early-nineteenth-century Quito, Americans and *peninsulares* competed intensely for business opportunities, government jobs, and honors. The crisis of the Monarchy widened the breach between the two groups. Moreover, since Conde Ruíz de Castilla, the president of the *audiencia* and governor of the kingdom, was an eighty-four-year-old man and the *audiencia* had been reduced to three quarrelsome *oidores,* few people in the city of Quito expressed confidence in the higher authorities. The criollos feared that the Spaniards would accept French rule, and the Europeans were convinced that the Americans favored independence.[71]

The climate of apprehension and suspicion heightened into a confrontation between the two groups when the *ayuntamiento* changed electoral practices. Quito traditionally alternated the positions of *alcalde primero* and *alcalde segundo* between Americans and Europeans. In 1808 the *alcalde primero* had been a criollo and the *alcalde segundo* a *peninsular.* In the elections

69 Rosemarie Terán Najas, *Los proyectos del Imperio borbónico en la Real Audiencia de Quito* (Quito: Abya-Yala, 1988); Demetrio Ramos Pérez, *Entre el Plata y Bogotá: Cuatro claves de la emancipación ecuatoriana* (Madrid: Ediciones de Cultura Hispánica, 1987), 162.

70 Douglas A. Washburn, "The Bourbon Reforms: A Social and Economic History of the Audiencia of Quito, 1760–1810" (Ph.D. diss., University of Texas, Austin, 1984), 165–251; María Luisa Laviana Cuetos, *Guayaquil en el siglo XVIII: Recursos naturales y desarrollo económico* (Seville: Escuela de Estudios Hispanoamericanos, 1987), 289–300.

71 José Gabriel Navarro, *La Revolución de Quito del 10 de agosto de 1809* (Quito: Editorial "Fray Jodoco Ricke," 1962), 41–7.

of January 1809, however, the *ayuntamiento* elected two Americans on the grounds that no European was qualified. The *alcalde segundo* for 1808, the Spaniard Pedro Muñoz, appealed the election "in the name of his nation." The *ayuntamiento*, in turn, proposed that in the future elections be held without distinguishing between Europeans and Americans.[72] The *peninsulares* responded by accusing the criollos of conspiracy. On March 9, 1809, six prominent *quiteños*, including the Marqués de Selva Alegre, were arrested. The authorities, however, subsequently exonerated the alleged conspirators and released them.

Tensions between Spaniards and Americans escalated. Rumors of alleged plots to assassinate the criollo nobles prompted the American elite of Quito to organize to protect itself.[73] On the evening of August 9, 1809, they signed an agreement to establish a junta of thirty-six members selected by the *vecinos* to govern in the name of Fernando VII. The garrison commander, Captain Juan Salinas, offered to support the movement with his troops. During the early hours of the next morning, August 10, Salinas and his men occupied all the government buildings and arrested most of the royal officials, including President Ruíz de Castilla. A new government consisting of the Marqués de Selva Alegre, president; Bishop José Cuero y Caicedo, vice president; and a junta of the leading members of the Quito elite, including most of the nobles, was proclaimed. The new body, which consisted entirely of criollos, declared in a *Manifiesto del Pueblo de Quito* that "the imperious circumstances had forced it to ensure the sacred interests of its religion, its prince, and its *patria*." It then proceeded to enumerate the grievances of the people of Quito: The Spaniards had "all public offices in their hands"; the criollos "had been viewed with contempt and treated with ignominy. . . . The Spanish Nation, devastated, oppressed, humiliated, and betrayed by an unworthy *favorite*, had seen a young monarch wrenched from its arms." Moreover, the *peninsulares* in Quito had declared "that if Spain submitted to Bonaparte, America was obliged to do the same." Therefore, Quito "swore to recognize Fernando VII as its lord and king, to conserve pure the religion of its forefathers, to defend and to seek the felicity of the *patria*, and to shed its last drop of blood for such sacred and worthy motives."[74]

In their manifestos to the *ayuntamiento* and to the people of Quito, the leaders of the Junta emphasized that they had acted because France might seize all of Spain. As the Marqués de Selva Alegre indicated, "Since the

---

72 AMQ, Actas del Consejo, 1809 a 1814, (January 9, 1809); Alfredo Ponce Ribadeneira, *Quito, 1809–1812* (Madrid: Imprenta Juan Bravo, 1960), 19–22.

73 Robert L. Gilmore, "The Imperial Crisis, Rebellion, and the Viceroy: Nueva Granada in 1809," *HAHR*, 40:1 (February 1960), 8–9.

74 "Manifiesto del Pueblo de Quito," 429–30.

French nation had subjugated through conquest nearly all Spain, since José Bonaparte had crowned himself king in Madrid, and, therefore, since the Junta Central, which represented our legitimate sovereign, had been extinguished, the people of this capital – faithful to God, the *patria,* and the king – had created another [junta] equally supreme and interim . . . until H. M. recovers the Peninsula or comes to America to rule."[75]

During the nearly three months that it governed, the Junta de Quito appealed to the people through public celebrations and economic reforms. It reduced some property taxes, abolished all debts, and eliminated the tobacco and *aguardiente* monopolies. Although the changes appealed to the masses, the actions benefited the elites. The properties of the upper class were heavily encumbered and subject to severe taxation. The monopolies were widely considered an unreasonable burden on producers and on consumers.

The *quiteños* were surprised to discover that the other provinces of the kingdom did not support their actions. The governors of Popayán, Guayaquil, and Cuenca organized forces to subdue the insurgents in the capital. The viceroys of New Granada and Peru prepared to mount major assaults. Isolated and blockaded by hostile forces, the junta split into factions. Selva Alegre resigned, and the others decided to return Ruíz de Castilla to office. On October 24, the junta reached an agreement with the deposed president that restored him to office while absolving its members of all charges stemming from their actions. On November 2, Ruíz de Castilla reinstated the taxes and the monopolies.

The following month, after the junta had dissolved its forces, troops from Lima and Guayaquil occupied the city, and units from other provinces stationed themselves nearby. On December 4, 1809, the forces of the Viceroy of Peru arrested the leaders of the junta, as well as the soldiers who backed them. The prosecutor Tomás Aréchaga, a mestizo from Cuzco, sought the death penalty for forty-six of the accused and perpetual exile for the others. President Ruíz de Castilla, however, decided to transfer the proceedings to Santa Fé for the viceroy to adjudicate the case. While the authorities investigated the matter, on August 2, 1810, groups in Quito attempted unsuccessfully to free the prisoners. During the struggle, the guards executed some of them.[76]

The actions of the Quito junta profoundly affected Americans in Santa Fé. Upon learning of the initial movement, Viceroy Antonio Amar y Bor-

---

75 These and other documents are reproduced in Ponce Ribadeneira, *Quito,* 136–41 and passim. Private letters of individuals stressing similar issues are published in Luis F. Borja, "Para la historia del 10 de agosto de 1809," *Boletín de la Sociedad Ecuatoriana de Estudios Históricos Americanos,* II, Núm. 6 (May–June 1919), 431–43.

76 Ponce Ribadeneira, *Quito,* 139–89; Navarro, *La Revolución de Quito,* 79–159.

bón of New Granada convened a junta of notables on September 6, 1809, to discuss the events in Quito. That meeting, and a subsequent one on the 11th, demonstrated the growing division between the *peninsulares* and criollos of Santa Fé de Bogotá. The Spanish-dominated *audiencia,* considering the *quiteños* traitors, insisted on using military force to crush the rebellion. The *ayuntamiento* and other American groups, including the lawyers and many militia officers, favored appeasing the Quito junta. Moreover, they proposed creating a local junta to negotiate with the *quiteños.* The viceroy dissolved the meeting rather than accept the American proposition. Subsequently, he dispatched the Marqués de San Jorge to negotiate with the Quito junta and placed on alert the troops along the border with Quito. Meanwhile, the forces sent by the Viceroy of Peru entered the city.[77]

The criollos of Santa Fé continued to agitate for a greater role in government affairs. The *oidores* of the *audiencia* alleged that some Americans were plotting independence. Indeed, it was rumored that they had proposed to the *virreina* that she convince the viceroy to become king in place of Fernando VII. In November 1809 the *ayuntamiento* issued its instructions to the representative of New Granada to the Junta Central. The document, officially known as the *Representación del Cabildo de Santafé,* had been written by its assessor, the *letrado* Camilo Torres, who had lost the election to the Junta Central to a European. Known popularly as the *Memorial de agravios* (Memorial of Grievances), it is a classic statement of American grievances and aspirations. The *Representación* denounced discrimination against criollos, condemned Crown policies that had hindered local economic growth, and demanded that the interests of New Granada be given equal weight with those of Spain. It argued passionately that there were no

other means to consolidate the union between America and Spain [but] the just and competent representation of its people, without any difference among its subjects that they do not have because of their laws, their customs, their origins, and their rights. Equality! The sacred right of equality. Justice is founded upon that principle and upon granting every one that which is his.[78]

And it warned:

[T]he true fraternal union between European Spaniards and Americans . . . can never exist except upon the bases of justice and equality. America and Spain are two integral and constituent parts of the Spanish Monarchy. . . . Anyone who believes otherwise does not love his *patria*. . . . Therefore, to exclude the Americas from such representation, in addition to being the greatest injustice, would arouse distrust and jealousy, and would forever alienate their desires for such a union. . . .

77 Gilmore, "The Imperial Crisis," 11–24; McFarlane, *Colombia before Independence,* 328–38.
78 Camilo Torres, "Memorial de agravios," in *Pensamiento político de la emancipación,* ed. José Luis Romero and Luis Alberto Romero (Caracas: Biblioteca de Ayacucho, 1977), 42.

If the English government had taken such an important step, perhaps today it would not rue the separation of its colonies. But a feeling of pride and a spirit of vanity and superiority led to the loss of those rich possessions which could not understand how it was that being vassals of the same sovereign, integral parts of the same Monarchy, all the other provinces [except they] could send representatives to the legislative body of the nation, a parliament which enacted laws and imposed taxes which they had not approved.[79]

Although Torres did not understand the nature of representation in the British Parliament, he and his colleagues in the Ayuntamiento of Santa Fé de Bogotá were clear: They insisted upon equality of representation by region, and they demanded the right to approve the laws that governed them and the taxes levied upon them. These were points upon which all the American kingdoms agreed.

While insisting on the establishment of a local junta, the *Representación* also affirmed the loyalty of the *ayuntamiento* to Fernando VII. Although the document possessed the support of the vast majority of that body, the viceroy refused to forward it to Spain. The Spanish-dominated *audiencia* took the opportunity to urge Amar y Borbón to ensure that only persons loyal to the government were chosen in the *ayuntamiento* elections of 1810. The viceroy forced the *ayuntamiento* to agree to alternate the office of *alcalde* between criollos and *peninsulares,* an action that engendered bitterness and hostility among the Americans.

The activities of the *peninsulares* of Santa Fé de Bogotá highlight a significant aspect of the crisis of the Monarchy. Although Americans expressed their loyalty at the same time that they demanded their rights, the Spaniards resident in the New World interpreted those actions as little better than treason. The narrow vision of the Europeans, more than anything else, drove the Americans to extreme positions. Indeed, it offered New World radicals a justification for their subsequent actions.

In New Spain, the criollos harbored even greater hostility to the *peninsulares.* The 1808 *golpe* had exacerbated the divisions between Europeans and Americans. The action particularly incensed the criollos because the Spaniards had broken the law and the new government in Spain, the Junta Central, had sided with the men who had overthrown the king's viceroy. The Americans, who had proposed establishing a junta in the name of Fernando, had been severely punished: Primo de Verdad had died in jail, probably the victim of his captors; Talamantes succumbed to yellow fever in a Veracruz jail in April 1809; and Azcárate and others remained imprisoned.

The *novohispano* autonomists never accepted the Spaniards' actions. Conspiracies and rumors of conspiracies became common in New Spain. Early in February 1809, for example, a proclamation appeared in a number of

---

79 Ibid., 27. See also Uribe, "Kill All the Lawyers!" who considers the American grievances exaggerated.

cities, such as Mexico, Puebla, Querétaro, Oaxaca, and Zacatecas, declaring that "The dedicated and valiant Spanish soldiers have been unable to hold back the superior forces of the tyrant Napoleon. . . . All Spain is about to fall under his yoke." Therefore the reputed author, Julian de Castillejos, a lawyer in the Audiencia of Mexico and a member of the college of lawyers, called for the establishment of an autonomous government to maintain New Spain for "our august and beloved Fernando VII and to keep our faith pure and unharmed. . . ." Moreover, he noted, "nowadays no one ignores the fact that, in the present circumstances, sovereignty resides in the people. That is what an infinite number of publications that arrive from the Peninsula teach us. It is a well known and recognized truth." The discovery of the proclamation concerned the authorities because Castillejos appeared to be part of an extensive network of autonomists who participated in the *tertulias* held by the Marqués de San Juan de Rayas. The group included members of the nobility, the college of lawyers, and other prominent individuals, most of whom had been active in the 1808 attempt to form a governing junta in New Spain. When interrogated, Castillejos denied responsibility, although he acknowledged that the views expressed in the proclamations were based on sound legal concepts. The royal officials eventually released him, but they kept a close watch on Castillejos, San Juan de Rayas, and the others.[80]

In the fall of 1809, the authorities uncovered a more serious conspiracy in the city of Valladolid. Convinced that the *peninsulares* had cheated them during the city's elections for a representative to the Junta Central, the American elite harbored strong resentments. Among the most disenchanted was the prominent Michelena family. It is not surprising, therefore, that Lieutenant José Mariano Michelena of the Royal Infantry and other American officers organized an autonomy movement in the city of Valladolid. Iturrigaray's overthrow in September 1808 and the subsequent arrogance of the Spaniards had galvanized the criollos. Many *novohispano* officers respected Iturrigaray, who had assembled the militia for maneuvers in 1806. For the first time since the conquest, a large army had gathered in New Spain, a sight that awed the Americans and gave them a sense of their potential power. Iturrigaray's overthrow was an affront not only because it removed an official who had honored *novohispanos* but also because a small group of European Spaniards had contemptuously dismissed the importance as well as the rights of Americans.

The conspirators obtained supporters in other provincial cities, such as Guanajuato, Querétaro, San Miguel el Grande, and Guadalajara. They had prepared an uprising for December 21, 1809, and expected backing from

---

80 Guedea, *En busca de un gobierno alterno,* 25–32. The proclamation is reproduced in García, *Documentos históricos mexicanos,* 1:102–3.

the army and militia. The Valladolid plotters intended to go beyond the La Paz group by appealing to the rural masses for support in an armed insurrection. They hoped to attract thousands of men among the Indians and *castas* by promising to abolish tribute. Once they had gained control of New Spain, the insurgents planned to convoke a congress of cities to govern in the name of Fernando VII. The plan differed from the earlier autonomy movement in Mexico City only in that the Americans had to rely on military force because the Spaniards had seized the government.

When the movement was exposed, the authorities brought the leaders to trial. But the prosecution could prove only that the conspirators had planned to save New Spain from a possible French invasion. Their defense attorney, Carlos María de Bustamante, convinced the viceroy that "the day the first insurgent is hanged, Spain must relinquish all hope of conserving this America."[81] Acting Viceroy Javier Lizana y Beaumont chose to exercise leniency because many important persons openly declared that the conspirators were guilty only of seeking to redress rightful grievances in an inappropriate way. Lizana ordered them released.

The dramatic events of 1808 and 1809 transformed the political culture of the Spanish world. As Virginia Guedea has noted, the 1808 crisis of the Monarchy was fundamentally a political crisis that initiated a process of politicization that rapidly intensified.[82] The leaders of Spain and America initially responded to the disintegration of the Monarchy in 1808 by opposing the French and insisting on the rights of Fernando VII. But almost immediately, the notion that, in the absence of the king, sovereignty reverted to the people became central to the political discourse. Imperceptibly but rapidly, the sovereignty of the king receded as the sovereignty of the people assumed prominence. Similarly, the belief that the traditional corporations represented the people soon began to change. Quickly, individuals became the people and, as a result, Americans argued that representation should be based on population. Thus, traditional political concepts and practices were adapted to new, even revolutionary, political purposes.

---

81 José Mariano Michelena, "Verdadero origen de la revolución de 1809 en el Departamento de Michoacán," in García, *Documentos históricos mexicanos,* 1:467–71; Carlos María de Bustamante, *Cuadro histórico de la revolución mexicana,* 3d ed., 3 vols. (Mexico: Comisión Nacional para la Celebración del Sesquicentenatio de la Proclamación de la Independencia Nacional y del Cincuentenario de la Revolución Mexicana, 1961), 1:22, 18–30; Carlos Juárez Nieto, *La oligarquía y el poder político en Valladolid de Michoacán, 1785–1810* (Morelia: Congreso del Estado, CNCA, INAH, Instituto Michoacano de Cultura, 1994), 270–93; Lucas Alamán, *Historia de Méjico desde los primeros movimientos que prepararon su independencia en el año de 1808 hasta la época presente,* 5 vols. (Mexico: Imprenta de Lara, 1849–1852), 1:314–20.

82 Guedea, "The Conspiracies of 1811."

The upheavals in America in 1809 were a harbinger of things to come. The recognition that the New World was an integral part of the Monarchy and the granting of representation in the national government was not sufficient to pacify the Americans. The conflict with the Spaniards in the New World became more pronounced as the mother country appeared to be in danger of being conquered by the French. Although most royal authorities had managed temporarily to control the first movements for home rule, clearly the government in Spain would have to employ other methods to retain its American possessions.

3

The Birth of Representative Government

The collapse of the Spanish Monarchy triggered a series of events that culminated in the establishment of representative government in the Spanish
world. The initial step in that process was the formation of local governing
juntas in Spain and America. Although the Spanish provinces made that
transition easily, the American kingdoms faced opposition from royal officials, resident *peninsulares,* and their New World allies. Initially, neither
the Spanish nor the American juntas had a clear vision of the nature of the
government they would form. Most possessed vague notions of what they
meant when, as the Ayuntamiento of Mexico declared, "in the absence . . .
[of the king], sovereignty lies represented in all the kingdom." Nonetheless, all the juntas asserted that sovereignty had reverted to the people. In
practice, this meant that the elites of the provinces of Spain and the kingdoms of America assumed the mantle of the people. Moreover, since the
act was taken in the name of Fernando VII, the assumption of popular sovereignty was provisional. When the king returned, presumably, sovereignty would revert to him.

Convening a Parliament

The provincial juntas of Spain administered their localities, whereas the
Junta Central attempted to function as a national government. In the
monarch's absence, however, Spanish legal tradition recognized the sovereignty of the representatives of the people – the cities, the tribunals, and
other major corporations. Neither the provincial juntas nor the Junta Central – composed of two representatives from each Spanish province, two
from Madrid as the capital, and, eventually, nine from America – fulfilled
those requirements.[1] Thus, voices emerged both in Spain and in America
insisting on convening general juntas, *cortes,* or national congresses. Some
provinces in Spain, such as Aragón and Galicia, convened their *cortes.* In
New Spain, the Ayuntamiento of Mexico proposed holding a national congress of cities.

1 Angel Martínez de Velasco, *La formación de la Junta Central* (Pamplona: Eunsa, 1972).

The members of the Junta Central were divided on the need to convene a *cortes*. Some believed that such action was necessary to unify the nation. Others feared that it might lead to revolution. A few, like the radical poet Manuel Quintana, were already talking about the "Spanish revolution." The French victories of late 1808 and early 1809, however, convinced the Junta "that the Monarchy's legal and traditional representation in its ancient *cortes* should be reestablished."[2] On May 22, 1809, the Junta Central issued a *Consultation to the Nation* to Spain and America requesting provincial juntas, *ayuntamientos,* tribunals, bishops, universities, and erudite individuals to recommend the best method of organizing the government. By taking that action, the Junta inadvertently moved from traditional political practices toward modern politics. In ways that we have yet to understand, that request initiated a process of devolution of political power to the localities and engendered new sociopolitical relations.[3]

The responses indicated that most people desired a *cortes.* The discussion within the Junta Central centered on the role that body would play. Those who favored convoking a *cortes* to marshal support for the war and not to function as a legislature preferred that any such parliament consist of the traditional three estates: the clergy, the nobility, and the cities. Others believed that the *cortes* should be transformed into a modern national assembly. New French victories, however, forced the Junta Central to act. On January 1, 1810, it decreed that elections be held for a national *cortes.* In Spain each provincial junta and each city entitled to representation in earlier *cortes* could select a deputy. In addition, a deputy was to be elected for every 50,000 inhabitants.[4] Each New World *province,* a vague and undefined term, would elect a deputy. No provision was made, however, for rep-

2 Cited in François-Xavier Guerra, *Modernidad e independencias: Ensayos sobre las revoluciones hispánicas* (Madrid: Editorial Mapfre, 1992), 141, 142.
3 The replies from Spain are well known: Miguel Artola has published many replies to the *Consulta a la Nación* in *Los orígenes de la España contemporánea,* 2 vols. (Madrid: Instituto de Estudios Políticos, 1959), 2 Federico Suárez has published others in *Cortes de Cádiz,* 2 vols. (Pamplona: Ediciones Universidad de Navarra, 1967–1968), 2. Those for America remain unknown. Guerra believes that the *intrucciones* and *representaciones* to the Junta Central constitute the New World's response to the *consulta.* Guerra, *Modernidad,* note 69, p. 143. He is mistaken. The elections of representatives to the Junta Central and, therefore, the dates when the *instrucciones* and *representaciones* were written are too early. The Ayuntamiento of Quito, for example, elected its candidate for representative to the Junta Central on June 9, 1809. Subsequently, on December 21, 1809, the Audiencia of Quito received the *consulta,* and the following month sent replies from all the pertinent institutions in the kingdom. AMQ, Actas del Consejo, 1809 a 1814 (June 9, 1809). I have located the transmittal letters for the *consulta* in Quito, Archivo Nacional de Historia, Quito (hereafter cited as ANHQ), Presidencia de Quito (hereafter cited as PQ), vol. 456, ff. 21–9, and in Jalapa, Archivo del Ayuntamiento de Jalapa, Actas del Cabildo, 1809. As far as I know, no one else has examined this question in America.
4 Gabriel Lovett, *Napoleon and the Birth of Modern Spain,* 2 vols. (New York: New York University Press, 1965), 1:344–5.

resentation based on population, as many prominent Americans urged.[5] Since the Junta Central had no idea how large America was, by granting each New World province individual representation, it inadvertently provided the Continent with more deputies than it expected. Apparently, the Junta Central considered summoning the clergy and nobility as separate estates. This never came to pass because the Junta could not compile a membership roll for those two groups.[6] Thus, despite the original intent, the Spanish Cortes met as one body and became a national assembly.

In spite of its best efforts, the Junta Central could not halt the French advance. Forced to retreat into the southern corner of Spain, it was bitterly criticized by many for its failure. In an attempt to create a more effective government, the Junta appointed a council of regency of five and dissolved itself at the end of January 1810. The delegate from New Spain to the Junta Central, Miguel Lardizábal y Uribe, represented America in the new government. The other members of the Junta, including the elected delegates from the New World who had not yet arrived, were relieved of their duties. As its last act, the Junta Central charged the Regency with convening the Cortes.

The new government, however, hesitated to implement that instruction. Some regents believed that the nation's constitutional process merely required the establishment of a regency rather than the convening of a national assembly. Finally, pressure from the Junta of Cádiz, where the government now resided, and from various deputies elected under the January 1 decree, forced the Regency's hand. It ordered that the Cortes convene in September 1810.[7]

Representative government in the Spanish world struggled to exist in the midst of a crisis of confidence. By 1810, most Americans expected a French triumph. Napoleonic armies, after all, controlled the majority of the Peninsula. Fear of French domination strengthened the desire of many in the New World to seek autonomy. In 1810, home rule movements reemerged in Caracas in April, Buenos Aires and Upper Peru in May, Santa Fé de Bogotá in July, and in three areas in September – the Bajío in New Spain on the 16th, Santiago de Chile on the 18th, and Quito, once again, on the 20th. All these regions sought to establish caretaker governments to rule in the name of Fernando VII. The autonomy movements of 1810, unlike those of 1809, inadvertently unleashed other social forces. Discon-

---

5 The decree specified: "Deputies from the Viceroyalties of New Spain, Peru, Santa Fé and Buenos Aires, and from the Captaincies General of Puerto Rico, Cuba, Santo Domingo, Guatemala, Provincias Internas, Venezuela, Chile, and the Philippines will come [to Spain] to take part in the national representation of the Extraordinary Cortes of the Kingdom. These deputies will be one for each *Capital cabeza de partido* of these various provinces." ANHQ: PQ, vol. 460, ff. 40–51.

6 Artola, *Los orígenes,* 1:282–4.

7 Ibid., 1:383–5; Lovett, *Napoleon and the Birth,* 1:370–2; ANHQ: PQ, vol. 460, ff. 122–5.

tented groups and regions capitalized on the opportunity to redress their grievances. Within a short time, civil wars consumed large parts of the American continent.

Elections for the new representative government occurred while warfare engulfed Spain and America. Because many of the occupied provinces of Spain could not hold elections, and because distance delayed the arrival of many American deputies, the Regency decreed that fifty-three *suplentes* (substitutes), among them thirty for America and the Philippines, be elected from among persons in Cádiz from the occupied provinces and from overseas.

The prosperous city of Cádiz, one of the major ports of Spain, was considered a center of Enlightenment thought and progress. Although other Peninsular ports had traded with the New World since the onset of *comercio libre* in the 1780s, nearly 90 percent of American trade passed through Cádiz. Naturally, the city's merchant community was both powerful and concerned with American policy. They would exercise much influence over the government since the Regency, and later the Cortes, depended upon taxes levied in Cádiz to sustain them. In addition, the city's merchant elite handled all the transfers of funds from the New World. The merchants of Cádiz kept in close touch with the Spanish merchant communities in America, sharing the belief that Spain should dominate the Monarchy. Thus, Cádiz, despite its reputed enlightenment, did not sympathize with American aspirations for equality. The views of the merchant community would shape the debate and actions of the Cortes.[8]

In 1810, Cádiz was swollen with refugees, American as well as Peninsular, who had retreated to the port from other regions of Spain to escape French control. As the September date for the inauguration of the Cortes neared, the Regency completed the list of the Americans in Cádiz who would elect *suplentes* from their regions to attend the parliament. Faced with the problem of the New World areas in revolt, the Regency decided that *suplentes* would represent the "healthy part" of the population in those provinces. It noted: "the rebels will say that they [the *suplentes*] are neither enough nor legal, but they will complain even more if they [the insurgent areas] were totally excluded."[9]

On September 8, the Regency announced the electoral procedures. It allocated the overseas provinces thirty *suplentes,* fifteen to *América Septentrional* (North America): New Spain seven, Guatemala two, Cuba two, the

---

8 Ramón Solís, *El Cádiz de las Cortes. Vida en la ciudad en los años 1810 a 1813* (Madrid: Editorial Alianza 1969). See also Michael P. Costeloe, *Response to Revolution: Imperial Spain and the Spanish American Revolutions, 1810–1840* (Cambridge: Cambridge University Press, 1986), 1–19, passim.

9 Quoted in Marie Laure Rieu-Millan, *Los Diputados americanos en las Cortes de Cádiz* (Madrid: Consejo Superior de Investigaciones Científicas, 1990), 34.

Philippines two, Santo Domingo one, and Puerto Rico one; and fifteen to *América Meridional* (South America): Peru five, Santa Fé three, Buenos Aires three, Venezuela two, and Chile two. *Suplentes* had to be at least twenty-five years of age and natives of the provinces that elected them. Members of the regular orders, convicted felons, public debtors, and servants were not eligible. The electors were to gather by province and choose seven *compromisarios* (arbiters), who would then select three to form a *terna* from whom one would be picked by lot. Because there were not enough Americans in Cádiz from each province to hold individual elections, the procedure, the same as the one used by the Spanish provinces, had to be abandoned. Therefore, the 177 American electors combined into four regional groups to pick the New World *suplentes:* New Spain, Guatemala, and the Philippines; Santo Domingo and Cuba; New Granada and Venezuela; and Peru, Buenos Aires, and Chile. Puerto Rico did not participate in this selection because its proprietary deputy, Ramón Power, was the only one from America who arrived in time for the opening of the Cortes. New World *suplentes* were a varied group; they included military men, lawyers, academics, clerics, and government functionaries. Two were *grandes* of Spain and one, Dionisio Inca Yupangui, was a Peruvian Indian who had served as a lieutenant colonel of dragoons in the Peninsula.[10]

Although the election of the *suplentes* was a temporary measure to ensure representation for those Spanish provinces and American kingdoms whose proprietary deputies could not arrive in time, a number of observers rejected them both as unrepresentative and as illegal. The *Gazeta de Caracas* and the *Gazeta de Buenos Ayres,* both publications of autonomous juntas, protested that the *suplentes* did not represent America. Uncertain about the situation in Spain, the *Gazeta de Caracas* questioned the veracity of the elections. Were they, it wondered, merely façades for French control? It noted: "If it were as easy to verify [facts] as to write falsehoods," there would be less reason to question the actions of a land "in which by a rare metamorphosis . . . Bonaparte was transformed into Fernando VII." The *Gazeta de Buenos Ayres* labeled the *suplentes* "representatives by an alien will." Further, it questioned the right of those Americans in Cádiz, whom it described as "a handful of adventurers without standing or authority," to elect deputies to the Cortes.[11] Similarly, the traditionalist American regent, Miguel Lardizábal y Uribe, declared: "Who really believes that the provinces, which have not sent their own deputies, will accept substantive reform and a constitution written by men whom they [the provinces] have not appointed nor given the authority to make such changes?"[12] Father Ser-

---

10 Ibid., 1–6.
11 *Gazeta de Caracas,* II, No. 17 (January 29, 1811); *Gazeta de Buenos Ayres* (February 25, 1811).
12 Quoted in Rieu-Millan, *Los Diputados americanos,* 9.

vando Teresa de Mier, then a publicist in Cádiz, became even more caustic and hyperbolic: "The killing of Americans [in the New World] continued because they [the authorities] obeyed 200 fugitives in the isle of León, among them 28 American refuges, who claimed, as a result of a popular riot, that they represented the nation even though they possessed no power other than that which they gave themselves. And with respect to the Americans, nearly all the provinces of America rejected them."[13]

The *suplentes* for Venezuela wrote their *ayuntamientos* to inform them of their election, only to receive the following reply: "The Junta Suprema de Caracas does not approve your appointment as *suplentes;* and far from ratifying actions which prejudice the liberty and independence of these . . . provinces, [the Junta] revokes [your appointment] and expressly orders . . . that you abstain from serving and await the arrival of proprietary deputies."[14] It is interesting to note that the Junta of Caracas did not reject the possibility of electing "proprietary deputies" if Spain had survived the French invasion. In contrast, the Ayuntamiento of Maracaibo thanked the *suplentes* and announced the election of a proprietary deputy. Despite objections, the *suplentes* played a major role in the Cortes on behalf of their areas and America as a whole. Indeed, some of them, like José María Couto of Mexico and José Mexía Llequerica of Quito, became outstanding parliamentarians. Moreover, when the proprietary deputies from America arrived, some *suplentes* remained in the Cortes representing New World kingdoms that had failed to elect proprietary deputies.

Elections for proprietary deputies to the Cortes were held in America during late 1810 and part of 1811.

This time, [as Guedea notes,] each province was allocated a deputy who would be elected by the *ayuntamiento* of every provincial capital. As had occurred for elections to the Junta Central, each *ayuntamiento* would select three individuals "endowed with probity, talent, and learning and without any blemish," from which a representative was to be chosen by drawing lots. As in 1809 the deputies were to receive instructions from their *ayuntamientos.* However, in contrast to the previous election, the deputies had to be natives of the provinces they represented.[15]

Although insurgencies had erupted in various areas of the continent, most kingdoms, with the exception of Chile and parts of Venezuela, New Granada, and the Río de la Plata, participated in the electoral process. The islands of Cuba, Puerto Rico, and Santo Domingo were the first to complete elections. New Spain, which was allocated twenty-two deputies, elected

13 Servando Teresa de Mier, "Manifiesto Apologético," in *Escritos inéditos de Fray Servando Teresa de Mier,* eds. José María Miquel y Verges y Hugo Díaz-Thomé (Mexico: El Colegio de México, 1994), 153–4.
14 *Gazeta de Caracas,* III, No. 18 (February 5, 1811).
15 Virginia Guedea, "The First Popular Elections in Mexico City, 1812–1813," in *The Evolution of the Mexican Political System,* ed. Jaime Rodríguez O. (Wilmington: Scholarly Resources, 1993), 47–8.

twenty, but only fifteen from the provinces of Guanajuato, Tlaxcala, Puebla, Querétaro, Villahermosa, México, Valladolid, Zacatecas, Guadalajara, Veracruz, Mérida, Coahuila, Sonora, Durango, and Nuevo México managed to reach Spain. The Kingdom of Guatemala elected six deputies from Guatemala, San Salvador, Costa Rica, Nicaragua, Honduras, and Chiapas. One city in Venezuela, Maracaibo, elected a deputy. New Granada selected two to represent Quito and Panama, the areas that remained in royalist hands. Guayaquil, which had been attached to the Viceroyalty of Peru, also elected a deputy, as did the Peruvian provinces of Lima, Piura, Tarma, Trujillo, Chachapoyas, Arequipa, and Puno. Only Charcas and Montevideo elected deputies from the Viceroyalty of the Río de la Plata.[16]

The circumstances surrounding each election varied considerably. Quito provides an extreme example. After the Junta of Quito of 1809 had disbanded and its members were arrested, some were executed by the authorities when the populace attempted to free them on August 2, 1810. Later, Carlos Montúfar, son of the Marqués de Selva Alegre, arrived in Quito as a representative of the Spanish government. He then helped establish a second junta on September 22, 1810, presided over by Governor Ruíz de Castilla, with his father and Bishop Cuero y Caicedo as members. A month later, on October 20, 1810, the new autonomous Junta of Quito held elections to select a deputy to the Cortes in Spain, choosing the Conde de Puñonrrostro.[17] Like Quito, most areas of America considered the elections for the Cortes very important. Many individuals lobbied to be elected. In some provinces, the authorities sought to influence the elections. Personal and political conflicts delayed for months the final selection in a few cities, like Oaxaca, New Spain and Puno, Peru. Some provinces, such as Texas, failed to elect a representative. Still others chose deputies but could not afford to send them to Spain.[18]

Since the electoral decree specified that the representatives had to be natives of the province, the process excluded Spaniards residing in the New World. Predictably, the *peninsulares* protested vehemently. As a result, the Regency modified the requirements on August 20, 1810, indicating "that the *convocatoria* should not be interpreted as it sounds, [restricted only] to Spaniards born in America and Asia, but also those domiciled and resident

16 Charles R. Berry, "The Election of Mexican Deputies to the Spanish Cortes, 1810–1822," in Nettie Lee Benson, *Mexico and the Spanish Cortes* (Austin: University of Texas Press, 1966), 11–16; Mario Rodríguez, *The Cádiz Experiment in Central America, 1808 to 1826* (Berkeley: University of California Press, 1978), 44–7; Rieu-Millan, *Los Diputados americanos*, 36–8.

17 AMQ, Actas del Consejo, 1809 a 1814 (October 20, 1810); Neptalí Zúñiga, *Juan Pío Montúfar y Larrea: Primer presidente la América revolucionaria* (Quito: Talleres Gráficos Nacionales, 1945), 508–48.

18 Nettie Lee Benson, "Texas' Failure to Send a Deputy to the Spanish Cortes, 1810–1812," *Southwestern Historical Quarterly,* 54 (July 1960), 1–22.

in those countries as well as the Indians and the sons of Spaniards and Indians."[19] The clarification reached the New World too late to affect the 1810 elections. It did, however, address an issue important to Americans: Indians and mestizos could vote and were eligible to be selected as deputies. The political rights of those of African ancestry remained unresolved.

The Cortes of Cádiz

Unlike earlier *cortes,* the congress that met on September 24, 1810, was truly a modern national assembly. It met as one body, and its members represented the entire Spanish world. When the Cortes convened, 104 deputies were present, 30 of them representing the overseas territories. Twenty-seven Americans and two Filipinos had been selected as *suplentes* in Cádiz. Only one of the thirty-six proprietary deputies elected in America arrived in time to attend the opening session. The others were admitted as they arrived. Approximately 300 deputies, including 63 Americans, eventually participated in the extraordinary Cortes in Cádiz. The composition of the Cortes was varied: One-third were clergymen, about one-sixth were nobles, and the remainder were persons of the third estate who, because of their professions, might be called middle class.[20]

In its first session the Cortes declared that, since it represented the people, it was the repository of national sovereignty. Then the national assembly divided the government into three branches: the legislative, the executive, and the judiciary. The Regency would act as the executive until the return of Fernando VII, the legitimate king and chief executive of the nation. The legislature, however, was the dominant sector of the government. When the Regency objected to what it considered usurpation of its authority, the Cortes arrested its members, tried them, found them guilty, and either imprisoned or banished them. It then appointed a second Regency.[21]

The new parliament faced an enormous task. It was charged with restructuring the government while prosecuting a war in Spain and preserving the overseas possessions. Two groups emerged in the Cortes: the *liberales,* who proposed to transform the nation into a modern constitutional monarchy, and the *serviles,* who favored the older absolutist form of government. The representatives of the New World did not constitute a third

---

19 Quoted in Rieu-Millan, *Los Diputados americanos,* 11.
20 See Lovett, *Napoleon and the Birth,* 1:371, note 33, for a review of the various estimates of the members of the Cortes. On the American deputies, see María Teresa Berruezo, *La participación americana en las Cortes de Cádiz (1810–1814)* (Madrid: Centro de Estudios Constitucionales, 1986), 55–299, who has a detailed analysis of each American deputy. See also Rieu-Millan, *Los Diputados americanos,* 31–9.
21 Lovett, *Napoleon and the Birth,* 1:373–4; Benson, *Mexico and the Spanish Cortes,* 4.

group except on the *American Question,* that is, the appropriate relationship between Spain and the Monarchy's overseas possessions. The American Question pitted Europeans against representatives of the New World, with most Americans demanding equality for the New World and most Spaniards rejecting that or any proposal that would deprive the *peninsulares* of control of the parliament.

From the outset, the Americans challenged the unequal representation between Spain and America in the Cortes. Led by the *quiteño* José Mexía Llequerica, on September 25, the day after the Cortes opened, they submitted a proposed decree to elect additional New World deputies on the same basis as the Peninsula: 1 for every 50,000 inhabitants. Moreover, they insisted on counting as inhabitants all the free subjects of the king, including Indians and *castas.* The *peninsulares* immediately opposed the measure because it would reduce them to a minority and transfer control of the government to the New World. Under the existing system, the Spaniards outnumbered the Americans three to one, whereas under equal representation the New World gained a three-to-two advantage. In part, the conflict stemmed from misleading estimates of the populations of Spain and America. At that time, Spain possessed a population of about 10.5 million, whereas according to Humboldt's inflated figures, accepted as accurate by the participants in the debate, the New World had a population of about 16 million.

Unfortunately for the American cause, the representative from Lima, Vicente Morales Duárez, opposed political rights for the colored *castas.* Despite eloquent speeches by the *quiteño* Mexía Llequerica, considered one of the best orators at the Cortes, and despite the nearly unanimous backing of the American delegates, the opposition prevailed. The *castas* would not be counted. The issue of race became so inflammatory that the Cortes had to debate it in secret sessions. A compromise on the question of representation emerged on October 15 when it was agreed that "the natives who originated in the said European and overseas dominions have the same rights as those from this Peninsula." The *castas,* who "originated" in Africa, were therefore not considered natives of the Spanish dominions. Since the colored *castas* were thought to number about 5.5 to 6 million, the compromise equalized the population counted for purposes of representation. Although twenty-one Spaniards supported the Americans' demand that additional representation based on population be granted immediately, the Peninsular majority refused. The Europeans soothed the Americans by reaffirming that the Spanish dominions in both hemispheres formed one Monarchy and by offering to forget the "commotions" in the New World.[22]

---

22 James King, "The Colored Castes and American Representation in the Cortes of Cádiz," *HAHR,* 33:1 (February 1953), 33–45; Rieu-Millan, *Los Diputados americanos,* 146–8.

The American deputies regrouped, and on December 16, 1810, they presented a program of eleven reforms that became the basis for subsequent discussions of the American Question. The propositions consisted of the following: equal representation; freedom to cultivate and to manufacture; free trade and navigation; free trade between America and the Philippines (the Asian possessions); free trade between America and the Philippines with Asia; abolition of monopolies; freedom to mine mercury; equal rights of Americans to civil, ecclesiastic, and military office; half of all positions to be allocated to natives of the kingdom; creation of advisory juntas in America to designate the holders of public office; and the restoration of the Jesuit order in the New World.[23]

American demands consisted of full political and economic rights, including local economic control, free trade, and access to public office. The Cortes extensively debated these questions during the next year and a half. The American Question could not be ignored because New World participation increased as the proprietary deputies arrived. More important, two *novohispanos* – José Miguel Guridi y Alcocer from Tlaxcala and José Miguel Ramos Arizpe from Coahuila – and two Central Americans – Antonio Larrazábal from Guatemala and Florencio Castillo from Costa Rica – joined Mexía Llequerica as leaders of the radical American reform group. Other New World deputies, including the moderate Morales Duárez, often supported them on many American issues, although not on the question of the rights of the colored *castas*.

The *American party,* as they were sometimes called, faced opposition on New World issues not only from Spanish deputies to the Cortes, but also from the Cádiz merchants and the *peninsulares* in America. Royal bureaucrats in the New World often objected to proposed reforms on the grounds that they aided the insurgents. Other Spaniards in America also expressed their hostility to New World demands for equality. The most vitriolic attack on America was the infamous *Representación del Consulado de México,* read in a public session of the Cortes on September 16, 1811, during a discussion of Article 29 of the constitution, which provided the "equal" basis for apportioning representation.

The *consulado*'s *Representación* began with an account of the history of the Indians that would have made any anti-American *philosophe* proud. According to the *consulado,* prior to the arrival of the Europeans, the Indians had been anarchic, savage beasts. More than 200 years of efforts to improve their lot had accomplished little because of the natives' genetic inferiority. Thus, the 3 million Indians of New Spain were unfit for self-government. The Indian, declared the *consulado,*

---

23 John Preston Moore, *The Cabildo in Peru under the Bourbons* (Durham: Duke University Press, 1966), reproduces the demands on pp. 208–9.

is endowed with a laziness and languor. . . . He never moves unless hunger or vice drive him. Congenitally stupid, without either innovative talent or strength of thought, he despises both the arts and work; they are not necessary to his way of life. He is a drunkard by nature. . . . Sensual because of lascivious thoughts and bereft of chaste ideas about physical closeness, modesty or incest, he takes his fleeting pleasures with the woman closest at hand. As careless as he is insensitive to religious truths . . . , and lacking love for his fellow-creatures, he only avoids those crimes which will bring him immediate punishment.

Two million *castas* were equally worthless:

With greater ability to acquire money, with more money to satiate their vices, with more vices to destroy themselves, it is not surprising that they are even more misguided and miserable [than the Indians]. Inebriates, incontinent, lax, lacking honor, gratitude, and fidelity, without a sense of religion or morality, without elegance, cleanliness, or decency, they appear even more mechanical and immoderate that the Indian himself. . . .

A million whites, who call themselves American Spaniards, demonstrate their superiority over the other five million . . . more by the wealth they have inherited, . . . by their extravagance, . . . and by the refinement of their vices, than by substantial differences of disposition. . . .

What is there in common, what comparison fits or what analogy can be found in the rights, condition, spirit, delicacy, exigencies, interests, institutions, habits, and localities of Spain the conqueror and the conquered colonies? . . . It is necessary to confess that the laws appropriate for the *Madre Patria* are not the best for its Americas. . . .[24]

Outraged by the vicious insults, the American deputies attempted to leave the Cortes en masse, but the president forbade it. The guards turned them back. Discussion on the article was suspended while the New World delegates prepared replies. The following day, the Galician deputy José Alfonso López offered a compromise that allocated an equal number of deputies to Spain and its overseas dominions. The Spanish majority rejected his proposal, reaffirming the denial of representation to the colored *castas*.[25]

Americans waged the struggle for political power on the issue of access to government jobs as well as over representation. They argued that equality meant nothing unless it also provided equality of access to civil, clerical, and military positions. Ramos Arizpe, Guridi y Alcocer, Mexía Llequerica, Inca Yupangui, and others vehemently but unsuccessfully argued that the colored *castas* should also be included in the equal rights provision. Even though some Spaniards supported their cause, many Americans

24 "Informe del Real Tribunal del Consulado de México sobre la incapacidad de los habitantes de N.E. para nombrar representantes a las Cortes," Juan E. Hernández y Dávalos, *Colección de documentos para la historia de la guerra de independencia de 1808 a 1821,* 6 vols. (Mexico: José María Sandoval Impresor, 1877–1882.) 2:450–66.
25 King, "The Colored Castes," 61–3.

opposed the proposal. On February 9, 1811, the Cortes approved one of the important aspects of the American proposal of December 1810 by granting American Spaniards, Indians, and mestizos the same rights as European Spaniards to civil, ecclesiastic, and military office. But the majority in the Cortes rejected the efforts to reserve half of all jobs in the New World for Americans.

The issue of preference troubled both Peninsular and New World *liberales* who believed that Spaniards, regardless of their place of birth, should possess the same rights. Thus, preferences for natives of America seemed inappropriate. As Juan José Guerra of Durango, New Spain, declared: "I would like, as a matter of policy, . . . that in the regulations established in the Peninsula as well as in America, either European Spaniards or Americans who possess the necessary good qualifications be treated the same. This is required if we are to remain true to fundamental principles since we are one nation in both hemispheres."[26]

In the end, the deputies achieved a compromise of sorts. Article 1 of the constitution read: "The Spanish Nation is the union of all Spaniards of both hemispheres." Article 5 declared; "Spaniards are. First: all free men born and residing in the Spanish dominions and their children. Second: foreigners who have obtained naturalization papers from the Cortes. Third: those who, without them [naturalization papers], legally reside ten years in any town of the Monarchy. Fourth: freedmen who acquire their liberty in the Spains."

The question of political rights surfaced in Article 18, which defined citizenship: "Citizens are those Spaniards who trace their origins on both sides [of the family] from the Spanish dominions on both hemispheres and reside in any part of those same dominions." The article clearly excluded the descendants of Africans. But Article 22 noted: "Those Spaniards who on either side [of the family] originate or are reputed to originate in Africa have the door of virtue and merit open to them to become citizens." Thus, persons of African ancestry might become citizens, but the requirements were stringent. "Consequently, the Cortes will grant citizenship papers to those who provide important services to the *patria,* or to those who distinguish themselves by their talent, assiduity, and good conduct on the condition that they are the offspring of a legitimate marriage of freeborn parents, that they are married to a freeborn woman, that they reside in Spanish dominions, and that they exercise a profession, occupation, or useful industry with their own capital."[27] In short, colored *castas* who wished to become citizens had to meet higher standards than others.

26 Quoted in Rieu-Millan, *Los Diputados americanos,* 269.
27 "Constitución Política de la Monarquía Española," in *Leyes fundamentales de México, 1808–1991,* 16th ed., ed. Felipe Tena Ramirez (Mexico: Editorial Porrúa, 1991), 60–3.

On May 25, 1811, Guridi y Alcocer proposed abolishing slavery. Since the representatives of slaveholding regions – the Caribbean, Venezuela, coastal New Granada, and Peru – were adamantly opposed to ending either slavery or the slave trade, Guridi y Alcocer and others recommended the gradual elimination of slavery. As an alternative, the great Spanish *liberal* Agustín Argüelles suggested only terminating the slave trade. At the request of Mexía Llequerica, a commission was appointed to consider the matter. But despite eloquent and often emotional arguments in favor of abolition, the opposition triumphed. In the end, the Cortes believed that political expediency required the retention of slavery. As Esteban Palacios, Simón Bolívar's uncle and the *suplente* from Caracas, declared: "As a lover of humanity, I approve the abolition of slavery; but, as a lover of political order, I disapprove it."[28]

The American deputies, particularly the *propietarios,* received specific instructions from their *ayuntamientos.* In many cases, communities in America sought recognition as full-fledged cities with their own *ayuntamientos.* Others desired a university or a bishopric. Some regions, such as the Provincias Internas of New Spain, hoped to be reorganized into smaller provinces with their own capital cities. In a few cases, such as Maracaibo, which had lost its status as a capital to Caracas, cities requested that they become administrative centers of new intendancies. The Cortes addressed such requests through an administrative reorganization of the Spanish world.

The parliament restructured the Spanish Nation in both hemispheres by creating two new home rule institutions: the *provincial deputations* and the *constitutional ayuntamientos.* The provincial deputation was an administrative body consisting of locally elected members and an executive appointed by the national government. Thus, Spanish provinces already ruled by juntas and rebellious American provinces could retain local administration while maintaining strong ties with the national government. With the creation of the provincial deputations, the Cortes abolished the viceroyalties, transformed the *audiencias* from judicial and quasi-administrative bodies into high courts, and divided the Spanish world into provinces that dealt directly with the central government in Spain. The second body, the constitutional *ayuntamiento,* substituted popularly elected officials for the hereditary elites, who had heretofore controlled city government.

Initially Americans had attempted to obtain recognition for the juntas being formed in the New World. On December 14, 1810, Mexía Lleque-

---

28 Quoted in Rieu-Millan, *Los Diputados americanos,* 168. See also Manuel Chust Calero, "De esclavos, encomenderos y mitayos. El anticolonialismo en las Cortes de Cádiz, *MS/EM,* 11:2 (Summer 1995), 179–202.

rica unsuccessfully proposed that the rules being established for the Peninsular juntas be extended to America. Formal regulations for the Spanish provinces were finally promulgated on March 4, 1811. Subsequently, Ramos Arizpe, who had been charged by the city of Saltillo to establish more provinces in northern New Spain, took the lead in arguing for the creation of regional institutions that he called *provincial deputations*. The suggestion aroused much debate. Many Spaniards, including prominent *liberales* such as Argüelles and the Conde de Toreno, feared that such a body might fragment the nation by endowing the localities with too much power.[29] Conversely, Americans were concerned that the *jefe político* (political chief), the official appointed by the national government to preside over the provincial deputation, might dominate that body to the detriment of the provinces.

The debate over the provincial disputations pitted those who favored a strong unitary government against those who championed provincial interests. Thus, some Spanish deputies from the outlying regions, who sought more autonomy for their areas, joined the Americans in support of greater powers for the provincial deputations. As proposed, the provincial deputation, presided over by the *jefe político*, would consist of seven members plus the intendant. Many American deputies, however, wanted the provincial deputation to possess more members, both because they perceived the institution as a quasi-legislative body and because the New World kingdoms varied greatly in size and composition. Moreover, the Spanish and American definitions of provinces differed. In the Peninsula the traditional kingdoms had become the current provinces. But the Americans did not equate kingdoms with provinces. In the New World, kingdoms like New Spain consisted of a number of provinces, as its twelve intendancies indicated. Since each provincial deputation would deal directly with Madrid, establishing twelve in New Spain would be tantamount to dismembering the kingdom unless some mechanism were established to coordinate the activities of the provincial deputations in each realm. To the Spanish majority such an arrangement constituted a threat to the unity of the Spanish Nation, and therefore they opposed it.

As finally approved, the Cortes entrusted the provincial deputation with overall responsibility for its province. The new institution, with the *jefe político* presiding and with the intendant as member, consisted of seven deputies. Although the office of viceroy was abolished, the chief officials of the former viceregal capitals retained broad military authority in the kingdoms as *capitanes generales* and *jefes políticos superiores*. The Cortes established nineteen provincial deputations for the overseas territories: New Spain,

29 Artola, *Los orígenes*, 1:417–23.

New Galicia, Yucatán, San Luis Potosí, Provincias Internas de Oriente, Provincias Internas de Occidente, Guatemala, Nicaragua, Cuba with the two Floridas, Santo Domingo and Puerto Rico, New Granada, Venezuela, Quito, Peru, Cuzco, Charcas, Chile, Río de la Plata, and the Philippines.[30]

The second home rule institution created by the Cortes, the constitutional *ayuntamiento,* dramatically expanded political participation in the Spanish world. The American representatives, particularly the proprietary deputies, had received instructions to seek the establishment of more *ayuntamientos* in their regions. As the Constitution was being discussed, however, it became evident that traditional officials, such as the hereditary *regidores,* would be abolished. This concerned Americans because their compatriots monopolized those positions in the New World. But when they realized that the electoral process provided advantages to the natives of the regions, the Americans accepted the changes. Their interest, thereafter, centered on preventing the *jefes políticos* from dominating the municipalities, as the intendants had in the past.[31]

Spaniards sought not only to introduce the new constitutional city governments, but also to increase the number of *ayuntamientos* in their provinces. Historically, municipal governments in the Peninsula had been crucial in developing autonomous and economically viable regions, particularly in those areas where nobles retained seigniorial jurisdiction. Since the constitution would abolish all such privileges, little stood in the way of creating more towns with *ayuntamientos.* As a result, the Spanish deputies recommended allowing centers with limited population to establish municipal governments.[32] The proposal did not affect significantly the level of political participation in the Peninsula because it already possessed numerous *ayuntamientos.* But in the New World, it had a dramatic impact because there *ayuntamientos* were limited to the principal cities. The Constitution, which allowed areas with 1,000 souls or more to establish *ayuntamientos,* therefore revolutionized America by dramatically expanding political participation.

The conflict between vital Spanish and Spanish American interests also

30 Nettie Lee Benson, *La Diputación Provincial y el federalismo mexicano* (Mexico: El Colegio de México, 1955), 11–21; Rieu-Millan, *Los Diputados americanos,* 239–53.

31 See Roger L. Cunniff, "Mexican Municipal Electoral Reform, *1810–1822,"* in Benson, *Mexico and the Spanish Cortes;* and Rieu-Millan, *Los Diputados americanos,* 217–31.

32 Manuel Chust, "La vía autonomista novohispana. Una propuesta federal en las Cortes de Cádiz," *Estudios de Historia Novohispana,* 15 (1995), 168–74; and his "América y el problema federal en las Cortes de Cádiz," in *Republicanos y repúblicas en España,* ed. José A. Piquera and Manuel Chust (Madrid: Siglo Veintiuno de España, 1966), 45–75. On the significance of *ayuntamientos* in Spain, see Helen Nader, *Liberty in Absolutist Spain: The Habsburg Sale of Towns, 1516–1700* (Baltimore: Johns Hopkins University Press, 1990). See also Manuel Morán Orti, *Poder y gobierno en las Cortes de Cádiz, 1810–1813* (Pamplona: Ediciones Universidad de Navarra, 1986).

emerged in the debate over commerce within the Monarchy. The British, now Spain's allies against the French, sought permission to trade freely with America. Some Spaniards supported a temporary relaxation of commercial restrictions to address the current economic and fiscal crisis. They did not, however, favor eliminating the existing monopoly trade. Many American deputies in the Cortes, however, sought a much broader liberalization of commerce. The Cádiz merchants joined their Spanish colleagues in the New World in opposing free trade. The debate also contained major political implications for the deputies of New Spain. In 1808, the Consulado of Mexico had played a leading role in preventing the formation of a junta in New Spain, overthrowing Viceroy Iturrigaray, imprisoning the autonomists, and dominating the government of the viceroyalty for some time thereafter. The members of the Consulado of Mexico and the *novohispano* deputies loathed each other. Many delegates from New Spain denounced the Consulado of Mexico in the Cortes. The Consulado, however, possessed an able defender in Cádiz, Juan López de Cancelada, who, based on his long experience in New Spain, effectively questioned the motives of the Americans in his paper, *El Telégrafo Americano.*

The Cádiz merchants countered attempts to introduce free trade by arguing that such an act would ruin Spain's economy. López de Cancelada published a pamphlet entitled *New Spain's Ruin if Free Trade with Foreigners Is Declared,* which demonstrated that both Spains would suffer if foreigners were allowed to trade freely within the Monarchy. The Americans responded with arguments in the Cortes and in the press in favor of liberalizing commerce. On August 1, 1811, thirty-three New World deputies submitted a proposal to the parliament advocating economic reforms, including free trade. But when the measure came to a vote on August 13, it was defeated by eighty-seven to forty-three. Some Spaniards supported the measure, a few Americans opposed it, and eight deputies from New Spain abstained.[33]

Conflicting regional and personal interests divided Americans on the issue of commerce. Although free trade benefited some areas, particularly the Caribbean ports, the representatives of other regions feared that their *patrias* would be harmed. Some worried that a native merchant marine could not compete with those of the great powers, such as Britain. Others feared that their manufactures, particularly textiles in New Spain and Quito, would be destroyed by cheaper European cloth. Although all Americans desired to end the control of the Spanish monopoly merchants, they found it difficult to agree on a unified approach.

The deputies from Spain and America to the General and Extraordinary

33 Rieu-Millan, *Los Diputados americanos,* 188–209; John H. Hann, "The Role of the Mexican Deputies in the Proposal and Enactment of Measures of Economic Reform Applicable to Mexico," in Benson, *Mexico and the Spanish Cortes,* 153–68; Michael P. Costeloe, "Spain and the Latin American Wars of Independence: The Free Trade Controversy, 1810–1820," *HAHR,"* 61:2 (May 1981), 209–16.

Cortes, in session from September 24, 1810, until September 20, 1813, transformed the Spanish Monarchy. Their Constitution of 1812 was not a Spanish document; it was a charter for the Spanish world. Indeed, it is unlikely that the Constitution of Cádiz would have taken the form it did without the participation of the representatives of the New World. The American deputies played a central role in drafting that charter. Their arguments and proposals convinced many Spaniards to embrace substantial change in America as well as in the Peninsula. Their project to abolish forced labor in the New World, for example, coincided with the wishes of some Europeans to end seigniorial obligations in the Peninsula. Whereas the Spaniards' desire to expand municipal government to urban centers with a population of 1,000 or more had revolutionary implications in the New World, the American proposal to endow the provinces with greater local control, the provincial deputation, had a profound impact in the Peninsula. The Constitution of 1812, therefore, was as much an American charter as a Spanish one.

Although many critics, then and now, have dismissed the Constitution of Cádiz as unrepresentative of the desires and needs of the people of Spain and America, that charter, as Mario Rodríguez has argued, "was the effort of pragmatists who were determined to create a modern Spanish nation while taking into account its traditions and experiences."[34] The Constitution of 1812 abolished seigniorial institutions, Indian tribute, and forced labor such as the *mita* in South America and personal service in Spain; ended the Inquisition; and established firm control over the Church. Freedom of the press, although already a fact, was formally proclaimed. The Constitution of the Spanish Monarchy, promulgated in March 1812, embodied these and other reforms. The new charter created a unitary state with equal laws for all parts of the Spanish world. It substantially restricted the king and entrusted the Cortes with decisive power. The unicameral legislature would meet annually in the capital.

In evaluating the achievements and limitations of the Cortes, it is useful to compare them with those of other nations. Although the Spanish majority failed to grant Americans the full equality that they desired, the *peninsulares* went further than the leaders of any other European nation. Certainly Britain, the birthplace of modern representative government, never considered giving its North American possessions equality of representation in Parliament. The Constitution of 1812 denied the people of African ancestry political rights as well as representation. In that regard, the Cortes acted in the same fashion as other Western nations, which also excluded their African-origin population from full citizenship. Under the Spanish

---

34 Rodríguez, *The Cádiz Experiment,* 94. For an example of criticism of the work of the Cortes, see Timothy E. Anna, *Spain and the Loss of America* (Lincoln: University of Nebraska Press, 1983), chap. 3.

Constitution, however, freedmen of extraordinary achievement might become full-fledged citizens.

The Spanish *liberales* and their American colleagues were determined to create a modern nation in America as well as in Spain. Despite extensive warnings from royal officials in the New World, as well as from tradition-alists both in Spain and in America about the special conditions of the Western Hemisphere, they refused to define the Indians and mestizos as less human than themselves. The Constitution of 1812 recognized Indians and mestizos as full citizens of the Spanish Nation. In contrast, the United States did not grant Indians citizenship until 1924. Before that date, both under Britain and after independence, the Indians of the territory that is now the United States were defined as foreigners.[35]

Britain proved unwilling even to grant the white inhabitants of its American colonies equal representation in Parliament. Spain, on the other hand, agreed to provide the New World with the same number of repre-sentatives as the Peninsula. No Spaniard, however, would agree to a provi-sion that reduced Spain to a minority in its own Cortes. Since a deputy was to be chosen on the basis of one for every 70,000 inhabitants, by depriving the colored *castas* of political rights, the *peninsulares* reduced the size of the politically eligible overseas population to a number comparable to theirs, thereby retaining equal representation for themselves in their parliament.

Perhaps the most revolutionary aspects of the Constitution of 1812 were endowing the Cortes with great power and introducing mass political par-ticipation. Unlike the U.S. Constitution, which established three equal branches of government, the Charter of Cádiz created three very unequal branches. The judiciary received little independent power, and the execu-tive was considered subservient to the legislature. Indeed, national sover-eignty was entrusted to the Cortes. Mass political participation was ensured in two ways: First, local government increased dramatically because popu-lation centers with 1,000 or more inhabitants were granted the right to form *ayuntamientos*. The change would have the greatest impact in Amer-ica, which possessed far fewer *ayuntamientos* than the Peninsula. And sec-ond, granting all males, except those of African ancestry, the franchise without requiring either literacy or property expanded the scope of popu-lar politics beyond that of any other government in the Western world.

The First Popular Elections in America

The new charter could not have come at a worse time for the royal officials in America, who for two years had been engaged in an extensive and bru-

---

35 Patricia Seed, "'Are These Not Also Men?': The Indians' Humanity and Capacity for Spanish Civ-ilization," *Journal of Latin American Studies*, 25:3 (October 1993), 651.

tal counterinsurgency campaign. They faced a great dilemma. The Cortes, which represented the legitimate government of the Spanish Monarchy, acted in ways that undermined the royal authorities and seemed to support the insurgents. The tenor of the official discourse was particularly disturbing. The decree of February 14, 1810, convoking elections to the Cortes, for example, declared: "American Spaniards, from this moment you are elevated to the dignity of free men . . . your destinies no longer depend either on the ministers, the viceroys, or the governors; they are in your hands."[36] To the viceroys of New Spain and Peru, it seemed less a government decree than an insurgent manifesto.

The free press in Spain, particularly that of Cádiz, and the published *actas* (debates) of the Cortes, which circulated widely in America, added fuel to the fire. The discussion of popular sovereignty was subversive enough, in the view of the royal authorities, but, in addition, Spanish *liberales* insisted on denouncing the 300 years of slavery they had endured. It mattered little that the *peninsulares* used the phrase to describe the period since the mythical democracy of Spain had been crushed by the despotic Habsburgs. In the New World, many Americans interpreted their words to mean the 300 years of Spanish domination. The speeches of the New World deputies further infuriated authorities in America. Royal officials there found it difficult enough to deal with the deputies' charge that the New World lacked adequate representation; it became almost unbearable when they read, in the *actas* of the Cortes and in the newspapers, attacks against themselves and demands that they be removed and disciplined.[37]

The royal authorities retaliated by obstructing the reforms. In Mexico City and Lima, the viceroys either restricted or suspended freedom of the press on various occasions. Such measures were of limited utility, however, because publications from Spain and from other areas in the viceroyalties or in America circulated widely. Havana became a major center for the publication and republication of works issued elsewhere. Starting in 1810, the number of pamphlets and periodicals circulating in Spanish America increased exponentially.[38] Thus, the residents of the New World, not only those in the principal cities and towns but also those in the "peasant com-

36 *Gazeta de Mexico,* I, Núm. 56 (June 18, 1810), 413.
37 Rieu-Millan, *Los Diputados americanos,* 304–28; Guerra, *Modernidad,* 305–18; Rodríguez, *The Cádiz Experiment,* 55–6.
38 Virginia Guedea, *En busca de un gobierno alterno, Los Guadalupes de Mexico* (Mexico: UNAM, 1992), 128–34; Timothy E. Anna, *The Fall of Royal Government in Peru* (Lincoln: University of Nebraska Press, 1979), 82–3. The massive growth of publications is evident in *Impresos novohispanos, 1808–1821,* 2 vols. ed. Amaya Garritz, Virginia Guedea, and Teresa Lozano (Mexico: UNAM, 1990), I, and in Rocío Meza Oliver and Luis Olivera López, eds., *Catálogo de la colección LaFragua de la Biblioteca Nacional de México, 1800–1810* (Mexico: UNAM, 1993) and their *Catálogo de la colección LaFragua de la Biblioteca Nacional de México, 1811–1821* (Mexico: UNAM, 1996).

munities, were receiving regular news regarding the decisions of the Cortes."[39]

Although royal officials might slow the pace of reforms, they could not ignore the Constitution of the Spanish Monarchy. In the months of August, September, and October 1812 in the regions under royal control – the Caribbean, New Spain, Central America, Quito, Peru, and Charcas – the Constitution was formally read to the civil, military, and ecclesiastic authorities and to the public. Then those present swore to obey the charter. "That same day [as Guedea notes] with the ringing of bells, *Te Deum* and mass in the cathedral, and the other solemnities which such an occasion warranted, the [Constitution] was published. . . . In the days that followed, the same thing was done throughout [all the kingdoms of America]."[40]

The Constitution of 1812 expanded the electorate and dramatically increased the scope of political activity. The new charter established representative government at three levels: the municipality, the province, and the Monarchy. It allowed cities and towns with 1,000 or more people to form *ayuntamientos*. Political power was thus transferred from the center to localities as large numbers of people were incorporated for the first time into the political process. The Spanish Cortes provided the American autonomists with a peaceful means to obtain home rule. Fearful of continuing race and class conflicts that raged in various parts of the continent, most autonomists welcomed the new representative government, which, while imposing limits on Monarchy, also possessed legitimacy. Their attitude is understandable. The autonomists of America, like some of the elites of other Western nations, wanted moderate representative government. They favored neither social revolution nor race and class warfare, but they were determined to rule at home. To this end, they organized themselves in 1812 to win the elections for constitutional *ayuntamientos*, provincial deputations, and the Cortes. Unlike the elections of 1809 for the Junta Central and those of 1810 for the Cortes, which were conducted by the *ayuntamientos*, the new constitutional elections were the first popular elections held in Spanish America.

Ironically, the new Spanish political system appears to have been more popular and democratic than those of most insurgent governments then vying for power in the New World. Relatively free elections occurred in those areas dominated by the royalists: New Spain, Guatemala, Cuba, Puerto Rico, Quito, Peru, and Upper Peru.[41] In contrast, the rebels either

---

39 Terry Rugeley, *Yucatán's Maya Peasantry & the Origins of the Caste War* (Austin: University of Texas Press, 1996), 39.

40 Guedea, *En busca de un gobierno alterno*, 127; Rodríguez, *The Cádiz Experiment*, 101–2; Anna, *The Fall of Royal Government in Peru*, 71–2.

41 Despite their significance, historians have not carefully examined these processes. We lack adequate

did not hold elections or failed to conduct them in a democratic or popular manner. Virginia Guedea's study of the insurgent elections for their own 1813 congress in New Spain indicates that the insurgents manipulated the process and allowed less local participation than the royalists, perhaps because they were attempting to form a national government and therefore feared the rise of local interests.[42]

The new popular electoral process was extremely complex since it required elections for three bodies: constitutional *ayuntamientos*, provincial deputations, and the regular Cortes. As Guedea indicates:

> The electoral procedures established by the Cortes were not only indirect but also lengthy and complex. There were two stages for elections to the constitutional *ayuntamientos:* the selection of parish electors and the designation of new alcaldes, *regidores*, and syndics by the electors. The election of deputies to the Cortes and to the provincial deputations was even more intricate. Elections to these two bodies occurred at three levels: parish, *partido* (district), and province. Because of their complexity, preparatory juntas were necessary to organize and conduct them.[43]

The preparatory juntas had fundamental and difficult responsibilities: They had to establish an electoral census by parish, divide their areas into districts for the selection of deputies to the Cortes and the provincial dep-

studies of these electoral contests, except for those of 1812–1813 in Mexico City. On the Mexico City elections, see Nettie Lee Benson, "The Contested Mexican Election of 1812," *HAHR*, 26:3 (August 1946), 336–50; Guedea, "The First Popular Elections in Mexico City," 45–69; Guedea, "El pueblo de México y la política capitalina, 1808–1812," *MS/SM*, 10:1 (Winter 1994), 27–61; Antonio Annino, "Prácticas criollas y liberalismo en la crisis del espacio urbano colonial. El 29 de noviembre de 1812 en la ciudad de México," *Secuencia*, Núm. 24 (September–December 1992), 121–58; and Richard A. Warren, "Vagrants and Citizens: Politics and the Poor in Mexico City, 1808–1836" (Ph.D. diss., University of Chicago, 1994), 56–71. On other elections, also see Charles Berry, "The Election of Mexican Deputies to the Spanish Cortes, 1810–1822," in *Mexico and the Spanish Cortes*, ed. Nettie Lee Benson (Austin: University of Texas Press, 1966) 10–42. Patrick J. Carroll discusses elections in Jalapa in *Blacks in Colonial Veracruz: Race, Ethnicity, and Regional Development* (Austin: University of Texas Press, 1991), 134–41; Rodríguez, *The Cádiz Experiment*, 79–80, 107–9, 137–9; John Preston Moore, *The Cabildo in Peru under the Bourbons* (Durham: Duke University Press, 1966), 197–220; John R. Fisher, *Government and Society in Colonial Peru: The Intendant System, 1784–1814* (London: Athlone Press, 1970), 201–32; Anna, *The Fall of Royal Government in Peru*, 83–6, 89–90; Antonio Gómez Vizuete, "Los primeros ayuntamientos liberales en Puerto Rico (1812–1814 y 1820–1823)," *Anuario de Estudios Americanos*, 47 (1990), 581–615. As Peter Guardino observes, people at the village level were fully aware of the significance of the new political system and participated actively in it. See his *Peasants, Politics, and the Formation of Mexico's National State: Guerrero, 1800–1857* (Stanford: Stanford University Press, 1996), chap. II.

42 Virginia Guedea, "Los procesos electorales insurgentes," *Estudios de Historia Novohispana*, Núm. 11 (1991), 201–49. Similarly, participation in elections to the first Junta of Quito was restricted to forty-three *vecinos nobles* of Quito. See Alonso Valencia Llano, "Elites, burocracia, clero y sectores populares en la Independencia Quiteña (1809–1812)," *Procesos: Revista ecuatoriana de historia*, 3 (II semester 1992), 67–8.

43 Guedea, "The First Popular Elections in Mexico City," 49.

utations, and, finally, oversee the elections. The task was complicated because, in many cases, districts overlapped; some districts voted together for deputies to the Cortes but separately for provincial deputies.[44]

The higher authorities had to determine the number of *ayuntamientos* for which elections were to be held, a complex and difficult task since many towns and villages were establishing *ayuntamientos* simultaneously. In 1810, New Spain, for example, had fewer than twenty *ayuntamientos* and Puerto Rico possessed only two. By 1814, 896 *ayuntamientos* had been created in New Spain and about 20 in Puerto Rico.[45] A similar explosion of *ayuntamientos* occurred in other areas of Spanish America.[46]

As Guedea observes, two parties emerged during the election: the American party and the European party.

> While these words [American and European] never lost their original meaning regarding place of birth, they acquired a heavy political content. They came more and more to refer to a strong attitude either of support for or of opposition to the colonial regime. . . . These views were held primarily, but not exclusively, by those born on this or that side of the Atlantic. They were based, more than anything else, on the orientation of their respective interests: either toward the Peninsula or the interior of . . . [America].[47]

Both groups campaigned extensively. Leading candidates and other prominent individuals held meetings to coordinate the vote.

Because the electoral system was complex, campaign organization became absolutely necessary. So many individuals had to be chosen as electors at the parish level that various groups created lists so that the voters would remember for whom they were voting. In addition, they provided illiterate voters in Mexico City and Quito slips of paper with the names of those for whom they were to vote. In Mexico City, Quito, and Lima, muleteers and tavern keepers distributed electoral information. Churchmen were extremely active on both sides. But since the majority of the clergy,

---

44 See, for example, "Plan de Elecciones de Diputados en Cortes y Provincia" and "El Censo [electoral] de esta Provincia de Quito" in ANHQ: PQ, vol. 579, ff. 41–7 and passim. A detailed electoral census for Peru by province and *partido* for 1813, as well as a comparable census for the Diputación Provincial de León de Nicaragua by *partido* and pueblo, are found in AGI: Indiferente, 1524.

45 Guedea, "The First Popular Elections in Mexico City," 50–6; Gómez Vizuete, "Los primeros ayuntamientos liberales," 584–8; Alicia Hernández Chávez, *La tradición republicana del buen gobierno* (Mexico: Fondo de Cultura Económica, 1993), 25.

46 At present, comparable information is lacking for other areas of Spanish America; one may assume that towns in royalist-held areas took advantage of the opportunity offered them by the Spanish Constitution to form municipal governments. I have located thirty-one reports of towns forming constitutional *ayuntamientos* in the Kingdom of Quito. Undoubtedly, more were established. See ANHQ: PQ, vol. 574.

47 Guedea, "The First Popular Elections in Mexico City," 68.

particularly the lower clergy, were American, they proved to be a great force in support of local interests. When the elections were held in the New World, frequently it proved impossible to determine if individuals seeking to vote qualified as citizens. In New Spain, for example, many people of color appear to have voted. Although the elite clearly dominated the process, thousands of middle- and lower-class individuals, including mestizos, Indians, and *castas,* became involved in politics in a meaningful way and made their presence felt.[48]

Americans overwhelmingly won the elections throughout the New World. In some cases, such as that of New Spain, urban groups collaborated with the insurgents in electing individuals favorable to American autonomy. In those areas, the elections weakened the royal authorities and strengthened the hand of autonomists.[49] To many *peninsulares,* the results demonstrated that Americans hated them. In Mexico City, Antonio Pol y España, for example, declared that there was no difference between those who fought against the royal government and those who sought power through constitutional means. He concluded that when the very sons of the Spaniards "unite with Indians, blacks, and the *canalla* [rabble] to destroy and to kill us, simply for having been born in Spain," it becomes necessary "to use force to repel their insolence, handling it with the degree of justice required by the most cruel, most barbarous, most extraordinary persecution that ever appeared upon the earth."[50] The authorities there temporarily suspended elections because of alleged irregularities. The new viceroy, Félix María Calleja, subsequently restored them, hoping to attract the support of partisans of the Constitution and that, with better control, more Europeans might be selected. He erred. Americans triumphed overwhelmingly in the subsequent elections.[51] Guatemala and Peru also experienced conflict between the royal authorities and local groups. There too, New World natives triumphed.[52]

It is striking that popular elections occurred in royalist areas in the midst of a violent insurgency. The 1813 elections in the Kingdom of Quito provide an example. Royalist forces under the command of General Toribio

48 Ibid., 65–6; Rieu-Millan, *Los Diputados americanos,* 38–57; Rodríguez, *The Cádiz Experiment,* 79–80. The documents for the election of 1813 in Quito are located in a volume titled. "Juramento a la Constitución, 1820," AMQ.

49 See, for example, the case of the Guadalupes of Mexico City: Guedea, *En busca de un gobierno alterno,* 137–71.

50 Quoted in Guedea, "The First Popular Elections in Mexico City," 65–6.

51 Ibid., 57–60.

52 Rodríguez, *The Cádiz Experiment,* 106–9; Anna, *The Fall of Royal Government in Peru,* 58–9, 83–6. Guillermo Durand Flores has published the *actas* of various parish, *partido,* and provincial elections for 1812–13 in *El Perú en las Cortes de Cádiz,* 2 vols. (Lima: Comisión Nacional del Sesquicentenario de la Independencia del Perú, 1974), 2.

Montes crushed the second Junta of Quito at the end of 1812. Insurgents continued to control much of New Granada in the north, however. Nevertheless, as required by the Spanish Constitution, General Montes initiated the process of holding popular elections in the Kingdom of Quito. First, he instructed local officials to publish the Constitution, that is, to have it read in formal ceremonies, in all the cities and towns of the kingdom. Then he ordered *curas* and local officials to conduct parish censuses to determine the size of the population eligible to participate in elections. The news startled most people in the realm. Countless local officials requested copies of the Constitution, as well as further instructions so that they might understand the new political system. Several wondered if Indians really were to be considered Spanish citizens. One official in the Marañon, the eastern jungle region, argued that he could not conduct an electoral census of the towns in his jurisdiction because most were twelve to fifteen days' walk in the jungle and, in any case, their residents were Indians. From Quito, General Montes replied that those individuals were citizens of the Spanish Nation and therefore possessed the same rights as any other citizen. The chastened official indicated that the census of those *"individuos selvaticos,"* individuals from the jungle, soon would be forthcoming.

The status of the Indians was complex, however. Some local officials inquired if *all* Indians were to be considered active citizens. Article 25 of the Constitution indicated that a man might lose his political rights if he was a convicted felon, legally bankrupt, or a domestic servant. Since many Indians in the Kingdom of Quito lived on haciendas in *concertaje,* a form a servitude, the crown attorney determined that they would be considered domestic servants and therefore not eligible to vote. It was a question that would lead to conflict in a number of jurisdictions when local groups attempted to prevent Indians who did not reside on haciendas from exercising their civic rights. The authorities determined that the vast majority of Indians were citizens who possessed political rights and overturned elections where Indians had been prevented from voting.

Questions were also raised about the political status of women, bastards, illiterates, and clerics. Since women had possessed the right to vote in traditional elections when they were family heads, *vecinos,* some wondered if they could also vote in the new popular elections. The higher authorities replied that under the Constitution of 1812, men voted as individuals and not as heads of families. Women family heads, therefore, were not entitled to vote. Since the Constitution did not differentiate between legitimate and illegitimate men, bastards possessed political rights. Similarly, illiterate men who were otherwise qualified could vote since the charter did not presently impose literacy requirements. Finally, according the Constitution, only secular clergy had the right to vote. Thus, the regulars were disenfranchised.

After months of effort, the electoral census of the Kingdom of Quito – which included the highland provinces from Pasto and Popayán in the north to Loja in the south, Marañon, Mainas, and Jaén de Bracamoros in the eastern jungles, and the northern coastal provinces of Barbacoas and Esmeraldas (the great southern coastal province of Guayaquil had been placed under the authority of Lima) – was completed in June 1813. Inasmuch as some regions were "currently occupied by the enemy," the authorities determined that a "prudent calculation" would be "four hundred sixty five thousand nine hundred individuals, a little more or less." Moreover, "sixty five thousand nine hundred individuals, who are either not citizens or may not exercise their rights," were to be deducted from the census. Thus, possessing a politically eligible population of 400,000 Quito had the right to five deputies to the Cortes on the basis "of one per seventy thousand" inhabitants. But since "fifty thousand inhabitants remained, [the kingdom] had the right to one more deputy . . . [according to article 32 of the Constitution]. As a consequence, this province has the right to six proprietary deputies and two suplentes . . . [as well as] eighteen *partido* electors." The electoral census also determined the number of *compromisarios* and parish electors for each *partido*.[53]

The elections for constitutional *ayuntamientos* during the months from September 1813 to January 1814 proved to be both exciting and confusing. The authorities in Quito were deluged with questions. Several cities wondered if the *corregidores* were to become *jefes políticos* and if they were to preside over the new constitutional *ayuntamientos*. Some small towns noted that they possessed more than the 1,000 souls required by the Constitution and asked if they might form *ayuntamientos*. Others inquired about their relationship to their former *ciudades cabezas de partido*. Jefe Político Superior Montes replied, to their amazement, that the old political relationships were over; any urban center with 1,000 inhabitants had the right to establish an independent *ayuntamiento,* subject only to the authority of the provincial deputation in Quito. Despite these and other clarifications, problems continued. Some citizens of the *partido* of Cuenca questioned elections in several small towns because the local *curas* had prepared slips with their names and those of their friends that illiterate citizens used in the

---

53 The Cortes issued a number of decrees establishing guidelines for the new popular elections. One of them, issued on May 23, 1812, required the establishment of "a *junta preparatoria* to facilitate the election of the Deputies to the Ordinary Cortes of 1813 in the . . . capitals" of the New World. But, inexplicably, the decree failed to include Quito and Charcas among the capitals where preparatory juntas were to be established. As a result, President Montes and the Crown attorney acted instead of a preparatory junta for Quito, Spain; Cortes, *Colección de decretos y ordenes de las Cortes de Cádiz.* 2 vols. (Madrid: Cortes Generales, 1987), 1:508–25. ANHQ: PQ, vol. 468, f. 19; vol. 477, ff. 10, 34, 40–1; vol. 478, f. 88; vol. 479, ff. 117, 145; vol. 482, f. 169; vol. 483, ff. 42, 48–9, 97; vol. 489, ff. 1–6; vol. 579, ff. 41–7.

elections. In the *partido* of Loja, several Indian *mandones,* as the officials of the former *repúblicas de indios* were called, demanded that elections be annulled because they had lost and new individuals, some of them not even Indians, had been elected to office. In the *partido* of Cuenca, former Indian officials threatened to revolt if they were not returned to office. The greatest conflict, however, occurred in the cities of Loja and Cuenca, where local cliques restricted the suffrage to their clients in order to win control of the *ayuntamientos.* In both cases, the authorities in Quito overturned the results because "all the members of the people [i.e., the Indians] had not participated in the election." The beneficiaries of those decisions were pleased to consider the Indians their "fellow citizens" and to rejoice that "the Spanish Monarchy is one of laws." Most cities and towns, however, managed to elect *ayuntamiento* officials with little or no difficulty.[54]

The election of deputies to the Cortes and the provincial deputation in the former Kingdom of Quito, now called the Province of Quito, proved to be lengthier and more complicated. The first phase, the parish elections, required the selection of as many as thirty-one and as few as one *compromisario* per parish. These, in turn, would choose the parish electors. Large, thinly populated parishes, which had been allocated between one and six *compromisarios,* were combined for parish elections and, as a result, experienced delays as the *compromisarios* traveled to the place where the parish electors were to be chosen. These then traveled to the *ciudad cabecera de partido,* where the *partido* electors would be selected. Most *partidos,* including heavily populated ones such as Quito and Cuenca, had distant parishes. Some, like the *partido* of Riobamba and Macas, stretched from the highlands to the depths of the eastern jungle. Naturally, the selection of *partido* electors suffered many delays. Some individuals chosen by their fellow citizens were unwilling to undertake the long trips required to hold elections, particularly *partido* elections. In a few cases, the authorities in Quito were forced to engage in lengthy arguments to convince them to assume their civic responsibilities. Finally, after months of effort, the eighteen *partido* electors met in Quito on August 24–6, 1814, to elect the six deputies to the Cortes, the two *suplentes,* and the seven deputies to the provincial deputation.[55] As occurred in other areas of the New World, the Americans overwhelmed the Europeans. Ironically, what they had been unable to win by force the *quiteños* accomplished through the ballot. They gained control of local government.

The constitutional *ayuntamientos* assumed office with great fanfare throughout the royalist-held areas of America. Then they proceeded to take

54 ANHQ: PQ, vol. 478, f. 72r–v, 74r–v; vol. 479, ff. 117, 145; vol. 481, ff. 42–3; vol. 482, ff. 81, 185; vol. 483, ff. 10r–v, 14, 62, 119–20; vol. 485, f. 108; vol. 492, vol. 494, ff. 3r–v, 4, 62, 82.
55 ANHQ: PQ, vol. 491, ff. 150–3; vol. 579, ff. 29r–v, 30–1.

control of the city government. In Mexico City the constitutional *regidores,* all Americans, included various insurgent sympathizers; several members of the secret society of Guadalupes, which was in contact with the insurgents; and a former Indian governor of the *parcialidad* of San Juan, Francisco Antonio Galicia. The new *regidores* governed with great care, but they clearly favored American interests. They challenged local royal authorities whenever they failed to follow constitutional mandates and sought to improve the condition of their fellow citizens.[56] Many constitutional *ayuntamientos,* such as those in the Kingdom of Quito, insisted on funds for schools, hospitals, and other public facilities. They also expressed widespread support for the success of "the national armies" in their struggle against the tyrant Napoleon.[57]

Although the larger cities appeared to function well under the control of the American upper and middle classes, the *ayuntamientos* in predominantly Indian regions, such as the highlands of the Kingdom of Quito, Guatemala, and the Yucatán Peninsula and the Huasteca region of New Spain, were forced to confront unforeseen consequences of the new constitutional order. Many Indians, former members of *repúblicas de indios,* refused to follow traditional patterns. They argued that now that they were Spanish citizens, they were no longer obligated to perform personal service or forced labor. Thus, they proved unwilling to work for the Church or on public projects such as roads and government buildings. They steadfastly refused to pay either tribute or the tithe on the grounds that the Constitution had ended those obligations. Many no longer contributed to the support of their parish *curas.* Some refused to attend mass and send their children to school. In various tropical and jungle areas, they abandoned the villages in which they had been congregated to form dispersed communities more suited to their environment. In a few instances they became drunk and disorderly because, they said, as free men they could do what they wanted. Some even refused to pay their debts in the belief that the Charter of Cádiz had ended such obligations. The dismayed local authorities could only complain about the Indians' "incredible effrontery" to higher officials in the hope that they would restore order.[58]

---

56 Guedea, *En busca de un gobierno alterno,* 173–231; and Guedea, "De la fidelidad a la infidencia: Los gobernadores de la parcialidad de San Juan," in Jaime E. Rodríguez O., ed., *Patterns of Contention in Mexican History* (Wilmington: Scholarly Resources, 1992) 95–123.

57 ANHQ: PQ, vol. 496, ff. 173r–v, 290; vol. 497, f. 133; vol. 498, f. 42.

58 The Yucatecan *cura* José de Jesús Texera, for example, noted: "Since the right of citizenship was proclaimed for the Indians, and tribute was abolished for them, along with obventions, many of them have disappeared, and go wandering two, three, and even four months without attending the Divine Offices, nor do they comply with the precepts of Our Mother the Holy Church. Children have abandoned the doors of the churches, where daily they were instructed with the rudiments of Our Holy Religion."

Instituting constitutional government at the provincial level proved more difficult. Although elections for provincial deputations were held throughout the continent, there were many delays before the deputies from the regions that constituted a province could convene in the provincial capital. In New Spain, Guatemala, and Peru, royal officials delayed inaugurating the new bodies. Nevertheless, several were functioning by the end of 1813 and others initiated their activities in 1814. The Provincial Deputations of New Spain and Quito, however, were only inaugurated in July and August 1814, shortly before news arrived that the king had abolished constitutional government.[59]

Despite widespread insurgencies, the new bodies sought to exercise authority in their areas. Some, like the Provincial Deputation of Guatemala, managed to obtain the removal of obstructive officials. Others, such as that of Nicaragua, concerned themselves with the economic development of their region. In New Spain, Central America, and Peru, provincial deputations proposed increasing the number of intendancies in their areas. In several cases, the new institutions fomented regionalism when local notables argued that their region should receive additional provincial deputations. The new provincial governments appeared to be thriving shortly before the constitution was abrogated by the king.[60]

American participation in constitutional government at the highest level, the Cortes, was less successful. In many parts of the New World, the conflict between the interests of the royal authorities and the Spaniards in America, on the one hand, and those of the natives of the New World, on the other, delayed elections for deputies to the Cortes. In some cases, royal authorities prevented the newly elected deputies from traveling to Spain. In others, lack of finances served the same purpose. Still, a number of Amer-

Quoted in Rugeley, *Yucatán's Maya Peasantry,* 41, 38–48; ANHQ: PQ, vol. 494, f. 83; vol. 495, ff. 266r–v; vol. 498, ff. 54, 68–70; Antonio Escobar Ohmstede, "Del gobierno indígena al Ayuntamiento constitucional en las Huastecas hidalguense y veracruzana, 1780–1853," *MS/EM,* 12:1 (Winter 1996), 1–26; Arturo Güémez Pineda, *Liberalismo en tierras del caminante Yucatán, 1812–1840* (Zamora: El Colegio de Michoacán, 1994), 49–62; Pedro Bracamonte y Sosa, "La ruptura del pacto social colonial y el reforzamiento de la identidad indígena en Yucatán, 1789–1847," in *Indio, nación y comunidad en el México del siglo XIX,* ed. Antonio Escobar O. (Mexico: Centro de Estudios Mexicanos y Centroamericanos and Centro de Investigaciones y Estudios Superiores en Antropología Social, 1993), 119–25; Juan Ortiz Escamilla, *Guerra y gobierno: Los pueblos y la independencia de México* (Mexico: Instituto Mora, 1997); Xiomara Avendaño Rojas, "Procesos electorales y clase política in la Federación de Centroamérica (1810–1840)" (Ph.D. diss., El Colegio de México, 1995), 47–9.

59 Benson, *La Diputación Provincial,* 43; Rodríguez, *The Cádiz Experiment,* 112–17; Anna, *The Fall of Royal Government in Peru;* Moore, *The Cabildo in Peru under the Bourbons,* 218–22; ANHQ: PQ, vol. 491, ff. 150–3.

60 Rodríguez, *The Cádiz Experiment,* 117–23; Fisher, *Government and Society,* 221–7; Moore, *The Cabildo in Peru under the Bourbons,* 218–22; Avendaño Rojas, "Procesos electorales," 42–51.

ican delegates managed to reach the Peninsula to participate in the regular Cortes of 1813–14.[61]

The Collapse of Constitutional Government

Once the Constitution had been promulgated, the extraordinary session of the Cortes should have ended. But practical realities forced the members of that body to continue in office. The Constitution stipulated that the Cortes inaugurate its yearly meeting in March. Since the charter was adopted in March 1812, it was impossible to elect members to a new session that year. The deputies, therefore, remained in office.

The three-tiered electoral process – parish, *partido,* and province – was slow and cumbersome. War in the Peninsula and insurgency in America increased the difficulties. Since more time was needed to hold elections and to permit the new representatives to travel to Spain, the Cortes issued a decree postponing the inauguration of the new session of parliament until October 1, 1813. Even this precaution did not allow all the elected representatives to arrive in time. Therefore, some deputies from the previous Cortes were permitted to remain as *suplentes* pending the arrival of the proprietary delegates.[62]

Had all the provinces of America eligible to elect deputies exercised that right, the New World would have been represented by 149 delegates, just a few less than the number from Spain. Unfortunately, circumstances in America prevented all the elections from taking place. Only sixty-five deputies from the New World participated in the ordinary Cortes of October 1, 1813, to May 10, 1814. Moreover, only twenty-three had been elected under the new constitutional system. The other forty-two were *suplentes.* Two more American deputies served in the 1813–14 Cortes than in the earlier one: Cuba had three representatives, the Floridas one, Puerto Rico one, Santo Domingo one, New Spain twenty, Guatemala seven, Venezuela three, New Granada one, Panama one, Quito one, Guayaquil one, Peru nineteen, Charcas one, Montevideo one, Río de la Plata three, and Chile one.

The first regular session of the Cortes, which met from October 1, 1813, to February 19, 1814, continued the process of reform begun in the previous extraordinary session. During that time the French were driven from

---

61 Some cities were ingenious in solving money problems. The Partido of Guayaquil, for example, elected Vicente Rocafuerte, who was already in Europe; see Archivo del Congreso de los Diputados [hereafter cited as ACDM]: Documentación Electoral, Leg. 5, No. 25. The *actas* of the elections of those American deputies who arrived for the Madrid Cortes are found in this archive in Documentación Electoral, Leg. 5.

62 Berry, "The Election of Mexican Deputies," 21–8.

Spain. Therefore, the Cortes moved to Madrid. As other Spanish provinces were liberated and conducted elections, more moderate and *servil* deputies arrived. When the second regular session of the Cortes convened in Madrid on March 1, 1814, nearly all of Spain was free. A majority of the parliament believed that reform had proceeded far enough. Some *servil* Spanish deputies felt that the *liberales* had gone too far. They did not view the king as a mad dog to be caged by legislative restrictions, and they did not believe that any self-respecting monarch could tolerate the role assigned to him by the Constitution. Nevertheless, the overwhelming majority was committed to the principle of a constitutional monarchy. They were convinced that the Cortes represented the people and were certain that no one would reject the authority of the national assembly. The revolution had been accomplished and could not be undone.[63]

Unfortunately for the Cortes, the legal structure created by its members did not win the widespread support of the Spanish people. All that had been achieved in the previous six years – the war of national liberation and the acts of the Cortes – had transpired in the name of Fernando VII. Everywhere, people awaited the return of their *desired* king. The monarch was an important symbol but an unknown personality. As the Napoleonic Wars ended, Fernando VII prepared to return. How would he react to the revolution carried out in his absence?

A majority in the Cortes believed that the king *must* accept the new order. Therefore, the Cortes decreed that only after having sworn allegiance to the Constitution in Madrid would he be recognized as Spain's legitimate sovereign. A minority disagreed. Sixty-nine deputies, including ten Americans, sent the king a document that has come to be known as the *Manifiesto de los persas* because it began by stating: "It was the custom of the ancient Persians to spend five days in anarchy after the death of the king so that the experience of murders, robberies, and other disasters would oblige them to be more faithful to his successor."[64] In the *Manifiesto* they urged Fernando not to accept the Constitution of 1812. The *persas* favored absolutism, which, they argued, differed from arbitrary government because the power of the monarch was limited by the rights of the people. Relying on Martínez Marina's constitutional study, *La teoría de las Cortes,* the *persas* argued that all the acts of the Cortes, including the Constitution, contravened Spain's traditions, laws, and history. They believed that the king

---

63 Artola, *Los orígenes,* I, 618–20; Lovett, *Napoleon and the Birth,* II, 809–10; María Cristina Diz-Lois, *El Manifiesto de 1814* (Pamplona: Estudio General de Navarra, 1967), 28–39.

64 "Representación y manifiesto que algunos diputados a las Cortes Ordinarias firmaron en los mayores apuros de su opresión en Madrid para que la Majestad del Sr. D. Fernando el VII a la entrada en España de vuelta de su cautividad, se penetrase del estado de la Nación, del deseo de sus provincias, y del remedio que creían oportuno," in Diz-Lois, *El Manifiesto de 1814,* 199–277.

should declare all the actions of the national assembly null and void. Then, in order to institute reforms, His Majesty should convoke a traditional *cortes* with three estates.

Fernando VII returned to a nation that had fought six bitter years of war in his name. Although they did not know him, the people expected the king to be the finest of men and the best of rulers. Only a small minority feared that the monarch might be different. Fernando was careful not to commit himself until he learned more about the Cortes. As he traveled to Madrid, he waited for an occasion to act. That opportunity came in Valencia on April 17, 1814. As usual, the populace received him with great enthusiasm. Then Francisco Javier Elío – captain-general of Valencia, an absolutist who hated the Cortes, where he had been severely criticized by the *liberales* for his activities in South America and subsequently in Spain – offered to support the king with his troops if he wished to abolish the Cortes. Fernando hesitated. But when he discovered that the *persas,* much of the regular army, many traditionalists, and the bureaucracy would support him, he made his decision. On May 4, 1814, Fernando abolished the Cortes and all its acts.[65]

The constitutional structure collapsed like a house of cards. The regular army pursued the *liberales,* and the people did not defend them. On the contrary, in many places the masses eagerly destroyed the symbols of the Constitution. Some *liberales,* like the Conde de Toreno and the *guayaquileño* Vicente Rocafuerte, escaped to France, where they remained in exile. Countless others, such as Agustín Argüelles and José Miguel Ramos Arizpe, were imprisoned. The number of *liberales* jailed or exiled has been estimated to have been as high as 12,000.[66]

Representative constitutional government collapsed for a number of reasons. First, there had been little time to win the people's support for the new institutions. Since most of Spain had been occupied by the French until 1813, the constitutional government had little opportunity to exercise its authority over the country. Hence neither the provincial deputations nor the constitutional *ayuntamientos* functioned long enough to demonstrate their value at the local level. Second, the guerrilla armies that might have defended the Cortes were fighting Napoleon in France while the hostile regular army took Madrid. Third, the Spanish clergy, which had supported earlier reforms, turned against the Cortes when its interests were threatened. Finally, the people retained an innocent faith in Fernando VII. They did not know that he had betrayed them while in France or that he

65 José Luis Comellas, *Los primeros pronunciamientos en España, 1814–1820* (Madrid: Consejo Superior de Investigaciones Científicas, 1958), 45–9; Lovett, *Napoleon and the Birth,* 2:808–29.
66 Vicente Llorens, *Liberales y románticos: Una emigración española en Inglaterra, 1823–1834,* 2d ed. (Madrid: Editorial Castalia, 1968), 10, 11; Comellas, *Los primeros pronunciamientos,* 58–105.

would become a despot. All they knew was that they had endured six years of immense sacrifices in his name. If he opposed the Cortes, he must have good reasons and they would not question them.

In America, the royal authorities eagerly ordered the abolition of the constitutional order. As in Spain, they moved rapidly to prosecute all those suspected of *infidencia* (disloyal conspiracy). Some Americans persisted in trying to retain the constitutional system. In Cuzco, a coalition of criollos, mestizos, and Indians overthrew the president and the *audiencia* and established an autonomous government under the Spanish Constitution of 1812. As late as March 1817, authorities both in New Spain and in Quito were still ordering the abolition of constitutional *ayuntamientos*. No longer hampered by the Constitution, the royal officials moved to crush the insurgents. Although pockets of resistance remained in many areas, most of the Continent was returned to royal control by the end of 1816. Only the Río de la Plata retained its autonomy by virtue of its isolation from royal power.

4

Civil War in America

The dramatic French victories of 1809, which drove the Junta Central to Cádiz, convinced many Americans and some *peninsulares* in the New World that Spain might not survive as an independent nation. Their fears appeared to be justified when the Junta dissolved itself at the end of January 1810 and appointed a Council of Regency. Americans questioned the legality of that action but, in addition, they believed that the Regency was probably a puppet of the Junta of Cádiz or, perhaps, of Napoleon Bonaparte himself. Fear of domination by the French emperor, widely known in the Spanish world as *el tirano*, strengthened the desire of many in America to govern at home. In 1810 movements for autonomy reemerged in Venezuela, Río de la Plata, Chile, Quito, New Granada, and New Spain, all seeking to establish local juntas in the name of the imprisoned King Fernando VII.

Historians generally have assumed that these movements invoked the name of Fernando VII to mask their real goal: achieving independence. But there is strong evidence to the contrary. Not only did the leaders of the American juntas insist that they were acting in the name of the sovereign, they even invited Fernando to govern.[1]

The American juntas based their actions on the same juridical principle that their Peninsular counterparts invoked: In the absence of the king, sovereignty reverted to the people. Although that principle justified the formation of local governments in the name of Fernando VII, it did not sup-

---

1 The question of the "mask" of Fernando VII is particularly heated in Argentine history. For a careful summary of the thesis that the criollos "masked" their real goal, see John Lynch, *The Spanish American Revolutions, 1808–1821*, 2d ed. (New York: W. W. Norton, 1986), 55–7. The Argentine historian Enrique de Gandia, on the other hand, has strongly questioned that argument: "In other words: all the inhabitants of Buenos Aires, Caracas, et cétera had desired independence and the formation of a new nation, but when news arrived about Spain's defeat, they falsely and hypocritically manifested their loyalty to Fernando VII. [Such actions] constitute a unique case in the [history of the] world of cities with thousands of inhabitants all of them liars and traitors." *Historia del 25 de mayo: Nacimiento de la libertad y la independencia argentina* (Buenos Aires: Editorial Claridad, 1960), 91.

port separation from the Monarchy. Those favoring autonomy grounded their arguments on the unwritten American constitution: the direct compact between the individual kingdoms and the monarch. According to their interpretation, the king, and only the king, possessed ties with the New World kingdoms. If that relationship were severed, for whatever reason, there was no bond between any American *reino* and Spain or even among individual New World realms. The authorities in Spain found such views unacceptable. The Regency and the Cortes could not constitutionally accede to the separation of the New World kingdoms. Therefore, when reforms and negotiations failed to restore the American juntas to compliance with the government, the authorities in Spain resorted to the use of force.

Several additional factors complicated the subsequent struggle: Some Spaniards and Americans in the New World who believed that the Council of Regency was, indeed, the legitimate government opposed the formation of local juntas; some provinces within the American kingdoms concluded that they too possessed the right to form their own local governments, a view that their capital cities rejected with force; in some regions, the elites were divided among themselves; and in some instances, conflict broke out between the cities and the countryside. Thus, civil wars erupted in the New World that pitted supporters of the Spanish national government against the American juntas, the capitals against the provinces, the elites against one another, and urban against rural groups.

The nature of transportation and communication also influenced events. Normally, the two- to four-month delay in communications between Europe and America was inconsequential, but in times of emergency it became very significant. The Atlantic ports were the first to learn of events in the Old World. Those on the Pacific coast received the news much later. In much of South America, transportation and communication between coastal cities and the interior were impeded by geography and climate; great distances, forests, mountains, heat, rain, and cold all affected communications. Highland cities, such as Santa Fé de Bogotá, Quito, and La Paz, might be cut off from the coast for months during the rainy season. Thus, it was not an accident that Caracas and Buenos Aires were among the first to respond to the crisis of the Monarchy. Lima, on the other hand, often learned of events in Europe at the same time that it received news of the reaction to those events by cities such as Caracas and Buenos Aires. But in the north, better roads and more efficient systems facilitated communication in the great Viceroyalty of New Spain.

Local conditions determined the nature and manner in which the conflict developed. As a result of the Europeans' successful *golpe* in 1808, the autonomy movements in New Spain began with urban conspiracies that subsequently erupted into widespread rural insurgencies. But América

Meridional experienced very different political processes. The kingdoms in the south, with the exception of Peru, established governing juntas in 1810 that assumed authority in the name of the imprisoned king and sought to dominate their regions. Many provinces, however, rejected their capitals' pretensions and, as a result, most realms in South America were engulfed in armed conflicts between their capital cities and their provinces. In some instances, these civil wars occurred because some provinces supported the government in Spain while their capitals opposed it. But in others, such as New Granada, the wars consisted primarily of regional power struggles.

Because all areas of the Spanish Monarchy possessed the same political culture, all these movements, including the insurgencies in New Spain, justified their actions on the same grounds and in virtually identical terms. They argued that because of the imprisonment of the king, sovereignty reverted to them. The South American juntas initially consisted of both *peninsulares* and Americans. But as it appeared that Spain was falling completely under French domination, more radical Americans took control, ousting the Europeans from power. In most cases, the governing juntas acted as though they were independent. And a few eventually formally declared independence from the Crown. Nevertheless, the vast majority of the politically active population of Spanish America desired to retain ties with the Spanish Monarchy and proved reluctant to sever those connections completely. Thus, they remained open to negotiating with the Crown some accommodation that granted the American kingdoms self-rule.

Venezuela

During 1809 the people of the Captaincy General of Venezuela, like those of other American kingdoms, alternated between joy and despair as news arrived sporadically describing the triumphs and defeats of the Peninsular forces. In May the Junta Central replaced Captain General Casas – who had gained the enmity of the Venezuelan elite when he arrested the proponents of a local junta in November 1808 – with Vicente Emparán, the highly regarded governor of Cumaná province. The new captain general won the support of the *caraqueño* elite by permitting foreign trade to continue, despite orders to the contrary from Spain. Since Britain was no longer an enemy, Venezuelan commerce expanded dramatically. Although pleased by the new prosperity, the people of the captaincy general continued to worry about the worsening military situation in the Peninsula.[2]

---

2 Caracciolo Parra Pérez, *Historia de la Primera República de Venezuela,* 2 vols. (Madrid: Ediciones Guadarrama, 1959), 1:367–8; Humberto Tandrón, *El Real Consulado de Caracas y el comercio exterior de Venezuela* (Caracas: Universidad Central de Venezuela, 1976), 199–200.

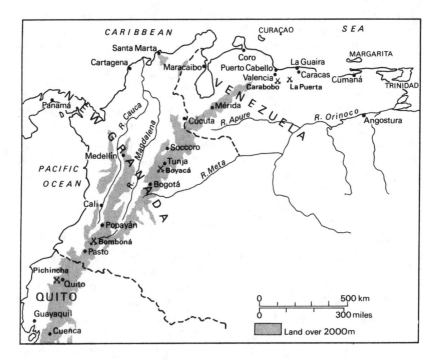

Map 2. Wars in South America: Northern theater. (From *Cambridge History of Latin America*, Vol. III, Cambridge: Cambridge University Press, 1985, p. 112. Reprinted with permission.)

News of the fall of Sevilla, the retreat to Cádiz, and the dissolution of the Junta Central at the end of January 1810 reached Caracas in mid-April. Convinced that Spain was lost to the French and that the *afrancesado* Captain General Emparán would recognize the regime of José Bonaparte, the elite decided to act. Although the captain general had thwarted two earlier movements to establish local juntas – in December 1809 and March 1810 – he proved unable to control the situation when the *caraqueño* elite, Spanish as well as American, convened a meeting of the *ayuntamiento* on April 19, 1810, and voted to oust Emparán, replacing him with a *Junta Suprema Conservadora de los Derechos de Fernando VII* (Supreme Junta to Conserve the Rights of Fernando VII). Since the *audiencia,* the *consulado,* the archbishop, and other leading individuals supported the action, Emparán resigned.[3]

3 Parra Pérez, *Historia de la Primera República*, 1:377–88.

The new government informed the "inhabitants of the United Provinces of Venezuela: The Spanish Nation in Europe, after two years of a bloody and destructive war to defend its liberty and independence, is about to fall under the tyrannical yoke of its conquerors. . . . The Junta Central Gubernativa del Reyno, which represented the will of the nation through its supreme authority, has been dissolved . . . , and the legally constituted sovereignty to preserve the state finally has been destroyed in that catastrophe."[4] The Junta Suprema ˙de Caracas emphasized that "Venezuela has declared its independence, neither from the *Madre Patria,* nor from the sovereign, but from the [Council of] Regency, whose legitimacy remains in question in Spain itself."[5] "In a word, we refuse to recognize the new Council of Regency; but if Spain saves itself, we will be the first to lend obedience to a government formed on legitimate and equitable bases."[6]

The Junta Suprema de Caracas rejected the new regime, which it believed had been created by the Junta of Cádiz. Clearly, old discords between the Cádiz merchants and Venezuelan exporters colored the attitudes of the Americans. Since the movement had the support of nearly all groups, including *peninsulares* resident in the area, it is evident that no one considered the action revolutionary. Quite the contrary: The Junta Suprema asserted that "Caracas, imitating Spain's conduct, has taken the path that she herself [Spain] has shown when she lacked a central government."[7] Venezuelans were, therefore, merely exercising their legitimate constitutional rights.

Caracas's actions, however, were not unanimously approved throughout Venezuela. Self-interest and complex local factors, rather than place of birth, determined individual decisions to support or reject Caracas. Although *ayuntamientos* in the other provinces of Venezuela, such as Barinas and Cumaná, voted to recognize the Junta Suprema, towns like Coro, in the Province of Caracas, and the provinces of Maracaibo and Guayana elected to support the Council of Regency in Spain. In Cumaná a junta composed almost entirely of Spaniards supported the Junta Suprema in Caracas. Although Barinas backed the Junta Suprema, it formed its own junta to govern in the name of Fernando VII and to establish its autonomy. Seeking autonomy from the city of Cumaná, the capital of the province, Barcelona created its own junta, which recognized both the Junta Suprema in Caracas and the Council of Regency in Cádiz. In other cities, including

4 *Gazeta de Caracas,* II, No. 93 (April 27, 1810).
5 *Gazeta de Caracas,* III, No. 123 (November 9, 1810).
6 Ibid. (May 11, 1810).
7 Academia Nacional de Historia, *Textos oficiales de la Primera República,* 2 vols. (Caracas: Academia Nacional de Historia, 1959), 1:136.

those that acknowledged the authority of the Council of Regency, Spaniards joined Americans in forming autonomous juntas.[8]

The Junta Suprema, composed of twenty-three members, represented the elite of Caracas province. It included leading Spanish merchants and planters, as well as the most prominent American *hacendados*. Although criollos predominated in the junta, that merely reflected the fact that they constituted the largest group in the white population.[9] The Junta Suprema introduced a number of reforms designed to liberalize the economy and gain the support of the masses. It declared free trade, abolished the *alcabala* tax on foodstuffs and on many necessary consumer items as well as reducing it on others, eliminated Indian tribute, and prohibited the slave trade. The Junta Suprema also made important administrative and political decisions: It reorganized the government, converting the *audiencia* into a high court of appeals, and it dispatched missions to non-Spanish islands in the Antilles and to Britain and the United States to seek political support, commerce, and weapons.[10] The Junta Suprema's actions during the first few months, as Michael McKinley notes, "reflected a consensus of the merchant–planter–Spanish–creole elite of Caracas, carried out with the aid of the largely intact secondary levels of the colonial bureaucracy."[11]

In an effort to unite the Kingdom of Venezuela, the Junta Suprema de Caracas convened a congress to determine the future of the area. Since the Junta Central's decree for elections to the Cortes had already been received by the provincial cities, the Caracas government had little choice other than to grant all cities and towns the right to hold elections during the months of October and November 1810 for a parliament to meet in Caracas in March 1811. The Junta Suprema modified the Junta Central's decree of January 1, 1810, for the election of deputies to the Cortes to suit Venezuela's needs. Local officials were to compile an electoral census in order to elect a deputy for every 20,000 souls. Free males twenty-five years or older who possessed 2,000 or more pesos in movable property were eligible to participate in indirect elections. First, electors would be chosen at the parish level, and these, in turn, would elect the deputies to the *Cuerpo Conservador de los Derechos de D. Fernando VII en las Provincias de*

---

8 Demetrio Ramos, "Wagram y sus consecuencia, como determinantes del clima público de la revolución de 19 de abril de 1810 en Caracas," in *Estudios sobre la emancipación de Hispanoamérica* (Madrid: Instituto Gonzalo Fernáandez de Oviedo, 1963), 33–85; Parra Pérez, *Historia de la Primera República*, 1:403–34; Salvador de Madariaga, *Bolívar*, 2 vols. (Mexico: Editorial Hermes, 1951), 1:272–4.

9 P. Michael McKinley, *Pre-Revolutionary Caracas: Politics, Economy, and Society 1777–1811* (Cambridge: Cambridge University Press, 1985), 159.

10 Parra Pérez, *Historia de la Primera República*, 1:389–93, 435–66.

11 McKinley, *Pre-Revolutionary Caracas*, 160.

Venezuela(Body to Conserve the Rights of D. Fernando VII in the Provinces of Venezuela).[12] Perhaps the most important difference between the *convocatorias* of Sevilla and Caracas was that the latter imposed property requirements that the former had not.

Before elections could be held, after months of inaction, the Council of Regency in Cádiz decided to impose its will upon the area. In November 1810, Antonio Cortabarria, the plenipotentiary of the Monarchy, demanded that Venezuela recognize the Spanish Regency and the recently convened Cortes, as well as the authority of newly appointed Captain General Fernando Miyares, the former governor of Maracaibo. In addition, the authorities in Spain ended free trade with foreigners on the grounds that Great Britain and Spain were no longer at war with one another and, therefore, that emergency measure was no longer necessary. Although this was technically correct, the action, which resulted from pressure by Cádiz merchants, was deeply resented in America. The enforcement of such an order threatened to cripple New World commerce at a time when Spain could not meet the needs of America. When the Junta Suprema of Caracas refused to accept their demands, the royal authorities, utilizing forces available in Cuba and Puerto Rico, instituted a naval blockade against Venezuela. The willingness of a desperately imperiled government in Spain to force one of its American possessions into compliance was not lost on New World autonomists. But the pro-Regency provinces and cities of Venezuela, such as Maracaibo, Guayana, and Coro, found solace in the fact that the government in the Peninsula still possessed the will to enforce its authority.[13]

The external challenge exacerbated existing tensions in Caracas. A younger and predominantly middle-class group of radicals who favored greater autonomy and, in some cases, independence, emerged to challenge the moderate elites who controlled the Junta Suprema. The radicals, consisting of lawyers, notaries, journalists, small merchants, clerics, and officials, as well as a few wealthy aristocrats such as Simón Bolívar, agitated against Spain. On October 22, upon learning that the royal authorities had massacred the Quito autonomists on August 2, the radicals provoked a riot of blacks, *zambos,* and *castas* in Caracas when they demanded the expulsion of all Spaniards and Americans not fully committed to home rule. The fearful authorities implored the public "to mourn the fate of your compatriots" from Quito but not to take the law into its own hands. The Junta

---

12 "Reglamento para la elección y reunión de diputados que han de componer el cuerpo conservador de los derechos del Sr. D. Fernando VII en las Provincias de Venezuela," Academia Nacional de Historia, *Textos oficiales,* 2:61–84. See also Pilar Chavarri Sidera, *Las elecciones de diputados a las Cortes Generales y Extraordinarias (1810–1813)* (Madrid: Centro de Estudios Constitucionales, 1988), 3–4 and passim.

13 Parra Pérez, *Historia de la Primera República,* 1:485–7; Madariaga, *Bolívar,* 1:279–80.

attempted to placate the colored masses by formally inviting the public to "the church of Our Lady of Altagracia [the *pardo* parish], where the funeral ceremonies for the victims of AMERICAN LIBERTY, sacrificed in QUITO, by the cruelty of the barbarous Spaniard RUIZ CASTILLA, will be held."[14] After an investigation, the Junta Suprema exiled some of the radical instigators of the tumult, and it prohibited the return of the old revolutionary Francisco Miranda from Britain. In an effort to reassert its authority, the Junta Suprema dispatched the Marqués del Toro at the head of a 3,000-man force to subdue the city of Coro. Unfortunately for the moderates, Toro proved to be an incompetent commander who withdrew from the battle on November 29 after the first attack resulted in serious casualties.

The inability of the moderates to establish firm control over Venezuela provided the radicals with opportunities to advance their cause. The latter had gained control of the *Sociedad Patriótica de Agricultores y Economía* (Patriotic Society of Agriculturists and the Economy), an association originally formed to contribute to the development of the region, and converted the body into a political organization. The Sociedad coerced the Junta Suprema into allowing Miranda to enter Venezuela in December and then, with the old revolutionary as its president, agitated for independence. During the next six months, the Sociedad waged a propaganda campaign for a break with Spain through the press, meetings, parades, and demonstrations. For Miranda and the other middle-class members of the Sociedad, it was an opportunity to harass the Caracas elite, which had treated them with disdain.[15]

The newly elected congress met on March 2, 1811, with thirty of the forty-two deputies selected in the seven provinces of Venezuela present. Although most were Americans, there were a few European Spaniards in the group. The vast majority of the members of congress, the representatives of the leading landowning families, favored autonomy rather than independence. The new assembly followed many of the precedents established by the Cortes of Cádiz. It arrogated authority to itself and established a weak executive by naming a triumvirate that would rotate in office. Congress convened at the cathedral of Caracas, where each deputy swore on the Bible to protect and conserve the rights of the *patria* "and those of Señor D. Fernando VII, to avoid all relations or influence with France, to remain independent of any government established in the Peninsula, and to recognize only the authority of the General Congress of Venezuela."[16]

14 Narciso Coll y Prat, *Memoriales sobre la Independencia de Venezuela* (Caracas: Academia Nacional de Historia, 1960), 143–4; Academia Nacional de Historia, *Textos oficiales*, 2:12–15.

15 Parra Pérez, *Historia de la Primera República*, 2:24–6; Juan Uslar Pietri, *Historia de la rebelión popular de 1814* (Paris: Ediciones Soberbia, 1954), 21–4.

16 Parra Pérez, *Historia de la Primera República*, 1:478–81, quoted in 2:15.

Dominated by the moderate elite, congress was concerned with preserving social order in the region. Venezuela was a multiracial society in which whites constituted about 22 percent of the kingdom's population. *Pardos,* free blacks, and fugitive black slaves represented more than half of the population, and slaves and Indians each accounted for nearly 10 percent. Much of the interior of the country consisted of *llanos* (grasslands) devoted to cattle raising. Whereas urban landowners possessed *hatos* or *estancias* (cattle estates) in the *llanos,* the residents, the *llaneros,* were men who lived a free pastoral existence and who considered the *llanos* and its animals theirs. The urban elites, however, perceived the *llaneros* to be a lawless group composed of people of mixed African ancestry.[17] Not surprisingly, congress sought to impose order on the "chaotic" *llanos* by creating formal social hierarchies. On July 1, 1811, it decreed *Los Derechos del Pueblo* (the rights of the people), which indicated that "all shall be equal under the law. . . ." Some Venezuelans, however, were more equal than others since "Citizens will be divided into two classes: those with the right to suffrage, and those without it."[18] Only property owners could be full citizens with voting rights.

The radicals in the Sociedad Patriótica did not object; their radicalism did not extend to social equality. It consisted merely in agitating for separation from the Spanish Monarchy. After months of public pressure, congress agreed to discuss independence on July 5, 1811. The radicals, who filled the hall with their partisans, intimidated the deputies into voting for independence. The *acta de independencia* (declaration of independence) was drafted and approved two days later and published on July 14, and a tricolor of yellow, blue, and red was adopted as the new national flag. Although the date of publication, July 14, and the tricolor apparently were intended to evoke the spirit of revolutionary France and are indicative of Miranda's influence, the *acta de independencia* itself failed to indict the rule of the Spanish Monarchy. Instead, the *acta* focused on the ancient compact, its rupture after 1808, and the failure of the subsequent Peninsular regimes.[19]

Congress completed drafting the constitution on December 21, 1811. The new charter abolished hereditary and institutional privileges, eliminated the slave trade – but not slavery – created a federal system, continued legislative dominance, and retained the weak triumvirate as the executive. Although it decreed legal equality for the free, it retained privilege

---

17 Federico Brito Figueroa, *Historia económica y social de Venezuela,* 2 vols. (Caracas: Universidad Central de Venezuela, 1966), 1:160; McKinley, *Pre-Revolutionary Caracas,* 9–31.

18 Academia Nacional de Historia, *Textos oficiales,* 2:93, 95. See also Miguel Izard, *El miedo de la revolución; La lucha por la libertad en Venezuela (1777–1830)* (Madrid: Editorial Tecnos, 1979), 139–43.

19 Parra Pérez, *Historia de la Primera República,* 2:55–75; "Acta de Independencia," in *La Constitución Federal de Venezuela de 1811* (Caracas: Academia Nacional de Historia, 1959), 89–96.

based on property requirements for active citizenship. Moreover, the government established a national guard to regulate slaves, and it introduced vagrancy laws and restrictions on the *llaneros*. It was a regime by and for the elite.[20]

The new government constituted a threat to the people of color, the majority of Venezuela's population. During the previous decades, the Crown had worked to improve their status. It provided them new opportunities in the army and the militia, and opened the doors to the professions and higher education by selling them certificates of whiteness, *cedulas de gracias al sacar.* It even issued laws and regulations specifying the rights of slaves and the obligations of slave owners in an effort to improve the conditions of forced servitude. But the whites, particularly the elites, who feared the colored masses, especially after the Haitian Revolution, vehemently opposed those efforts. Now in power, they intended to keep the people of color under strict control. Thus, *pardos, mulatos,* and blacks, both slave and free, remained strong supporters of the Monarchy. They constituted a potential danger to the new regime.[21]

Although the *acta de independencia* did not refer to a republic, the government of Venezuela after July 15, 1811, is generally known as the First Republic. The radicals remained outside government but wielded substantial influence through the Sociedad Patriótica, which acted as a Jacobin club. The new regime lasted a little more than a year until July 30, 1812. During that time, the country endured political, social, and economic instability. Most Venezuelans did not favor separation from the Monarchy; the declaration of independence had been prompted by political pressure in Caracas. Plots against the new republic erupted immediately. On July 11, 1811, a conspiracy to recognize the Regency in Spain led by Canary Islanders, known as *isleños,* and supported by criollos and *pardos,* erupted in the town of Los Teques near the capital. It was easily crushed by the government, which executed the principal leaders – seven *isleños,* one criollo, and two blacks.

---

20 It is often said that the Venezuelan Constitution of 1811 was based on the U.S. Charter of 1787. There is little basis for such an assertion. The only similarity is that both established federal systems. Leading Venezuelans, such as the prominent jurist Fernando Peñalver, however, were highly critical of the U.S. Constitution. See his "Memoria presentada al Supremo Congreso de Venezuela en que manifiesta sus opiniones sobre la necesidad de dividir la Provincia de Caracas para hacer la Constitución Federal permanente en Venezuela." Academia Nacional de Historia, *Pensamiento Constitucional hispanoaméricano,* 5 vols. (Caracas: Academia Nacional de Historia, 1961). 5:25–39. See also "Constitución de 1811" in *La Constitución Federal de Venezuela de 1811,* 150–220; Parra Pérez, *Historia de la Primera República,* 2:161–91; "Ordenanzas de Llanos," Academia Nacional de Historia, *Textos oficiales,* 2:143–205.

21 Federico Brito Figueroa, "Venezuela colonial: Las rebeliones de esclavos y la Revolución Francesa," *CARAVELLE: Cahiers du Monde Hispanique et Luso-Bresilien,* 54 (1990), 263–89.

A more serious threat emerged from the city of Valencia, which rejected independence and recognized the Council of Regency. The government dispatched the Marqués del Toro at the head of an all-white army to restore order. Once again, he failed. Pressured by the radicals, the executive power then entrusted military command to General Francisco Miranda, who marched upon Valencia at the head of a 4,000-man army. To meet the threat, the royalists in Valencia armed the *pardos,* an act that proved to be the beginning of virulent racial warfare in Venezuela. After a bitter siege of more than a month, Miranda forced the city to surrender unconditionally. Thereafter, military courts sentenced the royalist leaders to prison.[22]

The defeat of Valencia occasioned a contentious debate both within the republican government and among its supporters. Some leveled charges against Miranda for his arbitrary and autocratic actions. Provincial cities questioned the need for such violence and bloodshed against a sister city. As a result, the executive power relieved Miranda of command. The political crisis coincided with the virtual bankruptcy of the government, which, in order to sustain itself, issued paper money backed by tobacco but not convertible to that commodity. The action alienated merchants who were required to accept the paper and to provide change in silver. The application of such a law would force businessmen into economic ruin. Because many of the merchants who opposed the republican government's economic policy were Europeans, the radicals dismissed them as reactionaries. The poorly conceived introduction of paper money had serious negative effects on the region's economy, bankrupting some businessmen. The measure also eroded the government's political support.[23]

A new external threat compounded the regime's problems in 1812. Captain Domingo Monteverde, who arrived in Coro from Puerto Rico with a detachment of troops, began on March 10 a successful campaign to recover western Venezuela for the royalists. To a great extent, his victories resulted from the growing public disaffection with the republic. In most cases, towns changed hands without a battle. Then, on March 26, Venezuela experienced a massive earthquake. Parts of the cities of Caracas, La Guaira, Barquisimeto, Mérida, and San Felipe were destroyed. As it was Holy Thursday, many were killed in Church buildings. In Caracas, hundreds of soldiers died in their barracks. A second, more violent tremor struck Venezuela on April 4. Nature appeared to favor the monarch; royalist areas remained untouched. Naturally, proroyalist clergymen urged the faithful to

22 Parra Pérez, *Historia de la Primera República,* 2:80–9; William Spence Robertson, *The Life of Miranda,* 2 vols. 2d ed. (New York: Cooper Square, 1969), 1:130–4.

23 Manuel Lucena Salmoral, "El colapso económico de la Primera República de Venezuela," *América Latina: Dallo stato coloniale allo stalo nazionaile (1750–1940),* 2 vols. (Milan: Franco Angeli, 1987) 1:161–86; Parra Pérez, *Historia de la Primera República,* 2:135–40; Uslar Pietri, *Historia de la rebelión popular,* 40–2.

renounce the republic and recognize the Council of Regency in Cádiz. Since Spain continued to wage war against the "godless" French, and since the Cortes and the Constitution of Cádiz seemed to offer America equality, such proposals were eagerly accepted by a growing number of Venezuelans.[24]

Fearing that the republic might collapse, the Sociedad Patriótica forced the government to appoint Miranda commander of the army and subsequently to make him dictator, with full civil and military power. Miranda immediately proclaimed martial law and ordered the arrest of all Spaniards. In addition, he offered freedom to any slave who served ten years in the republican army. The decree alienated the American elite, who feared that the measure might deprive them of their slaves. Miranda's action instead benefited the royalists because the archbishop of Caracas, Narciso Coll y Prat, secretly instructed the clergy to encourage blacks, both free and slave, to fight for the Crown. The archbishop's appeal succeeded, in part, because lower-class European royalists, many of them *isleños* who had come to Venezuela to make their fortune, had closer relations with people of color than upper-class American republicans, many of whom were slaveholders. As a result, numerous *pardos* and blacks rebelled in favor of the Crown. By the end of June, large areas of the east coast were under the control of black royalists.[25]

The republic collapsed in July. Former slaves advanced on Caracas after Miranda transferred the government to Valencia. Bolívar, who was entrusted with the defense of Puerto Cabello, lost the city to the royalists. Monteverde's forces advanced with ease. Facing certain defeat, Miranda accepted the Capitulation of San Mateo on July 25, 1812, whereby republican forces surrendered to the royalists. Monteverde agreed to respect the property as well as the property transfers of the republicans, not to seek reprisals against them, and to grant passports to those who wished to leave the country. Miranda apparently failed to consult his leading officials, who, upon learning of the agreements, believed that the dictator had betrayed their cause. On the night of July 30, Bolívar and two other republican officers arrested Miranda and turned him over to the Spaniards. Bolívar, who expected to retain his property, accepted a passport from Monteverde and left Venezuela, apparently to join the British army that was fighting the French in the Peninsula. However, the subsequent discovery that his vast wealth had been confiscated rekindled his discarded republican sympathies, and he again turned against Spain. Miranda later died in a Spanish prison.[26]

24 Robertson, *The Life of Miranda*, 2:145–50; Uslar Pietri, *Historia de la rebelión popular*, 45–8.

25 Coll y Prat, *Memoriales sobre la Independencia*, 58–9.

26 Uslar Pietri, *Historia de la rebelión popular*, 53–61. The imprisonment of Miranda is one of Bolívar's dark deeds. Most Venezuelan historians interpret his action as one of indignation at Miranda's sup-

The fall of the First Republic marked the end of widespread political participation in Venezuela. Thereafter, a struggle for political dominance ensued that pitted ruthless *caudillos* against one another. The contest became exceedingly violent because it occurred in a land that had unleashed racial hatreds. First the royalists and then the republicans encouraged conflict between the colored *castas* and the whites. As a result, Venezuela endured nearly a decade of brutal warfare that killed thousands and devastated the country.[27]

The new regime, headed by Monteverde, lasted until August 7, 1813. Initially, fearing that the thousands of blacks who were advancing on Caracas might destroy the city, Monteverde agreed with Archbishop Coll y Prat that white republicans should be arrested to placate the victorious forces. When the threat of the colored *castas* was over, the Canary Islander Monteverde fell under the influence of his fellow *isleños,* who sought revenge against the Americans who had governed Venezuela under the republic. Hundreds of former revolutionaries were imprisoned and their properties confiscated, clearly a violation of the capitulation. The actions had an unintended effect: They convinced some Venezuelans who had forsaken revolution, among them Bolívar, to take up arms once again. In the months that followed, many lower-class *isleños* obtained important government posts and acquired considerable wealth. Although Monteverde was reluctant to implement the Constitution of Cádiz on the grounds that it should apply only to areas that had remained loyal to the Crown, members of the *audiencia,* particularly Regent José Francisco Heredia, insisted that the Constitution be obeyed. As a result, most imprisoned republicans were eventually released and compensated for their losses. Elections were held, and three Venezuelan deputies departed for the Cortes in Spain.

Monteverde, who was appointed *jefe político superior* and captain general

posed betrayal of the republican cause. Roberton, who published his biography of Miranda in 1929, accepted the Venezuelan thesis: Robertson, *The Life of Miranda,* 2:167–215. Gerhard Masur, the leading non-Hispanic biographer of Bolívar, also accepts the Venezuelan thesis, although he notes that the rivalry between the two men also contributed to Bolívar's "betrayal." Gerhard Masur, *Simón Bolívar* (Albuquerque: University of New Mexico Press, 1969), 103–7. Salvador de Madariaga has presented an extensively documented and damning case against Bolívar. Madariaga, *Bolívar,* 1:348–59. Vicente Lecuna, Bolívar's great apologist, offers a hypersensitive but weak reiteration of the Venezuelan thesis in which he does not address Madariaga's arguments even though, elsewhere in the work, he disagrees with him on other matters. Vicente Lecuna, *Catálogo de errores y calumnias en la historia de Bolívar,* 3 vols. (New York: Colonial Press, 1956), 1:243–68. Finally, a U.S. historian has noted: "Salvador de Madariaga claims that the Liberator turned Miranda over to Monteverde in order to ingratiate himself with the Spanish government. . . . Although Venezuelan historians reject this thesis, none have, in this author's opinion, offered adequate refutations of Madariaga's sources and line of reasoning." Stephen K. Stoan, *Pablo Morillo and Venezuela, 1815–1820* (Columbus: Ohio State University Press, 1974), 41.

27 McKinley, *Pre-Revolutionary Caracas,* 169–74.

of Venezuela, failed politically. Although a bland repressor – few people were executed under his regime – he nevertheless alienated large sectors of the population. The American elite loathed him because he had imprisoned many of them and despoiled them of their property. The blacks, *castas,* and slaves resented the fact that he ended their quest for freedom and equality. All were outraged by the excesses of the *isleño* parvenus who came to power with Monteverde.[28]

The unpopular royal government faced reconstituted republican forces in 1813. The criollos Francisco Bermúdez and Santiago Mariño and the *mulato* Manuel Piar raised large forces in the east, many of them *pardos* and blacks. And Bolívar, who had obtained support from the autonomists in New Granada, advanced from the west. Faced with a two-front war and in charge of a disintegrating regime, Monteverde proved unable to retain control of Venezuela.

On May 25, Piar defeated the royalists at Maturín. Although Monteverde withdrew to fortified positions, frightened royalists, particularly Spaniards, fled the countryside; some even abandoned Venezuela.[29] On June 15 Bolívar issued the decree of war to the death. He promised death to Spaniards who did not actively work for independence, even if they remained neutral, while informing Americans that they would be spared even if guilty of supporting the royalists. Since he lacked widespread support among both the elite and the masses, he intended to force Americans to choose sides.[30] As Mckinley has indicated:

He was ruthless in his pursuit of this goal across 1813 and 1814, and it is seldom realized just how systematic he was in implementing his reign of terror. . . . Bolívar himself spoke of how "I marched . . . through the cities and towns of Toyoquito, Valencia, . . . Maracay, Turnero, San Mateo, and la Victoria, where all the Europeans and Canary Islanders, almost without exception, have been executed."

Once Bolívar arrived in the city of Caracas in August 1813, small groups of Spaniards were put to death on one pretext or another.[31]

---

28 Coll y Prat, *Memoriales sobre la Independencia,* 63–6; José Francisco Heredia, *Memorias del Regente Heredia* (Caracas: Academia Nacional de la Historia, 1960), 83–4, 209–14; Stoan, *Pablo Morillo,* 43–8. John Lynch, relying solely on Simón Bolívar and Vicente Lecuna, characterizes Monteverde as an "unprincipled and ambitious demagogue" and accuses him of conducting a campaign of murder and terror: *The Spanish American Revolutions,* 199–203. On the other hand, Stoan, who bases his assessment on a wider array of sources, argues that "he imprisoned but did not execute, he was arbitrary but not bloodthirsty. The fact is that of all the consejista counterrevolutions, that of Venezuela was the least cruel." *Pablo Morillo,* 43.

29 Uslar Pietri, *Historia de la rebelión popular,* 75–7; Stoan, *Pablo Morillo,* 48–50.

30 Simón Bolívar, *Obras completas,* 2 vols. (La Habana: Editorial Lex, 1947), 2:1014–15.

31 McKinley, *Pre-Revolutionary Caracas,* 171.

The Second Republic would be different than the first. Bolívar had no intention of repeating the errors of the First Republic. That regime had failed, in his view, because it had adopted a weak federalist constitution, because it had been too tolerant of dissenting opinions, because popular elections had provided the weak and incompetent with too great a voice, and because the government had failed to recruit an effective military force and to manage the economy. The earthquake and the opposition had been important factors, but in his view the decisive flaw had been the nature of the regime.[32]

Bolívar established a military dictatorship with himself as its head. The Second Republic, like the first, had to deal with royalist strongholds. It controlled the province of Caracas, the most populous area of the country, but Maracaibo, Guayana, the region of Coro in Caracas province, and Puerto Cabello remained in royalist hands. Racial fears exacerbated political tensions. Republican whites, alarmed by the potential threat of the people of color, insisted on dominating the *pardos,* the blacks, and especially the slaves. Bolívar agreed. But in addition, as George Flinter, a British visitor, noted, the republicans were determined to crush the Europeans who had favored the colored *castas.* They terrorized Spaniards, imprisoning and executing men and whipping and raping women. "Finally," as Mckinley notes, "in February 1814, Bolívar had the over-1,000 Spanish prisoners he was still holding murdered in cold blood."[33] The violence and cruelty of the republicans arose from the fear, indeed the terror, of racial conflict. *Pardos,* blacks, and slaves often sided with the royalists. But even more terrifying, white Americans were divided. The royalist forces, like the republican armies, consisted primarily of criollos. Such divisions in a fundamentally nonwhite land augured ill for the upper class.[34]

An unlikely royalist leader, José Tomás Boves, emerged to challenge the republicans. As ambitious and ruthless as Bolívar, Boves was, in contrast, a lower-class trader from Asturias who initially eagerly supported the autonomous juntas of 1810. The high-handed actions of the Venezuelan elite, however, caused him to change his allegiance. Boves, who had lived in the *llanos* and had developed the skills and attitudes of the *llaneros,* served under Spanish royalist officers until Bolívar took Caracas in 1813. He then returned to the *llanos,* where he formed a superb cavalry force, composed

32 Simón Bolívar, "Memoria dirigida a los ciudadanos de la Nueva Granada por un Caraqueño," in Simón Bolívar, *Proclamas y discursos del Libertador* (Caracas: Litografía del Comercio, 1939), 11–22.
33 McKinley, *Pre-Revolutionary Caracas,* 171; George Flinter, *A History of the Revolution in Caracas; Comprising an Impartial Narrative of the Atrocities Committed by the Contending Parties* (London: T. and J. Allman, 1819), 136–51.
34 Stoan, *Pablo Morillo,* 50–1; Simón Bolívar, "Manifiesto de Carúpano," *Proclamas y discursos,* 111–16.

primarily of *pardos* and blacks who bitterly resented the white republicans who had earlier attempted to reduce them to serfdom. Boves promised to distribute the land of white aristocrats to his men. But most of all, he gave them the opportunity to vent their anger against their former oppressors. His forces gave no quarter. As Stephen K. Stoan has noted, "Boves let them indulge in their passion for murder, pillage, and rape."[35] Thus republican terror met with an equally violent royalist response. Venezuela now endured the worst aspects of civil war.

Bolívar, like Monteverde before him, faced war on two fronts. He managed to defeat the royalist forces of José Cevallos and Juan Manuel Cagigal on May 28, 1814. Then, joined by Mariño's troops, Bolívar moved south to face Boves's smaller army. Although outnumbered, the royalist *caudillo* routed his opponents in a bloody battle on June 15. More than 1,000 republicans died in that contest. As Bolívar abandoned Venezuela, whites – republicans as well as royalists – fled before Boves's "dark hordes." In the months that followed, the royalist *caudillo* destroyed the remnants of republican forces, spreading terror throughout the land. At the height of his power, on December 5, 1814, Boves was killed at the battle of Urica. His death brought relief to the royal authorities he nominally recognized. The *peninsulares,* like the Americans, feared the possibility of a Haiti-like revolution by the colored *castas.*

In April 1815, Field Marshal Pablo Morillo arrived with a Spanish army of 10,500 men to restore order to a war-weary land. In 1817, the *Gazeta de Caracas* calculated that more than 80,000 of Venezuela's 420,000 people, one-fifth of the population, had perished in the civil war, most of them during the years 1813–14 when Bolívar and Boves sought to impose their will through terror.[36] No one triumphed in the Venezuelan civil war. The American elite failed to achieve self-rule either within the Spanish Nation or through independence. The Spaniards were virtually exterminated. The *pardos,* blacks, and slaves did not achieve either equality or freedom. Venezuela was devastated; many years would be needed to restore order and prosperity.

35 Flinter, *A History of the Revolution,* 151–77; Stoan, *Pablo Morillo,* 52; Uslar Pietri, *Historia de la rebe-lión popular,* 89–109. The meaning of Boves's "revolutionary" actions has been widely debated. Germán Carrera Damas argues that cattle, not land, were important in the *llanos* and that Boves did not engage in radical land distribution. *Boves: Aspectos socioeconómicos de la guerra de independencia,* 2d ed. (Caracas: Universidad Central de Venezuela, 1968). Demetrio Ramos, however, maintains that Boves did indeed distribute land until royalist authority was restored. "Sobre un aspecto de las 'tácticas' de Boves," *Boletín de la Academia Nacional de Historia,* 51 (1968), 69–73.

36 *Gazeta de Caracas,* VI (May 21, 1817); Rufino Blanco Fombona, *Bolívar y la guerra a muerte* (Caracas: Impresoras Unidas, 1969), 241–2; Stoan, *Pablo Morillo,* 55–8, 63–71; McKinley, *Pre-Revolutionary Caracas,* 171–4.

Río de la Plata

The residents of the Viceroyalty of the Río de la Plata, like those of the Captaincy General of Venezuela, were greatly concerned by the events of 1809. Unlike the elite of the northern captaincy general before the civil wars, those of Buenos Aires were divided. The Americans had maintained a strong position since January of that year when they had prevented a European *golpe*. The *peninsulares*, however, expected the new viceroy, Baltazar Hidalgo de Cisneros – a veteran of Trafalgar – to restore them to their earlier dominant position. But the Americans were unwilling to relinquish their newfound influence, which they maintained through control of the militia.[37]

On May 13, 1810, news arrived in Montevideo that the Junta Central had disbanded after fleeing to Cádiz. Rumors circulated that all was lost. "The latest notices, loose and exaggerated talk, the reading of the latest gazettes, convinced the city [of Buenos Aires] that the Peninsula had totally succumbed [to the French]."[38] In such circumstances, the leaders of the port city, like those of Caracas, determined that they would not recognize the Council of Regency in Cádiz. The reasons were the same as those invoked earlier by the *caraqueños:* The compact had existed between the Río de la Plata and the king, not between America and Spain.[39]

The *porteños* organized themselves to gain control of the government of Buenos Aires. A group of Americans, backed by units of the criollo militia – the Patricios commanded by Cornelio Saavedra – pressured the viceroy to convene a junta of notables. On May 22, about 250 government officials, ecclesiastics, lawyers, merchants, professionals, military men, and citizens attended the gathering. Bishop Benito de Lué y Riega argued that as long as any royal authorities remained in Spain, they should be obeyed. But the majority believed that the Peninsular government of national defense no longer existed and that therefore sovereignty reverted to the people of the Río de la Plata. In those circumstances, they argued, Buenos Aires should form its own government in the name of Fernando VII.

As had occurred earlier in Caracas, the junta of notables decided to vote either to retain the existing government or to form a new one. After hours of debate, the majority voted to establish a governing junta. Although many Spaniards supported the majority and some Americans the minority,

---

37 Lynch, *The Spanish American Revolutions*, 49; Tulio Halperín-Donghi, *Politics, Economics and Society in Argentina in the Revolutionary Period* (Cambridge: Cambridge University Press, 1975), 147–8.
38 Gandia, *Historia del 25 de mayo*, 90.
39 Julio V. González, *Filiación histórica del gobierno representativo argentino*, 2 vols. (Buenos Aires: Editorial "La Vanguardia," 1937–8), 1:224–7; Halperín-Donghi, *Politics, Economics and Society*, 150; *Gazeta de Buenos Ayres*, Núm. 27 (December 6, 1810).

most *peninsulares* favored the status quo, whereas most criollos preferred change. Since the discussion lasted into the early hours of May 23, the group granted the *ayuntamiento* the authority to form a new junta. That body attempted to balance the competing forces by appointing a governing junta of five persons – two moderates, one of them an American and the other a Spaniard, and two criollo autonomists, Juan José Castelli and Colonel Saavedra, with the former viceroy as president.[40] All four members of the junta had voted earlier to remove the viceroy, but they now agreed to collaborate with him. On May 24, in a formal ceremony, the new authorities swore on the Bible "not to recognize any other sovereign but Señor Fernando VII, and his legitimate successors, according to the order established by law, *and to be subordinated to the government which legitimately represents him.*"[41]

Many *porteños,* however, were not pleased that Hidalgo de Cisneros continued in office as president of the junta and military commander. As one British visitor noted:

Late in the evening the regiment of *Patricios,* now en masse, with a great proportion of the inhabitants, went to the houses of the different officers of the cabildo and declared that, if an alteration was not immediately made in the junta that was formed, by excluding the late viceroy, they would teach them the way to shed blood; the consequence of which was, on the 25th, the cabildo were compelled to meet again.[42]

In addition, the *people* presented a petition with 409 signatures demanding a new governing body.

The members of the governing junta, therefore, submitted their resignation to the *ayuntamiento.* That body initially insisted on retaining the original junta but, faced with large groups, many of them members of the militia who filled the hall demanding change, it acquiesced on May 25. As the *people* requested, the *ayuntamiento* appointed Cornelio de Saavedra president; Juan José Castelli, Manuel Belgrano, Miguel de Azcuénaga, Manuel Alberti, Domingo Matheu, and Juan de Larrea members; and as secretaries, Juan José Paso and Mariano Moreno.[43] The new *Junta Provisional Gubernativa de las Provincias del Río de la Plata a nombre del Sr. D. Fernando VII* (Pro-

40 Roberto Marfany, *El Cabildo de Mayo* (Buenos Aires: Ediciones Theoría, 1961), 38–52; Marfany, "La primera junta de gobierno de Buenos Aires (1810)," *Estudios Americanos,* XIX (1960), 223–34

41 Luis V. Varela, *Historia constitucional de la República Argentina,* 4 vols. (Buenos Aires: Taller de Impresiones Oficiales, 1910), 1:213. The emphasis is Varela's.

42 Fabian to Crocker, *Mutine,* off Buenos Ayres, June 3, 1810, in *The Navy and South America, 1807–1823: Correspondence of the Commanders-in-Chief on the South American Station,* eds. Gerald S. Graham and R. A. Humphreys (London: Navy Records Society, 1962), 50.

43 González, *Filiación histórica,* 2:25–36; Ricardo Levene, *Ensayo histórico sobre la Revolución de Mayo y Mariano Moreno,* 3 vols., 4th ed. (Buenos Aires: Ediciones Peuser, 1960), 2:84–101.

visional Governing Junta of the Provinces of the Río de la Plata in the Name of Sr. D. Fernando VII) consisted of dedicated autonomists; nevertheless, they also swore "to maintain intact this part of America for our august sovereign señor Don Fernando VII and his legitimate successors, and to scrupulously observe the laws of the kingdom." In addition, they agreed to convene a congress of cities that was to "meet in this capital as soon as possible to establish the form of government it considers most convenient."[44]

It is significant that the second junta omitted the section of the earlier oath that accepted subordination "to the government which legitimately represents" Fernando VII. The new Junta Provisional Gubernativa had no intention of recognizing the Council of Regency in Cádiz. Moreover, in its decrees, the body changed its name to La Junta Provisional Gubernativa de la Capital del Río de la Plata. The name was indicative of the new regime's determination to dominate the entire viceroyalty.

Although the militia had taken the lead in the movement to change the regime, the leaders of the new government were members of the elite, not the military or popular sectors. The group included Spaniards as well as Americans. As Roberto H. Marfany notes, the division was not between patriots and royalists, but between autonomists and centralists, "considering the first, the defenders of local autonomous government, and the second, partisans of the centralist regime of Spain"[45] – that is, between supporters of a local junta and the Council of Regency in the Peninsula.

On May 26, the Junta Provisional Gubernativa dispatched circular letters to the provincial capitals informing them of recent events and requesting that they recognize the body as a provisional government. The following day, it issued a circular to the cities of the viceroyalty to elect "a deputy to the Junta Provisional Gubernativa of Buenos Aires." The new regime indicated that elections were to be held according to the requirements established in the royal order of October 6, 1809, the one for elections to the Junta Central in Spain.[46] The leaders of the Junta Provisional intended to broaden representation in the governing body rather than to convene a congress of cities, as its initial charge required. That is why they invoked the electoral decree to the Junta Central in Spain rather than the one to the Cortes. Further, the newly elected deputies were required to take an "oath of fidelity to king Fernando VII." Finally, "the elections for deputies would be guaranteed by a military expedition that would impose the authority of the provisional government and its resolutions in all the cities of the for-

---

44 Varela, *Historia constitucional*, 1:214; González, *Filiación histórica*, 2:41.

45 Marfany, *El Cabildo de Mayo*, 112; Halperín-Donghi, *Politics, Economics and Society*, 155–6.

46 González, *Filiación histórica*, quote in 2:52; 1:8–10, the decree of October 6, 1809, is reproduced in 1:269–70.

mer viceroyalty."[47] The new regime intended neither to break with recent electoral experience nor to abandon its outcome to the free will of the cities.

The situation changed shortly thereafter when the Council of Regency's February 14 decree for election of New World deputies to the Cortes formally arrived in early June 1810. The *audiencia* insisted that the Río de la Plata recognize the new government in Spain and elect deputies to the Cortes.[48] The Junta Provisional, however, decided to ignore the order, as well as others from the Council of Regency, on the grounds that there were "uncertainties about the legitimate authority [of that body]. . . . We know from the Spanish and British gazettes the artifices which the intruder king [José Bonaparte] manipulates in order to confound the strength and fidelity of the peoples of America." The Junta reminded the public that it had been "provisionally installed until a congress of deputies from the provinces, who were charged with establishing a government [met]." Furthermore, it noted: "The Junta has sworn allegiance to Sr. D. Fernando VII, and to conserve his august rights; equally it has been established on the specific condition of recognizing the sovereign authority legitimately established in Spain."[49] Since it was impossible to determine the legitimacy of the current government in Spain, the Junta Provisional would continue to exercise authority until circumstances changed. To justify the body's actions, Mariano Moreno, secretary of the Junta and editor of the *Gazeta de Buenos Ayres,* argued that "once the links that tied these peoples to the monarch were dissolved, each province became the master of its destiny since the social compact did not directly establish relations between them, but between the king and these peoples."[50]

The argument that justified autonomy from the government in Spain, however, also justified provincial autonomy from Buenos Aires. The provinces of Río de la Plata were not convinced that the Junta Provisional represented their interests. Montevideo and its interior, the Banda Oriental (the eastern bank of the Uruguay River), competed with Buenos Aires for control of seaborne trade, including livestock exports. Isolated Paraguay had little in common with the *porteños.* Charcas, which had fallen under the control of the Viceroy of Peru after the 1809 movements in La Paz and Chuquisaca, considered Buenos Aires a threat. The interests of the interior provinces of the Río de la Plata, such as Córdoba, Salta, Tucumán, Mendoza, and San Juan, clashed with those of Buenos Aires. Whereas those regions depended on commerce with Upper Peru and Chile and required

---

47 Ibid., 2:52.
48 "El Consejo de Regencia de España e Indias a los Americanos Españoles," *Gazeta Extraordinaria de Buenos Ayres* (June 9, 1810). See also Levene, *Ensayo histórico,* 2:142–3.
49 "Contestación de la Junta," *Gazeta Extraordinaria de Buenos Ayres* (June 9, 1810).
50 *Gazeta de Buenos Ayres,* Núm. 27 (December 6, 1810).

protection for their manufactures, the *porteños* insisted upon free trade.[51] Thus, the provinces of the Río de la Plata, which resented Buenos Aires' insistence on dominating the region, reacted to the claims of the Junta Provisional Gubernativa with considerable suspicion.

In the weeks that followed, some provinces voted to recognize the Junta Provisional. Montevideo, Paraguay, Charcas, Córdoba, and Salta, however, elected to support the Council of Regency in Spain. In many instances, royal officials cultivated long-standing regional enmities to sway the vote against Buenos Aires. Former Viceroy Hidalgo de Cisneros, members of the *audiencia,* and other officials corresponded with provincial authorities, apparently seeking to undermine the new regime. The Junta Provisional responded vigorously. First, it exiled the former viceroy, the judges of the *audiencia,* and other Spanish malcontents to the Canary Islands for conspiring against the government. Then it introduced more stringent security measures in Buenos Aires. In addition, it organized armies to subdue the rebellious provinces.

The Junta Provisional, however, was divided between moderate and radical factions; each had a public following, including some who formed clandestine organizations or clubs. Saavedra directed the moderates, and Moreno was the leader of the radicals. As secretary of the Junta, the latter operated almost as a de facto executive. The radicals controlled the *Gazeta de Buenos Ayres* and other publications that increasingly argued for complete autonomy, although they acknowledged the sovereignty of Fernando VII. The departure of militia units to impose the will of Buenos Aires upon the provinces weakened the moderates, especially Saavedra. The radicals instituted a harsh anti-Spanish policy. They removed many Peninsular officials from their posts, prohibited them from holding public office or from participating in elections, and subjected them to assault by radical thugs and to arrest and expulsion by the government. In August 1810 the radicals ordered the execution of former Viceroy Santiago Liniers and the intendant of Córdoba for opposing the government. In January 1811 they created a *Tribunal de Seguridad Pública* (Tribunal of Public Security) to pursue subversives.[52]

The policy of terror, however, backfired. As the newly elected provincial deputies arrived at the end of 1810, the balance of power swung toward the moderates. Moreno was forced to resign and dispatched on a diplomatic mission to Britain; he died at sea in March. A riot against the excesses of the Junta Provisional the following month permitted the moderates to oust

51 Miron Burgin, *The Economic Aspects of Argentine Federalism* (Cambridge: Harvard University Press, 1940), remains the best analysis of those economic interests.

52 Emilio P. Corbiere, *El terrorismo en la Revolución de Mayo* (Buenos Aires: Editorial "La Facultad," Bernabé y Cía, 1937).

several radicals. Although Saavedra and his supporters ended the discrimination against the Spaniards, they did not tolerate royalist activity. The Junta instituted many of the reforms enacted by the Cortes in Spain, such as freedom of the press, in many cases only modifying a few words of the original Peninsular decree. Like the Spanish parliament, the Junta Provisional recognized the provinces' desire for self-government by instituting provincial juntas modeled on those of Spain.[53]

Despite its accomplishments, the Junta Provisional functioned poorly because its increased size made the body unwieldy. The radicals emphasized this flaw and other shortcomings of the moderates through the Sociedad Patriótica. News of military disasters in Upper Peru undermined further the position of the Junta Provisional. In September, with mass public support, the radicals forced the election of a triumvirate, composed of Manuel Sarratea, Juan José Paso, and Juan Martín de Pueyrredón, to serve as the executive. The larger Junta would function as the legislature. Since the members of the triumvirate rotated in office and Sarratea and Pueyrredón assumed command of military forces, Bernardino Rivadavia, as its secretary, became the de facto executive, much as Moreno had been in the earlier body. The new regime enacted reforms modeled on those of the Spanish Cortes. It expanded education, restricted the slave trade, abolished tribute, and recognized the political rights of the Indians. In addition, it eliminated the Tribunal de Seguridad Pública, which the moderates controlled. When provincial leaders objected to its activism, the triumvirate dismissed their criticism. Similarly, it rejected the Junta Provisional's insistence upon its legislative prerogatives. In contrast to Spain, where the Cortes won the contest with the executive, in Buenos Aires the triumvirate dissolved the Junta Provisional in December. The following month, it abolished the provincial juntas.[54]

During 1812 the triumvirate sought to impose order and discipline in the country. It reorganized the administration of justice to stem what it considered growing delinquency. It introduced military, administrative, and financial reforms designed to concentrate power in the national government. It promoted primary education, the arts, agriculture, and industry. The regime imposed new taxes, abolished the tobacco monopoly, reduced tariffs, and encouraged foreign trade. Most of the transformations favored Buenos Aires, thus adding to the discontent in the provinces.

53 González, *Filiación histórica*, 2:403–9; Ricardo Levene, "Las juntas provinciales creadas por el reglamento de 10 febrero de 1811 y los orígenes del federalismo," in *Historia de la Nación Argentina*, 2d ed., 10 vols., ed. Ricardo Levene (Buenos Aires: Editorial El Ateneo, 1941), 5, segunda sección, 325–40.

54 Ricardo Levene, "Formación del triunvirato," ibid., 371–401; Ricardo Piccirilli, *Rivadavia y su tiempo*, 2d ed., 3 vols. (Buenos Aires: Ediciones Peuser, 1960), 1:117–95.

Military failures in Upper Peru, Paraguay, and the Banda Oriental further contributed to disenchantment with the government. Led by Bernardo de Monteagudo, extreme radicals in the capital, who considered the triumvirate too weak, added their criticism to that of provincials, who demanded a greater voice in government. The most serious opposition, however, emerged from recently returned veterans of the war in the Peninsula, such as José de San Martín and Carlos María de Alvear. Determined to improve the country's military forces, these distinguished officers also questioned the efficacy of the triumvirate.

A crisis occurred in April 1812 when an assembly convened to elect a substitute for Sarratea, who had assumed command of forces in the Banda Oriental, declared that it possessed supreme authority in the Provinces of the Río de la Plata. The triumvirate eliminated the threat to its authority by dissolving the assembly. Further, it restricted freedom of the press and the authority of the Ayuntamiento of Buenos Aires, justifying these measures on the grounds that a conspiracy against the government existed. In July the regime executed the Spaniard Martín de Alzaga and forty others for crimes against the state. The high-handed actions of the triumvirate united its opponents – the extreme radicals, the provincials, and the reformist military leaders. The departure of additional military forces to stem royalist advances on the frontiers set the stage for change. On October 8, 1812, a coalition led by Alvear and San Martín overthrew the regime and installed a new triumvirate, consisting of Paso, who remained from the previous one, Nicolás Rodríguez Peña, and Antonio Álvarez Jonte.[55]

The new triumvirate, lacking its own political base, became the tool of politicians from the secret lodges, such as the Lautaro established by the newly arrived military men who had become Masons in the Peninsula. In an effort to consolidate the regime, it convened a constituent assembly that met in January 1813. The new congress faced great obstacles. The executive, dominated by Buenos Aires, desired a strong government, whereas the provinces insisted upon a weak federalist system. Indeed, José Gervasio Artigas and the representatives of the Banda Oriental, who were not seated, demanded a confederation of equal provinces.

The general assembly distinguished itself as a reform-minded body. It abolished slavery and the slave trade, ended personal service by the Indians, eliminated primogeniture and entail, ended judicial torture, and terminated the Inquisition. These and other reforms have caused many scholars to hail the *assembly of the year xiii,* as it is known in Argentina, as a very progressive congress. Yet, as Julio V. González indicates, "All the fundamen-

55 Juan Canter, "El año xii, las asambleas generales y la revolución del 8 de octubre," in Levene, *Historia de la Nación Argentina,* 5, segunda sección, 403–510.

tal laws except one, with which the assembly of the year xiii gave such significance to the Argentine liberation movement, were extracted from the Spanish revolution."[56] That is understandable since what divided the liberals in Spain and the Río de la Plata was not the desire to forge a modern society but the issue of who would rule.

The difficulty for the leaders of the Río de la Plata was how to govern. The constitutional assembly failed to resolve that issue. The armies of Buenos Aires suffered serious defeats in Upper Peru, Paraguay, and the Banda Oriental in 1813. Some provincial leaders began to discuss forming coalitions without Buenos Aires. The region was divided for a number of reasons: The interests of the *porteños* and the other provinces did not coincide. Portuguese armies dominated the Banda Oriental, and the *orientales* (the people of the Banda Oriental) insisted on a confederation of equals. In addition, the government in Spain, which was beginning to drive the French from the Peninsula, managed to send troops to Montevideo. *Porteño* leaders confronted the growing crisis by strengthening the executive and disbanding the assembly even though it had not established a constitution or created a government. In January 1814 they appointed Gervasio Antonio Posadas supreme director. Most important of all, they named San Martín commander of the Army of the North.[57]

A stalemate existed between Buenos Aires and the provinces, but the region was relatively safe from the royalist forces. Given the widespread conflagrations in America, it was unlikely that the Monarchy could retake the Río de la Plata. The people of the region had time to regroup and complete the task begun in May 1810.

Charcas, Paraguay, and Uruguay

Although Buenos Aires, as the capital of the Viceroyalty of the Río de la Plata, believed it had the right to lead the region, many provinces were convinced that the ancient compact granted them the right to autonomy, not only from Spain but also from Buenos Aires. The Audiencia of Charcas, known as Upper Peru, the Intendancy of Paraguay, and the region east of the Uruguay River, known as the Banda Oriental, possessed strong separatist elements. Thus, in 1810 the Junta Provisional Gubernativa of the Capital of the Río de la Plata dispatched military expeditions under the command of Juan José Castelli to Upper Peru and Manuel Belgrano to Paraguay and Uruguay to enforce its mandates.

The military expedition destined for Charcas faced an obstacle – Cór-

56 González, *Filiación histórica*, 2:427.
57 Varela, *Historia constitucional*, 2:235–341; Juan Canter, "La Asamblea General Constituyente," in Levene, *Historia de la Nación Argentina*, 6, primera sección, 29–249.

doba – on the road to Upper Peru where Santiago Liniers, former viceroy and hero of the earlier victories against the British, the bishop, the intendant, and other officials had organized opposition to the Junta Provisional. They also were in contact with royal authorities in Upper Peru who were preparing to send forces to aid them. The Buenos Aires government rapidly dispatched a 1,000-man army that, in early August, easily overwhelmed the royalists in Córdoba and imprisoned its leaders. Determined to crush all opposition, the radical faction of the Junta Provisional issued orders to execute the "rebel" leaders. Although the people of Córdoba pleaded for clemency, Castelli had Liniers and the intendant shot; he pardoned the bishop. The execution of Liniers, the great hero who had saved the Río de la Plata from the hated British "heretics," incensed many, particularly the Indian communities of Charcas.[58]

The *porteño* army advanced northward, subduing Salta, Tucumán, and, ultimately, the highlands of Charcas. On November 7, 1810, it defeated royalist forces at Suipacha. Thereafter, the army controlled Upper Peru. Castelli, a graduate of the law faculty of the University of Chuquisaca, was returning as the all-powerful political agent of the Junta Provisional. Rather than liberating the Audiencia of Charcas, however, he instituted a rule of terror. The Junta's forces entered the great mining city, the Villa Imperial de Potosí, on November 25. Castelli immediately arrested the president of the *audiencia,* the intendant, and the commanding general and, despite pleas for clemency from the archbishop of Charcas and the leading citizens of the kingdom, executed them without a trial in the public square. Thereupon, he named the *porteño* Juan Martín de Pueyrredón president of the *audiencia.* The troops from the coast acted as though they were a conquering army; they assaulted, robbed, and killed innocent citizens at will.[59]

Potosí set the pattern. As the triumphant *porteños* advanced farther into Charcas, Castelli replaced local officials with his own men. He also decreed and sought to control elections to the Junta Provisional. On February 13, 1811, following instructions from Buenos Aires, Castelli granted the Indians the right to representation, just as the Junta Central in Spain had done earlier.[60] Elections and public pronouncements, however, could not overcome the arbitrary and violent nature of the "liberating" army.

58 Ricardo R. Caillet-Bois, "La revolución en el virreynato," in Levene, *Historia de la Nación Argentina,* 5, segunda sección, 116–20; Charles W. Arnade, *The Emergence of the Republic of Bolivia* (Gainesville: University of Florida Press, 1957), 58–9.

59 Arnade, *The Emergence of the Republic of Bolivia,* 60–1. Jorge Siles Salinas, *La independencia de Bolivia,* (Madrid: Editorial Mapfre, 1992), 197–226.

60 As González notes: "Comparing the proclamation of February 13, issued in Chuquisaca, with the decree of the Junta Central of Sevilla dated January 1, 1810, one determines that the former is a simplified version of the latter." *Filiación histórica,* 2:395.

Intoxicated by success, Castelli believed his forces would continue to march victoriously over the mountains all the way to Lima. But on June 20, when it faced the well-disciplined royalist army of General José Manuel de Goyeneche at Huachi, near the border of the Viceroyalty of Peru, the "liberating" army broke and fled from the battlefield. As the *porteños* retreated across Upper Peru, the population wreaked vengeance upon their former oppressors. The "liberators," however, had not entirely lost their nerve. In Potosí, Pueyrredón looted the *Casa de Moneda* (mint) at night before fleeing. In the months that followed, the royal army pursued the *porteños* into the lowlands, taking Jujuy and Salta. The royalists sought to capture Tucumán, but they had exhausted their resources. On February 20, 1813, the *porteño* Manuel Belgrano routed the invaders at Salta.

The bloody struggle for Upper Peru continued for two more years as *porteño* and royalist armies swept back and forth. Belgrano occupied Potosí on May 7, 1813. Unlike Castelli, he restrained his forces and governed correctly. But, like his predecessor, he was a conqueror, not a liberator; the people of Upper Peru feared but did not respect the *porteños*. A new royalist commander, the Spanish general Joaquín de la Pezuela, defeated Belgrano's forces. Once again, royalist armies pursued the *porteños* into the lowlands. In 1815, a new "liberating" army under the command of José Rondeau again marched up to Potosí. Like the first invaders from Buenos Aires, Rondeau's men plundered and exploited the people of Upper Peru. Pezuela's forces, substantially reinforced, routed the *porteños* at Sipe Sipe on November 29, 1815. For the third time, royalist forces pursued the *porteños* into the lowlands. Thereafter, a stalemate ensued in which royalist troops harassed the lowland provinces, but neither side advanced deeply into the other's territory.[61]

The three *porteño* invasions of Charcas ended any hope of uniting Upper Peru with the rest of the former Viceroyalty of the Río de la Plata. Instead, the forays heightened localism, particularly among the Indian communities, the *repúblicas de indios*. Led by their *caciques*, they had sided with one group or the other during the royalist–*porteño* clashes. In their quest for local control, they changed sides according to the circumstances. After Sipe Sipe, they struggled to maintain their autonomy vis-à-vis the restored absolutist regime. Because they controlled small areas, these movements have come to be known as *las republiquetas* (the little republics). [62]

Like Charcas, Paraguay remained beyond the control of Buenos Aires.

61 Bartolomé Mitre, *Historia de Belgrano y de la independencia argentina,* 3 vols. (Buenos Aires: Librería de Mayo, 1876), 1:401–29, 447–99; Arnade, *The Emergence of the Republic of Bolivia,* 67–79; Siles Salina, *La independencia de Bolivia,* 241–71; Lynch, *The Spanish American Revolutions,* 122–7.

62 Rene Danilo Arze, *Participación popular en la independencia de Bolivia* (La Paz: Organización de los Estados Americanos, 1979), 165–203; Siles Salinas, *La independencia de Bolivia,* 273–300.

Primarily a livestock and agricultural region, the area was dominated by the port city of Asunción, situated more than 1,000 miles upriver. Upon learning of the establishment of the Junta Provisional of Buenos Aires, Intendant Bernardo Velasco convened a junta of notables in Asunción on July 24, 1810. Approximately 200 individuals who gathered there voted to recognize the Council of Regency and to maintain cordial relations with Buenos Aires. The *porteños,* however, responded with force. The Junta Provisional appointed Manuel Belgrano to head a military expedition to Paraguay and Montevideo to impose the government's authority. Belgrano, like Castelli in Upper Peru, intended to crush the opposition and execute the principal "rebels." On January 15, 1811, his forces drove Intendant Velasco and his Peninsular staff from the field. But the Paraguayan criollo *estancieros* and their mestizo *peones* counterattacked in massive cavalry charges, routing Belgrano's army. After a second decisive defeat at Tacuarí on March 9, the *porteños* abandoned Paraguay.[63]

In an effort to reassert control, Intendant Velasco sought aid from Brazil. The criollo elite predictably opposed outside intervention. On May 14 they seized control of Asunción, appointed two "associates" to govern the region – the Spanish colonel Juan Valeriano de Zevallos and the criollo lawyer José Gaspar Rodríguez de Francia, known as Dr. Francia – and, on May 17, 1811, declared their autonomy from Buenos Aires or any foreign power. A congress, with representation from all parts of Paraguay, met on June 17. It established a Junta Superior of five men, including Francia, to govern the region. The Paraguayans proposed to Buenos Aires a confederation of the Río de la Plata, provided that all areas possessed complete equality. This the *porteños* rejected.[64]

During the two years that the Junta Superior governed Paraguay, Francia gained widespread popular support as the indispensable leader. A learned individual, a graduate of the University of Córdoba in a land with few educated men, he courted the popular classes. An astute politician, he outmaneuvered the other members of the Junta, gaining control of the government. He frightened the congress, which met in August 1813, with the specter of *porteño* and Brazilian aggression. As a result, the assembly declared Paraguay an independent republic on October 12, 1813, and established an administration of two consuls, Francia and Fulgencio Yegros, an unschooled *estanciero* who deferred to his coconsul.

In 1814 Francia convened another congress, which elected him supreme

63 Mitre, *Historia de Belgrano,* 1:303–34; John Hoyt Williams, *The Rise and Fall of the Paraguayan Republic, 1810–1870* (Austin: University of Texas Press, 1979), 24–6.

64 John Hoyt Williams, "Governor Velasco, the Portuguese and the Paraguayan Revolution of 1811," *The Americas,* 28:4 (April 1972), 442–50; Julio César Chávez, *La revolución del 14 y 15* (Asunción: Librería Nizza, 1957).

dictator of the republic for five years. Two years later, he convinced the assembly to appoint him perpetual dictator and to meet only when he required it. The legislature did not meet again for more than a quarter century. Francia, known as *el Supremo,* governed Paraguay until his death in 1840.[65]

The Banda Oriental, present-day Uruguay, was the third region that broke away from the former Viceroyalty of the Río de la Plata. Like Paraguay, the Banda Oriental was primarily a livestock-raising area with a prominent port city, Montevideo, and also like Paraguay, the region shared a border with Brazil. The circular from Buenos Aires requesting recognition and inviting the area to elect a deputy to the Junta Provisional arrived in Montevideo on May 31, 1810. Two days later, a junta of notables instead voted to recognize the Council of Regency. Earlier, the *ayuntamiento,* dominated by Spaniards, had elected Rafael de Zufriátegui deputy to the Cortes from Montevideo. A conservative and a bitter opponent of Buenos Aires, Zufriátegui supported the regime in the Peninsula and the activities of Francisco Xavier Elío as governor and later as viceroy.[66] Thus, the royalists in Montevideo possessed strong support in Spain.

Like many other Americans, the criollos of the Banda Oriental wished to establish their own junta. Earlier, in 1808, when it appeared that Liniers might recognize José Bonaparte, Governor Elío had convened a junta to govern in the name of Fernando VII. In 1810, however, Montevideo failed to take such an action. Instead, the authorities tried to blockade Buenos Aires by sea and to establish military control of the interior of the Banda Oriental. Early in 1811 Elío returned to Montevideo as viceroy of the Río de la Plata. He rapidly imposed military rule in the interior, insisted that *estancieros* prove title to their land, increased taxes, and sought aid from neighboring Brazil to fight Buenos Aires. Naturally, these actions alienated the Americans of the Banda Oriental.[67]

On February 15, 1811, José Gervasio Artigas, a prominent criollo officer who had returned from Spain in 1810 after fighting the French, crossed the Uruguay River into Buenos Aires territory to obtain aid in liberating the Banda Oriental. The following day, *estancieros* gathered about 200 gauchos on the banks of the Arroyo Asencio to declare their opposition to the royalists, an event known in Uruguayan history as the *Grito de Asencio.* Artigas returned from the province of Entre Ríos, on the west bank, with his

65 Chávez, *La revolución,* 27–99; Richard Alan White, *Paraguay's Autonomous Revolution, 1810–1840* (Albuquerque: University of New Mexico Press, 1978).

66 John Street, *Artigas and the Emancipation of Uruguay* (Cambridge: Cambridge University Press, 1959), 114–17; María Teresa Berruezo, *La participacion americana en las Cortes de Cádiz (1810–1814)* (Madrid: Centro de Estudios Constitucionales, 1986), 182–4.

67 Street, *Artigas* 123–6; Lynch, *The Spanish American Revolutions,* 92–3.

forces to lead the movement. Other *orientales* soon joined. Buenos Aires also sent troops, the remnants of Belgrano's abortive expedition to Asunción, as well as a detachment commanded by José Rondeau. On May 18 Artigas defeated a large royalist force at Las Piedras and marched on Montevideo. The *oriental* leader urged Rondeau to join in the attack but the *porteño* commander hesitated, giving the royalists time to reorganize their defenses. As a result, they retained control of the city.

Desperate, Viceroy Elío appealed to the Portuguese government in Brazil for help. The Portuguese Crown, which had established its capital in Rio de Janeiro after fleeing from the French in 1807, took the opportunity to reassert its claims to the region by sending a large army to occupy the Banda Oriental. In these circumstances, Elío turned to his enemies across the river for aid. On October 20, 1811, Buenos Aires agreed to an armistice that recognized the sovereignty of Fernando VII and the unity of the Spanish Nation. The accord also acknowledged Elío's authority over the Banda Oriental and provided for joint operations against the Portuguese. The agreement pointedly excluded Artigas and his *orientales*. The *chief of the orientales*, as he was now called, withdrew to Entre Ríos with thousands of his compatriots to escape the invading Portuguese armies.[68]

The Buenos Aires government, asserting that it remained loyal to the king, requested British help in getting the Portuguese to withdraw. As an ally of both Spain and Portugal, the British managed to convince the Portuguese to evacuate the region at the end of 1812. Since Montevideo remained under the control of royalist forces, Buenos Aires, abrogating its agreement with Elío, joined the *orientales* in besieging the city. Once again, the *porteño* regime sought to incorporate the region into its union of provinces. The leaders of the Banda Oriental, however, convened a congress on April 1813, which determined that the region would participate in a larger union only on the basis of complete autonomy within a federal system. This was unacceptable to the *porteño* government, which excluded the *oriental* deputies from its congress. Thereafter, Artigas broke completely with Buenos Aires.[69]

After a lengthy siege, the royalists in Montevideo surrendered to *porteño* forces in June 1814. Buenos Aires, however, was unable to dominate the Banda Oriental because Artigas controlled the interior. The two sides struggled for months until the *porteños* finally abandoned Montevideo in February 1815, initiating a brief period of local government known as *la*

68 Street, *Artigas*, 128–46; Edmundo M. Narancio, *La independencia de Uruguay* (Madrid: Mapfre, 1992), 71–90.

69 Edmundo M. Narancio, *El origen del Estado Oriental* (Montevideo: Anales de la Universidad, 1948), 276–7; Pablo Blanco Acevedo, *El federalismo de Artigas y la independencia nacional,* 2d ed. (Montevideo: Impresora Uruguarya, 1950); Narancio, *La independencia de Uruguay,* 91–108.

Patria Vieja (the Old Fatherland). Although it was evident that the *orientales* insisted on autonomy, for years Buenos Aires and Brazil continued their attempts to incorporate the region into their territories. Finally, with British mediation, on August 27, 1828, all sides agreed to a treaty recognizing the independence of the Provincia Oriental del Uruguay.[70]

Chile

Isolated on the west coast of South America, the residents of the Captaincy General of Chile responded to the disasters in Spain with concern and anguish. Like many other Americans, Chileans feared not only for the motherland but also for themselves. In 1810, when some began considering how to respond to the crisis of the Monarchy, the capricious and harsh governor, Francisco García Carrasco, reacted by instituting repressive measures. On May 25 he arrested three prominent citizens of Santiago – José Antonio Rosas, Juan Antonio Ovalle, and Bernardo de Vera – on charges of disloyal conspiracy and ordered them sent to Lima for trial. The action so outraged the elite that the Spanish-dominated *audiencia* deposed the captain general on July 16, replacing him with an octogenarian criollo, Mateo de Toro Zambrano, Conde de la Conquista.[71]

Shortly thereafter, news of three events arrived. The Council of Regency had assumed power from the Junta Central in Spain and convoked elections to a *cortes*; the Regency had appointed the reactionary Francisco Javier Elío captain general of Chile; and the people of Buenos Aires had refused to recognize the Regency and established an autonomous junta. Elío's appointment distressed Chileans, who had just ousted the repressive García Carrasco. Like many other Americans, they wondered if Spain would survive as an independent nation. The actions of Buenos Aires and the words of the Regency's election decree – "your destinies no longer depend either on ministers, viceroys, or governors: they are in your hands" – convinced many that Chile should form its own governing junta.

A number of publications advocating autonomy circulated in the captaincy general at the time. One of them, *El Catecismo político cristiano,* clearly noted that Americans had the same rights as Spaniards to establish juntas. Moreover, it argued that "although a Junta was established in Sevilla, which called itself Supreme, America did not have to accept its authority because, according to the Laws of the Indies, she was independent of the

70 Street, *Artigas,* 189–369.
71 Sergio Villalobos R., *Tradición y reforma en 1810* (Santiago: Universidad de Chile, 1961), 157–60, 191–206; Alfredo Jocelyn-Holt Letelier, *La independencia de Chile* (Madrid: Mapfre, 1992), 140–6.

Map 3. Wars in South America: Southern theater. (After John Lynch, *The Spanish American Revolutions, 1808–1826,* New York: W. W. Norton, 1986.)

domination of any province of Spain, even though she [America] was considered an integral part of the Monarchy."[72]

Despite opposition from the *audiencia,* the Conde de la Conquista convened a junta of notables on September 18, 1810, to consider whether or not to recognize the Council of Regency. Approximately 450 leading citizens, government officials, military men, ecclesiastics, lawyers, merchants, and professionals attended the meeting. Spaniards and Americans were found on both sides of the issue, although the majority of *peninsulares* backed the Regency, whereas the majority of criollos favored a local junta. The partisans of the Regency faced two serious obstacles: Many believed that France would conquer Spain, and they questioned the legitimacy of a body appointed by a Junta Central that, after being discredited, dissolved itself before the American representatives could participate in its decisions.

The autonomist position was forceful: The compact was between Chile and the monarch, not between the captaincy general and Spain, and in the absence of the king, sovereignty reverted to the people. Its proponents were able to buttress their arguments with reference to ancient Spanish jurisprudence, such as the *Siete Partidas.* When it came time to vote, the autonomists won by a large majority. They established a new governing junta consisting of the Conde de la Conquista as president, Bishop Elect José Antonio Martínez as vice-president, five other members, and two secretaries. The new Junta Provisional Gubernativa swore to govern and defend the kingdom in the name of Fernando VII until a congress of the provinces of Chile was elected.[73] The action initiated a period of autonomous government in Chile that lasted until 1814, an era known as *la Patria Vieja.*

The Junta Provisional Gubernativa began governing Chile carefully. It informed other American governments, as well as the Council of Regency in Spain, of its actions. The Junta appeared to be so moderate that it was one of the few American juntas that managed to obtain recognition from the Council of Regency in Spain. It particularly sought close relations with its counterpart in Buenos Aires, which the Junta considered a natural ally. Fearful that the Viceroy of Peru might intervene militarily in Chile, as he had in Charcas and Quito, it organized a more effective armed force. The Junta introduced a number of economic reforms, the most contentious of which was free trade. Finally, it convened elections for a congress to meet in April 1811. The Junta justified the action on the grounds that "sover-

72 Jaime Eyzaguirre, *Ideario y ruta de la emancipación chilena* (Santiago: Editorial Universitaria, 1957), 110; Walter Hanisch Espindola, *El Catecismo político cristiano. Las ideas y la época: 1810* (Santiago: Editorial Andrés Bello, 1970).

73 Simon Collier, *Ideas and Politics, of Chilean Independence, 1808–1833* (Cambridge: Cambridge University Press, 1967) 49–56; Eyzaguirre, *Ideario y ruta,* 110–19; Jocelyn-Holt Letelier, *La independencia de Chile,* 147–52.

eignty having reverted to the people because of the civil death of the monarch, they must . . . elect their representatives so that, gathered together in a general congress, they determine the type of government that should rule until the sovereign is restored to the throne and resumes by right of postliminy his sovereign authority."[74]

Since the decrees for elections to the Cortes had already been received, the Santiago government modified them to meet Chile's needs. The *ayuntamientos* of each of the kingdom's *partido* (district) capitals were to elect one deputy, except Santiago, Concepción, Chillán, Talca, and Coquimbo, which, because of their larger populations, were to elect six, three, two, two, and two, respectively. Only those who could pay their own expenses and who, "by their patriotic virtues, their talent, and their distinguished prudence, have merited the esteem of their fellow citizens" were eligible to be elected deputies. Men "older than twenty-five years who, by their fortune, employment, talent, or quality, enjoy a certain regard in the districts in which they reside" were eligible to vote. As in the case of election to the Cortes, domestic servants, debtors, and criminals were ineligible.[75]

The makeup of the Junta Provisional Gubernativa changed radically when first President Toro Zambrano and then Vice President Martínez died. Juan Martínez de Rozas, a prominent figure from Concepción, became the dominant force in the Junta. Opponents of the new regime, among them members of the *audiencia,* organized a *golpe de mano.* On April 1, 1811, the day elections were to be held in Santiago, Lt. Colonel Tomás de Figueroa rebelled. Led by Martínez de Rozas, the Junta responded energetically; it crushed the revolt and executed Figueroa. The *audiencia* ceased to exist and was replaced by a court of appeals. The reaction had been stifled, and Martínez de Rozas appeared dominant.

Congress met on July 4 with forty-two members instead of the thirty-six proposed by the Junta. Santiago had obtained permission to elect twelve deputies instead of the six it originally had been allocated. Although most deputies were Americans, a few Spaniards were chosen. As its first act, congress swore, in the name of Fernando VII, to defend the kingdom and to protect the Catholic religion against foreign and internal enemies. A minority, including criollos as well as *peninsulares,* preferred to recognize the Council of Regency. Another minority, composed entirely of Americans, wanted complete autonomy, although not independence. And a sub-

74 Eyzaguirre, *Ideario y ruta,* 123; Collier, *Ideas and Politics,* 73.
75 "Convocación al Congreso Nacional de 1811 por la Junta de Gobierno en [el] 15 de Diciembre de 1810," in *Sesiones de los cuerpos lejislativos de la república de Chile, 1811 a 1845,* 37 vols., ed. Valentín Letelier (Santiago: Talleres Gráficos Nacionales, 1887–1908), 1:9–11. As Fernando Campos Harriet has noted: "The eligibility requirements and the proceedings were, with little difference, those which the Spanish Council of Regency had established for the formation of the Cortes." *Historia constitucional de Chile* (Santiago: Editorial Jurídica de Chile, 1956), 488.

stantial middle group wished to govern without severing relations with the government in Spain. The radicals, with ties to the powerful Larraín family and Martínez de Rozas, came primarily from Concepción in the south and included among their members Bernardo O'Higgins, an avid separatist.

Chile's moderate government was soon divided by regional, family, and political differences. With the meeting of congress, the governing junta ceased to exist. Therefore, one of the new legislature's first tasks was to appoint an executive branch. But before it could act, the body had to resolve an internal dispute. The deputies from Concepción disapproved of Santiago's doubling its representation to twelve. When the rest of congress failed to support their objection, the group unsuccessfully sought to prevent the selection of another governing junta. Then, in an effort to retain Martínez de Rozas in office, they proposed that two members of the three-man junta be chosen from the center of the country while Concepción pick the third. The opposition group abandoned the legislature on August 9 when the majority of congress insisted that the entire body elect the governing junta.[76]

The remaining members of congress established a weak junta to function as the executive. In an effort to maintain regional balance, the new junta consisted of three men, one from each of Chile's regions. Because they all were moderates, however, they were not acceptable either to the radicals who had abandoned congress or to the powerful families that had supported the walkout. The opposition – which in Santiago coalesced around the Larraín family and in Concepción around Martínez de Rozas – reacted forcefully. It convinced the Carrera brothers, Juan José, Luis, and José Miguel – military men and members of a prominent family – to compel congress to do their bidding. José Miguel Carrera, a twenty-six-year-old who had just returned from Spain, where he had distinguished himself in battle against the French, surrounded congress in Santiago with his troops on September 4, 1811. The following day, Concepción formed its own provincial junta.

Carrera imposed his will upon congress. He demanded the expulsion of seven deputies from Santiago and the appointment of a new governing junta composed of Martínez de Rozas, Martín Calvo de Encalada, José Gaspar Marín, Juan Enrique Rosales, and Juan Mackenna, the latter two members of the Larraín family. In addition, the family head, Joaquín Larraín Salas, was incorporated into congress as a deputy from Santiago. Thus, a minority had seized control of the government and converted itself into the majority.[77]

76 Mary Lowenthal Felstiner, "Kinship Politics in the Chilean Independence Movement," *HAHR*, 56:1 (February 1976), 58–80; Collier, *Ideas and Politics*, 93–4.

77 Campos Harriet, *Historia constitucional*, 118–22.

The restructured, more radical congress introduced a number of significant reforms, many of them similar to those then being discussed in Cádiz: It replaced the hereditary elites who had controlled *ayuntamientos* with popularly elected officials; assumed authority over the Church, ordering its hierarchy to prohibit criticism of the government; reduced many Church fees and established salaries for parish priests; and cut government expenditures and taxes. Its most notable change was the Law of the Free Womb, which prohibited the introduction of any new slaves and provided for the eventual elimination of that odious institution. However, the measure was not particularly significant because there were few slaves in Chile. Congress also introduced a number of administrative innovations, the most important of which was the creation of a third province, that of Coquimbo. Finally, it appointed a commission to prepare a constitution to govern the country "in the name of the king" and appointed an envoy to the Junta of Buenos Aires.[78]

Convinced that "Spain is lost, and if we allow ourselves to be dominated by groundless misgivings, we will become prey to the first adventurer who wishes to subjugate us,"[79] and unwilling to remain on the sidelines any longer, José Miguel Carrera took control of the government by force on November 15, 1811. He established a triumvirate composed of himself, representing Santiago; Martínez de Rozas, Concepción; and José Gaspar Marín, Coquimbo. O'Higgins temporarily replaced Martínez de Rozas while the latter was absent. Although in theory the triumvirate represented the three provinces of Chile, it soon became evident that Carrera intended to dominate the body. On December 2, 1811, without consulting the other members, he dissolved congress and invested the triumvirate with executive, judicial, and legislative power. Two days later, Marín and O'Higgins resigned in protest. Carrera then became a dictator. In Concepción, however, the Junta Provincial refused to recognize the *golpe*. It appeared that civil war was imminent.[80]

Carrera gained the support of the Santiago elite and declared the Concepción junta in rebellion. While both sides prepared their armed forces for conflict, Martínez de Rozas sought a peaceful resolution to the crisis. Negotiations continued as two armies prepared for war. Ultimately, Carrera proved to be the better politician. He delayed talks long enough to undermine Martínez de Rozas by blockading the south for several months. The merchants and landowners of the region began to suffer economically, and

78 Ibid., 419–20, 549–52.

79 Quoted in Julio Alemparte, *Carrera y Freire. Fundadores de la República* (Santiago: Editorial Nascimento, 1963), 39.

80 Letelier, *Sesiones de los cuerpos lejislativos,* 1:190–6; Raúl Silva Castro, *Egaña y la Patria Vieja, 1810–1814* (Santiago: Editorial Andrés Bello, 1959), 58–64.

the troops in Concepción grew restless when they did not receive their pay. Finally, in July 1812 the military arrested Martínez de Rozas, deporting him to Mendoza across the Andes, where he died the following year. Carrera now controlled Chile.

The Carrera dictatorship introduced new ideas to Chile. To further "revolutionary" sentiment, the *caudillo* hired U.S. printers who published government decrees as well as a series of newspapers, the most important of which was *La Aurora de Chile,* edited by fray Camilo Henríquez, a veteran of the Quito revolution of 1809 who returned to Chile in 1810. Henríquez and other publicists rapidly spread contemporary ideas that questioned traditional views of government.[81]

Not all writers espoused radical ideas, however. Manuel de Salas, one of Chile's leading intellectuals, published *Diálogo de los porteros,* in which he envisioned a reconciliation with the king. Juan Egaña, another prominent intellectual, wrote a *Plan of Government* in 1810 and later published a *Declaration of the Rights of the People of Chile,* which proposed a federation of autonomous American kingdoms that recognized Fernando VII as the constitutional head of the Spanish Nation. The idea of federated American kingdoms was an old one and later in 1821 would be presented as the last best hope of retaining ties between the Monarchy and America. Bonds with the Crown remained strong despite Carrera's separatist tendencies. As a British naval officer noted in 1812: "The People of Chile . . . might with no great difficulty, be prevailed to accept the new Constitution of Spain."[82]

Carrera nevertheless was determined to restructure the government. In this he was encouraged by the arrival of the U.S. agent, Joel R. Poinsett, who implied that his country would assist Chile to obtain independence. The Anglo American so ingratiated himself with Carrera that he proposed a draft of a constitution modeled on the U.S. charter. Chileans, however, sanctioned a *Reglamento Constitucional* on October 26, 1812, that recognized Fernando VII as the monarch and established a senate and a three-member governing junta. Carrera, who as a member of the new junta dominated the government, alienated various groups, particularly the supporters of the Larraín family and the southerners who, after Martínez de Rozas's exile, looked to O'Higgins for leadership.

Only royalist threats averted civil war between the two Chilean factions. Viceroy Abascal of Peru sent an expedition to reconquer Chile under the command of Brigadier Antonio Pareja, which landed in the south in March 1813. The royalists, who rapidly captured Concepción, were joined by

---

81 Lawrence S. Thompson, *Printing in Colonial Spanish America* (Hamden: Anchor, 1962), 87–93; Collier, *Ideas and Politics,* 95–112.
82 Collier, *Ideas and Politics,* quote on pp. 116, 113–21.

many discontented Chileans as they advanced north. Appointed supreme commander by the senate, Carrera marched to meet the enemy. Although O'Higgins distinguished himself in several minor engagements, Carrera proved unable to defeat the royalists. The military failure diminished his power and provided the governing junta the opportunity to relieve Carrera of command in November. That body replaced him with O'Higgins, who accepted the post with some reluctance. The autonomists had little time to regroup. The royalists received reinforcements and a new commander, Gabino Gainza, in January 1814.[83]

Unable to prevent the royalists from advancing, the Chilean government accepted British mediation and signed an armistice on May 3. Under the *Treaty of Lircay,* as the armistice was called, Chile recognized the Council of Regency and the Spanish Constitution of 1812, as well as the sovereignty of Fernando VII. In addition, Chile was to elect constitutional *ayuntamientos,* a provincial deputation, and deputies to the Cortes. Finally, trade restrictions would be lifted, and Gainza promised to evacuate Chile within thirty days. Francisco de la Lastra, who had been named supreme director by the senate, justified the treaty on the grounds that Chile had not sought independence but rather a form of government concordant with the principles of the Spanish Nation. As he noted, under the treaty Chileans had obtained self-government, the right to hold public office, free trade, and command of the armed forces.[84]

Two events contributed to the abrogation of the Treaty of Lircay: a *golpe de estado* in Chile and the abolition of the constitutional system in Spain. Although many Chileans, among them prominent figures such as Manuel de Salas, considered the treaty an honorable and just agreement, others, among them the Carreras, viewed it as a humiliating capitulation. On July 23, 1814, José Miguel Carrera overthrew the government and instituted a three-man junta, which he dominated. The constitutionalists in the south were outraged by Carrera's arrogance. Some cities refused to recognize the new regime. After a council of war, O'Higgins led an army north to restore the legitimate government.

In Lima, Viceroy Abascal repudiated the Treaty of Lircay. It was no longer applicable inasmuch as Fernando VII had abolished the Constitution and the Cortes. He dispatched General Mariano Osorio with a contingent of troops to Chile to restore order. The new Spanish commander landed in the south on August 13. After taking control of all royalist forces, he advanced rapidly toward Santiago. The royalist invasion briefly united Chile's warring factions. The temporary alliance failed, however; Carrera and O'Higgins proved unable to unite sufficiently to prevent disaster. After

83 Jay Kinsbruner, *Bernardo O'Higgins* (New York: Twayne, 1968), 64–72.
84 Letelier, *Sesiones de los cuerpos lejislativos,* 1:340–1; Collier, *Ideas and Politics,* 116–17.

a series of engagements, Osorio won a decisive victory over O'Higgins at Rancagua on October 1. Although O'Higgins managed to break out of the siege with part of his forces, Carrera was unwilling to continue the struggle. As a result, Carrera, O'Higgins, and other leaders abandoned Chile, fleeing to Mendoza across the Andes. General Osorio occupied Santiago on October 6, 1814. The *Patria Vieja* had ended.[85]

Quito

Quito, alone among the capitals of Spanish America, was an occupied city in 1810. Neither the residents of the capital nor President Ruíz de Castilla and his government considered themselves free. The troops from Peru, the *pardo* fusiliers of the Real de Lima, behaved as though they were the conquerors, not the defenders, of the Spanish Nation to which they and the *quiteños* belonged. They oppressed and threatened the population, remaining in a city that belonged to another viceroyalty, New Granada, even though the revolt that they had been sent to quell was over. This occurred because Viceroy Abascal of Peru, an ardent champion of the old order, lacked confidence either in President Ruíz de Castilla or in Viceroy Amar y Borbón of New Granada. The situation augured ill for the future.[86]

The Crown attorney, Tomás de Aréchaga, and the commander of the Peruvian troops, Manuel Arredondo, insisted on severe punishment for the "rebels." The representatives of the Viceroy of Peru arrested most of the participants, although the Marqués de Selva Alegre and a few others fled before the "foreign" officials violated the capitulation, which guaranteed that the leaders of the 1809 movement were not to be prosecuted. Inquiries continued for months as the authorities tried to prove a disloyal conspiracy. The participants of the 1809 movement either denied culpability – claiming that they had acted in the belief that France had conquered Spain – or declared that they had been coerced into taking part in the movement. The abundant and contradictory information they offered made it difficult, if not impossible, for the royal authorities to determine responsibility.[87]

Convinced of their guilt, Aréchaga demanded the death penalty for 40 of the leading participants and 40 of the 160 soldiers who served in the gar-

85 Collier, *Ideas and Politics*, 121–5; Kinsbruner, *Bernardo O' Higgins*, 74–84.

86 Demetrio Ramos-Pérez, *Entre el Plata y Bogotá: Quatro claves de la emancipación ecuatoriana* (Madrid: Ediciones de Cultura Hispánica, 1987), 201–3.

87 The information is located in AMQ, "El Proceso de la Revolución de Quito de 1809." It is carefully analyzed by Carlos de la Torre Reyes, *La Revolución de Quito del 10 de Agosto de 1809* (Quito: Ministerio de Educación, 1961), 343–506.

rison the night of August 10 – the latter to be selected by lot. In addition, he requested the imprisonment of fifty others, the sequestration of their property, and their dismissal from their posts. The recommendations were so draconian that they had to be sent to Santa Fé de Bogotá for the viceroy's review. *Quiteños* were shocked by and indignant at such harsh sentences, particularly because it was becoming evident by mid-1810 that other Spanish American cities were doing what Quito had attempted in 1809.

At the end of June, the city stirred with news that Carlos Montúfar, son of the Marqués de Selva Alegre, was arriving from Spain as royal commissioner with full powers to remedy the situation in Quito. As Montúfar wrote to his sister:

I bring with me the papers or instructions for the Kingdom [of Quito]. And in them the president will see how different are the intentions of H. M. [the Council of Regency] than what is being done there. . . . Our friend, my protector and almost father, General [Francisco Xavier] Castaños [the hero of the battle of Bailén] . . . is the president of the Regency. Miguel Lardizábal [y Uribe], cousin on father's side and related to me on both sides, with whom I have lived for a year, with whom I am on familiar terms, and who is like a brother to me, is the representative for the Americas [in the Regency] and the one who handles all matters concerning the New World. Now, infer if we can possibly suffer any more and if the day will come when in Quito they will be sorry how they have treated us. . . . My commission is the most honorable and my instructions very broad. . . . [In addition he noted,] my good friend General [Francisco Xavier] Venegas is coming to govern the Kingdom [of New Granada].[88]

It appeared that the city would finally be restored to normality and that it would obtain its rightful place within the great Spanish Nation.

The good news, however, frightened the authorities, who requested that the viceroy in Santa Fé prevent Montúfar's arrival. Their action increased discontent in Quito; many criticized the government, demanding that Peruvian forces evacuate the city immediately. The concerned authorities ordered increased vigilance, particularly of the imprisoned members of the 1809 movement. An abortive attempt to free the prisoners on August 2, 1810, resulted in the death of many of the movement's leaders, the slaughter of numerous civilians, and the plundering of the city.[89]

Bishop José Cuero y Caicedo, who had served as vice president of the 1809 Junta, ventured into the streets with the Holy Sacraments to calm the population. News of the assassinations and the sack of the city of Quito

---

88 Carlos Montúfar to Rosa Montúfar, Cartagena, May 10, 1810, in Alfredo Ribadeneira, *Quito, 1809–1812* (Madrid: Imprenta Juan Bravo, 1960), 201–20. Since the juntas of New Granada refused to accept the appointment, Venegas instead was named viceroy of New Spain.

89 William B. Stevenson, *Historical and Descriptive Narrative of Twenty Years Residence in South America*, 3 vols. (London: Hurst, Robinson, and Co., 1825), 3:27–9.

spread rapidly, creating great discontent throughout the region. Responding to the bishop's demand, Ruíz de Castilla convened an assembly of notables on August 4. After extensive debate, the body resolved that the Peruvian troops would leave immediately; that military forces would be raised locally; that all that had occurred since August 10, 1809, would be forgotten; and that Royal Commissioner Carlos Montúfar would be received with all appropriate honors.[90] President Ruíz de Castilla agreed to all the demands; the Peruvian troops withdrew the next day.

The royal commissioner arrived on September 12. Immediately establishing his authority, Montúfar insisted on sharing command of the armed forces with the president. They convened a junta of notables on September 19, which resolved that "this city and its province recognize the supreme authority of the Council of Regency as the representative of our well beloved King Fernando VII . . . as long as it controls any part of the Peninsula which is free from French domination. . . ." It also agreed to form a "Junta Superior de Gobierno subject only to the Council of Regency. . . ." In this manner, Quito declared its autonomy of both Santa Fé and Lima. The Junta would consist of Ruíz de Castilla, president; and the royal commissioner, the bishop, and eleven representatives of the corporations, classes, and parishes of the city as members, elected "in the accustomed manner."[91]

Three days later, the representatives of the ecclesiastical *cabildo,* the *ayuntamiento,* the nobility, and the five urban parishes met with the authorities. They reviewed and approved the previous actions, elected members to the Junta Superior, and unanimously named Juan Pío Montúfar, the Marqués de Selva Alegre, vice president. Seven of the eleven individuals elected to the Junta Superior had served in the 1809 junta. Finally, they declared "that the purpose of this Junta Superior is the defense of our Catholic, Apostolic, and Roman religion which we profess; the preservation of these dominions for our legitimate sovereign Sr. D. Fernando VII; and to seek all the well-being possible for the nation and the *patria.*"[92] As a representative of the Regency, Montúfar favored retaining ties with the Monarchy. His influence is evident in the statement of purpose, which mentions both "the nation and the *patria.*" Since at that time the word *nation* referred to the Spanish Nation, the entire Spanish world, and *patria* to the local area, the representatives voted to "seek all the well-being" for both the Spanish Nation and the *patria,* the Kingdom of Quito.[93]

90 Torre Reyes, *La Revolución de Quito,* 554–62.

91 Manuel María Borrero published the actas of those meetings in *La Revolución quiteña, 1809–1812* (Quito: Editorial Espejo, 1962), quote on p. 278.

92 Ibid., 281.

93 The distinction between *nation* and *patria* was common throughout the Spanish world at that time. In the Cortes, all groups called the Spanish world *la Nación Española* and their regions, whether in the Peninsula or in America, their *patria.*

The Junta Superior informed the other provinces of the Kingdom of Quito of its actions, inviting them to establish local juntas to collaborate with the new government in the capital. Montúfar wrote to Viceroy Abascal of Peru, not only notifying him of what had occurred but also insisting that the Province of Guayaquil be fully restored to the Kingdom of Quito. As had occurred in 1809, the other provinces refused to accept Quito's authority. Popayán and Pasto to the north, Cuenca to the south, and Guayaquil to the west organized forces to oppose Quito. Guayaquil also requested assistance from Abascal.[94]

Encircled by hostile provinces and cut off from the autonomists in Santa Fé de Bogotá, Quito took the offensive. It formed armies to subdue the recalcitrant regions. Carlos Montúfar assumed command of one force, which marched south to oppose Guayaquil and Cuenca, while his uncle Pedro Montúfar led another to the north. In the months that followed, the *quiteño* armies established control over most of the sierra. Cuenca, however, remained under royalist control and opposed the Junta Superior.

Concerned about events in Quito and convinced that Ruíz de Castilla was incompetent, the new Council of Regency – which no longer included Castaños and Lardizábal y Uribe – named General Joaquín Molina president of the Kingdom of Quito. Molina, who arrived after the Junta Superior had been formed, established his headquarters in proroyalist Cuenca, where some of the judges of the *audiencia* had fled. Carlos Montúfar, who subsequently besieged that city, maintained that he was the legal representative of the Council of Regency. As he informed the *cuencanos,* "they force you to engage in a destructive civil war which clashes directly with the will of the monarch." The people of Cuenca, however, believing otherwise, continued to defend themselves from the *quiteño* "rebels." Indians of the province joined urban groups in fighting for their "beloved king." In March 1811 Montúfar was forced to retreat north in harsh weather and under continued attack by royalist Indians.[95]

The Junta Superior of Quito found itself in an anomalous situation. It recognized the Regency in Spain, but acted as though it were autonomous in seeking to impose its authority over the entire kingdom and in refusing to acknowledge the authority of President Molina. Nevertheless, in October 1810, the city of Quito held elections for deputy to the Cortes, selecting the Conde de Puñonrrostro, who was then in the Peninsula. The perplexed Council of Regency, which received conflicting reports from Montúfar and from the royal officials in the other provinces, as well as from Viceroy Abascal in Peru, declared in April 1811 that given "the worthy motives which caused the citizens of that city [Quito] to establish a Junta,

94 The correspondence is published in Ponce Ribadeneira, *Quito,* 206–17.
95 Borrero, *La Revolución quiteña,* 294–307; Ramos–Pérez, *Entre el Plata y Bogotá,* 213–15.

and the good order which they demonstrated in electing the individuals that form it, [the Regency] has decided to condescend that it continue to exist until the august congress of the General and Extraordinary Cortes of the Kingdom establish, in the constitution which it will frame, the government most convenient to the provinces of the Spanish Nation."[96]

The Regency's recognition increased political confusion in the area. Who was the president of the Kingdom of Quito – Ruíz de Castilla, who nominally presided over the Junta Superior, or Molina, who had established an alternative royalist government in Cuenca? How was the Junta of Quito to react to the other American juntas? With the exception of Chile, most did not recognize the legitimacy of the Council of Regency and the Cortes. Moreover, only Quito, among all the American juntas, had elected a deputy to that congress!

Family and political rivalries divided *quiteños*. The Montúfar family and its supporters appeared wedded to the Regency, whereas others, led by Jacinto Sánchez de Orellana, the Marqués de Villa Orellana, favored an autonomous junta. The *sanchistas,* as the latter were called, sought to dilute the power of the *montúfares* in the Junta Superior and were especially critical of Carlos Montúfar both for his military failures and for maintaining his role as royal commissioner. In May 1811 the *sanchistas* forced Carlos Montúfar to abandon his command. After months of intrigue, the partisans of autonomy fomented a riot in Quito on October 11 that forced Ruíz de Castilla to resign as president of the Junta. Juan Pío Montúfar, the Marqués de Selva Alegre, as vice president, should have succeeded him to that office. But the *sanchistas* blocked him and, instead, elevated Bishop Cuero y Caicedo to the presidency.

The new regime convened a congress to determine the appropriate course of action. The *ayuntamiento,* the ecclesiastic *cabildo,* the clergy, and the regular orders each elected one deputy; the nobility, two; and Quito's five parishes, one each. In addition, the provincial capitals of Ibarra, Otavalo, Latacunga, Ambato, Riobamba, Guaranda, and Alausí, the sierra regions that the Junta controlled, each were to elect one representative.

The eighteen-member congress met in Quito in December 1811. Dominated by the *montúfaristas,* whose partisans had won many of the elections, the assembly elected Bishop Cuero y Caicedo president and the Marqués de Selva Alegre vice president. The growing threat of the royalist provinces that encircled Quito convinced many representatives, including some *montúfaristas,* that the time had come to end relations with the Council of Regency. On December 11, congress voted to establish an autonomous government "subject only to the supreme and legitimate authority of Sr.

---

96 Quoted in Ramos-Pérez, *Entre el Plata y Bogotá,* 216.

Dn. Fernando VII. . . ."[97] After much discussion, on February 15, 1812, congress promulgated the Solemn Pact of Association and Union Among the Provinces that form the State of Quito, which "recognizes and will recognize as its monarch Señor Don Fernando VII, provided that, free of French domination, . . . he is able to govern [the kingdom] without prejudice to this constitution." The new charter established a representative government with a plural executive, a legislature, and a judiciary. As the royalist President Molina noted, the constitutions of Quito and of Cádiz possessed many similarities "in purpose, structure, and expression which must have arisen from one and the same democratic aspiration."[98]

Personalist rivalries quickly resurfaced. Only the *montúfarista* majority ratified the new constitution. The *sanchistas* withdrew to Latacunga, where they formed another government. They rallied the army of the south and marched on Quito. To avoid civil war, the newly elected authorities resigned. Since the victors accused the Marqués de Selva Alegre of conspiring to crown himself king, the Montúfar family fled to avoid prosecution. Political divisions in Quito permitted the royalists, led by a new and more effective president, General Toribio Montes, to triumph by the end of 1812.[99]

The royal authorities arrested and imprisoned many of the leaders of the autonomist regime, although some managed to flee. After calm was restored, President Montes, as ordered by the Cortes, issued pardons to those who swore allegiance to the Constitution of Cádiz. As noted in Chapter 3, he also instructed the cities of the Kingdom of Quito to hold elections, as required by the Constitution of 1812. Elections for constitutional *ayuntamientos* were held in 1813 and again in 1814. Although elections were held for the Cortes and the provincial deputation, there were many delays before the deputies from the provinces convened in Quito. They finally met in August 1814 to elect six deputies to the Cortes and seven deputies to the provincial deputation. As had occurred in the municipal elections, virtually all those elected to office were Americans, including many who had participated in the defeated and disbanded Quito juntas and assemblies.[100]

Despite the defeat of the second Junta, the people of the Kingdom of Quito enjoyed representative government during 1813 and 1814. Presi-

---

97 Quoted in ibid., note 358, p. 220; Borrero, *La Revolución quiteña,* 321–5.

98 Quoted in José Gabriel Navarro, *La Revolución de Quito del 10 de agosto de 1809* (Quito: Editorial "Fray Jodoco Ricke," 1962), 400. The text of the *Pacto* is found in Ramiro Borja y Borja, *Derecho constitucional ecuatoriano,* 3 vols. (Madrid: Ediciones de Cultura Hispánica, 1950), 3:9–23.

99 Borrero, *La Revolución quiteña,* 345–94.

100 AHN: PQ, vol. 473, f. 33; vol. 477, ff. 81, 100; vol. 491, ff. 150–3; AMQ, Juramento a la Constitución, 1820.

dent Montes pursued a policy of reconciliation, which contributed to the restoration of peace and order. It appeared that Quito's desire for local government had been fulfilled within the new Spanish constitutional system. Unfortunately, that state of affairs lasted only a short time. News arrived in late August 1814 that the king had abolished constitutional government. Since many autonomist leaders were either in prison or in exile, and since royalist forces controlled the Kingdom of Quito, few objected to the restoration of the old order.

New Granada

Viceroy Antonio Amar y Borbón governed a divided New Kingdom of Granada in 1810. The events of the previous year – the conflict over elections to the Junta Central, contradictory reactions to the Junta of Quito of 1809, and the *Memorial de agravios* – exacerbated existing tensions between *peninsulares* and criollos. Suspicion and hostility were widespread. In the capital, the Peninsular-dominated *audiencia* opposed the predominantly criollo *ayuntamiento,* whereas in the provinces, Spanish governors confronted the American-controlled *ayuntamientos.* Many criollos were convinced that the Spaniards harbored pro-French sentiments and that they would accept Napoleonic rule, whereas most Europeans believed that the Americans really sought independence when they proposed establishing a local junta to govern in the name of Fernando VII. News of the military disasters in the Peninsula aggravated these concerns.[101]

The royal commissioners Antonio de Villavicencio, Carlos Montúfar, and José de Cos Iriberri, who landed in Cartagena de Indias on May 8, 1810, brought news of the dissolution of the Junta Central, the establishment of the Council of Regency, and, more shocking, the formation of a junta in Caracas on April 19. The arrival of the royal commissioners, who had been sent to New Granada, Quito, and Peru to strengthen ties between the Regency and the American kingdoms, precipitated political change. Although Governor Francisco Montes hesitated, wishing to learn more before acting, on May 10 the Ayuntamiento of Cartagena took the lead in forming a junta that recognized the Regency in Spain. In an effort to maintain harmony, the new body consisted of Americans and Spaniards, with the governor as a member. Concerns about his French leanings, however, resulted in his removal on June 14.

101 Abelardo Forero Benavides, *El 20 de Julio tiene 300 días* (Bogotá: Ediciones Universidad de los Andes, 1967), 63–107; José D. Monsalve, *Antonio de Villavicencio y la Revolución de la Independencia,* 2 vols. (Bogotá: Imprenta Nacional, 1920), 1:101–5; Anthony McFarlane, *Colombia Before Independence: Economy, Society, and Politics under Bourbon Rule* (Cambridge: Cambridge University Press, 1993), pp. 335–8.

Villavicencio supported Cartagena's actions. The royal commissioner, like his colleagues Montúfar and Cos Iriberri, found no reason to oppose the desire for local autonomy as long as the Junta of Cartagena acknowledged the supremacy of the Regency. Other provincial cities also formed juntas: Cali on July 3, Pamplona the following day, and Socorro, near the capital, on the 9th.[102]

Although most juntas were established peacefully, maintaining a balance among Americans, Spaniards, and royal officials, Socorro became the center of conflict between local elites and the Spanish governor. On July 11 the *ayuntamiento* took control in the name of King Fernando VII, ousted Peninsular officials, and refused to acknowledge the viceroy's authority. Socorro then invited nearby towns to join it in an alliance against the authorities in Santa Fé de Bogotá.[103] The proposed association was the first expression of the regionalism that would plague the *Patria Boba* (Foolish Fatherland), as the period 1810 to 1816 has come to be known in Colombian history.

While the provinces formed juntas the capital appeared calm, but local groups were organizing to change the government. On July 20 members of the elite and middle-class professionals in Santa Fé mobilized crowds to force the viceroy to convene a junta of notables that, after hours of debate and pressure from the multitudes gathered in the plaza mayor, voted to form a *Junta Suprema del Nuevo Reino de Granada*. The Junta consisted of Amar y Borbón as president, José Miguel Pey – *alcalde primero* of the *ayuntamiento* and one of the leaders of the autonomy movement – as vice president, and twenty-five leading citizens as members. The Junta Suprema invited the provinces to elect deputies to a congress that was charged with writing a constitution "on the basis of liberty and independence among them [the provinces], united only by a federal system. . . . [The Junta] solemnly declares that it will not abdicate the imprescriptible rights of popular sovereignty to any person other than our august and unfortunate monarch, don Fernando VII, provided that he comes to reign among us." Nevertheless, the Junta did not sever relations with the government in the Peninsula. It declared: "For the moment, this new government remains subject to the Superior Junta of Regency [in Spain]." In addition, it agreed that "the persons of the Europeans shall remain inviolable . . ., because the

---

102 Rafael Gómez Hoyos, *La independencia de Colombia* (Madrid: Editorial Mapfre, 1992), 139–44.

103 Forero Benavides, *El 20 de Julio,* 109–33; Gabriel Jiménez Molinares, *Los mártires de Cartagena de 1816*, 2 vols. (Cartagena: Imprenta Departamental, 1948–1950), 1:38–120; Horacio Rodríguez Plata, *La Antigua Provincia del Socorro y la Independencia* (Bogotá: Editorial Bogotá, 1963), 17–39; Sergio Elías Ortiz, *Génesis de la revolución del 20 de Julio de 1810* (Bogotá: Editorial Kelly, 1960), 103–38.

public felicity must result from the reciprocal unity of Americans and Europeans."[104]

The members of the Junta Suprema represented the interests of moderate elite and middle-class Americans in Santa Fé. Although they shared power with officials of the old regime, they sought to establish a new political order in New Granada by inviting the provincial capitals to elect representatives. Although they had relied on popular support to gain control, they were reluctant to allow mass participation in the government. Like the Junta of Caracas, the Junta Suprema of Santa Fé modified the decree for election of deputies to the Cortes, limiting the suffrage to property holders and, like the Cádiz decree, excluding servants, debtors, and criminals.

The Junta's conservatism, however, displeased many *santafereños*. A group of young radicals, including lower-level bureaucrats, lawyers, scientists, and clerics, who favored an American-controlled junta, incited the lower classes to demand the removal of royalist functionaries. The authorities imprisoned *audiencia* Judge Juan Hernández de Alba and Crown Attorney Diego de Frías, the two Spaniards most disliked by the crowd, in order to defuse popular discontent.

The struggle for control of the government intensified in the days that followed. The radicals, led by José María Carbonell, mobilized crowds demanding the imprisonment of other officials, including the former viceroy and his wife. The Junta Suprema calmed the masses by placing Amar y Borbón and his wife, Doña Francisca Villanova, under house arrest on July 25, as well as incarcerating other *audiencia* judges and high-ranking Spanish officials. It also abrogated its recognition of the Council of Regency in Spain; refused to accept the newly appointed viceroy, Francisco Xavier Venegas; and agreed to receive Villavicencio, but not in his capacity of royal commissioner.

Fearing loss of control, the Junta Suprema stationed armed detachments in strategic locations in the city and ringed the palace with artillery. It also strengthened the regime by appointing key members of the Junta to the most important branches of government, such as justice and ecclesiastic affairs, finance, and war. Undeterred, Carbonell and the radicals continued to incite the populace. On August 13 riots forced the Junta Suprema to place in protective custody the viceroy and *virreina*. To the horror of the upper-class Junta, hundreds of women harassed them as they traveled to jail, particularly the ex-*virreina*, who, as one clergyman noted, was fortunate to escape alive.

The Junta Suprema responded decisively. On August 16 it arrested Carbonell and other radical leaders. Troops restored order in the city. Calm

104 Manuel Antonio Pombo and José Joaquín Guerra, *Constituciones de Colombia*, 3 vols. (Bogotá: Biblioteca Banco Popular, 1986), 1:270–4. Gómez Hoyos, *La independencia de Colombia*, 157–66.

seemed assured when the Junta exiled the ex-viceroy, members of the *audiencia,* and other Spanish officials who had gained the enmity of the population.[105]

Although it had established control in Santa Fé, the Junta Suprema failed to unify the kingdom. The provinces of New Granada, which possessed conflicting economic interests, resented the capital's attempts to dominate them. Many had formed their own juntas before Santa Fé took such action. Although Pamplona, Nóvita, and Mariquita acknowledged the authority of the Junta Suprema, Cartagena and Cali desired autonomy from Santa Fé. Some provinces, such as Santa Marta and Rioacha on the north coast, Panama in the west, and Popayán and Pasto – northern provinces of the Kingdom of Quito – in the south recognized only the Council of Regency. The desire for local control threatened provincial integrity as well as the unity of the realm. Some cities seceded from established provinces to form new ones – for example, Mompós from Cartagena, Vélez from Socorro, and Tocaima from Mariquita.

The Junta of Cartagena opposed the Junta Suprema of Santa Fé because it sought to dominate the kingdom. In September 1810 Cartagena invited the provinces of New Granada, as well as the coastal cities of Guayaquil in the Kingdom of Quito and Maracaibo in Venezuela, to meet in Medellín to form a confederation. Cartagena proposed establishing "a perfect and federal government" that would grant each province equality and autonomy.[106] Although Cartagena's bid for power failed, its action demonstrated the strength of federal sentiment.

Before the provincial representatives could assemble in Medellín, the Junta Suprema of Santa Fé convened an assembly in an effort to neutralize the drive toward federalism. The first congress of New Granada met in Santa Fé on December 22, 1810. The Junta Suprema had invited all the recognized provinces of the kingdom to attend, but only six – Santa Fé, Socorro, Neiva, Pamplona, Nóvita, and Mariquita – sent representatives. In addition, the newly formed provinces also sent deputies to the congress, an act that bitterly divided the body. Congress, which considered itself the sovereign representative of the nation, immediately clashed with the Junta Suprema over control of the government, particularly the armed forces. Since the military supported the Junta, congress lost the struggle. Unable to accomplish anything, the body dissolved itself in February 1811.

The provincial juntas, however, proved to be more effective than congress in imposing unity. Cartagena attacked Mompós, dissolved that city's

105 Ortiz, *Génesis de la revolución,* 205–32; Gómez Hoyos, *La independencia de Colombia,* 166–72.
106 José Manuel Restrepo, *Historia de la Revolución de la República de Colombia,* 4 vols. (Bensazon: Imprenta de José Jacquin, 1858), 1:88–92; Pombo and Guerra, *Constituciones de Colombia,* 1:281–8.

junta, and established control over the entire province. Other provincial capitals also subdued their breakaway areas by force.

Since most provinces were establishing their own autonomous governments, the Junta Suprema convened an assembly to write a constitution for Santa Fé province, the central area of New Granada. In March 1811 the assembly created the State of Cundinamarca, which recognized "Don Fernando VII, by the grace of God and by the will of the people, legitimately and constitutionally authorized, King of the *cundinamarqueses*."[107] The new government consisted of a strong legislature and a weak executive. Until the king could come to govern Cundinamarca, a president – as viceregent of Fernando VII, associated with two counselors – would exercise executive power. The first president of the new State of Cundinamarca, Jorge Tadeo Lozano, attempted to unify New Granada by inviting representatives from the provinces, including those in the Kingdom of Quito, to attend a second congress in Bogotá, as the capital was now called, to form a true confederation of equals.

Although many provincial leaders questioned Lozano's intentions, seven provinces sent representatives to the congress. At the time, conditions in the Viceroyalty of New Granada were chaotic. In the south, the Kingdom of Quito was embroiled in a civil war between the second Junta de Quito and the provinces of Guayaquil, Cuenca, Popayan, and Pasto, as well as the forces of the Viceroy of Peru. Moreover, struggles between royalists and autonomists rent Pasto and Popayán. Royalists controlled Santa Marta and Rioacha in the north and Panama in the west. The autonomists also were bitterly divided. Moderates, who sought to retain ties with the Council of Regency, and radicals, determined to declare independence, were embroiled in a power struggle in Cartagena, and in Bogotá centralists sought to end Cundinamarca's weak profederalist regime.

As the congress of provinces met in Bogotá in an effort to restore the kingdom's unity, the centralists overthrew the government. On September 19, 1811, Antonio Nariño, who had berated President Lozano for his indecisiveness, in his paper *La Bagatela,* and his radical allies forced the president and the vice president to resign when they provoked a riot in Bogotá. The legislature of the State of Cundinamarca, fearful of the mob, elected Nariño president and acceded to his demands, strengthening executive power. Although Nariño favored a strong central government, the provincial delegates nevertheless wrote a federalist constitution for New Granada.

---

107 Gómez Hoyos, *La independencia de Colombia,* 173–82; "Constitución de Cundinamarca," in Pombo and Guerra, *Constituciones de Colombia,* 1:309. Cundinamarca was thought to be an Indian name for the central region of New Granada, but apparently it was a Quichua word, probably from Quito. Subsequently, the capital came to be called Bogotá, after an Indian community that once lived in the area.

Congress promulgated the Act of Federation of the United Provinces of New Granada on November 27, 1811. The new charter created a confederation of autonomous provinces with an extremely weak national government. Congress received most of the authority the confederation possessed. The president, "if there were one with separate attributes, or . . . the executive power, if it were created," would be completely subordinate to the congress of the confederation. Five provinces – Antioquia, Cartagena, Neiva, Pamplona, and Tunja – approved the Act of Federation and two – Cundinamarca and Chocó – rejected it. Thus, the congress convened to promote national unity only succeeded in splitting New Granada. Three contending political blocs existed at the end of 1811 – the areas under royalist control, the State of Cundinamarca, and the United Provinces of New Granada.[108]

Shortly before the enactment of the Act of Federation, on November 11, 1811, Cartagena declared independence from the Monarchy. Although Americans and Spaniards had initially established a coalition government there, younger, more radical elements – criollo lawyers, notaries, small merchants, clerics, and officials – favored separation from the Crown. The Council of Regency inadvertently contributed to their success when it demanded that Cartagena fully recognize its authority and accept a governor appointed from Spain. The radicals mobilized popular groups, particularly the colored *castas* who had benefited from the new regime, in defense of local autonomy. On the morning of November 11, 1811, a large mob gathered in front of the palace of the *ayuntamiento* where the Junta de Gobierno met. The people, through their representatives, the lawyers Ignacio Muñoz and Nicolás Mauricio de Omaña, demanded the declaration of independence and the abolition of the Inquisition. The Junta acquiesced.

Interestingly, although Cartagena's *acta de independencia,* unlike the one from Caracas, indicted the rule of the Spanish Monarchy, its criticisms were mild and perfunctory. The *acta* concentrated on the rupture of the ancient compact in 1808, the subsequent chaotic governments in Spain, the threats of the Council of Regency, and the failure of the Cortes to grant equal representation to Americans. The *acta* concluded by declaring: "The Province of Cartagena de Indias is from today, in fact and by law, a free, sovereign, and independent state."[109] In many ways, Cartagena's declaration of independence was directed against Bogotá as much as, if not more than, against the Monarchy.

108 "Acta de Federación de las Provincias Unidas de la Nueva Granada," in Pombo and Guerra *Constituciones de Colombia,* 1:391–418; Restrepo, *Historia de la Revolución,* 1:118–26.
109 "Acta de la Independencia de la Provincia de Cartagena en la Nueva Granada," in Pombo and Guerra, *Constituciones de Colombia,* 2:75–82; Restrepo, *Historia de la Revolución,* 1:126–9.

Although constituent assemblies were meeting in many provinces, none followed Cartagena's example of declaring independence. Instead, several promulgated constitutions, as called for in the Act of Federation. Tunja took the lead in establishing a republic on December 9, 1811. Antioquia and Cartagena formed states on May 3 and June 14, 1812, respectively. The constitutions of the federal states, like the Act of Federation, established weak executives and powerful legislatures. Although they sought autonomy, they remained hesitant about independence. For example, the Province of Tunja declared itself "independent from all civil authorities in Spain or any other nation, but on this point subjecting itself to whatever two thirds of the provinces of the New Kingdom of Granada determine."[110] Antioquia explained its actions as follows: "We are convinced that once the Crown abdicated, once the persons who enjoyed the attributes of sovereignty were reduced to captivity, without any hope of postliminy, once the government which they had established was dissolved, the prerogatives of natural liberty reverted to the Spaniards of both hemispheres and the people resumed the right of social contract. The peoples of the [Spanish] Nation, and among them those of the Province of Antioquia, regained their sovereignty."[111] Even Cartagena felt compelled to declare: "Once the exercise of legitimate authority in Spain ceased because of the imprisonment of King Fernando and the usurpation of the largest part of his dominion in Europe by the emperor of the French . . . , the body politic, of which we were an integral part, dissolved for lack of a just and legitimately constituted national center of authority. [Therefore], we confirm and ratify the declaration of independence made by the former Junta of the province."[112]

Centralists in the capital opposed the federalist provinces. Dominated by Bogotá, the State of Cundinamarca represented the central highlands that had historically controlled New Granada. The federalist–centralist conflict was not limited to ideology. The economic interests of the coast, for example, conflicted with those of the center. But local control was the most important issue. Provincial elites had no desire to exchange royal officials for those from Bogotá. The leaders of Cundinamarca, however, were determined to dominate the country.

President Nariño and his supporters were bitterly opposed to congress and the federation, fearing that Cundinamarca, the richest and most populous province, would lose its resources and its power if it were to join the union. But they were certain that an expanded and strengthened State of Cundinamarca could dominate New Granada. Nariño therefore proceeded

---

110 Mariquita, the last of the provinces of New Granada to write a constitution, did not finish its charter until August 4, 1815. Pombo and Guerra, *Constituciones de Colombia,* 1:432.
111 Ibid., 1:473.
112 Ibid., 2:103–4.

along three fronts: He convened an assembly to revise and strengthen the constitution of the state; he decided to incorporate into Cundinamarca, by force if necessary, part or all of the central provinces of Tunja, Socorro, Pamplona, Mariquita, and Neiva; and he sought to undermine the other provinces through intrigue.[113]

He was only partially successful in those efforts. On April 17, 1812, the assembly reformed the constitution and declared that "the State of Cundinamarca is a republic." But contrary of Nariño's wishes, it did not strengthen the executive branch. Instead, it retained "a president and two counselors, all three with a deliberative vote." The reforms consisted essentially of eliminating the monarchical nature of the first charter. Although he dispatched troops to subdue the recalcitrant provinces, only portions of Socorro, Neiva, and Tunja joined Cundinamarca. Nariño's high-handed tactics so outraged the leaders of Tunja that they formed armies to defend themselves.[114]

Civil war between the centralists and the federalists embroiled New Granada during the next two years. Most of the fighting pitted Cundinamarca against Tunja. In March 1812 Nariño dispatched an army under the command of General Antonio Baraya to subdue Tunja. But the general changed sides, according to Francisco de Paula Santander, when faced with "the disapproval of the people . . . for the elimination of their own government and their incorporation into Santa Fé." To confront the crisis, Nariño convinced the legislature of Cundinamarca to grant him extraordinary powers "to operate as a dictator." When he and his large force failed to vanquish Tunja and bring General Baraya to justice, the Province of Socorro took the opportunity to rebel against Cundinamarca. Nariño retreated to Bogotá, pursued by Baraya's troops. During his absence, the capital had fallen into anarchy as contending political groups attacked one another. Upon his return, Nariño resigned. His successor proved to be ineffectual. Unable to find another capable leader, the government of Cundinamarca turned once again to Nariño; in June 1813 it appointed him dictator for life. The following month, the Republic of Cundinamarca declared independence from the Monarchy.[115]

As the centralist forces of Cundinamarca were attempting to crush Tunja, the federalist congress of the United Provinces of New Granada established itself in Leiva. When it became evident that the federal government could not function without an executive, congress elected Camilo Torres president. The remaining royalist centers soon challenged the

113 Restrepo, *Historia de la Revolución,* 1:147–50.
114 "Constitución de la Repúlica de Cundinamarca," Pombo and Guerra, *Constituciones de Colombia,* 2:5–70; Restrepo, *Historia de la Revolución,* 1:150–4.
115 "Independencia de Cundinamarca," Pombo and Guerra, *Constituciones de Colombia,* 2:202–6.

United Provinces. In the north, Santa Marta sought to isolate Cartagena, and in the south, royalists won control of Pasto and Popayán . In its efforts to defend itself, Cartagena enlisted the aid of Venezuelan *émigrés,* among them Simón Bolívar. After months of struggle, Cartagena's forces drove the royalists from the Magdalena River, ensuring its communication with the interior. When Bolívar stopped the royalists' advance at Cúcuta in February 1813, President Torres promoted him to the rank of brigadier general of the federation. The Venezuelan returned to his country in May.[116]

New Granada was a profoundly divided land in mid-1813. The United Provinces and Cundinamarca maintained an uneasy truce. The royalists retained their strongholds in Santa Marta and Rioacha on the north coast and in Panama in the west. In Pasto and Popayán, the northern provinces of the Kingdom of Quito, Colonel Juan Sámano gathered forces to march north to Bogotá. The royalist threat temporarily united the autonomists of New Granada. In September, Nariño led an army south, composed primarily of forces from Cundinamarca with units from Socorro, Tunja, Neiva, and Antioquia. The United Provinces contributed funds for the campaign. The struggle for control of the south was extremely violent. For months, autonomist and royalist armies fought bloody battles. After several victories, Nariño's forces were defeated by Sámano on May 11, 1814. The dictator was captured and sent to prison in Spain.

The royalist victory in the south shattered the temporary unity of the autonomists. Cundinamarca, determined to assert its power in New Granada, named a new dictator, Manuel Bernardo Álvarez. The congress of the United Provinces of New Granada established a triumvirate to govern the union. Although the leaders of the United Provinces attempted to reach an accord with Cundinamarca, Álvarez was unwilling to compromise with the federation. The centralist–federalist split contributed to the resurgence of royalist offensives. In the north, Santa Marta renewed its attempts to encircle Cartagena. By October it appeared that royal authority would be fully restored when news arrived that Fernando VII had abolished the constitution and that the royalists had won in Venezuela.

In these circumstances, the arrival of Venezuelan *émigrés* temporarily altered the balance of power in favor of the federation. While Bolívar escaped by sea to Cartagena, Rafael Urdaneta and his regiment fought their way out of Venezuela to New Granada. The United Provinces once again granted Bolívar a command to restore order with an army of *neogranadinos* and Venezuelans. Although a centralist and a firm believer in strong government, he nevertheless agreed to lead the federal forces. First, the Venezuelan marched against centralist Cundinamarca. Bolívar captured

---

116 Restrepo, *Historia de la Revolución,* 1:155–88; Thomas Blossom, *Nariño: Hero of Colombian Independence* (Tucson: University of Arizona Press, 1967), 81–99; Masur, *Simón Bolívar,* 116–21.

the city of Bogotá on December 12, 1814, incorporating Cundinamarca, the richest and most populous province of New Granada, into the union. As a result of the victory, the federation promoted Bolívar to the rank of captain general of New Granada. On January 23, 1815, the federal government of the United Provinces established its capital in Bogotá.

The federation then ordered its captain general to subdue the royalists in Santa Marta. As Bolívar advanced to the coast, he demanded that Cartagena place its military and financial resources under his command. The city refused. Thus, instead of attacking Santa Marta, federation forces assaulted Cartagena in March. While Americans fought each other, royalist troops landed in Barranquilla, quickly capturing the Magdalena River, the primary route between the sea and the center of the kingdom. Unable to subdue Cartagena and threatened by royalist units, Bolívar abandoned New Granada on May 8, 1815.[117]

Spanish forces ended the civil war. In July, Field Marshal Pablo Morillo arrived from Venezuela with fresh troops. Cartagena maintained a heroic resistance until December. Royalist forces then converged on the capital from the north and the south. Bogotá did not fall until May 1816. No longer hampered by the Spanish constitution, royalist authorities prosecuted the "rebels" to the full extent of the law; some were imprisoned, others were exiled, and a few were executed for treason. The last president of the United Provinces of New Granada, José Fernández de Madrid, was exiled to Cuba. The *Patria Boba* had ended.[118]

New Spain

The great Viceroyalty of New Spain maintained the appearance of calm in 1810. But as Christon I. Archer has noted:

A form of collective neurosis gripped the population. . . . European Spaniards, the gachupines, thought that they identified diabolical plots foreshadowing genocide against their minority. . . . Criollos harbored similar dark thoughts of atrocities . . . planned against their class by the gachupines in league with French, English or American invaders. Throughout New Spain, criollos discussed collective action to protect their legitimate government against a gachupín sellout to the godless French or the heretical English. . . . The Indians, mestizos, and other racially mixed groups perceived even greater apprehension of impending calamities.[119]

117 Masur, *Simón Bolívar,* 168–71.
118 Restrepo, *Historia de la Revolución,* 1:191–347.
119 Christon I. Archer, "Bite of the Hydra: The Rebellion of Cura Miguel Hidalgo, 1810–1811," in *Patterns of Contention in Mexican History,* ed. Jaime E. Rodríguez O. (Wilmington: Scholarly Resources, 1992), 73.

Some disaffected Americans in Guanajuato, like many others in New Spain, worried about the situation in the mother country. Part of an enlightened group who earlier had gathered around Juan Antonio Riaño, the Spanish intendant of Guanajuato, they included the *Corregidor* of Querétaro, Miguel Domínguez, and his wife, María Josefa Ortíz; the militia captains, Ignacio Allende, Juan Aldama, and Mariano Abasolo; and the *cura* of the prosperous town of Dolores, Miguel Hidalgo – former rector of the Colegio de San Nicolás Obispo in Valladolid. The Americans had been in contact with the 1809 plotters in Valladolid and harbored strong resentments against the *gachupines* who had overthrown Viceroy Iturrigaray in 1808. News of events in Spain concerned them because, even though they admired the French Enlightenment, they did not favor either the radicalism of the French Revolution or Napoleon's imperialism. In that respect, like most of their countrymen, they abhorred the godless French. Although elections for deputies to the Cortes were being held throughout the realm, they viewed Spain's situation as precarious. Conditions in Europe and their resentment against the *gachupines* in New Spain led them to consider remedies, including seizing local control. Eventually, they embraced a solution that, like the earlier Valladolid movement, sought to depose the Spaniards with the aid of the urban and rural workers of the Bajío and to establish an American junta to govern New Spain in the name of Fernando VII.

The conspirators planned the uprising for October 1810, but on September 13 the authorities, who had discovered their plot, arrested most of the Querétaro group. Royal officials were not frightened by news of another intrigue. Intendant Riaño had known about the plot for some time but had been reluctant to arrest his friends. Had events gone no further, most participants might have remained free, like the Valladolid group. However, Doña María Josefa Ortíz de Domínguez, who had been an extremely active conspirator, managed to warn Aldama that the plot had been exposed.[120]

Aldama arrived in Dolores about two in the morning of September 16 with news that the authorities had discovered their conspiracy. Hidalgo, Aldama, and Allende, who was visiting the *cura,* decided to launch the revolt in Dolores in the belief that most *novohispanos* would embrace their cause. It was Sunday, a market day, and many people had gathered in the town. After ringing church bells to attract a crowd, Hidalgo exhorted the people to join his rebellion, an event known in Mexican history as *el Grito de Dolores.* According to Aldama, about eight o'clock in the morning:

---

120 Hugh M. Hamill, Jr., *The Hidalgo Revolt* (Gainesville: University of Florida Press, 1966), 101–16;
    Lucas Alamán, *Historia de Méjico desde los primeros movimientos que prepararon su independencia en el año de 1808 hasta la época presente*, 5 vols. (Mexico: Imprenta de Lara, 1849–52), 1:237–501.

There were gathered more than 600 men on foot and on horseback, for it was Sunday and they had come to Mass from the nearby *ranchos* [middle-sized farms], and the *Cura* [Hidalgo] exhorted them to join him and help him defend the kingdom because they [the Spanish] wanted to turn it over to the French; that now oppression had reached an end; that there was no longer any tribute; that those who enlisted with horses and arms would be paid a peso daily, and those on foot four reales.[121]

Thus Hidalgo appealed to the traditional view that *mal gobierno* (bad government) should be removed, while the Monarchy remained inviolate. As Hugh Hamill has declared: "What Hidalgo said in Dolores will probably never be known. It is reasonable to suppose, however, that the climax of his speech included one or all of the following: Long Live Ferdinand VII! Long Live America! Long Live Religion! and Death to Bad Government!"[122]

Father Hidalgo's exhortation resonated among the rural and urban poor, not because he promised to abolish tribute – which affected only a small group in the Bajío – or to pay them, but because it addressed the fears of *novohispanos* that the very foundations of their society, God – and its representative, the Catholic Church – and the Crown, were threatened. As Peter Guardino has observed: "New Spain's poor and elite shared a common political culture to a striking degree. They were united, in fact, by the same basic beliefs that were the ones shared by the poor across village boundaries, namely, that the king was the ultimate guardian of justice and the Catholic Church was the only guarantee of eternal salvation."[123]

The belief in the king's goodness permitted all groups to defend their interests on the grounds that they were acting on behalf of the monarch against officials who distorted or violated his just order. Indeed, in the past, even riots against undesired government actions invoked the traditional formula: *Death to bad government, long live the king.* For more than two decades the clergy and the royal authorities had denounced the atheism of the French Revolution and, more recently, the tyranny of Napoleon. That *tirano* and his godless French had captured King Fernando VII and were conquering Spain. In New Spain the *gachupines* had overthrown the king's viceroy, and many *novohispanos* feared that Spaniards might betray the nation to the French. Rumors of a *gachupín* betrayal became widespread. In such circumstances, it was easy to blame the European Spaniards for all New Spain's ills. It was also logical to conclude that taking power away from the *gachupines* was to act in the best interests of the Crown and the

121 "Declaración rendida por Juan Aldama en la causa que se le instruyó por haber sido caudillo insurgente," in Genaro García, ed., *Documentos históricos mexicanos,* 7 vols. (Mexico: Museo Nacional de Arqueología, Historia y Etnología, 1910), 6:529.

122 Hamill, *The Hidalgo Revolt,* 123.

123 Peter Guardino, *Peasants, Politics, and the Formation of Mexico's National State: Guerrero, 1800–1857* (Stanford: Stanford University Press, 1996), 58.

Church. Thus a new formula emerged: *Death to the gachupines, long live the king.*[124]

Deprivation heightened the sense of insecurity caused by the fear that the mother country might lose its independence to the French. Between 1720 and 1810, New Spain endured ten agricultural crises, the worst in 1785–6 when the Bajío's population experienced widespread famine. About 300,000 people, 15 percent of the rural population, starved to death or died from disease during the catastrophe. The Bajío again experienced a severe drought in 1808 and 1809, drastically reducing the harvest and quadrupling food prices. Crises in other sectors of the economy exacerbated this perennial problem. Rising costs, shortages caused by the European wars, and growing competition from foreign producers crippled the area's vast mining and extensive textile industry. Famine and disease were accompanied by rising unemployment.[125]

Millenarian movements in the countryside further exacerbated tensions in the Bajío. After 1800 a number of Indian messiahs appeared in central New Spain to lead the *campesinos* to a better life. Such movements represented a mechanism to cope with otherwise unmanageable socioeconomic crises in rural society. *Campesinos* sought a leader, preferably a religious man, who would transport them to a better life.[126] Clearly, Father Hidalgo fit this criterion.

124 The term *gachupín* did not refer to Spaniards in the Peninsula; it meant European immigrants who came to New Spain to *hacer la América,* that is, to get rich in the New World. Thus, there was no contradiction in anyone's mind between the "hated" *gachupines* and the "beloved" king. As Guardino notes: "The image of a European Spanish conspiracy to turn New Spain over to the French was both plausible and powerful in 1810." Moreover, as he indicates: "The similarity between this anti-French discourse and the anti-*gachupín* proclamations of the insurgency is striking." Peter Guardino, "Identity and Nationalism in Mexico: Guerrero, 1780–1840," *Journal of Historical Sociology,* 7:3 (September 1994), 314–42.

125 Enrique Florescano, *Precios del maíz y crisis agrícolas en México, 1708–1810* (Mexico: El Colegio de México, 1976), 71–197; John Tutino, *From Insurrection to Revolution in Mexico: Social Bases of Agrarian Violence, 1750–1940* (Princeton: Princeton University Press, 1986), 61–98; Manuel Miño Grijalba, *Obrajes y tejedores de Nueva España (1700–1810)* (Madrid: Instituto de Estudios Fiscales, 1990), 257–359; Richard J. Salvucci, *Textiles and Capitalism in Mexico: An Economic History of the Obrajes, 1539–1840* (Princeton: Princeton University Press, 1987), 157–66; David Brading, *Miners and Merchants in Bourbon Mexico, 1763–1810* (Cambridge: Cambridge University Press, 1971), 261–302. For an assessment of the economy of New Spain, consult Richard Garner with Spiro E. Stefanou, *Economic Growth and Change in Bourbon Mexico* (Gainesville: University Press of Florida).

126 Eric Van Young, "Millennium in the Northern Marches: The Mad Messiah of Durango and Popular Rebellion in Mexico, 1800–1815," *Comparative Studies in History and Society,* 28:3 (July 1986), 385–413; and his "Quetzalcóatl, King Ferdinand, and Ignacio Allende Go to the Seashore: Or Messianism and Mystical Kingship in Mexico, 1800–1821," in *The Independence of Mexico and the Creation of the New Nation,* ed. Jaime Rodríguez O. (Los Angeles: UCLA Latin American Center, 1989), 109–27; Felipe Castro Gutiérrez, "El rey indio de la máscara de oro: La historia y el mito en la ideología plebeya," *Históricas,* 21 (February 1987), 12–20; and his "La rebelión del indio Mariano (Nayarit, 1808)," *Estudios de Historia Novohispana,* 10 (1991), 347–67; José Luis Mira-

All these factors acted as accelerants for the movement that erupted in the Bajío but rapidly engulfed large areas of central New Spain. After arresting authorities in Dolores, nearly 700 rebels marched to San Miguel el Grande. Along the way, the insurgents seized the standard of the Virgin of Guadalupe from the church of Atotonilco and adopted it as their banner. San Miguel capitulated without difficulty. The movement quickly attracted new adherents; within a week the rebel army numbered more than 25,000. Hidalgo assumed the title of *captain general of America,* and Allende became his lieutenant; other militia officers took command of the newly formed units.

New Spain's urban upper and middle classes originally perceived the Hidalgo Revolt, which began as a criollo movement for autonomy, favorably. But whatever support the cause might have engendered among the elite disappeared when it became apparent that the insurgent leaders could not restrain their followers. Within a short time the rebels began to plunder indiscriminately, making no distinction between the property of bad and good Spaniards or even between that of *peninsulares* and Americans. The sack of Guanajuato marked the turning point in the revolt. After capturing the Alhóndiga de Granaditas (the granary), where the royalists had barricaded themselves to await reinforcements, the insurgent masses butchered them – making no distinction between Spaniards and criollos – sacked the city, and destroyed the mining equipment.

News of the massacre of Guanajuato terrified New Spain's upper and middle classes and even many in the lower class. The elite, who vividly remembered the violence of the earlier Haitian revolution, dreaded a race and class war. The Indians with communal lands and *campesinos* who owned property also feared that they might be dispossessed by the landless poor in Hidalgo's forces. The royal army and most of the militia, which were 95 percent American, remained loyal to the Crown.

After Guanajuato, Hidalgo turned south to Valladolid. To avoid a bloodbath, the city surrendered on October 16. This established a pattern: Cities threatened by the insurgents surrendered to escape violence. The rebel forces, now swollen to 80,000, marched towards Mexico City. The royalists stopped the insurgents at Monte Cruces, an elevation overlooking the passes to the Valley of Mexico. Discouraged, Hidalgo's army turned northward toward Querétaro, but a royalist force routed them at Aculco before they arrived there. The insurgents then retreated to Guadalajara, where they were ultimately defeated by the royalists. Hidalgo was subsequently captured, tried, degraded from the priesthood, and executed.

fuentes Galván, "Identidad india, legitimidad y emancipación política en el noroeste de México (Copala, 1771), *Patterns of Contention in Mexican History,* ed. Jaime Rodriguez. O. (Wilmington: Scholarly Resources, 1992), 49–67; and Virginia Guedea, "Los indios voluntarios de Fernando VII," *Estudios de Historia Moderna y Contemporánea de México,* 10 (1986), 11–83.

In the final analysis, the Hidalgo Revolt failed because, although initially appealing to upper-class concerns, it unleashed a lower-class revolt that was limited mainly to the Bajío and Jalisco. The rebels' bitterest enemy, General Félix María Calleja, understood this clearly when he declared: "[The] natives and even the Europeans themselves are convinced of the advantages that would result from an independent [i.e., autonomous] government; and if the absurd insurrection of Hidalgo had been built upon that base, it seems to me, as I now look at it, that it would have met little opposition."[127]

Ignacio Rayón, a lawyer who served as the rebel secretary of state, assumed leadership of the movement after Hidalgo's execution in 1811. Initially, Rayón attempted to effect a reconciliation with General Calleja. He wrote on April 22, 1811, that the insurrection's principal concern had been to prevent a French occupation of New Spain, and he invited the general's cooperation in the formation of a national junta to govern the kingdom in the name of Fernando VII. When Calleja rejected this attempt to obtain autonomy, Rayón and other insurgent leaders organized the *Suprema Junta Nacional Americana.* In January 1812, Calleja captured Zitácuaro, where the Junta was based. Although Rayón escaped, he gradually lost his position as leader of the rebels. Father José María Morelos, who had been waging a guerrilla campaign in the south since 1810, emerged as the most important insurgent chieftain.

Despite the social dangers posed by the insurgency, the autonomists continued to advance their interests through clandestine organizations. The authorities, for example, uncovered conspiracies in April and August 1811; the first proposed forming a governing junta in Mexico City, and the second sought to join forces with the insurgents. Politically active *novohispanos* used the insurgency to advance their interests. In the Cortes, American deputies demanded reforms, arguing vehemently that *mal gobierno* had caused the insurrection. In New Spain, prominent individuals maintained ties with the rebels. Landowners provided supplies, and rich entrepreneurs financed some of their operations. Clandestine groups, among them the Guadalupes, operated in Mexico City and in provincial centers, providing insurgents with crucial information about royalist activities.[128]

Whereas the autonomists formed a variety of loose coalitions to further

---

127 Carlos María de Bustamante, *Cuadro Histórico de la revolución mexicana,* 3d ed., 3 vols. (Mexico: Comisión Nacional para la Celebración del Sesquicentenario de la Proclamación de la Independencia Nacional y del Cincuentenario de la Revolución Mexicana, 1961), 1:130.

128 Virginia Guedea, "The Conspiracies of 1811 or How the Criollos Learned to Organize in Secret" (paper presented at the conference Mexican Wars of Independence, the Empire, and the Early Republic, University of Calgary, April 4–5, 1991). Alamán, *Historia de Méjico,* 3:443–580, 4:2–123; Guedea , *En busca de un gobierno alterno: Los Guadalupes de Mexico* (Mexico: UNAM, 1992); 48–125; Guedea, "Una nueva forma de organización política: La sociedad secreta de Jalapa, 1812,"

their cause, the Guadalupes, whose correspondence was discovered by the authorities, symbolized the activities of upper- and middle-class partisans of local control. General Calleja identified the plotters as "condes, marqueses, judges, councilmen, and other individuals such as doctors, lawyers, merchants," characterizing their network "as a kind of Freemasonry . . . that protects them from all investigation regarding disloyal conspiracy. They are all united, they work for the same principles, and they never give themselves away."[129]

In contrast to the Hidalgo Revolt, the Morelos insurgency flourished because he directed an orderly movement that virtually eliminated the specter of race and class warfare, and his men effectively waged guerrilla campaigns throughout New Spain while maintaining ties with the clandestine urban autonomists. During 1811 and 1812, Morelos and his commanders concentrated on cutting the capital's lines of communications and on achieving control of the south. They occupied Taxco, as well as other centers along the road to Acapulco. Although they failed to take Puebla to the east, the insurgents temporarily severed communications between the capital and Veracruz.

The royal army, composed primarily of Americans, sought to wage a counterinsurgency campaign "designed to maintain control over the countryside and to harden town defenses so as to eliminate guerrilla raids by lightly armed forces."[130] Although the royalists held the cities and towns, including Mexico City, the insurgents dominated the countryside with their dispersed and mobile forces.

Morelos achieved his greatest success in 1812 when he captured Oaxaca. The following spring, he initiated a seven-month siege of Acapulco. Despite his military achievements, he could not claim authority merely by force of arms, particularly since the Spanish Cortes had ratified the notion of popular sovereignty. The Suprema Junta Nacional, composed of Rayón, José Sixto Verduzco, José María Liceaga, and Morelos, continued to exist, but it was divided by conflicts among its members. After the promulgation of the Spanish Constitution of 1812 and the holding of popular

in *Un hombre entre Europa y América: Homenaje a Juan Antonio Ortega y Medina* ed. Amaya Garritz (UNAM, 1993), 185–208; and her "Ignacio Adalid, un *equilibrista* novohispano," in *Mexico in the Age of Democratic Revolutions: 1750–1850,* ed. Jaime E. Rodríguez O. (Boulder: Lynne Rienner, 1994), 71–96.

129 Calleja to ministro de Gracia y Justicia, July 30, 1814, in *Los Guadalalupes y la independencia,* 2d ed., ed. Ernesto de la Torre Villar (Mexico: Editorial Jus, 1985), 120, 104. Guedea, *En busca de un gobierno alterno,* 67–104.

130 Christon I. Archer, "Insurrection – Reaction – Revolution – Fragmentation: Reconstructing the Choreography of Meltdown in New Spain during the Independence Era," *MS/EM,* 10:1 (Winter 1994), 75; Alamán, *Historia de Méjico,* 2:227–479; Ernesto Lemoine, *Morelos y la revolución de 1810,* 3d ed. (Mexico: UNAM, 1990), 200–30.

elections throughout New Spain, the clandestine autonomists urged the convening of a congress, even if it were only in the regions controlled by the insurgents. The urban leaders sought, according to Guedea, to establish "an alternative government in which they could make their influence felt."[131]

In June 1813 Morelos convened elections in the regions controlled by the insurgents for a congress to be held in September at Chilpancingo, a small, easily defended, friendly town. Like elections under the Constitution of 1812, the insurgent electoral process was indirect and based on parish boundaries. Electors were to be chosen in the towns of the provinces where each subdelegate, together with the parson of the parish, would convene the *curas,* the military commanders, the heads of the Indian *repúblicas,* and the *vecinos principales* (leading citizens). The electors had to be "Americans of probity, education, patriotism, and, preferably, natives of the province." They had to be either ecclesiastic or secular theologians or jurists, but they did not have to possess a degree. Elections appear to have been held in the areas of Oaxaca, Puebla, Veracruz, and Michoacan held by the insurgents; in the insurgent Province of Tecpan; and secretly in Mexico City and possibly in other urban centers. Unlike elections under the Spanish Constitution, the insurgent elections were less popular and appear to have been controlled or influenced to some degree. Moreover, not all the individuals elected to the eight-member congress that met on September 14, 1813, were natives of the provinces they represented.[132]

Conflict ensued from the outset between the insurgent executive and the legislature. Morelos issued a *Reglamento* that reduced congress to a subordinate body that would confer supreme authority upon him as *generalísimo* of the army and as chief executive. He also presented to the body his *Sentimientos de la Nación,* which established twenty-three principles upon which to organize the government. Congress assumed national sovereignty and attempted to exercise supreme power, but the insurgent military proved unwilling to accept its authority. As Virginia Guedea observes: "The men of law and the men of arms were unable to understand each other. The divisions that emerged between the legislative and executive branches increased with the passage of time."[133]

Although congress ratified Morelos's command as *generalísimo* and declared the independence of América Septentrional, the insurgents soon suffered reverses that severely weakened him. In December 1813 and January 1814, the royalist army defeated Morelos's forces at Valladolid and Puruarán. Then, in a series of well-executed campaigns, the royalists recov-

---

131 Guedea, *En busca de un gobierno alterno,* 238.
132 Virginia Guedea, "Los procesos electrorales insurgentes," *Estudios de Historia Novohispana,* 11 (1991), 222–48.
133 Ibid., 248.

ered much insurgent-held territory. As Morelos lost military prestige, congress asserted its independence: It stripped him of his authority, discarded the *Reglamento,* and ignored the *Sentimientos* as it proceeded to prepare its own constitution. The movement lost cohesion and power when insurgent commanders also disregarded Morelos's authority.

The short period of civilian dominance ended when the royalists threatened Chilpancingo, and the insurgent legislators were forced to flee. The abolition of the Constitution of Cádiz after Fernando VII returned to Spain in 1814 briefly rekindled the hopes of the insurgent congressmen. They completed a constitution in a desperate bid to win support for their cause by offering an alternative to the restored absolutism. On October 22, 1814, congress issued the Constitutional Decree for the Liberty of Mexican America, known as the *Constitution of Apatzingán,* after the town where its was promulgated. The new charter established a republic with a plural executive and a powerful legislature. Congress clearly rejected Morelos's pretensions to power and attempted to attract supporters of the Spanish constitutional system by issuing a liberal constitution that included many aspects of the Constitution of 1812, particularly its electoral processes, which were well known in New Spain.[134]

Congress had stripped Morelos of his supreme authority, but it retained his support by appointing him a member of the executive triumvirate. In September 1815 the beleaguered congress decided to travel east to Tehuacan in search of a more secure location. On November 5 a large royalist force intercepted the group. Morelos fought a courageous rearguard action that allowed congress to escape. He, however, was captured and subsequently tried, degraded from the priesthood, and executed on December 22, 1815. Earlier that same month, other insurgent leaders dissolved congress. The Constitution of Apatzingán was never implemented and exercised little influence on subsequent constitutional development in Mexico.

Morelos's defeat and the failure of the insurgent congress ended the possibility of an alternative government in New Spain. The elimination of a unified insurgent movement left the urban conspirators without a military alternative. But, as Virginia Guedea observes, it was the loss of popular support that destroyed the insurgency. In the final analysis, the local inhabitants "determined the course of the war. . . . [They supported the insurgent movement] while it was a viable option for positive change, withdrawing it when it ceased to be [positive] and increasingly became an onerous presence."[135]

134 Alamán, *Historia de Méjico,* 3:545–84, 4:2–123, 166–335; Ana Macías, *Génesis del gobierno constitucional en México, 1808–1820* (Mexico: Secretaría de Educación Pública, 1973); Guedea, "Los procesos electorales insurgentes," 203–49.

135 Virginia Guedea, *La insurgencia en el Departamento del Norte: Los Llanos de Apan y la Sierra de Puebla, 1810–1816* (Mexico: UNAM, 1996), 237.

Freed from the restraints of the Constitution of 1812 and strengthened by newly arrived Spanish battalions, the royalists relentlessly pursued the insurgents throughout 1815. The insurgency continued in a fragmented form in many parts of New Spain, but the urban autonomists lacked a cohesive group with whom to attempt to form a national government. Although some continued their covert activities, most attempted to lead quiet, inconspicuous lives, hoping that the authorities would discover no evidence or grounds to prosecute them for their earlier actions.[136]

The American autonomy movements of 1810, like those of Spain, arose from a desire to remain independent of French domination. The kingdoms of the New World, like the provinces of the Peninsula, also questioned the legitimacy of the Council of Regency and its right to speak for the Nación Española. The great difference between the Peninsula and the New World was that the regions of Spain fought an external enemy, whereas the American realms faced internal divisions. The Cortes conducted a political revolution as the provinces of Spain drove the French from their land. The return of Fernando VII and the abolition of the Cortes and the Constitution resolved in the Peninsula the question of legitimacy, at least for a time.

Civil war erupted in America because some groups favored autonomy, while others insisted upon recognizing the government in Spain. Many provinces proved unwilling to follow the lead of their capitals. And divisions within the elite, as well as between classes, added to the tensions. Thus, political and social differences combined with regional antipathy to aggravate the conflict. In addition, some royal officials – of whom Viceroy Abascal of Peru is the most notable – were determined to prevent what they erroneously perceived to be the fragmentation of the Spanish world. By interrupting a political restructuring that seemed to be moving toward a federated Monarchy, the royalists created the conditions that would ultimately destroy the Spanish Monarchy. The conflict waxed and waned during the constitutional period, 1810–14. At times, when the royal authorities acted with restraint, accommodation seemed possible. After the abolition of the Cortes and the Constitution, most autonomist movements were defeated. Although fragmented insurgent groups continued to struggle in various parts of Spanish America, only the government of the isolated Río de la Plata ruled its territory. Beyond the reach of a weakened Spanish Crown, the area retained its autonomy.

136 Guedea, "Los procesos electorales insurgentes," 249; and Guedea, *En busca de un gobierno alterno*, 309–42.

5

Independence

The return of Fernando VII, *the desired,* provided an opportunity to restore the unity of the Spanish world. Virtually every act that had occurred since 1808 – the struggle against the French and the political revolution carried out by the Cortes, as well as most of the autonomy movements in America – had been conducted in his name. Many individuals in Spain and America believed that an accommodation based on the legitimacy of the Crown and a more modern representative political system was not only possible but also imperative. Even in the New World, where a few insurgent groups continued to struggle against royalist forces, most Americans favored reconciliation. Manuel de Sarratea, representing Buenos Aires, a region that had maintained its autonomy since 1810 by virtue of its isolation, for example, wrote the king on May 25, 1814, that his government desired reconciliation with the monarch. Bernardino Rivadavia would repeat the offer the following year.[1]

Everyone, even the *persas* who denounced the actions of the Cortes and the autonomists in America, moreover, believed that change was required. Too much had transpired in the previous six years to return to the status quo ante. When the *serviles* urged Fernando VII to restore absolutism, they did not seek a return to arbitrary and autocratic rule. On the contrary, they decried the ministerial despotism of the pre-1808 years. The system they favored was the traditional one, characterized by a flexibility and an adaptability that had served the Monarchy well for three centuries.

The Restoration

Fernando VII proved unequal to the task of uniting the worldwide Spanish Monarchy. In a less turbulent period, the legitimate government structures and institutions might have compensated for his poor education and lack

---

1 Miguel Artola, *La España de Fernando VII* (Madrid: Espasa-Calpe, 1968), 543–62; Enrique de Gandia, *Historia del 25 de Mayo: Nacimiento de la libertad y la independencia argentina* (Buenos Aires: Editorial Claridad, 1960), 427.

of political experience. Unfortunately, the events of the previous six years had shattered those institutions. The times demanded a politically sophisticated king with the vision to address the conflicts that divided Hispanic society. Instead, almost from the moment he arrived, Fernando was surrounded by a coterie of friends and advisors, a *camarilla,* who counseled him to abolish the Constitution and the Cortes, the institutional structure that offered the best opportunity to reconcile the interests of the Crown with those of America. In the years to come, these reactionaries rather than his ministers would influence the monarch's decisions.

Initially it appeared that Fernando might accept the moderate reforms proposed by the *persas.* In his May 4, 1814, decree abolishing the Cortes and the Constitution, he explained that the body had usurped the king's authority and abused the good will of the people. While rejecting their nefarious acts, Fernando announced his intention to convene a traditional *cortes* with three estates to address the need for reform. He restored the pre-1808 form of government but was careful to reduce the power of the officials to prevent the earlier ministerial despotism of individuals such as Godoy. By limiting the authority of his ministers, the king undercut their ability to forge and implement policies to address the Monarchy's pressing political and economic problems. Fernando's ministers were never certain if they possessed the king's confidence. That was particularly true of Miguel de Lardizábal y Uribe, the *novohispano* elected to the Junta Central and named to the first Council of Regency, only to be removed and exiled by the Cortes, who was appointed Ministro Universal de las Indias (minister of the Indies). Fernando either rejected, revised, or postponed many of his proposals to reconcile the interests of the Monarchy and the New World.[2]

As might be expected, prosecuting those who had attempted to deprive the king of his sovereignty became a priority for the restored Monarchy. In Spain the authorities arrested the leading *liberales* for *lesa majestad,* "an offense violating the dignity of the sovereign," or treason. In Fernando VII's view, the *liberales* had committed treason when they transferred sovereignty from the king to the nation. Although many of those who surrounded the king were "men filled with a desire for revenge, with envy, and with ambi-

---

2   A conservative school of historians formed by Federico Suárez at the Estudio General de Navarra, now the Universidad de Navarra, argues that the *persas* were not reactionaries but "renovators," whereas the *liberales* were "innovators." Further, they maintain that Fernando VII intended to carry out the moderate reform proposed by the renovators. See Federico Suárez, *La crisis política del antiguo régimen en España, 1800–1840,* 2d ed. (Madrid: Ediciones Rialp, 1958), 88–100; María Cristina Diz-Lois, *El Manifiesto de 1814* (Pamploma: Estudio General de Navarra, 1967); María del Carmen Pintos Vieites, *La política de Fernando VII entre 1814 y 1820* (Pamplona: Studio General de Navarra, 1958). Josep Fontana Lazaro, *La quiebra de la monarquía absoluta, 1814–1820* (Barcelona: Ediciones Ariel, 1971), 76–8; and Timothy E. Anna, *Spain and the Loss of America* (Lincoln: University of Nebraska Press, 1983), 115–25, however, strongly disagree.

tion,"[3] they did not dominate policy in the early days. Instead, moderates prevailed and limited prosecution to the principal *liberales*.

As María del Carmen Pintos Vieites has indicated, those prosecuted received due process. Their cases were investigated, brought before the appropriate magistrates, and tried according to the law. Some were found innocent. The penalties given those judged guilty generally were not extreme. The nature of the sentences depended on the ability of judges to insist upon the supremacy of civil as opposed to military law. In those instances when civilian courts prevailed, penalties were relatively lenient. A few were only exiled and fined. Others found guilty were sentenced to four to ten years' confinement. Civilians were sent to either *presidios* or castles, whereas clergymen were held in convents and Carthusian monasteries.

After careful investigation, including extensive testimony from the moderate and *servil* members of the former Cortes, the authorities in Spain convicted fifty *liberales,* among them twenty-two former deputies, and sentenced them for acts against the Crown.[4] Others, like the Conde de Toreno (Spain) and Vicente Rocafuerte (Guayaquil), fled abroad. Some, such as José Miguel Guridi y Alcocer (New Spain), had returned home to America. *Liberal* constitutionalists in the New World also were prosecuted. Some, like the Indian former governor Francisco Antonio Galicia (New Spain), were sentenced to six years in the Marianas Islands. A few, like José Fernández de Madrid (New Granada), were exiled to Cuba. Others, such as José María Fagoaga (New Spain) and Ignacio Adalid (New Spain), had to defend themselves from charges of disloyalty in the Peninsula.[5] A few Americans suspected of disloyal conspiracy, such as Judge Jacobo Villaurrutia in New Spain, were merely forced to accept a post in Spain. In Venezuela, Juan Bautista Arismendi, accused of murdering countless Spanish prisoners, obtained a pardon. Others, like Adalid and the Central American José de Aycinena, were not only absolved but also decorated with the Cross of Isabel la Católica for their services to the Monarchy.[6]

3 Quoted in Fontana Lazaro, *La quiebra de la monarquía absoluta,* 79.
4 Ignacio Lasa Iraola, "El primer proceso de los liberales," *Hispania,* 30:115 (1970), 327–83; Marie Laure Rieu-Millan, *Los diputados americanos en las Cortes de Cádiz* (Madrid: Consejo Superior de Investigaciones Cienfíficas, 1990), 277–9; Pintos Vieites, *La política de Fernando VII,* 177–8.
5 Virginia Guedea, "De la fidelidad a la infidencia: Los gobernadores de la parcialidad de San Juan," in *Patterns of Contention in Mexican History* ed. Jaime E. Rodríguez O. (Wilmington: Scholarly Resources, 1992), 120–1; Guedea, "Ignacio Adalid, un *equilibrista* novohispano, in *Mexico in the Age of Democratic Revolutions, 1750–1850,* ed. Jaime E. Rodríguez O. (Boulder: Lynne Rienner, 1994), 93–6.
6 Jaime E. Rodríguez O., "The Transition from Colony to Nation: New Spain, 1820–1821," in Rodríguez O., *Mexico in the Age of Democratic Revolutions,* 100; Stephen K. Stoan, *Pablo Morillo and Venezuela, 1815–1820* (Columbus: Ohio State University Press, 1974), 69; Guedea, "Ignacio

While the prosecution of *liberales* occupied public attention, government officials struggled to return the Monarchy to normality. Spain needed rebuilding after a long and destructive war, but revenues had declined to nearly half their prewar level. American silver no longer arrived, and Peninsular industries suffered because foreign competitors had captured their markets in the New World. Deprived of outlets, Cataluña's large textile industry nearly collapsed.[7] Although most of America was under royal authority by mid-1814, scattered insurgencies continued in New Spain, fighting had not ended in New Granada, and the Río de la Plata remained beyond the authority of the Crown. If the Monarchy were to recover, it had to regain control of America, restore trade, and revive the flow of silver.

Fernando VII's ministers proposed a policy of reconciliation as the best way to establish peace in the New World. Minister Lardizábal y Uribe urged the appointment of more criollos to government positions both at home and in the Peninsula. The council of state not only agreed with the suggestion, but also proposed granting free trade to the American kingdoms as a means of regaining the loyalty of the people of the New World. Narciso de Heredia, a member of the council of state, recommended an extensive program of reform that included amnesty for the leaders of the American juntas, the introduction of free trade, the reduction or elimination of wartime taxes, and greater autonomy for the American kingdoms.[8]

Minister of the Indies Lardizábal y Uribe attempted to implement a program of reconciliation. He issued a manifesto in July 1814 urging Americans to end the destructive warfare that was bringing economic ruin to the nation. He proposed that they submit statements of their needs and desires to the Crown. Earlier, in June, former members of the Cortes had been asked to present their requests to the minister of the Indies. Lardizábal y Uribe soon received representations both from former deputies and from various New World institutions. Most reaffirmed their earlier demands to the Cortes; they sought economic concessions, local autonomy from provincial capitals, the establishment of new intendancies, bishoprics, and universities, and improvements such as ports and roads. A few requests, such as the Costa Rican Florencio Castillo's proposal for the establishment of a port at Punta Arenas, were speedily approved, in his case by July 1815. However, given the nature of the Spanish bureaucracy, months and years

Adalid," in Rodríguez O., *Mexico in the Age of Democratic Revolutions,* 94; Mario Rodríguez, *The Cádiz Experiment in Central America, 1808 to 1826* (Berkeley: University of California Press, 1978), 125.

7 Charles W. Fehrenbach, "Moderados and Exaltados: The Liberal Opposition to Ferdinand VII, 1814–1823," *HAHR,* 50:1 (February 1970), 52–9.

8 Enoch F. Resnick, "The Council of State and Spanish America, 1814–1820" (Ph.D. diss., American University, 1970), 56–118.

passed while they reviewed other proposals. Many were still under consideration when independence was achieved.[9]

Unfortunately, the ministers' conciliatory policies did not enjoy Fernando VII's full support. A weak and indecisive individual, the king frequently either procrastinated or reversed himself when his personal advisors convinced him that certain reforms were similar to the changes introduced by the Cortes. As time passed, his reactionary advisors supplanted the moderates. Thus, the king restored the Inquisition, brought back the Jesuit Order – something the Americans sought but Spanish *liberales* vehemently opposed – restricted the press, and delayed implementing virtually all the recommendations for reconciliation. Despite the warnings of some Americans, like the Conde de Puñonrostro of Quito and José Baquíjano, Conde de Vistaflorida, of Peru, against military action, others, including Antonio Pérez of New Spain, convinced the king that only force would restore peace and order to the New World. The decision to dispatch a large army to South America in 1815, commanded by Field Marshal Morillo, seriously undermined the policy of reconciliation. Although royal officials defeated the organized autonomy movements in New Spain and Field Marshal Morillo succeeded in restoring royal authority in New Granada, fragmented insurgencies continued in the two viceroyalties and throughout the Andes. It was evident that other military expeditions would be necessary to complete the pacification of America. By late 1816, it appeared that the king's reactionary advisors had triumphed. Fernando, who increasingly favored a military solution to the conflict in America, was considering sending another army to subdue the Río de la Plata.[10]

Although officials in Spain continued for years to debate the merits of various means of restoring order in the New World, the failure of reconciliation was evident to Americans by the end of 1816. As the Buenos Aires periodical *El Censor* noted:

In 1810 we did what we had to. We only aspired to remain free of foreign domination and not to follow Spain's misfortune if she were lost. We have seen each and everyone vacillate

9 Ibid., 73–95; Rodríguez, *The Cádiz Experiment*, 125–7. Even *liberales* like José Joaquín de Olmedo and Vicente Rocafuerte, who had been denounced by the *serviles* and included in the government's list of subversives, responded to the request for statements of their province's needs. See "Informe que en cumplimiento de Real Orden hacen a S.M. por el Ministerio Universal de Indias los Diputados de Guayaquil [José Joaquín de Olmedo y Vicente Rocafuerte] sobre las pretenciones de su provincia," Madrid, September 10, 1814, Archivo General de Indias, Quito, 596, ff. 723–32; and José Joaquín de Olmedo to the Secretario de Estado y del Despacho Universal de Indias, Madrid, September 10, 1814 in Biblioteca Mínima Ecuatoriana, *José Joaquín de Olmedo. Epistolario* (Puebla: Editorial J. M. Cajica, 1960), 318–24.

10 Michael P. Costeloe, *Response to Revolution: Imperial Spain and the Spanish American Revolutions, 1810–1840* (Cambridge: Cambridge University Press, 1986), 59–72; Anna, *Spain and the Loss of America*, 158–88.

... because no one knew what would be the result of Spain's struggle for her liberty, or if King Fernando would return or not to the throne of Spain. At that time we still looked to that king with expectation and hoped that some day he would end our ills .... But suddenly these expectations were destroyed. In Spain, [upon his return in 1814, the king] punished those who had obeyed the Cortes, and he waged a bloody war against the natives of America who, not recognizing [those Cortes] legitimate, just as that king did, had disobeyed them. Thus, ... we began to detest so unjust a king who without a hearing sought to destroy men more faithful than many of those who surround him [at court].[11]

The Conflict in America

The return of Fernando VII placed the politically active population of America in a quandary. A minority who favored independence insisted on separation from the Spanish Monarchy, whereas another minority who preferred absolutism demanded the restoration of the old order. The majority, which sought autonomy, were divided over the best means to attain self-rule. The political future was perplexing, in part because the urban and rural masses, the vast majority of the population, retained faith in the monarch. As Bolívar noted in 1815: "In my opinion, ... the restoration of the Spanish government in America ... appears certain .... Opinion in America is not yet well fixed. And even though all the beings who think are all in favor of independence, the general mass [of the people] still ignores its rights and does not know its interests."[12]

The people of the South American regions that had not participated in the political revolution carried out by the Cortes during the years 1810–14 – Venezuela, the Río de la Plata, Chile, and New Granada – lacked a clear sense of their options. They had neither elected representatives to the Cortes nor established provincial deputations and constitutional *ayuntamientos*. Their own experience with representative government was limited. Whereas the Spanish Cortes had introduced popular elections, the South American autonomists had restricted representation to the established groups of society. In addition, they had failed to resolve the conflicts between the capital cities, which insisted upon centralism, and the provinces, which favored federalism.

South American autonomists could not agree on the type of government best suited for their countries. Whereas some favored establishing republics, many others preferred monarchies. With the exception of the alien and Protestant United States, most previous republican experience seemed negative. The recent French republic had dissolved into anarchy.

11 *El Censor,* September 19, 1816, in Argentina, Senate, *Biblioteca de Mayo,* 10 vols. (Buenos Aires: Imprenta del Congreso de la Nación, 1969), 8:6870–1.
12 Simón Bolívar to Maxwell Hyslop, Kingston, May 19, 1815, in Simón Bolívar, *Cartas del Libertador,* 8 vols. (Caracas: Fundación Vicente Lecuna, 1964–1970), 1:182.

The earlier Dutch republic had been established by heretics hostile to the Spanish world and the Holy Faith. Ancient classical history seemed to suggest that republics were suited only for small states. On the other hand, all the leading European nations were monarchies. Britain, although Protestant, provided an example of a successful constitutional monarchy much admired by South American leaders. Many prominent Americans believed that autonomous monarchies with ties to the Spanish Crown could be successfully established in the New World.

Proposals for establishing autonomous monarchies in America had been discussed for decades. In 1781 the intendant of Caracas, José de Abalos, suggested the establishment of politically and militarily autonomous monarchies in the New World to defend the region from Britain and the emerging United States. Two years later, the Conde de Aranda recommended to Carlos III that Spain retain the Antilles while establishing three kingdoms in the rest of the continent: New Spain, *Costa Firme* (northern South America), and Peru. These realms were to be ruled by Spanish princes who would preserve political, economic, and military ties to the Spanish Monarchy. In 1797 Manuel Godoy suggested that Louisiana become a federated kingdom with a Spanish prince on the throne. Later, in 1804, he proposed the creation of American regencies ruled by Spanish princes. In October 1806, Carlos IV considered the establishment of New World kingdoms in the viceroyalties of New Spain, New Granada, Peru, and Río de la Plata, once again governed by Spanish princes. The project resurfaced in 1811 when José Beye de Cisneros, representative from the Province of Mexico, proposed to the Cortes erecting juntas in every viceroyalty and superior government in America. Under his plan, the American juntas would recognize the Cortes as an overarching parliament superior to them. Similar ideas continued to be discussed in the New World after Fernando returned from captivity in France.[13]

---

13 Carlos E. Muñoz Ora, "Prognostico de la Independencia de América y un proyecto de Monarquías en 1781," *Revista de Historia de América,* Núm. 50 (December 1960), 439–73; Ramón Ezquerra, "La crítica española de la situación de América en el siglo XVIII," *Revista de Indias,* nos. 87–8 (1962), 158–286. Several South American leaders, among them San Martín and Sarratea, seemed to have favored some form of monarchy for their countries. As Henry Chamberlain reported to Viscount Castlereagh on February 17, 1817: "Don Manuel Sarratea arrived in the River Plate from London sometime about the end of December last, and has been ever since busily employed in . . . procuring the adoption of a scheme . . . , whose object is to place a Spanish Prince (the Infant Don Francisco de Paula) at the head of the new South American Kingdom, which is to be composed of the ancient Vice-Royalty of Buenos Ayres, and Chili. . . ." Quote in *Britain and the Independence of Latin America, 1812–1830,* 2 vols., ed. C. K. Webster (London: Oxford University Press, 1938), 1:101. Commander William Bowles, who had become friendly with San Martín, described the general's political views as follows: "He is . . . decidedly in favor of a monarchical government, as the only one suited to the state of society in this country, as well as the genius and disposition of its inhabitants. . . . The lower orders have . . . obtained an undue preponderance and are begin-

The political conflicts among South Americans were especially evident in the Río de la Plata, the one region that had little to fear from royalist forces. There, political leaders were not only divided upon the type of government best suited for their area, they also were engaged in a bitter struggle for dominance between the capital city, Buenos Aires, and the provinces. *Porteño* armies had failed to dominate the viceroyalty in 1814. Supreme Director Posadas proved unable to control either the government or the military of Buenos Aires. In December news of the revolt of *porteño* troops in the north further undermined the authority of the supreme director, who resigned on January 9, 1815. An assembly then elected Carlos de Alvear supreme director.

The new chief executive found it equally difficult to restore order to the region. Although he attempted to institute a strong central government, the provinces refused to recognize the authority of Buenos Aires. Córdoba and Santa Fé declared independence. Even in the capital, opposition groups formed that questioned the supreme director's actions. To control discontent in the city, Alvear imposed martial law, arrested malcontents, and executed those believed to be plotting against the government. As the disintegration of the Río de la Plata continued, the supreme director even contemplated reconciliation with the Spanish king. The final crisis occurred early in April 1815 when troops sent to subdue the Banda Oriental rebelled. By the 15th, the insurrection had spread to many provinces and to Buenos Aires. Two days later, Alvear was forced to resign and a transitional government appointed.[14]

The leaders of Buenos Aires faced two problems: the excesses committed by the executives and the rebellion of the provinces. After electing José Rondeau, commander of the Army of the North, supreme director and Ignacio Álvarez Thomas *suplente,* they established a five-member Junta of Observation to restrain the executive branch. In an effort to mollify the rebellious provinces, particularly the newly formed Confederation of Provinces composed of the Banda Oriental, Corrientes, Entre Ríos, Misiones, Santa Fé, and Córdoba, they convened a national congress in San Miguel de Tucumán to determine the fate of the Río de la Plata.

The inauguration of the national congress on March 24, 1816, in San

---

ning to manifest a revolutionary disposition dangerous in any country. . . . One day, . . . he threw out the idea of dividing South America amongst the principal European powers. . . . Spain might have Mexico, the other powers the different viceroyalties. . . ." Bowles to Croker, at sea, February 14, 1818, in Gerald S. Graham and R. A. Humphreys, eds., *The Navy and South America, 1807–1823: Correspondence of the Commanders-in-Chief of the South American Station* (London: Navy Records Society 1962), 226.

14 Juan Canter, "La revolucion de abril de 1815 y la organización del nuevo directorio," in Ricardo Levene, *Historia de la Nación Argentina*, 2d ed., 10 vols., ed. Ricardo Levene (Buenos Aires: Editorial El Ateneo, 1941), 6, primera sección, 252–98; Luis V. Varela, *Historia constitucional de la República Argentina*, 4 vols. (Buenos Aires: Taller de Impresiones Oficiales, 1910), 2:407–57.

Miguel, the capital of Tucumán province, appeared to provide the legitimacy necessary to unify the country. As Joaquín V. González noted, "the Congress of Tucumán was the most national, most Argentine, and most representative assembly that has ever existed in our history."[15] The newly elected congress met with thirty deputies representing thirteen provinces, including Charcas. Absent were representatives of Paraguay, who refused to participate, and some of the members of the Confederation – the Banda Oriental, Entre Ríos, Corrientes, and Santa Fé. The deputies represented the elite of their provinces; many were lawyers, some were clergymen, others were landowners, and a few were military men. On May 3, 1816, congress elected Juan Martín de Pueyrredón supreme director. The appointment initiated a three-year period of greater stability in the national government.

The actions of the Congress of Tucumán are indicative of the ambivalence of South American political leaders. Although the liberation of Montevideo in June 1814 had virtually ended the possibility of a Spanish invasion from the Atlantic, royalist forces in Upper Peru still threatened the new regime. Therefore, General Manuel Belgrano, the new commander of the Army of the North, and General José de San Martín, commander of the Army of the West, insisted upon a declaration of independence to facilitate their task of defending the nation. Congress agreed. On July 9, 1816, it declared "the United Provinces in South America . . . a nation free and independent of King Fernando VII, his successors, and the metropolis." Nevertheless, congress subsequently went to great lengths to explain in a Manifesto to the Nations that the Río de la Plata had established a provisional junta in 1810 "similar to those in Spain" and "in [the] name of the captive King Fernando." It was the unjust actions of the king after returning from captivity in France that had driven the United Provinces to declare independence.[16]

While agreeing on independence, congress was divided over the appropriate form of government for the nation. A minority proposed a republic, but the majority, including prominent figures outside congress like San Martín, favored a constitutional monarchy. Some advocated inviting a Spanish prince to govern; others preferred a member of another royal family, possibly from France; and a tiny minority even proposed "restoring" an Inca to the throne.[17] Congress also was divided between *unitarios,* who

---

15 Quoted in Leoncio Gianello, *Historia del Congreso de Tucumán* (Buenos Aires: Academia Nacional de Historia, 1966), 122, 20–96; Ricardo R. Caillet-Bois, "El directorio, las provincias de la unión y el Congreso de Tucumán (1816–1819)," in Levene, *Historia de la Nación Argentina,* 6, primera sección, 605–16

16 Gianello, *Historia del Congreso de Tucumán,* 123–249.

17 Dardo Pérez Guilhou, *Las ideas monárquicas en el Congreso de Tucumán* (Buenos Aires: Editorial Depalma, 1966).

believed in a highly centralized government with Buenos Aires dominant, and *federalistas,* who insisted on the equality of the provinces.

International events also affected the congress. In June 1816 Portuguese armies again invaded the Banda Oriental. Montevideo fell to the invaders in January 1817. Confident that the invasion would destroy the Confederation, the Buenos Aires government refused to aid the *orientales,* despite their desperate pleas for help. During the next three years, the struggle against the Portuguese consumed the resources of the Confederation of provinces along the Uruguay River. The Confederation crumbled in 1820 when Artigas was driven west of the Uruguay River and Santa Fé and Entre Ríos refused to continue the struggle. Since the conflict in the Banda Oriental eliminated the threat of the Confederation, many *porteños* insisted that congress move to the capital. After much discussion, the deputies agreed in January 1817 to transfer the assembly to Buenos Aires.

The move to Buenos Aires coincided with new congressional elections that shifted the balance of power in favor of the *unitarios.* The new assembly, which convened in April 1817, drafted a constitution that was promulgated on April 22, 1819. The Constitution of the United Provinces in South America was a conservative *unitario* charter that granted considerable power to the national government in Buenos Aires. Although ostensibly a republic, the executive branch was designed to be transformed easily into a monarchy if a suitable candidate were found. The constitution established an aristocratic senate, composed of "citizens distinguished" by virtue of either belonging "to the military or ecclesiastical class" or possessing "wealth and talent," and a chamber of representatives, consisting of citizens "who did not enjoy a *fuero,* or those from the common class."[18]

The provinces of Buenos Aires, Salta, Tucumán, Mendoza, Córdoba, Santiago del Estero, San Luis, La Rioja, and Catamarca, as well as the armies of San Martín and Belgrano, swore allegiance to the constitution between May 25 and June 6, 1819. The new charter, however, provoked a confrontation with most of the provinces of the Confederation, which refused to accept the constitution. The most disturbing feature to regional leaders was the power granted the executive to appoint and remove local officials, including provincial governors. When Santa Fé declared independence and established a republic, the national government in Buenos Aires sent an army that unsuccessfully tried to subdue the rebellious province. Santa Fé's triumph sparked similar movements in other provinces, such as Entre Ríos, Tucumán, Córdoba, and La Rioja. The Buenos Aires government, led by José Rondeau after Pueyrredón resigned in June 1819, raised new armies

---

18 Gianello, *Historia del Congreso de Tucumán,* 277–348; "Constitution de las Provincias Unidas en Sud-América," in *Estatutos, reglamentos y constituciones argentinas (1811–1898)* (Buenos Aires: Universidad de Buenos Aires, 1956), 117–52.

to subdue the recalcitrant provinces. Since neither San Martín nor Belgrano would commit their troops to defend the national government, the provinces overwhelmed the regime's forces on February 1, 1820, at Cepeda, near Buenos Aires. The victorious provincials occupied the capital, abrogated the Constitution of 1819, and forced Buenos Aires to establish its own provincial regime.[19] The national government had ceased to exist. Thereafter, the provinces administered their regions and, because it controlled access to the sea, the Province of Buenos Aires became the first among equals.

The conflict between Buenos Aires and the other provinces appeared insoluble at times. As a British observer noted in April 1819:

> [Buenos Aires'] misfortunes have arisen from the pride, obstinacy and corruption of its numerous rulers since 1810, whose rapacity and bad management awakened in full force all the local jealousies and antipathies which have always remarkably prevailed in the different districts of this viceroyalty. Each province aspired to independence and sovereign power, and as, instead of resorting to measures of negotiations and conciliation, Buenos Ayres [sic] has always repelled these pretensions by force and treated those who advanced them as rebels and traitors, she has been considered by the inhabitants of the interior as unjustly usurping a dominion to which nothing entitles her, and her authority has been resisted by arms whenever a fair opportunity offered.[20]

The region's independence was assured by 1820, but unity proved much harder to achieve. Only at midcentury, when the Constitution of 1853 established the República Argentina, did a nation begin to coalesce.

Buenos Aires' desire to dominate the former Viceroyalty of the Río de la Plata contributed to the independence of the rest of South America. Since 1810, the autonomous governments of Buenos Aires had attempted to take control of Upper Peru. Before he was defeated by royalist forces, Castelli, the first *porteño* liberator-conqueror, even considered marching victoriously to Lima. In January 1814, after a second *porteño* army suffered defeat at royalist hands, the government of the Río de la Plata appointed San Martín commander of the Army of Peru, or of the North. Within a short time the new commander concluded that Upper Peru could not be held with the limited forces available to him. A strategic thinker, San Martín realized that Lima held the key to the control of South America. As long as Peru remained a royalist stronghold, it could threaten autonomists in New Granada and Chile and even in the Río de la Plata. Since autonomists controlled Chile, early in 1814 San Martín concluded that the best route to

---

19 Gianello, *Historia del Congreso de Tucumán*, 349–520; Ricardo Levene, "La anarquía de 1820 en Buenos Aires," in Levene, *Historia de la Nación Argentina*, 6, segunda sección, 287–342; José López Rozas, *Entre la monarquía y la república* (Buenos Aires: La Bastilla, 1976), 230–356.
20 Bowles to Croker, Buenos Aires, April 3, 1819, in Graham and Humphreys, *The Navy and South America*, 267–8.

Lima was west over the Andes and then north by sea. He resigned command of the Army of the North, arranging to transfer to the city of Mendoza, where in August he assumed the post of intendant of the Province of Cuyo. There he raised an army to assault Peru.[21]

The Chilean autonomists were defeated at Rancagua on October 1, 1814; nevertheless, San Martín persisted with his plan. Now he faced a more difficult task since he would have to liberate Chile before invading Peru. The majority of the Río de la Plata's military forces were concentrated in the Army of the North; he had to create a new force, the Army of the Andes, or of the West. But the human, military, and economic resources at his disposal as intendant of the Province of Cuyo were extremely limited. Moreover, the wars against the royalists and among the provinces had severely damaged the economy of the Río de la Plata. This was particularly true of the interior provinces, which had been harmed by Buenos Aires' policy of free trade. Finally, and most important, the Río de la Plata's political instability hampered the general's efforts to build a truly effective army. Nevertheless, San Martín began recruiting and training men, raising funds, and manufacturing arms and equipment. In addition to militia units and regular troops, San Martín recruited about 1,500 slaves, who joined the Army of the Andes in return for their freedom. They would become one of the strongest units in his army. The arrival of unemployed French and British veterans of the Napoleonic Wars contributed to military discipline and organization. Chilean autonomists, who fled across the Andes after the royalist triumph at Rancagua, also enlisted in San Martín's cause. The most important support, however, came from the Congress of Tucumán and Supreme Director Pueyrredón, who provided both financial and military resources for the Army of the Andes. San Martín carefully trained and prepared his army for the difficult crossing of the high Andes and the struggle thereafter. Discipline and organization, in his view, were the main components of victory.[22]

The royalist government in Chile, whose repressive policies increased discontent in the area, inadvertently contributed to the success of the Army of the Andes. General Mariano Osorio, who assumed command of Chile after the battle of Rancagua, began his government with a conciliatory policy much like that of Montes in Quito, but orders from Viceroy Abascal in Peru and pressure from extreme royalists in Chile soon caused him to adopt

21 Bartolomé Mitre, *Historia de San Martín y de la emancipación sud-americana,* 3 vols. (Buenos Aires: Imprenta de "La Nación," 1887), 1:207–80; José P. Otero, *Historia del Libertador don José de San Martín,* 4 vols. (Buenos Aires: Cabaut y Cía, 1932), 1:243–60.

22 Alfredo Estévez and Oscar H. Elía, *Aspectos económico-financieros de la campaña sanmartiniana,* 2d ed. (Buenos Aires: Editorial El Coloquio, 1976), 97–128; Mitre, *Historia de San Martín,* 1:375–415, 445–68; Otero, *Historia del Libertador,* 1:503–79; Jaime Eyzaguirre, *O'Higgins* (Santiago: Editorial Zig-Zag, 1946), 149–65.

harsher measures. In November 1814 he began to prosecute former autonomists, among them some of the kingdom's leading citizens. Most were
exiled to the Juan Fernández Islands without a hearing. In March 1815,
when two "persons of modest condition" were killed in prison for allegedly
attempting to escape and foment revolution, the principal corporations of
the kingdom dispatched representatives to Spain to seek pardons for the
autonomists. Although the king ordered the prisoners released and their
goods restored to them, the royal decree arrived in August 1816, after a
new and more repressive governor, Francisco Mancó del Mont, had assumed
command. The new official not only ignored the royal order, he also introduced greater controls and removed all Americans from military commands. His harsh policies convinced many Chileans that independence was
necessary. As a result, some Chileans began secretly collaborating with the
Army of the Andes. Bernardo O'Higgins, who joined the Army of the
Andes in February 1816, became San Martín's principal Chilean collabora-
tor, providing the necessary leadership for his compatriots. The two leaders
and Supreme Director Pueyrredón agreed that O'Higgins would govern
Chile once freed, allowing San Martín to conduct a seaborne invasion of
Peru.

General San Martín had prepared carefully. By the end of 1816, the
Army of the Andes numbered 5,000 well-trained and well-equipped men.
With the aid of secret Chilean supporters, San Martín was fully informed
of royalist positions and activities. In Chile, his allies spread false and misleading information to confuse the royalists and create uncertainty. During
January 1817, the summer in South America, when the passes were free of
snow, the Army of the Andes began its march across that towering moun-
tain range. In one of the great military achievements of the struggle for
independence – an accomplishment that Bartolomé Mitre rightly compared with Hannibal's and Napoleon's crossings of the Alps – the army
divided into various units and traversed the Andes over six different passes,
several more than 10,000 feet high – higher than the St. Bernard pass in
the Alps. With superb coordination, the units regrouped on the Chilean
side and quickly marched toward Santiago. Early in February, Governor
Mancó del Mont began receiving reports that invaders had entered Chile
along various points on the Andes, but he was unable to determine the size
of the invading force. On February 12, 1817, forward elements of the Army
of the Andes, commanded by O'Higgins, surprised the royalists at Cha-
cabuco, easily defeating them. Two days later, the victors entered Santiago.
On February 15, a junta of notables in the capital elected San Martín governor with total power. When the general declined the honor, the following day the junta chose O'Higgins supreme director.[23]

23 Mitre, *Historia de San Martín,* 1:504–52, 2:5–66, 110–86; Otero, *Historia del Libertador,* 2:6–76.

Although central Chile had been liberated, royalists still controlled the south. They reconstituted an army during the next year. Early in 1818, General Osorio, the royalist commander, advanced on Santiago, defeating San Martín at Cancha Rayada on March 19. After hastily regrouping, San Martín attacked the royalists on Sunday, April 5, 1818, at Maipó, near the capital. San Martín's forces destroyed the 6,000-man royalist army. As a British observer reported: "It was . . . almost impossible for a victory to have been more complete."[24] Although royalists in the south continued to wage a guerrilla war for several years, Chile was essentially free, providing a base for the assault on Peru. In that respect, San Martín was correct when he declared that the battle of Maipó "decided the fate of South America."[25]

Bernardo O'Higgins served as supreme director of Chile from February 18, 1817, to January 28, 1823. As Fernando Campos Harriet observed: "At that time, O'Higgins was the greatest Chilean captain in the country, the most dedicated precursor of independence, the only citizen worthy of the great honor of becoming the supreme director of Chile. No other election was possible."[26] But he was not chosen in a free and open election. He was selected by a junta in Santiago that was clearly influenced by San Martín, who had already agreed with Supreme Director Pueyrredón that O'Higgins would become his counterpart in Chile.[27]

O'Higgins was determined to ensure his country's liberty. Early in 1818, he formally declared that "Chile's continental territory and adjacent islands form, in fact and by law, a free, independent, and sovereign state: they remain forever separated from the Spanish Monarchy or any other [foreign] domination; and they possess the full capacity of adopting the form of government most convenient to their interests." Like other American declarations of independence, the Chilean document justified the action primarily because of rupture of the ancient compact and the failure of recent Spanish regimes to treat the country fairly.[28]

The new chief of state began his administration by crushing royalist opposition. He confiscated the properties of royalists who fled and placed those who remained under strict surveillance. Those royalists found guilty of crimes, particularly military men, suffered severe punishments; a few

---

24 Samuel Haigh, *Sketches of Buenos Ayres, Chile, and Peru* (London: Effingham Wilson, 1831), 223–5, 238.

25 José de San Martín to Viscount Castlereagh, Santiago de Chile, April 18, 1818, in Webster, *Britain and the Independence of Latin America,* 1:558.

26 Fernando Campos Harriet, *Historia constitucional de Chile* (Santiago: Editorial Jurídica de Chile, 1956), 145.

27 Simon Collier provides an excellent assessment of O'Higgins in *Ideas and Politics of Chilean Independence, 1808–1833* (Cambridge: Cambridge University Press, 1967), 225–30.

28 "Acta y Manifiesto de la Independencia," in *Anales de la República,* 2 vols., ed. Luis Valencia Avarla (Santiago: Imprenta Universitaria, 1951), 1:13–34.

were executed. O'Higgins exiled the royalist bishop of Santiago, José Rodríguez-Zorilla, to Mendoza. He charged a tribunal of justification with examining offending political ideas. Finally, he forced Spaniards resident in Chile to contribute 600,000 pesos to the government.

Neither O'Higgins nor any other Chilean was certain about the nature of government their country should have. Some advocated a monarchy, whereas others preferred a republic. The supreme director appointed a commission of seven leading intellectuals to prepare a constitution for Chile. The new charter ratified the authority of the supreme director and established a senate of five members chosen by the executive that would function until a general congress met at some future date. After a plebiscite ratified the new charter, O'Higgins promulgated the constitution on October 23, 1818.[29] Although the charter granted the supreme director great power, O'Higgins usually operated within the general guidelines of the senate.

The arrangement worked reasonably well for a couple of years. Both the executive and the senate respected each other's power. However, after San Martín departed for Peru in 1820, the senate attempted to restrict the supreme director. As representatives of the landed oligarchy, the senators objected to O'Higgins's assaults on the landowning aristocracy, such as eliminating entail and proposing higher property taxes. Relations between the executive and the legislature deteriorated further when the senate attempted to usurp the supreme director's authority to regulate provincial officials.

In May 1822, after failing to resolve his conflict with the senate, O'Higgins convened a congress to write a new constitution. "The elections," as Campos Harriet has noted, "were a scandal."[30] Since O'Higgins directed the governors to control the proceedings, only the candidates favored by the executive won office. The assembly established a centralist conservative government with a supreme director, presumably O'Higgins, who would serve for a period of six years. The legislature consisted of two houses, a senate and a chamber of deputies; in addition, the charter created a "court of representatives" to serve as a moderating body. Most important, the document distinguished between *Chileans,* those who were either born in the country or obtained its nationality, and *citizens,* who besides being Chileans had to be "older than twenty-five years or married and know how to read

29 "Constitución Provisoria para el Estado de Chile," in Valencia Avarla, *Anales de la República,* 1:52–69. Article 1 on the Poder Ejecutivo stated: "The Supreme Director of the State will exercise executive power in all its territory. His election has already been carried out, according to the circumstances which have occurred; but, in the future, it must be done on the basis of the free consent of the provinces in accord with the regulations which the legislative authority will prepare for that purpose." Ibid., 59.

30 Campos Harriet, *Historia constitucional de Chile,* 438.

and write." Only citizens could participate in elections or hold public office. Criminals, debtors, domestic servants, and those who had no permanent domicile had their citizenship suspended.[31]

Expecting to remain supreme director for the new six-year term, O'Higgins promulgated the constitution in October 1822. But he soon faced opposition in the provinces. After Concepción and Coquimbo rose in revolt and tensions mounted in the capital, the supreme director resigned on January 28, 1823. Another decade would pass before the nation achieved stability.[32]

Unlike the situation in Chile and the Río de la Plata, the independence movement in northern South America appeared stymied. Field Marshal Morillo's forces had regained control of most of New Granada and Venezuela by the end of 1816. The Spanish commander restored order by instituting councils of purification to investigate those suspected of disloyal conspiracy, councils of war to try them, and juntas of sequestration to confiscate and sell their property. Since the autonomous city-states of New Granada, which had refused either to surrender or to accept pardons, had to be defeated militarily, the council of war in Bogotá meted out harsh penalties. It sentenced 101 prominent leaders – including Royal Commissioner Antonio Villavicencio and the former presidents of Cundinamarca and the United Provinces, Jorge Tadeo Lozano and Camilo Torres – to death.[33] In Venezuela, where most of the insurgents either fled or surrendered, the authorities did not resort to such extreme punishments. Those found guilty were either fined or briefly imprisoned. In 1817, on the occasion of his marriage, Fernando VII issued a general pardon.[34]

The measure that most alienated the middle and upper classes, however, was expropriation. To pay for the war and to maintain the army, juntas of sequestration both in New Granada and in Venezuela seized and sold the properties of those accused of disloyal conspiracy. Some members of the elite lost most of their wealth. In Venezuela, for example, Bolívar's five estates, two houses, and slaves, valued at 200,000 pesos, were expropriated and sold for 80,000. The action reduced to penury one of the wealthiest men in the country.[35]

The imprisonments, executions, and expropriations alienated many, particularly in New Granada, where the repression was harshest. Some *neogranadino* insurgents escaped to the *llanos* of the eastern lowland province of Casanare, where they formed opposition groups under the leadership of

---

31 "Constitución política del Estado de Chile," in Valencia Avarla, *Anales de la República*, 1:69–94.
32 Collier, *Ideas and Politics,* 258–9.
33 Oswaldo Díaz Díaz, *La reconquista española,* 2 vols. (Bogotá: Ediciones Lerner, 1964), 1:99–127.
34 Stoan, *Pablo Morillo,* 134.
35 Ibid., 159–63.

men like Francisco de Paula Santander. Others, such as the brothers José Vicente and Ambrosio Almeyda, organized guerrilla bands in the central highlands near Bogotá. In Venezuela, insurgent forces coalesced in the *llanos* and in the eastern province of Guayana. Their numbers swelled as the many *llaneros,* who had been discharged from the royalist forces after Boves's death, were persuaded to join the insurgent armies of new leaders like José Antonio Páez.[36] Thus, large peripheral areas of New Granada and Venezuela remained beyond the control of royal authorities.

Earlier, in 1815, other independence leaders, among them Bolívar, had fled to the Caribbean. At the time, he was but one of many men who aspired to lead an invasion of their homeland. As John Lombardi has noted:

Simón Bolívar was still little more than a brilliant, ambitious South American general whose short military and political career had been characterized by an erratic record of brilliant successes and dramatic failures. . . . Other men were wiser, better educated, more intrepid, vainer, stronger, more ambitious, and wealthier.[37]

But Bolívar was luckier; he managed to outlive most of his coevals. Perhaps most important, he was determined to achieve greatness by freeing first his country and then the rest of South America.

In 1815 Venezuelan and *neogranadino émigrés* sought aid in Jamaica to mount an invasion of Tierra Firme and, when the British proved reluctant, in Haiti. The *émigrés* could not agree upon a leader for the expedition. Unlike San Martín, Bolívar did not possess the stature to win the support of many *émigré* leaders, who considered him an irresponsible, womanizing aristocrat willing to endanger the lives of others for his pleasures. Some even accused him of cowardice and incompetence. Bolívar, however, had two strong supporters: President Alexandre Pétion, who was captivated by Bolívar's vision of independence for Spanish America and who backed him on the condition that he free the slaves once his own country was liberated, and the wealthy merchant-adventurer Luis Brion, who placed his fleet at Bolívar's disposal. Ultimately, President Pétion's and Brion's backing won Bolívar the position of supreme commander.[38]

Armed, supplied, and financed by President Pétion, the expeditionary force landed on the northeast coast of Venezuela at the end of May 1816. Assuming the title of supreme chief of the Republic and captain general of the armies of Venezuela and New Granada, Bolívar issued a number of decrees to establish his regime. On June 2 he proclaimed "the absolute lib-

---

36 Díaz Díaz, *La reconquista española,* 1:139–394; Stoan, *Pablo Morillo,* 203–10.

37 John V. Lombardi, *Venezuela: The Search for Order, the Dream of Progress* (New York: Oxford University Press, 1982), 149, 138. Although Bolívar has had many admirers and detractors, few have offered as balanced an assessment of his abilities as Lombardi. See ibid., 137–49.

38 Gerhard Masur, *Simón Bolívar* (Albuquerque: University of New Mexico Press, 1969), 192–5.

erty of the slaves," but only on the condition that "all robust males, from the age of fourteen until sixty years" serve in the army. Although elsewhere he declared that "from now on there will only be one class of men in Venezuela, all will be citizens," the decree freeing the slaves stated: "The . . . [slave], who refuses to take up arms to comply with the sacred duty to defend his liberty, will be subject to servitude, not only he, but also his children younger than fourteen years of age, his wife, and his elderly parents."[39] Whereas others were invited to join the republic's forces, the slaves were coerced into doing so. As might be expected, these cynical decrees attracted few slaves to the liberating army; the majority supported the royal government.[40]

Initially, it appeared that Bolívar's critics were correct. He proved equally inept as a political and as a military leader. Few Venezuelans supported his movement. Although insurgent generals like Santiago Mariño, Manuel Piar, and Carlos Soublette won initial victories, after a few engagements royalist forces began to encircle the invaders near the port of Ocumare. On the evening of July 14, Bolívar, his mistress, and some of his officers escaped by sea, abandoning most of the invading army and the arms and equipment provided by President Pétion of Haiti.[41] The expedition was a great disaster, softened only by the fact that generals like Mariño and Piar were able to fight their way into the interior, where they established their own military and political bases.

The military debacle and Bolívar's desertion divided the leaders of the independence movement. Although some were still willing to follow him, others, like Mariño and Francisco Bermúdez, considered him a traitor. They refused to obey him or to allow him to return to Venezuela. Bolívar had little choice but to go into exile in Haiti. Fortunately for him, President Pétion remained confident that Bolívar would eventually succeed and continued to provide support. In Venezuela, independence leaders like Piar, Mariño, and Páez began to establish strongholds in the east. None, however, proved able to unite the others into a coherent force. Many believed that, despite his faults, Bolívar was the only one with the vision to become the supreme commander they needed. Finally, in October 1816, a council of war presided over by Piar agreed to recall Bolívar on the condition that he assume only military command and that a congress be convened to organize the government. Bolívar accepted, apparently agreeing to the terms.

---

39 See the decrees of June 2 and July 6, 1816 in Simón Bolívar *Proclamas y discursos del Libertador* (Caracas: Litografía del Comercio, 1939), 148–51.

40 Masur, *Simón Bolívar,* 198.

41 Even his sympathetic biographer, Masur, acknowledges that "Bolívar's conduct on that night was inexcusable. . . . It is unforgivable that, after the collapse, Bolívar deserted his army without even saving the vital equipment." Ibid., 201.

As he wrote before departing for Venezuela: "Arms will destroy the tyrants in vain, if we do not establish a political order capable of repairing the ravages of the revolution. The military way consists of force and force is not a government."[42]

Bolívar landed at Barcelona on December 31, 1816, with supplies and equipment, but he did not immediately command the allegiance of all the independence leaders. Some had already established their own areas of influence; Mariño dominated the northeast, Páez the *llanos,* and Piar Guayana along the Orinoco River. Although they recognized Bolívar as their titular leader, they often ignored his instructions. Since Mariño appeared the most hostile, Bolívar and his small force moved southeast into the Orinoco, where Piar assured him that the possibilities for success were great. The move provided Bolívar with great flexibility. He had access to the sea and the support of Brion's fleet, as well as the *llanos* and its livestock. Their combined forces slowly secured control of the region. On July 17, 1817, they captured the city of Angostura, which became the temporary capital of a restored Republic of Venezuela.

Bolívar's success did not end the division among the republican leaders. On May 8 Mariño had convened a congress in the coastal town of Cariaco, forming a separate government. Some backed the assembly of Cariaco because it offered the possibility of establishing the civilian congress that many desired.[43] But others opposed the assembly as a cynical attempt to transfer power to Mariño. Military men, like civilians, were divided. Whereas some officers recognized the congress, others, such as Urdaneta and Antonio José de Sucre, supported Bolívar.

After the victory at Angostura, Bolívar felt strong enough to assert his authority over the dissenters. He chose to discipline not Mariño, who retained command of his forces, but his former ally Piar, who had resigned his command in disagreement with Bolívar's policies and who had received a passport to travel abroad on June 30.[44] Fearing that Piar would join Mariño's movement and alleging that the *mulato* general was fomenting a rev-

42 Bolívar to Cortés Madariaga, Puerto Príncipe, November 26, 1816 in *Cartas del Libertador,* 1:339; Masur, *Simón Bolívar,* 202–3; Salvador de Madariaga, *Bolívar,* 2 vols. (Mexico: Editorial Hermes, 1951), 1:558–61.

43 Whereas most scholars interpret the Congreso de Cariaco merely as an attempt by Mariño to grasp power, Baltazar Vallenilla Lanz observes: "In that dawn of legality beats the . . . idea of a Republic. . . . There could have been a mistake, but not the preconceived plan to wrest from Bolívar all his authority." In José Gil Portoul, *Historia constitucional de Venezuela,* 2 vols., 5th ed. (Caracas: Librería Piñango, 1967), 1:17.

44 On June 19, 1817, Bolívar wrote Piar: "Do not insist on leaving your post. If you were the commander, I would not abandon you, as I will not abandon whoever might be in command tomorrow, . . . as long as that person possessed legitimacy and the *patria* needed him. The *patria* needs you. . . . Do not doubt my sincerity. . . . I am your true friend (soy su amigo de corazon)." Bolívar to Manuel Piar, San Félix, June 19, 1817, Bolívar, *Cartas del Libertador,* 1:381–2.

olution of the people of color, Bolívar ordered his arrest. Piar was captured; court martialed for desertion, rebellion, and treason; and executed on October 16, 1817. As Bolívar's aide, Daniel Florencio O'Leary, noted: "General Mariño, no doubt, merited the same fate as Piar, but was less dangerous than he, and only one example was sufficient."[45] The execution had the intended effect; Mariño, as well as the others, recognized Bolívar as the supreme chief.

Although Bolívar had returned to Venezuela after agreeing to convene a congress, he preferred ruling with unquestioned power. Nevertheless, a number of prominent civilians insisted on a more orderly form of government. Therefore, on November 1, 1817, he established a council of government and state to act in lieu of a congress. The supreme chief, however, retained final authority. Bolívar was determined to use his power to force Americans to support the Third Republic of Venezuela. To that end he issued two decrees. The first ordered the expropriation of royalist properties, both Spanish and American, which were to be divided among his troops in descending order according to rank. The second established martial law requiring that "All men residing in the free territory of Venezuela, from the age of fourteen years until sixty inclusively will report . . . to be enrolled [in the army]. All those who, after eight days from the publication of this decree, are apprehended without being enrolled in some [military] body will be either considered traitors to the *Patria,* or as deserters, and as such irremissibly executed regardless of how numerous they may be."[46] It was war to the death in another form. In his zeal to free South America, Bolívar carried out acts as violent and bloody as those of his most ruthless royalist opponents.

Neither the republicans nor the royalists triumphed in 1818. During that year, Bolívar had only limited military success. His forces, which joined Páez in the *llanos,* conducted a series of attacks against the royalists. Bolívar managed to drive Morillo's army from Calabozo, at the entrance to the *llanos,* but his other campaigns were unsuccessful. His military failures so disenchanted republicans that some proposed that Páez be named supreme commander. Although Bolívar's efforts to take Caracas ended in disaster in March and April, the royalists lacked the resources to defeat the republicans in their redoubts.[47]

45 Daniel Florencio O'Leary, *Memorias,* 3 vols. (Caracas: Imprenta de "El Monitor," 1883), 1:429. Masur, however, observes: "It is questionable whether Mariño was less dangerous than Piar. But Piar was a better victim to Bolívar's assumption of authority." Masur, *Simón Bolívar,* 219, 205–20; Madariaga, *Bolívar,* 1:570–91; Gil Fortoul, *Historia constitucional de Venezuela,* 1:377–92.

46 Bolívar, *Proclamas y discursos del Libertador,* 178–81.

47 Vicente Lecuna, *Crónica razonada de las guerras de Bolívar,* 3 vols. (New York: Colonial Press, 1950), 2:101–208; Stoan, *Pablo Morillo,* 213–20.

At the end of 1818, the republicans held portions of the northeast, the southeast, and the *llanos,* while the royalists controlled the central and western regions of the coast and the highlands. The republicans possessed a very effective cavalry, the *llaneros,* but a poorly trained and undisciplined infantry. Although the royalists lacked an effective cavalry, they had a highly disciplined and superb infantry. Thus, the royalists were at the mercy of republican cavalry in the *llanos,* but their infantry dominated the highlands. Although both sides controlled much territory, it was the royalists who governed the most densely populated provinces, including Caracas, the most populous and wealthy province of Venezuela. Most of New Granada continued under royal control, although its people remained exceedingly restive because of the harsh royalist repression. The few Spanish troops that remained in New Granada after Morillo returned to Venezuela in January 1817 garrisoned the port of Cartagena. The interior of the kingdom was patrolled by American royalist troops from Venezuela.

The military impasse prompted civilian republicans to challenge Bolívar's autocratic rule. Increasingly civilians, particularly lawyers, whom the supreme chief learned to detest, insisted on convening a congress. Like some royalist officials during the constitutional period (1810–1814), Bolívar repeatedly argued: "It is presently impossible to establish a representative government and a genuinely liberal constitution, an end towards which are directed all my efforts and the most ardent desires of my heart."[48] Ultimately, he was forced to capitulate to civilian pressures. On October 1, 1818, Bolívar asked the council of state to convene elections. Since the nation was at war, the body determined that it could not implement the electoral requirements of the Venezuelan Constitution of 1811. Instead, it allocated five deputies to each of Venezuela's six provinces and five to Casanare in New Granada because that province had joined the Venezuelan republicans in fighting for independence. At the time, only the provinces of Margarita and Guayana, which were in republican hands, elected their own representatives. Most deputies were selected by military and political officials in republican territory, and several represented provinces other than their own.

The Congress of Angostura met on February 15, 1819, with twenty-six deputies representing the provinces of Caracas, Barcelona, Cumaná, Barinas, Guayana, and Margarita. The supreme chief of the republic inaugurated the congress by reading a proposed constitution. Bolívar recom-

---

48 Quoted in Madariaga, *Bolívar,* 1:592. The distinguished jurist Fernando Peñalver was among those who convinced Bolívar that he could no longer delay convening congress. As Bolívar subsequently acknowledged: "You know that you were the one who most encouraged me to convene the Congress of Angostura.. . ." Bolívar to Fernando Peñalver, Guayaquil, May 30, 1823 in Simón Bolívar, *Obras completas,* 2 vols. (Havana: Editorial Lex, 1947), 1:758–9.

mended that Venezuela establish a parliament similar to that of Britain, with an elected chamber of deputies and a hereditary senate. Although he declared: "When I speak about the British government I refer to its republican aspects; and, in truth, can a system which recognizes popular sovereignty, the division and equality of the branches of government, civil liberty, freedom of conscience and of the press, and all that is sublime in politics be called a monarchy? can there be more liberty in any sort of republic?", he also insisted on a highly centralized government in which power was concentrated in a powerful lifetime executive unfettered by congressional authority. On that point he was adamant. Bolívar rejected the United States' constitution, which vested considerable power in the legislature. He also dismissed the Spanish Constitution of 1812, which, although unicameral, contained most of the provisions of the English constitution he lauded but possessed the grave disadvantage of severely restricting the power of the chief executive. He concluded by proposing "the union of New Granada and Venezuela in a great state."[49] As one of its first acts, congress elected Bolívar president and the *neogranadino* Francisco Antonio Zea vice president. Then it debated the president's proposals while he returned to the field of battle.[50]

During 1818 and 1819, republican military forces increased while royalist strength declined. Enough foreign officers and supplies had arrived by mid-1818 to restructure significantly the republican army. In August, Santander became governor of Casanare province, where he probed royalist defenses. Páez continued to hold royalist forces at bay in the *llanos.* By the beginning of 1819, the republicans were in a relatively strong position. The royalist lines, on the other hand, were overextended: The 10,000 Spanish troops that Morillo had brought with him in 1815 were dispersed across South America from Caracas to Lima. The royalist units in Venezuela and New Granada now consisted mostly of Americans. It was becoming harder to recruit royalist troops locally, and it was unlikely that Spanish reinforcements would arrive in the near future.

San Martín's victory at Maipó suggested the strategy that would allow Bolívar's forces to end the stalemate in northern South America. It had long become evident that although the republicans could defend the *llanos,* they could not take the highlands or Caracas. But New Granada could be invaded from the *llanos* by going over the Andes. Such an attack would outflank Morillo's forces and, if successful, lead to the liberation of Bogotá and eventually of Caracas. The opportunity the republicans sought came in May 1819 when Santander defeated royalist forces in Casanare. Bolívar joined

49 Bolívar, *Proclamas y discursos del Libertador,* 202–35.
50 Pedro Grases, ed., *Actas del Congreso de Angostura* (Caracas: Universidad Central de Venezuela, 1969), 95–103.

him at the end of the month. During late June and early July, in an epic maneuver, their combined forces marched over Andean passes higher than those crossed by San Martín's army. Countless men perished, among them more than a quarter of the British officers. The republican invasion caught the royalists unprepared. By the end of July, Bolívar's army was advancing rapidly on Bogotá. On August 7, Venezuelan royalist forces in New Granada succumbed to *neogranadino* and Venezuelan republican troops at Boyacá, south of Tunja, near Bogotá. Three days later, Bolívar occupied the capital. It was a tremendous victory. Virtually all New Granada, with the exception of Cartagena, was in republican hands.[51]

The victory in New Granada came just in time for Bolívar to solidify his political position. In his absence, the legislators at Angostura began to reconsider the power they had granted him. Although it accepted many of Bolívar's constitutional proposals, including discarding the federalism of the First Republic and introducing centralism, congress rejected the hereditary senate and the lifetime presidency. The congressmen also clashed with Vice President Zea, who represented Bolívar, ultimately forcing him to resign in favor of General Juan Bautista Arismendi. After appointing Santander vice president of New Granada, Bolívar returned to Angostura to confront his critics. The triumphant president forced the legislature to accept his dictates. On December 17, 1819, congress approved the Fundamental Law of the Republic of Colombia, whereby the former New Kingdom of Granada, in its entirety, became a single state. The new constitution, however, recognized the significance of the former viceroyalty's semiautonomous regions when it declared: "The Republic of Colombia will be divided into three large departments: Venezuela, Quito, and Cundinamarca. . . . The capitals of these departments will be the cities of Caracas, Quito, and Bogotá." A new national congress would meet the following year in the town of Rosario de Cúcuta. In the interim, Bolívar would serve as president of the republic, Juan Germán Rocio as vice president of Venezuela, and Santander as vice president of New Granada. Quito would receive a vice president "after the liberating armies entered there."[52] The congress that established the new nation of Colombia contained no representatives from Quito, very few from New Granada, and only *suplentes* from most provinces of Venezuela, including the most populous, Caracas. In that regard, the leaders of the new nation ignored regional and provincial interests, which would quickly reemerge.

51 Lecuna, *Crónica razonada*, 2:300–49; Alfred Hasbrouck, *Foreign Legionaries in the Liberation of Spanish South America* (New York: Octagon Books, 1969), 190–217; Daniel Florencio O'Leary, *Memorias*, 3 vols. (Caracas: Imprenta de "El Monitor," 1883), 1;526–86.
52 Grases, *Actas del Congreso de Angostura*, 355–60; Gil Fortoul, *Historia constitucional de Venezuela*, 1:405–26.

The creation of the new Republic of Colombia did not end the royalist threat. Although no longer capable of reconquering republican territories, they remained a formidable force in Venezuela that the republicans could not overcome. If Field Marshal Morillo received Spanish reinforcements from the large expeditionary force then assembling in Cádiz, he might turn the tide. That possibility ended on January 1, 1820, when Spanish *liberales* convinced the troops in Cádiz to rebel and restore the Constitution of 1812.

The Spanish Constitution Restored

The struggle in America was but one source of dissatisfaction in Spain. The king not only possessed a *camarilla* of friends that undermined his official ministers but was also widely believed to associate with disreputable elements. Once again, a Spanish monarch had discredited himself in the eyes of the people. The restored Inquisition added to the unrest by relentlessly pursuing *liberales* and Masons. However, the most vexing issue for many Spaniards was the reestablishment of centralized administration. The provinces, which had become accustomed to home rule as a result of six years of war, began to realize that the Constitution had permitted them more local control than any·previous government. The mounting economic crisis, which the Crown failed to resolve, added to the growing criticism of the regime. Many Spaniards, particularly those in the cities, came to believe that absolutism had failed and that a return to constitutional government was urgently needed.

Spaniards, who had fought the French for six years, were dismayed when Fernando restored the higher clergy, the nobility, the old bureaucracy, and the regular army to power. The monarch rewarded those who had failed to defend Spain from the French while dismissing most guerrilla generals, the heroes of the struggle, who had expected rewards and high positions in the king's government. Only a few received provincial posts. After having wielded authority over entire provinces, most were expected to return quietly to their old lives.[53]

Opposition to Fernando's rule coalesced in clandestine organizations. Although *tertulias* had long been occasions for political discussion, the first secret societies appeared in Cádiz during the early days of the constitutional period. Spanish *liberales* and army officers formed clandestine groups, often called *sociedades patrióticas*. Masonic lodges, established initially by the French but controlled by Spanish officers and *liberales* after 1814, became

---

53 Artola, *La España de Fernando VII*, 555–62, 593–606; José Luis Comellas, *Los primeros pronunciamientos en España, 1814–1820* (Madrid: Consejo Superior de Investigaciones Científicas, 1958), 31–54.

covert centers of opposition. As Evaristo San Miguel, a prominent *liberal* officer, declared: "The Masonic lodges became *liberal* and conspiratorial juntas. The terms constitutional and Mason were synonymous."[54]

The conspirators possessed a variety of motives. Many merely wanted jobs, some sought to end the struggle in America, and others wished to restore constitutional rule. A few equated the American demand for home rule with the Spanish desire for local representative government. Indeed, one of them, Javier Mina, believed that the insurgent struggle in America was really an attempt to restore the Constitution.

The Mina insurrection is an example of the complex relationship that existed between Spanish *liberales* and American autonomists. Mina was a hero of the Spanish War of Independence who, like other guerrilla leaders, could find no employment at home after the war with France ended. When offered a command in New Spain to fight the insurgents, he indignantly refused, insisting that the cause defended by the Americans was the same as that of Spain. Instead, he and his uncle Francisco Espoz y Mina, another great guerrilla general, rebelled in 1814, demanding the restoration of the constitution. The insurrection failed, and its leaders fled. At the request of Father Mier, the exiled Mina agreed to lead an invasion of New Spain to restore constitutional rule there and then extend it to Spain and to other parts of the Monarchy. The expedition, which obtained the aid of Spanish Americans, Britons, and citizens of the United States, landed in northern New Spain in mid-1816. Although initially victorious, the royalists eventually captured and executed Mina and imprisoned Father Mier.[55]

Conspiracies and insurrections to restore the Constitution continued. Another rebellion occurred in Spain even before Mina attacked New Spain. Juan Díaz Porlier, a native of Buenos Aires and a hero of the war against the French, rebelled in La Coruña in September 1815, demanding the return of the Constitution. In 1816 Vicente Richard planned to assassinate the king in a brothel. The following year, Lieutenant General Luis Lacy rebelled in Cataluña. Shortly thereafter, the Inquisition uncovered another conspiracy known as the *Great Masonic Plot*. In 1818 officials thwarted an attempt to restore Carlos IV to the throne as a constitutional monarch. When the plan failed, Colonel Joaquín Vidal led an insurrection in Valencia. All these

---

54 Evaristo San Miguel, *Vida de D. Agustín Argüelles*, 4 vols. (Madrid: Imprenta del Colegio de Sordo-Mudos, 1851–1852), 2:62–3; José A. Ferrer Benimeli, *Masonería española contemporánea*, 2 vols. (Madrid: Siglo Veintiuno, 1980), 1:82–4; Alberto Gil Novales, *Las Sociedades Patrióticas (1820–1823)*, 2 vols. (Madrid: Editorial Tecnos, 1975), 1:5–16.

55 Harris G. Warren, "The Origin of General Mina's Invasion of Mexico," *Southwestern Historical Quarterly*, 52 (July 1938), 1–20; Comellas, *Los primeros pronunciamientos*, 165–86; Harris G. Warren, "Xavier Mina's Invasion of Mexico," *HAHR*, 23 (February 1943), 52–76; Guadalupe Jiménez Codinach, *La Gran Bretaña y la independencia de México, 1808–1821* (Mexico: Fondo de Cultura Económica, 1991), 265–333.

attempts to restore the Constitution failed, and their leaders forfeited their lives.[56]

Opposition in Spain increased despite the government's repression. But in spite of the great discontent in the cities, none of the insurrections had attracted widespread popular support. Opposition to the war in America provided the *liberales* with a new opportunity to advance their cause. In 1819, they exploited discontent in the large expeditionary army encamped in Andalucía awaiting transportation to the New World. Arguing that the American struggle would end if the Constitution were restored, Cádiz Masons attempted to convince leading officers to take action. Colonels Antonio Quiroga and Juan O'Donojú, who had been implicated in the Great Masonic Plot, were receptive but cautious. On January 1, 1820, Major Rafael Riego, commander of the Asturias Regiment, raised the banner of rebellion, demanding the restoration of the Constitution. Other units followed, but the government rapidly isolated the movement by dispatching new troops to occupy the cities of the south. Although the rebels marched throughout southern Spain seeking support, they found none. It seemed certain that the Crown would defeat this insurrection as it had previous rebellions.

Regionalism succeeded where armed insurrection failed. Discontented with the political and economic failures of Fernando's centralized absolutist government, the provincial cities of Spain seized the opportunity presented by the January uprising to restore the home rule granted them by the Constitution of 1812. On February 21, La Coruña rebelled, immediately restoring its provincial deputation and constitutional *ayuntamiento.* Other northern cities also restored their constitutional governments. By March 5 large cities, such as Zaragoza and Barcelona, had reestablished provincial deputations and constitutional *ayuntamientos.* Fernando VII capitulated on March 7 after the *liberales* mobilized the masses in Madrid, demanding the restoration of the Constitution. The king appointed a *Junta Provisional Consultiva,* composed of *liberales,* to advise him until the Cortes met.[57]

The Junta Provisional rapidly restored the constitutional structures of government. Under the Constitution, the council of state consisted of forty members, twelve of them from America. During the transition, an interim council of state began functioning with only thirty members, nine from the New World. The king also appointed a ministry of *liberales,* recently

56 Comellas, *Los primeros pronunciamientos,* 187–302.

57 Antonio Alcalá Galiano, *Recuerdos de un Anciano* (Madrid: Edicions Atlas, 1955), 91–131; Ramón Mesonero Romanos, *Memorias de un setentón* (Madrid: Ediciones Atlas, 1957), 97–9; Artola, *La España de Fernando VII,* 634–64; Charles W. Fehrenbach, "A Study of Spanish Liberalism: The Revolution of 1820" (Ph.D. diss., University of Texas, Austin, 1961), 73–85.

released from prison – the "jail birds," as he called them. Elections were scheduled for a new Cortes that would meet in July.

The new *liberal* regime sought to end the conflict in America through conciliation. On April 11, 1820, it instructed the viceroys and captains general in the New World to publish the monarch's decree restoring the Constitution and encouraging everyone, including the dissidents, to swear allegiance to the charter. The former constitutional bodies were to be restored and elections held immediately. Although insurgent leaders were encouraged to acknowledge the Constitution, even those who refused would be allowed to retain their authority if they recognized the Monarchy. The government ordered a cease-fire, an exchange of prisoners, and the initiation of negotiations. Finally, as they had done in 1809 and during the first constitutional period, the authorities in Spain appointed royal commissioners to resolve American grievances.[58]

The Junta Provisional decided not to restore the old Cortes but to convene new elections. It issued a new *convocatoria* on March 22, indicating that because of the delays in holding elections in America, thirty New World *suplentes* would be chosen from among individuals residing in the Peninsula. Americans in Spain, some of them recently released from confinement, vehemently protested that the number of *suplentes* allocated to the New World was inadequate. They insisted on doubling New World representation, and some refused to participate in the election of *suplentes* unless the government acceded to their demands. Despite numerous protests, the Junta Provisional refused to modify its decision. Convinced by the distinguished parliamentarian from Coahuila, New Spain, Father Ramos Arizpe that it was better to possess fewer representatives than none at all, the Americans ultimately agreed to participate, electing twenty-nine *suplentes:* fifteen for América Septentrional – New Spain seven, Guatemala two, Cuba two, the Philippines two, Santo Domingo one, and Puerto Rico one – and fourteen for América Meridional – Peru five, New Granada three, Buenos Aires three, Venezuela two, and Chile one.[59]

58 The decree and other instructions arrived in Quito on September 4, 1820. ANH: PQ, vol. 579, ff. 18–47.

59 D.U.L.A., *Idea general de la conducta política de D. Miguel Ramos Arizpe, natural de la provincia de Coahuila, como diputado que ha sido por esta provincia en las Cortes generales y extraordinarias de la monarchía {sic} española desde el año de 1810 hasta el de 1821* (Madrid: Imprenta de Herculana de Villa, 1822); Juan de Dios Cañedo, *Manifiesto a la nación española, sobre la representación de las provincias de ultramar en las próximas Cortes* (Madrid: Imprenta de Vega, 1820); Manuel de Vidaurre, *Manifiesto sobre la nulidad de las elecciones que a nombre de los países ultramarinos se practicaron en Madrid por algunos americanos el día de 28 y 29 de mayo del año de 1820* (Madrid: Imprenta de Vega, 1820); *Lista de los señores diputados nombrados para las Cortes del año 1820 y 1821* (Mexico: Reimpresa en la oficina de J. B. Arizpe, 1820). Extensive documentation on the American arguments for greater representation is located in AGI: Indiferente, 1523.

The people of America did not wait for formal decrees. On April 16, the day after news of Fernando's restoration of the Constitution arrived, great crowds in Havana forced Captain General Juan Minuel Cagigal to swear allegiance to the charter. Without waiting for instructions, the coastal cities of Mérida and Campeche in New Spain restored the Constitution in early May. Veracruz and Jalapa followed later that month. Although he would have preferred to await formal instructions, public pressure in Mexico City forced Viceroy Juan Ruiz de Apodaca to proclaim the Constitution on May 31. Guatemala, Venezuela, and Puerto Rico restored the Constitution in June. News reached Lima and Quito in late July and August. Shortly thereafter, San Martín's expeditionary force landed at Pisco, on the Peruvian coast. In accord with their instructions, the Peruvian authorities, like those in Venezuela, arranged for a cease-fire, the exchange of prisoners, and negotiation to end the conflict.[60]

The public in those regions of America under royalist control viewed the restored constitutional system with great enthusiasm. Thousands of pamphlets, newspapers, and broadsides circulated in which writers discussed the significance of the restored constitutional order and lauded the constitutional heroes of the Peninsula. As the *guayaquileño* Vicente Rocafuerte later recalled: "The rebirth of . . . [the Constitution's] second epoch was welcomed with great joy. It received the most tender praises. No public paper nor poem was published which did not have as its object to praise it and recommend it [to the people]." Some referred to the Constitution as the *Sacred Code,* the *Divine Charter,* or *la Niña bonita* (the pretty girl). Even insurgent supporters, like Carlos María de Bustamante in New Spain, argued in a pamphlet entitled *The Constitution of Cádiz, or Why I Love the Constitution* that the charter served the best interests of America.[61]

Although the royal authorities, with varying degrees of enthusiasm, restored the constitutional order in those regions under their control, there was a considerable difference between América Septentrional and América Meridional. Whereas the former experienced fully the new political system in its first and second periods, the latter did not. Autonomists who did not

---

60 Jaime E. Rodríguez O., *The Emergence of Spanish America: Vicente Rocafuerte and Spanish Americanism, 1808–1832* (Berkeley: University of California Press, 1975), 1; Rodríguez O., "The Transition from Colony to Nation: New Spain, 1820–1821," in *Mexico in the Age of Democratic Revolutions,* ed. Jaime E. Rodríguez O. (Boulder: Lynne Rienner, 1994), 101–2; Rodríguez, *The Cadiz Experiment,* 131; Antonio Gómez Vizuete, "Los primeros ayuntamientos liberales en Puerto Rico (1812–1814 y 1820–1823)," *Anuario de Estudios Americanos,* 47 (1990), 602–3; ANH: PQ, vol. 577, ff. 1–5; Timothy E. Anna, *The Fall of Royal Government in Peru* (Lincoln: University of Nebraska Press, 1979), 160–1; Stoan, *Pablo Morillo,* 228–9.

61 Vicente Rocafuerte, *Bosquejo ligerísimo de la Revolución de Mégico* [sic] *desde el grito de Iguala hasta la proclamación imperial de Iturbide* (Filadelfia: Imprenta de Teracrouef y Naroajeb, 1822), 4; Rodríguez O., "The Transition from Colony to Nation," 102–5.

implement the Spanish constitutional system and who introduced more limited forms of representative government, controlled large regions of South America. In 1820 the Río de la Plata, Chile, and parts of Venezuela and New Granada were in the hands of independent regimes that were unwilling to return to the Monarchy, even under the Constitution. Some South American political leaders, however, still favored establishing independent kingdoms with European, preferably Spanish, rulers and retaining ties to the Spanish Crown in a federal system of monarchies. In that sense, no region of Spanish America had completely cut its links with the Spanish Monarchy.

The constitutional elections dominated the political life of most royalist areas, particularly in América Septentrional. Viceroy Apodaca distributed more than 1,000 copies of the Constitution to the cities and towns of New Spain, and Captain General Carlos Urrutia disseminated about 500 copies in the Kingdom of Guatemala. By the end of the year, hundreds of constitutional *ayuntamientos* and the eight provincial deputations in New Spain and Guatemala had been restored.

North America was the site of intense political activity. Since there were neither literacy nor property qualifications for voting, nearly all adult males were eligible to participate. In New Spain, for example, elections for its six provincial deputations occurred between August and October 1820. Two separate elections were held for deputies to the Cortes: one rapidly in the autumn of 1820 for the 1821–1822 parliament and a second starting in December for the 1822–1823 session of the Cortes. In addition, more than 1,000 elections were held in December 1820 for the constitutional *ayuntamientos* of 1821. Thus, from June 1820 to March 1821, electioneering and elections preoccupied the politically active population of New Spain – perhaps numbering hundreds of thousands. Similar intense political participation occurred in the Kingdom of Guatemala, Cuba, and Puerto Rico.[62]

Although elections were held in South America, there politics was more restrained because of the area's extensive warfare. Quito's experience during the second constitutional period is illustrative of the conflicts and difficulties of holding elections at a time of widespread insurgency. In mid-1820, General Melchor Aymerich, president of the Audiencia, faced insurgencies in Colombia in the north and Peru in the south. Only the coastal provinces on the west and the jungles on the eastern side of the cordillera appeared quiet. Fears of insurgent threats became intense in July and August as reports from Barbacoas and Guayaquil indicated widespread unrest on the

62 Rodríguez O., "The Transition from Colony to Nation," 101–5; Rodríguez, *The Cádiz Experiment,* 131–7; Gómez Vizuete, "Los primeros ayuntamientos liberales," 22–6.

coast. In an effort to maintain order, the *audiencia* imposed travel restrictions throughout the kingdom.[63]

In those tense circumstances, news reached Quito on August 27, 1820, that the Constitution had been restored. As the auditor of war later recounted:

The king's dispositions were immediately executed. . . . Not only was the Constitution published and the oath taken by all the civil[, clerical,] and military authorities . . ., but the constitutional *cabildos* that were functioning before . . . [they were abolished by Fernando VII in 1814] were restored. Everything possible was done given the critical circumstances in which these territories found themselves. The Province of Guayaquil and then Cuenca rebelled [in September and October], and, shortly thereafter, and almost at the same day and hour, all the *partidos* of this [Province of] Quito. [The revolt was so extensive] that this capital suffered a rigorous siege in the month of November. . . . Then it was not possible to think about anything other than restoring peace and tranquility. It was not practical to carry the constitutional system to its ultimate perfection. First, it was necessary to defeat the enemy and to recover the lost towns. . . .[64]

After consulting the *audiencia* and the Ayuntamiento of Quito, Aymerich instructed the cities and towns of the realm not to hold the elections scheduled for December 1820, but to keep their constitutional officials in office for another year. These emergency measures were taken until the Province of Quito, as the realm was called under the Constitution, was pacified. The Ayuntamiento of Quito initially agreed that provincial elections would be suspended given the nature of the "circumstances of the day."[65] Support for the emergency measures, however, waned as months passed. By May 1821, criticism of Aymerich's failure to hold elections became widespread and, as a result, despite the continuing insurgency and the constant threat of "treason," the *jefe político superior* was forced to schedule elections. He informed the cities and towns not under siege by the insurgents that "these military enterprises do not for the present constitute an insuperable obstacle to introducing the constitutional system in its totality." Therefore he convened elections for the provincial deputation and for the Cortes. Since it was impractical to conduct a new electoral census, the authorities decided to form one based on the previous count. But since "the *partidos* of Popayán, Cali, Buga, Barbacoas, other towns of the coast, and Jaén de Bracamoros . . . are presently occupied by the enemy," only twelve *partidos* in the highlands would hold elections. As in the previous constitutional period, the Province of Quito would elect six deputies to the Cortes, two *suplentes,* and seven deputies to the provincial deputation. The

63 Correspondence on these matters is located in ANH: PQ, vols. 574, 575, and 579.
64 Auditor de Guerra to Melchor Aymerich, July 21, 1821, ANH: PQ, vol. 579, ff. 34–8.
65 AMQ, Actas del Consejo (January 1, 1821); ANH: PQ, vol. 579., ff. 18–47.

authorities redistributed the number of *compromisarios* and parish electors among the "free" *partidos* in order to reach the appropriate number of eighteen *partido* electors, who were to convene in Quito on October 12, 1821, to complete the electoral process.[66]

The elections proved to be lengthy and complicated. Some cities and towns found it difficult to organize them and reported that they had been forced to delay elections "because of the political circumstances" of the day. Authorities in Riobamba, for example, declared that a large proportion of the city's population so feared the insurgents that they had fled to the countryside. Cuenca officials were concerned with subversives who were determined to open the city to the rebels from Guayaquil. As had occurred in the earlier constitutional period, there were many complaints that elections were being manipulated. Discontented persons in the Partido of Cuenca requested that elections there be annulled because of irregularities. As before, some electors were unwilling to assume their obligation to travel to the *partido* elections. Because of these and other problems, the elections were not completed until the end of the year. Despite the growing power of the republican forces from Guayaquil, the constitutional order was in full operation in all royalist-held areas as 1822 began.[67] Although circumstances varied widely, comparable elections also were held in Peru and Upper Peru and in the royalist areas of Venezuela and New Granada.[68]

When the Cortes convened in Madrid in July 1820, the American deputies, led by the North American contingent, again raised the American Question. They demanded equal representation, free trade, and the abolition of monopolies. They also insisted that a provincial deputation be established in every intendancy in the New World. Because Spain was becoming embroiled in internal political conflicts between the moderate *doceañistas,* the men of the first constitutional period, and the *exaltados,* the younger and more radical men of 1820 who wanted rapid political change, the *suplentes* from America found it difficult to obtain a full hearing of their proposals. Nevertheless, the Cortes considered projects for economic and institutional improvements in the New World. It also authorized the establishment of one new provincial deputation in Valladolid, New Spain, before recessing at the end of 1820.

The arrival of the proprietary deputies in 1821 reinforced the American delegation. During the months of February to June 1821, more than forty proprietary deputies arrived from New Spain, six from Guatemala, one from Cuba, one from Panama, and three from Venezuela. They and the

66 ANH: PQ, vol. 579, ff. 32–47.
67 Ibid., vols. 579, 582.
68 Anna, *The Fall of Royal Government in Peru,* 168.

suplentes who remained in the new session constituted a powerful coalition. They continued to press the American Question and to criticize the government for failing to resolve the issues that led to the conflict in the New World. Although the American delegation in the Cortes eventually grew to seventy-eight deputies, it constituted a minority that was continually overruled by the Spanish majority on such questions as representation and autonomy.[69]

Nevertheless, the deputies from New Spain, who constituted the overwhelming majority of Americans, were determined to win concessions from the Cortes. They possessed instructions from their provinces demanding greater autonomy and insisting on provincial deputations for every former intendancy in the New World. In 1820 José Mariano Michelena of Michoacán developed a plan that combined elements of the widely discussed proposals for American autonomy with the new system of constitutional government. The *suplentes* discussed the project at a series of meetings in Madrid, obtaining support for the proposal from the proprietary deputies when they arrived.

Internal Spanish politics, however, prevented the government from addressing the American Question. Shortly after the Cortes reconvened in March 1821, the king dismissed the ministry, provoking a political crisis. When the monarch named a new moderate government of unknown *doceañistas,* a group of extreme radicals known as the *comuneros* appealed to the masses, inciting them to turn against the government. The new ministry managed to retain control of Madrid, but the *comuneros* dominated the provincial cities. In Barcelona, they seized the *ayuntamiento* and deported alleged absolutists. Similar acts occurred in Galicia, Cádiz, Sevilla, Málaga, Algeciras, and Cartagena. In Alcoy workers burned textile mills. Spain rapidly was becoming an armed camp where the radical masses in the towns opposed both the moderate government in Madrid and the conservative countryside.[70]

Despite the Peninsula's political turbulence, the American deputies continued to insist that the government pay more attention to New World issues. On May 3, at the suggestion of the Conde de Toreno, the Cortes named a committee of four Spaniards and five Americans – four *novohispanos,* Lorenzo de Zavala, Lucas Alamán, Francisco Fagoaga, and Bernardino Amati, and the Venezuelan Fermín Paul – to consider the matter. The Americans were ecstatic. As Ramos Arizpe declared:

69 The records of the American deputies who arrived at these Cortes are located in ACDM: Documentación Electoral, legs. 7–9. See also Mario Rodríguez, "The 'American Question' at the Cortes of Madrid," *The Americas,* 38:3 (January 1982), 293–306.

70 Fehrenbach, "A Study of Spanish Liberalism," 202–25; Artola, *La España de Fernando VII,* 695–705; José L. Comellas, *El trienio constitucional* (Madrid: Ediciones Rialp, 1963), 208–95.

Madrid and the entire Peninsula constitute a glorious spectacle. It is an entirely free theater where the most important questions of practical politics relative to the future of Spain's America are treated. Questions which a few years ago were a crime to indicate in the most private of conversations, today are treated with the most absolute liberty. They are treated in *tertulias;* in the public patriotic societies in speeches and in very sound addresses; in the public papers; in the meetings of the deputies; and in a publicly named special commission of the Cortes cordially attended by the honorable secretaries of state and by many Spanish and American deputies.[71]

The optimism of the New World deputies seemed justified. It appeared that the government was disposed to grant greater autonomy to America. The first major concession occurred on May 8, 1821. After considerable debate, the Cortes agreed that a provincial deputation should be established in every intendancy in America.[72] It was a great triumph for the deputies of New Spain, who doubled the number of provincial deputations in their area. In mid-May the *ministro de Ultramar* (overseas minister) convened a meeting, which included former viceroys, captains general, and *visitadores* then in Madrid, to "agree upon a general project which ought to be presented [to the Cortes]." The officials concluded that three *regencies,* which the king would rule by means of Spanish princes under the Constitution, should be established in the New World.[73] If approved, the project would grant Americans the autonomous governments they desired.

Earlier, the deputies from New Spain had achieved a significant concession that would have far-reaching consequences. From the time the Cortes reconvened in 1820, New World representatives had argued that peace would be restored in their lands only if the authorities respected the constitutional rights of Americans. They charged that many royal officials currently serving in the New World were not only associated with the earlier repression but were also anti-American. Deputies Michelena and Ramos Arizpe of New Spain were among the most active in seeking the removal of the "anticonstitutional" and "brutal anti-American" officials, among them Viceroys Joaquín de Pezuela of Peru and Ruiz de Apodaca of New Spain, as well as Generals Morillo of Venezuela and José de la Cruz of New Galicia. The representatives of New Spain sought to replace Ruiz de Apodaca with

---

71 *Carta escrita a un americano sobre la forma de gobierno que para hacer practicable la Constitution y las leyes, conviene establecer en Nueva España atendida su actual situación* (Madrid: Ibarra, Impresor de Cámara de S. M., 1821).

72 Nettie Lee Benson, *La Diputación Provincial y el federalismo mexicano* (Mexico: El Colegio de México, 1955), 54–9.

73 Lucas Alamán, *Historia de Méjico, desde los primeros movimientos que prepararon su independencia en el año de 1808 hasta la época presente,* 5 vols. (Mexico: Imprenta de Lara, 1849–52), 5:548–9; Jaime Delgado, *España y México en el siglo XIX,* 3 vols. (Madrid: Consejo Superior de Investigaciones Científicas, 1950), 1:103–4.

an individual who shared their particular vision of New World autonomy. Michelena, a distinguished army officer and Mason, and Ramos Arizpe, another Mason and a renowned *doceañista,* relied on their extensive contacts among military men, *liberales,* and fellow Masons to achieve their ends. They ultimately succeeded when, in January 1821, the government appointed General Juan O'Donojú captain general and superior political chief of New Spain. The new official, a distinguished officer, *liberal,* and Mason, had served as minister of war during the first constitutional period, had conspired against the absolute monarch in 1818–1819, and was then serving as political chief of the Province of Sevilla.[74]

O'Donojú was well aware of the aspirations of the *novohispanos.* Michelena and Ramos Arizpe had discussed with him their plan of regencies for America. That project appeared to have the support of the government, as well as of the American deputies at the time O'Donojú departed for New Spain. In addition, the Cortes was then preparing to increase the number of provincial deputations in America. Indeed, Ramos Arizpe urged the legislature to pass the measure in time for O'Donojú to "take with him the order to establish deputations in all the intendancies."[75] Clearly, O'Donojú left the Peninsula believing that he had been charged with strengthening the constitutional order in New Spain and that, in all likelihood, he would also introduce the new system of American regencies.

In early June, many American deputies expected the government to approve an arrangement acceptable to the independent regimes in South America. Unfortunately, the king rejected the proposed regencies. Convinced that the project was a plot by his enemies to "drive him to the guillotine," Fernando VII refused "to send a crown prince to America."[76] As a result, the mixed committee of the Cortes could not offer the parliament a meaningful recommendation.

Undeterred, the Americans insisted upon presenting the Michelena plan to the Cortes. On June 25, 1821, they proposed dividing the New World into three kingdoms: New Spain and Guatemala; New Granada and the provinces of Tierra Firme; and Peru, Chile, and Buenos Aires. Each kingdom would possess its own *cortes,* which would govern under the Constitution of 1812. A Spanish prince or a person appointed by the king would preside over each area. Spain and the American realms would maintain special commercial, diplomatic, and defense relationships. Finally, the new

74 Alamán, *Historia de Méjico,* 5:33–4; Delgado, *España y México* 1:54–9.

75 Quoted in Benson, *La Diputación Provincial,* 57. Michelena, for example, informed the Cortes that he had met with O'Donojú to discuss that and other issues concerning New Spain. See España, Cortes, *Diario de las sesiones de Cortes: Legislatura de 1821,* 3 vols. (Madrid: Imprenta de J. A. García, 1871–1873), 2:2046.

76 Delgado, *España y México,* 1:103–4.

kingdoms would pay a portion of Spain's foreign debt. The following day, Ramos Arizpe and José María Couto submitted an alternative proposal for the autonomy of New Spain. In contrast to the earlier American plan, theirs did not require the appointment of a Spanish prince as ruler and provided close ties with the *madre patria* (mother country) by requiring that some deputies from the legislature in North America also serve in the Spanish parliament.[77]

The arrival of news that an independence movement had erupted in February 1821 in New Spain increased profoundly the divisions between American and Peninsular deputies. Although some Spaniards believed that a restructuring of the Spanish Monarchy, such as the one proposed by the New World representatives, was necessary to prevent the complete separation of America, most European deputies were convinced that such extreme concessions were unnecessary. Many considered the proposals of the New World deputies to be little more than thinly disguised mechanisms to achieve independence. Thus, neither the Michelena proposal, which had the support of all the American deputies, nor the Ramos Arizpe–Couto proposal on New Spain obtained the approval of the Cortes.

The failure to grant the New World greater autonomy further increased the conflict in the Cortes between Americans and Spaniards. New World deputies angrily denounced their Spanish colleagues, who responded with equally harsh criticism. The hostility of the Europeans became evident when discussion focused on the agenda for the special session of the Cortes to convene in September 1821. Although the principal question for the legislature was to be the internal political crisis in Spain, New World deputies insisted that the American Question be addressed in the special session. After an acrimonious debate, the Americans got their wish.

The special Cortes proved unable to arrange a compromise between American and Spanish interests. At the outset, the Spanish majority ruled that American *suplentes* could not participate because they had been elected only for one term. As a result, distinguished legislators such as Ramos Arizpe were excluded. News of the independence of New Spain and Guatemala only inflamed the passions of the Spaniards, who rejected O'Donojú's action in signing a treaty with the new American regime. Although *novohispano* deputies such as Lucas Alamán, Juan Gómez de Navarrete, and José María Puchet argued eloquently that unless the Cortes recognized the legitimacy of the New World's demands the Monarchy

---

77 Alamán, *Historia de Méjico,* 5:549–50; "Exposición presentada a las Cortes por los diputados de ultramar en la sesión de 25 de junio de 1821, sobre el estado actual de las provincias de que eran representantes, y medios convenientes para su definitiva pacificacón," in Alamán, *Historia de Méjico,* 5, Apéndice, 49–65; "Proyecto de ley para hacer que la Constitución de la monarquía española se cumpla y ejecute en la América española del Norte, conservando la integridad de la misma monarquía con mutua y verdadera utilidad en ambas Españas," in Delgado, *España y México,* 1:104–6.

would lose its New World kingdoms, most Spanish legislators still refused to make any concessions to the Americans.

As time passed, more and more American deputies lost hope that a compromise could be reached and returned to their *patrias.* In an attempt to retain New World participation in the Cortes, some Spanish *liberales* proposed a conciliatory measure exploring the means of retaining the Spanish Nation as a federal Monarchy. As with previous efforts to deal with the American Question, the majority blocked any action on the matter. On February 13, 1822, parliament decided to postpone the American Question until the next regular Cortes met. No New World deputy objected because virtually none remained in the Spanish parliament.[78] Most had departed convinced that only independence could provide their lands the governments they desired.

When the next Cortes opened its regular session in March 1822, Spain was sinking into anarchy. In the north, absolutists declared that the king was a prisoner of the *liberales,* that he could not exercise sovereignty, and that therefore they were establishing a regency to wage war against the constitutionalists. On June 30, 1822, Fernando VII attempted to regain absolute power with the help of his Royal Corps, only to be defeated by the militia led by *exaltado* Colonel Evaristo San Miguel. Thereafter, the *comuneros* gained control of the ministry and the Cortes and governed a bitterly divided nation.

The political factions in Spain and the intense agitation of the radical clubs reminded many observers of the French Revolution on the eve of the Terror. Such comparisons frightened the conservative powers of Europe, particularly France. After months of diplomatic threats, France invaded Spain in April 1823 to restore absolutism. The constitutional government retreated first to Sevilla and then to Cádiz, where it deposed Fernando and established a regency. Unlike 1808, the people of Spain did not oppose the French invaders. The *liberal* factions did not unite and the people, tired of political upheaval and economic decline, allowed a well-behaved French army to pass and restore Fernando VII to his throne. The king abolished the Cortes, nullified all its acts, and imprisoned those *liberales* who failed to escape. There followed a decade of absolutist rule during which French troops were necessary to keep the king on his throne.[79] The restored constitutional system had failed to solve the political crises of Spain and America.

78 Juan Gómez de Navarrete and Tomás Murfi, "Noticias importantes sobre nuestra Independencia dadas por los S.S. Diputados a las Cortes de España," AGN, Gobernación, sin sección, caja 23; W. Woodrow Anderson, "Reform as a Means to Quell Revolution," in Nettie Lee Benson, *Mexico and the Spanish Cortes* (Austin: University of Texas Press, 1966), 198–206.
79 Artola, *La España de Fernando VII,* 767–830; José Luis Comellas, *El trienio constitucional* (Madrid: Ediciones Rialp, 1963), 336–443.

Final Emancipation

In 1820 Americans welcomed the restoration of the Constitution, but they did not place all their hopes in the success of the restored order. Even the citizens of América Septentrional who participated most fully in constitutional government during its two periods considered alternatives. Thus, the autonomists of New Spain embraced two strategies in their efforts to achieve home rule: the Spanish constitutional process and, as in 1813 when they had considered joining the insurgent regime, the possibility of establishing their own autonomous government. Initially, they viewed the constitutional process as a more manageable and more attractive alternative. The autonomists gained control of the provincial deputations and the constitutional *ayuntamientos* and won elections to the Cortes. Although they were willing to follow the constitutional road to autonomy, they remained determined to govern at home.[80]

The restoration of the Constitution of 1812 unleashed widespread political activity in New Spain. Thousands of publications argued the pros and cons of the new system. Countless elections accustomed people throughout the viceroyalty to greater political participation. Such intense political activity could not fail to engender fears among various groups. In the provinces, teachers complained that pupils no longer heeded them, *curas* reported that Indians did not respect them and refused to attend mass, and officials charged that people no longer obeyed the authorities because they believed the Constitution relieved them of most obligations. The military and the clergy became hostile to the Constitution when the Cortes enacted measures suppressing the Jesuits and the monastic orders and abolishing ecclesiastical and military immunity from civil prosecution. Although vexing to the national elite, the disenchantment of members of the army and the clergy was not sufficient to disrupt the restored constitutional system.

In Mexico City members of the national elite, who were concerned about the need to retain autonomy, kept in close touch with like-minded individuals in the provincial capitals. Many issues worried them. The intense involvement of the people in the political process was new and unsettling. The discontent of segments of the clergy and the military augured ill for the success of the restored constitutional system. One faction, apparently led by the higher clergy, had sought in May 1820 to postpone implementation or to suspend the constitution. But mass popular support for the charter ended that possibility immediately. Perhaps most distressing to the autonomists were reports about the political disintegration of the Peninsula. Was a social revolution imminent? If so, what should be done to pro-

---

80 The following is based on my article "The Transition from Colony to Nation," 97–132. The sources for my interpretation may be consulted there.

tect orderly representative government in New Spain? Perhaps the time had come to act. One group concluded that independence might be necessary to retain home rule under the Constitution of 1812, that is, to establish a limited constitutional monarchy in New Spain. In a sense, the ideas being discussed were no more than variations of the plans for autonomy that had been debated since 1808.

Concerned that Spain would not grant them the full autonomy they sought, the elite of New Spain pursued alternative means of achieving home rule. Although members of the national elite gathered to discuss their country's future in a variety of places, one of the most prominent was the Mexico City salon of María Ignacia Rodríguez de Velasco, popularly known as *la Güera Rodríguez* (the Rodríguez blonde). With her help they convinced an efficient and ruthless royalist officer, Colonel Agustín de Iturbide, to assume the leadership of an autonomy movement.

In early 1821 he began coordinating his activities with the leading civil, clerical, and military leaders of the viceroyalty. With their help, he formulated a program that he issued at the village of Iguala on February 24, 1821. A carefully crafted compromise document, the Plan of Iguala combined the long-discussed autonomous regency with the Constitution – as did the Michelena proposal to the Cortes. In addition, the Plan of Iguala provided protection for the clergy, the army, and the Europeans. It established the Roman Catholic faith as the official religion, "without tolerance for any other," declared "the absolute independence of this kingdom," instituted a constitutional monarchy, and invited Fernando VII, a member of his family, or someone from another ruling dynasty to govern.

The Plan of Iguala provided a compromise, a way of retaining representative constitutional government that did not preclude a reconciliation with the Spanish Monarchy. Following Hispanic traditions and practices introduced in 1808, the plan established a ruling junta until a Mexican *cortes* convened. The proposed governing committee consisted primarily of former autonomists and constitutionalists. Although the Plan of Iguala was signed on February 24, 1821, Iturbide did not formally present it to his senior officers until March 1. The following day, he wrote to Captain General and Superior Political Chief Ruiz de Apodaca, formally inviting him to participate in the movement. Later, on March 16, Iturbide informed the Cortes and the king of his actions. Expressing his patriotism and his desire to protect the Constitution and the Crown, Iturbide urged the authorities to recognize New Spain's desire for home rule. Ruiz de Apodaca rejected the rebel's entreaty, as did initially most of the civil, military, and ecclesiastic authorities of the realm.

The most critical task for the new insurgents was to win the support of powerful religious and civil authorities, such as the bishops and ecclesiastic *cabildos,* the provincial deputations and constitutional *ayuntamientos,*

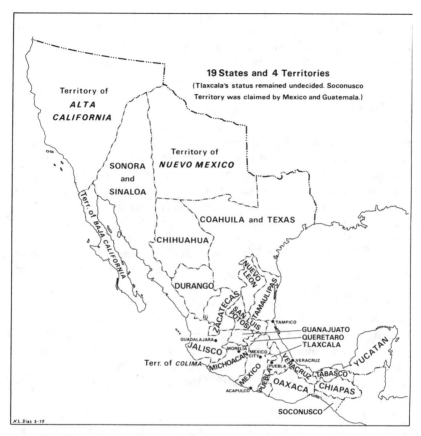

Map 4. The United States of Mexico, 1824. (From Jaime E. Rodríguez O., *The Emergence of Spanish America: Vicente Rocafuerte and Spanish Americanism, 1808–1832,* Berkeley: University of California Press, 1975, p. 213.)

and important officials like the former intendants, now political chiefs, and the principal regional commanders. To the higher ecclesiastic authorities Iturbide offered respect and protection. Although initially cautious, the prelates ultimately responded positively. Only Archbishop Pedro José de Fonte steadfastly refused to accept the Plan of Iguala. Winning the backing of the other authorities required bridging conflicting civilian and army interests. Civil and military leaders were divided over the nature of government. The men who controlled the provincial deputations and constitutional *ayuntamientos* insisted upon the traditional civil dominance over the military. They no longer accepted wartime exigencies as reasons to overrule civilian authority and were adamantly opposed to emergency measures, including war taxes. Regional elites sought to expand their power by demanding the immediate establishment of provincial deputations in all former intendancies, as the Spanish Cortes had approved. Since Iturbide was a military man, most civilian authorities were not certain how far to trust him. Many waited to learn what the government in Spain would do.

Iturbide's force, now called the *Army of the Three Guarantees,* numbered fewer than 1,000 men. On March 9 Vicente Guerrero, the most important insurgent leader in the south, agreed to support the Plan of Iguala on the condition that he retain authority over the region then under his control. Their combined force of 1,800 men was insufficient to defeat the constituted authorities. But the situation of the royal army also was dismal. Not only had *ayuntamientos* refused to continue supporting the military, as was their right under the Constitution, but since many units were short of funds, supplies, clothes, and even food, soldiers began to desert. The discontent of the American-born officers, however, constituted the greatest weakness of the royal army. After years of dedicated service, many found their careers frustrated and themselves excluded from high political office. As a result, some senior American commanders, such as José Joaquín de Herrera, Anastasio Bustamante, and Luis Cortázar, as well as junior officers like Antonio López de Santa Anna, joined the new insurgency. Although some royalist commanders defended their areas, others simply abandoned their posts because they could not control their troops. During the months of April, May, and June, large parts of the Bajío and New Galicia accepted the Plan of Iguala.

Frustrated by Ruiz de Apodaca's inability to defend the realm, royal army units in Mexico City forced him to resign on the evening of July 5, 1821, and transfer his command to Field Marshal Francisco Novella. Although the Provincial Deputation of New Spain and the Constitutional Ayuntamiento of Mexico City refused to accept the *golpe,* Novella took control of the city but could not extend his authority beyond the confines of the capital.

In the provinces, the cause of independence gained support. Spanish officers such as Luis Quintanar and Pedro Celestino Negrete, as well as former insurgents like Guadalupe Victoria and Nicolás Bravo, joined the movement. The most important victory, however, occurred in Puebla at the end of July. Provincial leaders, led by the Constitutional Ayuntamiento of Puebla, negotiated with the new insurgents, agreeing to support the movement in exchange for the establishment of a provincial deputation. Once the accord was reached, Iturbide entered Puebla in triumph on August 2.

When Captain General and Superior Political Chief O'Donojú landed in Veracruz at the end of July, the new insurgents already controlled large parts of the realm and, in the capital, Spanish troops had overthrown the legally constituted authorities. O'Donojú faced a delicate task. As a Spaniard he was committed to maintaining ties between New Spain and the Spanish Monarchy, and as a *liberal* he was determined to ensure that constitutional rule was firmly implanted in América Septentrional. He chose to negotiate with Iturbide. The two men met in the city of Córdoba on August 23, 1821. The following day they signed a treaty that recognized the independence of New Spain. They reached this accord quickly because the Plan of Iguala was essentially the same as the Michelena proposal, which O'Donojú had every reason to believe that the Cortes had already approved. As Iturbide later declared, the Spaniard accepted the proposal "as if he had helped me write the plan."

The Treaty of Córdoba not only ratified the Plan of Iguala but also established the procedures by which the independent government would be formed. It declared: "This America is recognized as a sovereign and independent nation, called hereafter, the Mexican Empire." It provided for a moderate, representative constitutional monarchy that would be governed by Fernando VII, a Spanish prince, or someone designated by the Spanish Cortes. It recognized the Spanish Constitution and its acts as the law of the land. And it established a regency and a governing junta to administer the country until a Mexican *cortes* convened.

O'Donojú moved immediately to implement the accord. After some difficulty, he forced Novella to yield to his authority. Then he and Iturbide selected the governing junta of thirty-eight men, the *Soberana Junta Suprema Gubernativa*. The body consisted of the most important men of the realm, among them leading autonomists, constitutionalists, and a few *servil* clergymen and officers. The captain general and superior political chief entered the capital on September 26 to the music of bands, the ringing of bells, and the firing of cannon. The Army of the Three Guarantees and its commander arrived in Mexico City the following day. At its first session, on September 28, the Soberana Junta Suprema Gubernativa signed the declaration of independence. Unfortunately, O'Donojú became ill immediately after entering the capital and could not attend the ceremonies. He died of pleurisy on October 8, 1821. Although the government in Spain refused to approve O'Donojú's actions, it did not matter. The Mexican Empire was independent.

The newly independent Mexicans carefully followed the precedents of the Spanish constitutional system. They formed a Council of Regency to serve as an executive and a Soberana Junta Provisional Gubernativa to function as the legislative branch until the Mexican Cortes convened. At its first session in Mexico City, the Soberana Junta reviewed and approved the participation of the thirty-two members present. Then it selected five individuals to serve on the Council of Regency, naming Iturbide president.

The national elite who gained power at independence preferred a constitutional monarchy with the Spanish king or a member of the royal family as sovereign. When the government in Spain rejected their proposal and they were faced with popular and military demands, the country's political leaders reluctantly accepted a native son, Agustín de Iturbide, as the nation's first emperor.

Emancipation was received joyously throughout the country. Iturbide was widely acclaimed as a great hero, a farsighted statesman, and the nation's liberator. His popularity, however, was as short-lived as the temporary consensus based on the Plan of Iguala. It evaporated after he made himself emperor with the aid of the army, and the nation was forced to grapple with difficult political and economic questions. After the emperor's ouster in 1823, Mexicans elected a constituent congress that promulgated a federal constitution in 1824.

The new charter was not only modeled on the Spanish Constitution of 1812 but also repeated some sections verbatim. This was only natural since prominent *novohispanos* such as Guridi y Alcocer and Ramos Arizpe, who had served in the Spanish Cortes and participated in writing the Spanish constitution, also served in the Mexican congress. Indeed, many Mexicans considered the Spanish charter their first constitution. The principal innovations – republicanism and federalism – were adopted to address Mexico's new reality. The monarchy was abolished because both Fernando VII and Agustín I had failed as political leaders. But the only difference between the constitutional monarchy and the republic was the manner in which the executive was selected. Both the Spanish Constitution of 1812 and the Mexican Constitution of 1824 established powerful legislatures and weak executives. Federalism arose naturally from Mexico's earlier political experience. The provincial deputations, created by the Constitution of Cádiz, simply converted themselves into states. Since several had formed state governments before the Mexican constituent congress met, that body had no choice but to establish a federal system. The distinguished *novohispanos* who had assumed a role of leadership in the Spanish Cortes continued to promote their views in the new Mexican nation they were forming.[81]

The people of the Kingdom of Guatemala, like those of New Spain, were determined to benefit from the restoration of the Spanish Constitution. In 1820 they also insisted on expanding their provincial deputations from two

---

81 Jaime E. Rodríguez O., "The Constitution of 1824 and the Formation of the Mexican State," in *The Evolution of the Mexican Political System,* ed. Jaime E. Rodríguez O. (Wilmington: Scholarly Resources, 1993), 73–90; Rodríguez O., "The Struggle for the Nation: The First Centralist–Federalist Conflict in Mexico," *The Americas,* 49:9 (July 1992), 1–1992; Benson, *La Diputación Provincial.*

– Guatemala and Nicaragua – to six – Guatemala, Nicaragua, San Salvador, Costa Rica, Honduras, and Chiapas – the number of provinces in the kingdom. Without waiting for approval from the Cortes, Honduras elected its own provincial deputation at the end of 1820. When news arrived the following year that the Cortes had approved the formation of provincial deputations in every intendancy, Chiapas, San Salvador, and Costa Rica established provincial governments.[82]

The Peninsula's social and political instability, particularly the growing anticlericalism, worried many Central Americans. They, like their northern brethren, eventually concluded that only independence could preserve the moderate constitutional monarchy they desired. News of the Plan of Iguala and the subsequent victories of the *novohispanos* pleased many people in the Kingdom of Guatemala. Reports of Iturbide's success in Puebla convinced the leaders of Chiapas to declare independence on September 1, 1821, and adhere to the Plan of Iguala.

Superior Political Chief Gabino Gaínza, convinced that a majority of the politically active elites favored change, convened a junta of notables in Guatemala City on September 15, 1821.[83] The assembly declared absolute independence from the Spanish Monarchy, but since its members represented only the province of Guatemala, the junta could not act for the entire kingdom. Therefore, it established a *Junta Provisional Consultiva* to advise Gaínza until deputies from all the kingdom's provinces, elected according to the laws of the Spanish Cortes, convened at the capital on March 1, 1822. The interim government followed the precedents established by the Spanish constitutional system, making minor modifications as circumstances warranted.

The cities of the other provinces proved unwilling to follow the lead of Guatemala City. Chiapas, which had joined the Mexican Empire, severed all relations with Guatemala. Nicaragua and Honduras also decided to join Mexico. Within provinces, cities competed for dominance. Tegucigalpa and Comayagua fought for control of Honduras, and León and Granada disputed the right to govern Nicaragua. Most cities, however, favored joining the Mexican Empire. On January 5, 1822, the Junta Provisional announced that 147 *ayuntamientos* had voted in favor of union with Mexico, 2 opposed it, and 21 left the matter up to the future congress of provinces. Respond-

---

82 Rodríguez, *The Cádiz Experiment,* 130–44; Xiomara Avendaño Rojas, "La independencia y la autonomía provincial en el Reino de Guatemala, 1821–1823, " paper presented at the seminar "La Independencia y la formación de las autonomías territoriales mexicanas," held at the Insituto de Investigaciones doctor José María Luis Mora, Mexico City, August 24–5, 1994; Carlos Meléndez, *La independencia de Centroamérica* (Madrid: Mapfre, 1993), 186–92.

83 Gaínza, who was the Spanish brother-in-law of the prominent *guayaquileño liberal* Vicente Rocafuerte and sympathetic to New World aspirations, appears to have decided to join the Americans in their quest for independence.

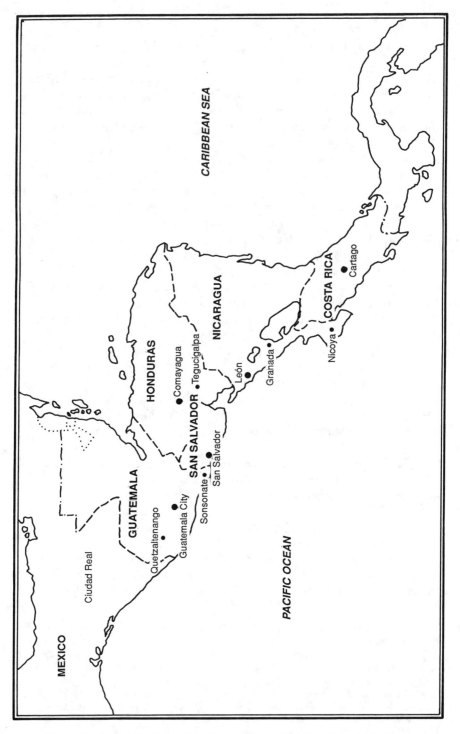

Map 5. The United Provinces of the Center of America. (After Carlos Meléndez, *La independencia de Centroamérica,* Madrid: Editorial Mapfre, 1993.)

ing to the electorate, the Junta Provisional determined that "in this case, there is nothing to do but inform the government of Mexico what *the people* want."[84] Through their vote, the cities of Central America affirmed both the existence of a distinct region known as América Septentrional and their preference for a constitutional monarchy patterned on the Spanish Constitution of 1812. Small minorities throughout the Kingdom of Guatemala, however, favored the establishment of a republic.

After Iturbide's abdication, the Central American provinces except Chiapas decided to form their own country. The new Mexican congress accepted their decision; the two regions separated peacefully. In 1823 the former Audiencia or Kingdom of Guatemala became an independent country known as the United Provinces of the Center of America. Like its neighbor to the north, the new nation based its new republican government on the Spanish Constitution that its representatives earlier had helped to create. Distinguished *centroamericano* parliamentarians like Antonio Larrazábal had contributed to the formation of that political heritage.[85]

Unlike América Septentrional, América Meridional lived through a profoundly different political experience during the years 1810 to 1824. Whereas Americans in the north participated fully in the political transformation of the Spanish world, those in the south generally did not. Only the areas under royalist control during the two constitutional periods (1810–14 and 1820–3) – Quito, Peru, and Charcas, as well as parts of Venezuela and New Granada – held constitutional elections and established provincial deputations and constitutional *ayuntamientos*. The other regions of South America, those controlled by the autonomists – the Río de la Plata and Chile, together with parts of Venezuela and New Granada – did not share that experience. Their experiments with representative government were more restricted and less participatory. The two halves of Spanish America also followed different paths to emancipation. Whereas the elites of América Septentrional gained independence through a political compromise in which civil and military officials changed sides and supported the decision to separate from the Spanish Monarchy, the autonomists of América Meridional had to fight prolonged bloody wars to defeat the royal authorities.

The restoration of the Spanish constitution in 1820 coincided with San Martín's invasion of Peru. He had spent the two years after the victory at Maipó preparing an expeditionary force, a costly enterprise requiring the formation of a joint *ríoplatense* and Chilean army and a navy to transport and

---

84 Quoted in Avendaño Rojas, "La independencia y la autonomía provincial."
85 Rodríguez, *The Cádiz Experiment*, 145–211; Nettie Lee Benson and Charles Berry, "The Central American Delegation to the First Constituent Congress of Mexico, 1822–1823," *HAHR*, 49:4 (November 1969), 679–702; Meléndez, *La independencia de Centroamérica*, 192–203.

protect the invaders. Since the chief executives of the United Provinces in South America and Chile, Pueyrredón and O'Higgins, fully supported San Martín, the two governments contributed substantially to the enterprise. It is estimated that each nation invested nearly 2 million pesos in the Chilean and Peruvian campaigns.[86] After the defeat of the government of the United Provinces by the provinces of the Río de la Plata in February 1820, Chile bore most of the cost for the Peruvian expedition.

San Martín and his naval commander, Lord Cochrane, were bitterly divided over military policy. Whereas the Briton wanted to take Lima directly, the American, convinced that Peruvians would, if given the opportunity, embrace the cause of independence, preferred an indirect approach. Therefore, he landed in Pisco, south of Lima, on September 10, 1820, and reinforced by large numbers of Peruvian autonomists proposed marching on the capital. He did not implement this strategy because the day after the expeditionary forces landed, Viceroy Joaquín de la Pezuela proposed a cease-fire, as instructed by the new constitutional government in Spain. Pezuela officially proclaimed the Constitution of Cádiz on September 15, 1820, and immediately scheduled elections, thus offering Peruvians partial autonomy within the Spanish Nation.

Peruvians were perplexed by San Martín's actions. He had invaded Peru but immediately accepted an armistice. The general then sent letters and private envoys to prominent Peruvians proposing the establishment of a constitutional monarchy. His proposal appealed to many members of the elite because, unlike the restored Spanish constitutional system, it called for an independent Peruvian government with Lima, instead of Madrid, as the capital. Thus, the plan offered the local upper and middle classes numerous opportunities for government employment. San Martín also proposed retaining aristocratic and other hierarchical privileges. Socially conservative Peruvians, alienated by a government in Spain increasingly dominated by anticlerical radicals, were reassured by his vision of an autonomous, conservative monarchy. The proposal was particularly attractive to Peru's urban elite and middle groups, who feared the discontent of the *pueblo bajo* – the slaves, the Indian communities, and the colored *castas*.[87] But San Martín's failure to take military action made them reluctant to embrace his cause. They awaited the outcome of the contest between the American and the Spanish viceroy.

Viceroy Pezuela proved to be equally indecisive. Although his officers

86 Estévez and Elía, *Aspectos económico-financieros* 129–202; Fritz C. Hoffman, "The Financing of San Martín's Expeditions," *HAHR*, 32:4 (November 1952), 634–8.

87 Ricardo Piccirilli, *San Martín y la políca de los pueblos* (Buenos Aires: Ediciones Gure, 1957), 239–300; John Lynch, *The Spanish American Revolutions, 1808–1821*, 2d ed. (New York: W. W. Norton, 1986), 175–6.

argued that they could defeat the invaders, he procrastinated, hoping that negotiations would resolve the conflict. His representatives met with San Martín's commissioners at Miraflores, outside Lima, on September 25, but they failed to reach an agreement. Despite his conservatism, the American leader insisted upon independence. But as the representative of the Spanish Monarchy, Pezuela was unwilling to accept independence in any form, even an autonomous monarchy ruled by a Spanish prince. In October the viceroy's generals, led by José de la Serna, proposed evacuating the capital. In their view, the invaders' naval and land forces could easily encircle Lima, cutting off vital supplies for its large population. They recommended withdrawing into the interior, which provided a strong base from which to defend the kingdom. Pezuela refused to abandon the capital.

As the royalist generals predicted, San Martín's forces began to encircle the capital. He sent one detachment inland to isolate the city from the highlands. In November he moved his army north of Lima, cutting it off from its food supplies. Lord Cochrane entered the harbor at Callao and captured the best Spanish warship, the forty-four-gun frigate *Esmeralda,* thus eliminating royalist naval power in the Pacific. Thereafter, the Chilean navy, under the Briton's command, dominated the west coast of South America. Peru was now entirely dependent on foreign shipping to provide its needs and carry its products abroad.

San Martín's success prompted provincial leaders in northern Peru to assert their autonomy. In December the Marqués Torre Tagle, former deputy to the Cortes and current political chief of the northern province of Trujillo, convinced the constitutional *ayuntamiento* of Trujillo to declare independence. Like San Martín, Torre Tagle favored the creation of an autonomous monarchy within the Spanish Nation. Other constitutional *ayuntamientos* in northern cities followed Trujillo's example. Large areas of the north, including Lambayeque, Piura, and Cajamarca, had declared themselves independent by March 1821. In most cases, the actions did not signify a commitment to abandon ties with the Spanish Monarchy. Rather, they constituted an accommodation to the invading army by individuals elected to the constitutional *ayuntamientos.* They would readily return to royal authority should it ultimately triumph. In 1821, however, the region was an important source of support for San Martín's forces.[88]

Pezuela became increasingly isolated as Lima's situation deteriorated. Food and other necessities became scarce and correspondingly expensive. Both civil and military officials criticized the viceroy's failure to deal with the invaders. The Peruvian *liberales,* who won the elections to the constitutional *ayuntamiento* of Lima on December 7, 1820, insisted on reaching an

---

88 Rubén Vargas Ugarte, *Historia General del Perú,* 6 vols. (Lima: Carlos Milla Batres, 1966), 6:115–31; Otero, *Historia del Libertador,* III, 65–226; Anna, *The Fall of Royal Government in Peru,* 160–6.

accommodation with San Martín. Others, including high-ranking army officers, urged an immediate military response. Convinced that Pezuela's passivity would lose Peru, the leading royalist commanders removed him from office on January 29, 1821. In his place, they named La Serna captain general and superior political chief, the post that replaced the viceroy under the Constitution of 1812. Although the *ayuntamiento* and the higher clergy protested, they accepted the change because La Serna promised to obey the Constitution and because they were not yet prepared to side with San Martín. The accommodation quickly collapsed as city officials increasingly disagreed with La Serna's policies.

Upon his arrival in April, 1821, naval Captain Manuel Abreu, the peace commissioner sent by the constitutional government in Spain, resumed negotiations with San Martín. The envoy first met privately with the independence leader and then with General La Serna. On May 23 both parties agreed to a twenty-day armistice and to the creation of a junta of pacification. At the first meeting of the junta, held on June 2, San Martín proposed a version of the widely discussed plan of autonomous monarchies as a solution to the conflict in America. He suggested that a three-man governing junta be established, composed of one member appointed by La Serna, one by him, and one by Peruvian leaders; and that a commission be sent to Spain to request the recognition of the independence of the United Provinces, Chile, and Peru and the naming of a Spanish prince to govern Peru under the Constitution. La Serna, some of his officials, and the Ayuntamiento of Lima initially favored the proposal, but the Spanish general ultimately rejected it as unconstitutional. Abreu continued negotiations for some time but La Serna withdrew, determined to abandon Lima and prosecute the struggle from the interior. He evacuated the capital on July 6, leaving a small garrison in the fortress of Callao. In evacuating Lima, La Serna was preserving the royal army. The surrounded city not only lacked food and supplies, it was ravaged by epidemic disease. By June most of the royal army was ill, and twenty soldiers a day were dying.[89]

The evacuation of the royal army left the residents of Lima, particularly the middle and upper classes, in terror. In their view, the city was surrounded by wild Indians, violent former slaves, colored *castas*, and terrorists. The authorities invited San Martín to occupy Lima to guarantee order. He entered the capital on July 12. Two days later he requested the *ayuntamiento* to hold a *cabildo abierto* to determine the country's future. On July 15, 1821, the city declared independence. As Timothy Anna notes: "The Declaration was the work of a group of ambitious letrados – lawyers, priests, and professionals – who forced it upon a desperate and starving cap-

---

89 Vargas Ugarte, *Historia General del Perú*, 6:145–70; Anna, *The Fall of Royal Government in Peru*, 161–78.

ital whose citizens were intimidated by armed force, threatened by imminent social chaos, and coerced by violence and fear."[90] San Martín had finally gotten his wish; the Peruvians had declared independence.

On August 3 San Martín assumed supreme military and civil power with the title of *protector.* Since he believed that the entire country soon would be independent, San Martín devoted his efforts primarily to establishing a government rather than destroying the royalist army. He appointed three ministers: the Peruvian Hipólito Unánue, finance; the *neogranadino* Juan García del Río, foreign relations; and the *porteño* Bernardo Monteagudo, war and marine. In November 1821 García del Río departed on a secret mission to Europe to obtain recognition, loans, and, most important, a prince for the future Peruvian monarchy.

The protector of Peru faced difficult political and economic problems that would have taxed the resources of a healthy man. Unfortunately, San Martín – ill with tuberculosis and increasingly addicted to opium, the only reliable pain killer available – proved unable either to govern effectively or to command the army. As a result, Monteagudo, the most powerful minister in the administration, became de facto executive. Many attributed to him the most unpopular government measures.[91]

The evacuation of the royalists had not ended either the shortages or the high prices in Lima. The surrounding areas experienced considerable unrest as royalist and independence armies plundered haciendas and small towns to feed and maintain their troops. Numerous guerrilla bands, often bandits rather than partisans either of the royalists or of the independents, appeared throughout the country. Spanish landowners, merchants, and other businessmen, fearing political persecution and social disintegration, began to leave. Their fears were justified; at the end of 1821, the government expelled first single and then married Spaniards and confiscated their property. The loss of that important segment of the economically active population and the dispersal of their assets devastated the economy. Forced loans to pay for the regime's expenses, particularly the army, depleted the resources of entrepreneurs and property owners and alienated important segments of the population. Conflict between *ríoplatense* and Chilean troops over the spoils of victory heightened social tensions. Both demanded honors, pensions, and jobs as rewards for their services. Peruvians rapidly came to see San Martín's forces not as liberators but as rapacious conquerors.

---

90 Anna, *The Fall of Royal Government in Peru,* 179. See also his "The Peruvian Declaration of Independence: Freedom by Coercion," *Journal of Latin American Studies,* 7:2 (November 1975), 221–48, and Piccirilli, *San Martín y la política de los pueblos,* 257–74.

91 José A. de la Puente Candamo, *La independencia de Perú* (Madrid: Mapfre, 1992), 158–65; Adolfo José Galatoire, *Cuales fueron las enfermedades de San Martín* (Buenos Aires: Editorial Plus Ultra, 1973).

Perhaps San Martín's most perplexing failure was military. The brilliant strategist of past campaigns seemed determined to destroy his reputation in Peru. Since landing, San Martín had refused to engage in combat, insisting that he would not win by shedding American blood. Inasmuch as the vast majority of royalist officers and men were natives of the New World, who gave little indication of changing sides, his hope for a bloodless victory was unrealistic. Independence would have to be won by force, but San Martín seemed incapable of taking the initiative. On one occasion, he permitted the royalist General José Canterac to enter and depart Callao with his army unmolested. Although he allowed some of his commanders, like Colonel William Miller, to campaign in the south against the royalists and although guerrilla forces harassed them inland and in the north, San Martín's army failed to engage the principal royalist forces in the interior.

The year 1821 ended in a stalemate. General La Serna controlled the central highlands and Upper Peru from his headquarters in Cuzco. The royalists governed a territory that contained heavily populated Indian communities, many of which, believing that the Monarchy offered them the greatest opportunities, overwhelmingly supported the Crown. But the sierra also included a large mestizo population that pursued its own interests, sometimes by fighting against the royalists. San Martín governed Peru from Lima, but other quasi-independent groups dominated the rest of the coast. Although nominally recognizing his authority, they generally acted on their own initiative without consulting national officials.[92]

San Martín's government was on the verge of collapse by the end of 1821. The regime could not pay its troops, many of whom deserted. Only 600 Chileans and even fewer *ríoplatenses* remained in Peru by 1822. Faced with bankruptcy, the government established a bank to issue paper money. The measure only worsened the situation. The persecution of Spaniards had not only damaged the economy, it had also created widespread discontent among the middle and upper classes. The people of Lima now considered San Martín a burden rather than a savior. Royalist and republican factions emerged, determined to oust the protector and introduce their own system of government. In these circumstances, San Martín appealed to the Colombians for help. In January 1822 he proposed meeting with Simón Bolívar

---

92 Otero, *Historia del Libertador*, 3:474–651. On the *guerrillas,* see Raúl Rivera Serna, *Los guerrilleros del Centro en la emancipación peruana* (Lima: Talleres Gráficos P. L. Villanueva, 1958), 80–92, 108–13; Gustavo Vergara Arias, *Montoneras y guerrillas en la etapa de la emancipación del Perú* (Lima: Editorial Salesiana, 1973); Heraclio Bonilla, "Bolívar y las guerrillas indigenas en el Perú," *Cultura: Revista del Banco Central del Ecuador,* 6:16 (May–August 1983), 81–95; and Peter Guardino, "Las guerrillas y la independencia peruana: Un ensayo de interpretación," *Pasado y presente,* 2:3 (1989). 101–17.

to discuss the best means of completing the independence of South America.[93]

The Republic of Colombia, whose aid the protector of Peru sought, was still consolidating its power. The Spanish Constitution had been restored in 1820, shortly after the great victories in New Granada and the formal establishment of the republic at Angostura. The cease-fire mandated by the new Spanish constitutional regime provided the republicans with time to strengthen their forces. But the triumphant republicans faced the task of driving the royalists from Cartagena, Panama, and other regions in New Granada and from large areas of Venezuela. That enterprise was made easier by the departure of Field Marshal Morillo, who had long before requested a transfer and finally was granted his wish. Although all the constitutional *ayuntamientos* of Venezuela urged him to remain, he departed at the end of the year, leaving General Miguel de la Torre, a less able officer, in command. Thus, a weaker royalist force faced a stronger enemy.

The republicans sought to capitalize on their new military power by renewing hostilities. They violated the armistice, rebelling in Maracaibo on January 28, 1821. Fighting spread throughout Venezuela. Dismayed by Field Marshal Morillo's departure and by Madrid's unwillingness to reinforce its army in the country, the royalists under General De la Torre proved unable to contain the republicans. After a series of minor engagements, republican forces converged on Caracas from the *llanos,* the Andes, the west, and the east. On June 24, 1821, armies led by Bolívar, Páez, and Mariño defeated the royalists at Carabobo, southwest of Caracas. Five days later, Bolívar entered the capital of Venezuela in triumph. Although royalist resistance continued for some time in scattered areas of Puerto Cabello, Cumaná, and Coro, Venezuela was essentially free. On August 1, President Bolívar traveled to New Granada to complete the liberation of the Republic of Colombia. Carlos Soublette remained as vice president of Venezuela, while Páez received military command of Caracas province and independence leaders, like Mariño and Bermúdez, were granted other commands.[94]

Although military commanders dominated the republic, civilians continued to insist on the creation of a representative government. As decreed by the Congress of Angostura, elections were held throughout republican New Granada and Venezuela at the end of 1820. Each province in the union was allocated three deputies, a cause for some complaint in the more populous areas of New Granada. The provinces of the Kingdom of Quito, which had been incorporated into the Republic of Colombia at Angostura,

93 Anna, *The Fall of Royal Government in Peru,* 189–207; Timothy E. Anna, "Economic Causes of San Martín's Failure in Lima," *HAHR,* 54:4 (November 1975), 657–81; Estévez and Elía, *Aspectos económico-financieros,* 203–50.

94 Stoan, *Pablo Morillo,* 227–32; Lecuna, *Crónica razonada,* 3:1–64; O'Leary, *Memorias,* 2:41–109.

were not included in the elections even though Guayaquil already had declared its independence.[95] Unlike elections under the Spanish constitutional system, those for the Congress of Cúcuta were restricted to men who possessed at least 500 pesos in real property, practiced a profession, or served in the army. Although many Colombians were denied the franchise, foreigners serving in the army were granted the suffrage. Like elections under the Constitution of Cádiz, these were indirect. Eligible voters chose electors, who, in turn, selected the deputies. The men elected to congress represented the elite of their provinces; they included clergymen, landowners, lawyers, and a few military men.

The constituent congress, which was to meet on January 1, 1821, could not obtain a quorum of fifty-seven deputies until May 1, when it was declared in session in the provincial city of Cúcuta near the border of Venezuela and New Granada. One of the most difficult and sensitive tasks facing congress was determining the nature of the new government. At Angostura, Bolívar had imposed a provisional constitution that established a highly centralized system with a president who had the power to suspend the constitution as he chose and a dual system of active citizens, who exercised the suffrage, and passive ones, who did not. Although many deputies believed that a more liberal and democratic charter, possibly a federal system, was needed, they faced strong opposition from the president, who not only dismissed their views as impractical but openly expressed disdain about lawyers and the law. As Bolívar wrote Santander:

Many in Cundinamarca are said to prefer a federation. . . . At last, at last, the *letrados* [lawyers] will go so far that they will be proscribed from the Republic of Colombia as were the poets from Plato's. These gentlemen think that their opinion constitutes the will of the people. They don't realize that in Colombia the people are in the army, because they are the army . . .; they are also the people who choose, the people who act, and the people who have the final say. The rest are persons who vegetate with more or less malignancy, or more or less patriotism, but all without any right to be anything other that passive citizens. This policy, which is certainly not Rousseau's, will ultimately have to be implemented so that those gentlemen will not again be our ruination. . . . Don't you think, my dear Santander, that those legislators [at Cúcuta], more ignorant than evil, and more presumptuous than ambitious, will lead us down the road to anarchy, then tyranny, and, in any case, ruin? I believe so; I am certain of it.[96]

The president was not alone in believing that the military should govern while civilians were restricted to the role of passive citizens. Many

95 Restrepo was one of the few deputies who expressed concern about the absence of representatives from Quito. He wrote to Santander on August 26, 1820, declaring: "I am of the same opinion as you; without Quito we should not treat the matter of the constitution." Quoted in *Actas del Congreso de Cúcuta, 1821*, 3 vols. (Bogotá: Biblioteca de la Presidencia de la República, 1989), 1:lxxiv.
96 Bolívar to Francisco de Paula Santander, San Carlos, June 13, 1821 in Bolívar, *Obras completas*, 1:565–6.

high-ranking army officers deprecated the congress and preferred governing as autocrats. As Deputy José Manuel Restrepo recalled:

The deputies feared the army and the military men. Many of the latter had publicly declared
that they favored neither establishing a congress nor that the people be granted institutions
which would end the abuses and disorders associated with a revolution. They were well content with the military government which until then had ruled Colombia, but the people
detested such an oppressive and violent regime.[97]

Although republicans controlled most of New Granada and large parts
of Venezuela when congress met in Cúcuta, the assembly drafted a wartime
constitution designed to facilitate the completion of the struggle for independence rather than a charter to govern the nation in normal times. Their
intention became evident in the final article, which stated, "When all or a
major part of the territory of the republic presently under Spanish power is
free," after ten years congress would summon "a great convention of the
Republic of Colombia which would be authorized to evaluate and reform
the government or change it completely."[98] Pressured by the extraordinary
wartime circumstances, Bolívar, and the military, most federalists voted for
a strong central government to prosecute the war. Forty-one of the fifty
deputies voted to approve the centralist document.

On August 6, 1821, the Congress of Cúcuta promulgated the constitution, which established a republic with a bicameral legislature and granted
vast power to the president. The new government possessed a highly centralized administration divided into departments, governed by intendants
appointed by the president. The former Captaincy General of Venezuela
was divided into three departments: Orinoco, Venezuela, and Zulia; New
Granada into four: Boyacá, Cundinamarca, Cauca, and Magdalena; and the
Kingdom of Quito into three: Guayaquil, Cuenca, and Quito. The new
regime retained pre-1808 Spanish law, provided it did not contradict the
constitution. For example, the Royal Ordinance of Intendants of New
Spain governed the administration of the departments. As a result, the
widely accepted principle of separation of powers, a concept enshrined in
the U.S. and Spanish constitutions, was abrogated. Many government officials in Colombia now possessed civil, military, and judicial authority.
Although congress abolished the odious distinction between active and
passive citizens, the people were granted little role in their government.
"The people," as Article 10 indicated, "will not by itself exercise any attributes of sovereignty other than primary elections."[99] The new regime con-

---

97 Quoted in *Actas del Congreso de Cúcuta, 1821*, 1:1xxxix–xc.
98 "Constitución de la República de Colombia," in Manuel Antonio Pombo and José Joaquín Guerra,
    Constituciones de Colombia, 3 vols. (Bogotá: Biblioteca Banco Popular, 1986), 3:103.
99 Ibid., 64–104; David Bushnell, *The Santander Regime in Gran Colombia* (Westport: Greenwood
    Press, 1970), 14–22.

stituted a return to enlightened despotism. Although effective during the conduct of war, the new system of government would quickly foster provincial unrest once peace was restored.

On September 7 congress chose Bolívar president and Santander vice president. The chief executive appointed leading military men intendants of the liberated departments and delegated the day-to-day administrative responsibilities of the nation to Santander so that he could devote himself to prosecuting the war with the Spanish Monarchy. The new constitution provided the legal framework to raise the men, money, and equipment necessary to extend the struggle to the regions of Colombia that remained in royalist hands. After the royalists in Cartagena surrendered on October 1 and Panama declared independence on November 28, Bolívar decided to march on Quito while his lieutenants extinguished the remaining pockets of royalist resistance. The liberation of the Kingdom of Quito was essential to preventing the port of Guayaquil, which had declared independence the year before, from falling under Peruvian control.

A naval base, a shipbuilding center, and one of the principal ports in the Pacific, Guayaquil had important commercial ties ranging from New Spain in the north to Chile in the south. Although the city was the principal port of the Kingdom of Quito, the region's topography made it much easier to travel from Guayaquil to Lima by water than to the capital in the highlands. The journey to Santa Fé de Bogotá, the capital of the former Viceroyalty of New Granada, was even more difficult. As a result, many prominent *guayaquileños* possessed strong ties with the Peruvian capital. Merchants and members of the elite often sent their sons to study in Lima. The distinguished poet and jurist José Joaquín de Olmedo, for example, attended universities both in Quito and in Lima.[100] Thus, Bolívar and many Colombians feared that the port might accept San Martín's invitation to join Peru.

Guayaquil had remained royalist during the Quito revolutions of 1809 and 1810–12. The situation had changed, however, by 1820. The restored absolutism of 1814–20 convinced many *guayaquileños,* among them the liberal deputy to the Cortes Olmedo, that significant change was needed. Economic and military developments also pushed the port toward independence. After 1815, Spanish shipping virtually disappeared from the Pacific and commerce could only be conducted by foreign vessels, yet Peninsular merchants continued to block all efforts to obtain governmental approval of free trade. The port also experienced raids by British privateers in the service of governments of the Río de la Plata and Chile during

---

100 Julio Estrada Ycaza, *La lucha de Guayaquil por el Estado de Quito,* 2 vols. (Guayaquil: Banco Central del Ecuador, 1984), 1:172–3.

the absolutist period. Guayaquil merchants facing economic disaster reassessed their royalist sympathies.

The city's upper and middle classes were seriously considering declaring independence when official word of the restoration of the Spanish Constitution arrived in September 1820. The city proclaimed the Constitution on the 13th and held elections four days later. All those elected to the constitutional *ayuntamiento* were *liberal* autonomist Americans. On October 9, 1820, they declared independence as the first step in establishing the State of Quito. Shortly thereafter, a junta of notables elected Olmedo president of the new republic.[101]

The new government of Guayaquil dispatched proclamations to Quito, Cuenca, and other cities in the kingdom informing them of its action and convening a constituent congress in Guayaquil on November 8, 1820. The Guayaquil government immediately formed an army, the *División Protectora de Quito* (Division to Protect Quito), to liberate the rest of the realm. The response in the interior was positive. Cuenca declared independence on November 3. Machachi, Latacunga, and Riobamba joined the movement on the 11th, Ambato on the 12th, and Alausí on the 13th. Quito, however, remained under royal control. The División Protectora advanced into the highlands, reaching Ambato on November 20; two days later, royalist forces commanded by Colonel Francisco González routed the republicans. After a series of victories, González reoccupied Cuenca on December 20. At the end of the year, the royalists controlled the highlands while the republicans held the coast.

The congress that met in Guayaquil in November consisted of fifty-seven deputies representing the coast. It declared independence and established a republic. The deputies intended the former Kingdom of Quito to be one entity, but without input from the other provinces, they were unwilling to decide whether to form an independent state or join either Colombia or Peru. Olmedo, who preferred an independent nation, acknowledged that the highlands could not be freed without outside aid.[102]

For nearly two years, President Olmedo attempted to obtain assistance from San Martín and Bolívar without compromising his country. San Martín sent envoys, and Bolívar dispatched General Antonio José de Sucre with 700 men to aid Guayaquil. The governments of Peru and Colombia, however, insisted upon controlling Guayaquil. The failure of President

---

101 Mariano Fazio Fernández, *Ideología de la emancipación guayaquileña* (Guayaquil: Banco Central del Ecuador, 1987), 44–5.

102 Estrada Ycaza, *La lucha de Guayaquil,* 1:193–212; Camilo Destruje, *Historia de la Revolución de Octubre y la campaña libertadora,* 2d ed. (Guayaquil: Banco Central del Ecuador, 1982), 163–252; Francisco Aguirre Abad, *Bosquejo histórico de la República del Ecuador* (Guayaquil: Corporación de Estudios y Publicaciones, 1972), 179–82.

Olmedo's second campaign to liberate the sierra in 1821 forced the Guayaquil government to reach an accord with Colombia. The treaty signed in May 1821 established a protectorate but did not commit either Guayaquil or the Kingdom of Quito to join Colombia. As part of the agreement, General Sucre assumed command of the republican forces until the sierra was liberated.

Despite Guayaquil's determination to maintain its independence, Bolívar and San Martín continued to pressure the Olmedo government to join their nations. The relative strength of the two leaders changed as the year progressed. San Martín's political and military situation worsened, while Bolívar's power increased. Emboldened by his growing strength, Bolívar informed Olmedo that Colombia would not permit Guayaquil to be independent. He asserted that the province lacked the power to maintain its freedom, that legally it was part of Colombia, and that the majority of the population of the Kingdom of Quito favored union with the northern republic. Olmedo's government steadfastly refused to submit to Colombian pressure. Guayaquil insisted upon its right to self-determination in the belief that it possessed the resources to act freely. It was paying the cost of maintaining the republican army, and the majority of the troops under Sucre's command were local.[103]

After two unsuccessful attempts to ascend the sierra directly to Quito, Sucre changed his strategy. In 1822 he marched southeast to Cuenca, where forces sent by San Martín joined his army. General Sucre's men captured the city on February 20; he and his troops remained there until Cuenca agreed to its "spontaneous" annexation by Colombia on April 11. Royalist forces retreated slowly toward the capital. The final confrontation between royalists and republicans occurred on the morning of May 24, 1822. General Sucre's 3,000-man army, most of whom were natives of the Kingdom of Quito, defeated the royalist forces of General Melchor Aymerich on the foothills of Mount Pichincha above the city of Quito.

After victory ceremonies, Sucre forced the Ayuntamiento of Quito to recognize, on behalf of the entire kingdom, the sovereignty of Colombia. The capital of the realm, the city of Quito, however, did not possess the authority to act for the entire region. Only a congress of provinces, such as the one proposed by Guayaquil, could decide the fate of the entire kingdom. Nevertheless, the capital's "spontaneous" declaration provided Colombia's leaders the justification for annexing the Kingdom of Quito. Despite attempts to maintain the appearance of unity, some prominent *quiteños* opposed the decision to join Colombia. Four members of the constitutional *ayuntamiento,* described as "disorderly enemies of Colombia," became victims of

103 Otero, *Historia del Libertador,* 3:653–89; Destruje, *Historia de la Revolución,* 253–346; Estrada Ycaza, *La lucha de Guayaquil,* 2:425–61.

a "bloody dispute" for criticizing the northern republiç. Not long afterward, placards appeared throughout the city reading: "*Último día del despotismo y el primero de lo mismo*" ("the last day of despotism and the first of the same thing"). After defeating the royalists in Pasto to the north, President Bolívar entered Quito with his army on June 16. He officially declared the entire Kingdom of Quito to be the Department of Quito, naming General Sucre its first intendant.[104]

On the coast, the *republiqueta,* (petty republic), as Bolívar contemptuously referred to Guayaquil, braced itself for the last act of Colombia's "liberation" of the Kingdom of Quito. Although President Olmedo continued to insist that only Guayaquil's assembly had the right to decide the region's future, he feared Colombia's military might. On April 2, 1822, before the battle of Pichincha, he wrote to San Martín explaining Bolívar's threat to take the province by a "*golpe de fuerza*" and informing the protector of Peru that the "time has come to fulfill your solemn promise to sustain the liberty of these peoples."[105] It was too late. San Martín himself was then seeking aid from Colombia.

Bolívar had no intention of allowing Guayaquil to decide its own destiny. He wrote San Martín: "I do not believe, like Your Excellency, that the will of a province must be consulted . . . . The Colombian Constitution grants the Province of Guayaquil the most perfect representation." He informed Olmedo: "I will have the satisfaction of entering that city at the head of the allied troops and I expect to be received as the president of Colombia and protector of Guayaquil."[106] To ensure that things went according to plan, nearly 2,000 Colombian troops occupied Guayaquil as Bolívar traveled with another army down the mountains from Quito.

The president of Colombia entered Guayaquil on July 11 to the firing of cannon and the ringing of bells. The city government ordered three days of celebrations in honor of the victory of Pichincha. Immediately Colombians began agitating for annexation. Two days later, Bolívar announced that he was assuming "political and military command . . . to save the people of Guayaquil from the dreadful anarchy in which they find themselves." Cynically, he added, "without this protective measure limiting in any way the absolute liberty of the people to manifest freely and spontaneously its

---

104 Destruje, *Historia de la Revolución,* 347–81; Estrada Ycaza, *La lucha de Guayaquil,* 2:485–96; Demetrio Ramos-Pérez, *Entre el Plata y Bogotá: Cuatro claves de la emancipación ecuatoriana* (Madrid: Ediciones de Cultura Hispanica 1987), 359–60; Bolívar to Santander, Quito, January 30, 1823, in Lecuna, *Cartas del Libertador,* 3:345–6.

105 Olmedo to San Martín, Guayaquil, April 2, 1822, in José Joaquín de Olmedo, *José Joaquín de Olmedo. Epistolario* (Puebla: Editorial J. M. Cajica, 1960), 485–8.

106 Bolívar to San Martín, Quito, June 22, 1822, in Lecuna, *Cartas del Libertador,* 3:242–3; Bolívar to Olmedo, Quito, June 18, 1822, in *Colección de tratados,* 2 vols. ed. Aurelio Noboa (Guayaquil: Imprenta de Noboa, 1901), 1:300–1.

will."[107] However, the decree published that day stated: "The former authorities have ceased to exercise their political and military responsibilities."[108]

The government of Guayaquil had no choice but to acquiesce. Olmedo wrote Bolívar that "all the philosophy of a Stoic or the impudence of a Cynic would be necessary not to see how the candor of these people has been abused." He announced that he was going into exile because "my honor requires it."[109] General José de La Mar, a native of Cuenca then in command of the forces of the Republic of Guayaquil, declined Bolívar's offer of command of the province and also departed.

The bayonets rather than the people had voted. As Bolívar explained to Santander: "The junta of this government, on its part, and the people, on theirs, compromised me to such a degree that I had no choice but to take the action I did on the 13th. It was not entirely violent, and force was not actually employed; one may say that these gentlemen bowed to the threat of force." The former Kingdom of Quito had achieved independence from the Spanish Monarchy but not liberty. The Department of Quito or of the South, as it was sometimes called, was placed under martial law. Officials from other parts of Colombia, as well as from other countries, replaced local authorities. To pay for the liberation of Peru, Bolívar restored Indian tribute, as well as the salt and tobacco monopolies, and increased duties that the Cortes and, later, the Congress of Colombia had abolished.[110]

Bolívar held the upper hand when San Martín arrived in Guayaquil for their long-postponed meeting. The two men met in private on July 26 and 27, 1822. Initially, San Martín had hoped to discuss the future of Guayaquil, the establishment of monarchies in America, and assistance for the war in Peru. The question of Guayaquil had already been settled by force. Bolívar, although autocratic and a believer in a strong, unfettered, and, if possible, lifetime executive, opposed monarchies. Therefore the two men limited their discussions to the conduct of the war in Peru. A weakened San Martín requested aid, which Bolívar denied on the grounds that he needed his forces to complete the liberation of Colombia. It became

107 Noboa, *Colección*, 1:309.

108 Lecuna, *Crónica razonada*, 3:192. William H. Gray presents a balanced account in his "Bolívar's Conquest of Guayaquil," *HAHR*, 27:4 (November 1947), 603–22. See also David J. Cubitt, "Guerra y diplomacia en la República de Guayaquil, 1820–1822," *Revista de historia de América*, 72 (January–June 1971), 391–411; and his "La anexión de la Provincia de Guayaquil. Estudio del estilo político boliviano," *Revista del Archivo Histórico del Guayas* 13 (1978), 5–27.

109 Olmedo to Bolívar, Guayaquil, July 29, 1822 in Olmedo, *Epistolario*, 497–9.

110 Bolívar to Santander, Guayaquil, July 22, 1822, in Lecuna, *Cartas del Libertador*, 3:246. Bushnell, *The Santander Regime*, 310–17; Estrada Ycaza, *La lucha de Guayaquil*. 2:547–85; Roger P. Davis, "Ecuador under Gran Colombia: Regionalism, Localism, and Legitimacy in the Emergence of an Andean Republic" (Ph. D. diss., University of Arizona, 1983), 82–178.

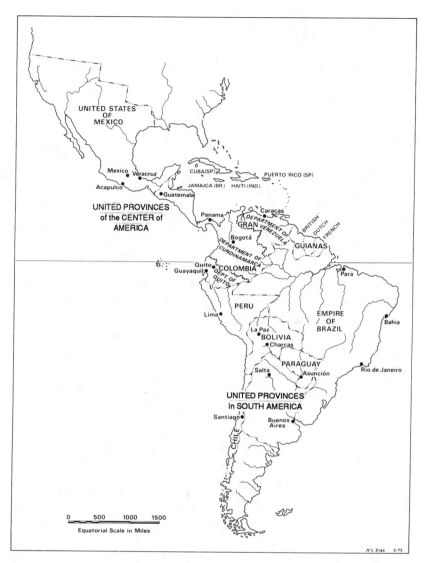

Map 6. Spanish America in 1825. (From Jaime E. Rodríguez O., *The Emergence of Spanish America: Vicente Rocafuerte and Spanish Americanism, 1808–1832,* Berkeley: University of California Press, 1975, p. 72.)

obvious that Bolívar would not cooperate with a rival like San Martín, whose reputation and political and military achievements challenged the Venezuelan's position as liberator of South America.

The protector of Peru departed, convinced that he had become an obstacle to the final liberation of South America. Upon his arrival in Lima, he also discovered that his government had been repudiated; a coalition of leading citizens had ousted Minister Monteagudo. Faced with growing discontent and convinced that "there is not enough room for Bolívar and for me in Peru,"[111] he resigned on September 20, 1822. Entrusting his authority to the country's first congress, he immediately traveled to Chile and then to Europe, where he remained in exile until his death in 1850.

The Peruvian congress, which convened on September 20, 1822, met with only 50 of its 107 deputies present. Although indirect elections, like those for the Spanish Cortes, were held in six of the country's eleven provinces, five – Cuzco, Arequipa, Huamanga, Puno, and Huancavelica – were under royalist control and, therefore, represented by *suplentes.* As one of its first acts, congress established a triumvirate composed of José de La Mar, Felipe Alvarado, and Francisco Salazar Baquíjano.

The triumvirate lasted five months. Unlike San Martín, who had possessed vast power as protector, the new executive body was severely restricted by the legislature, which had assumed sovereignty. Congress soon splintered into factions and proved unable to govern the nation. The weak, divided government was virtually bankrupt and unable to mount an effective campaign against the royalists. Republican forces commanded by General Alvarado suffered serious defeats at Intermedios, allowing royalist troops to threaten the capital. Many individuals, both in and out of congress, insisted on strengthening the executive branch. Some favored inviting Bolívar to assume power in Peru, but most preferred to appoint a native son president. Finally, in February 1823, the leading generals forced the legislature to appoint José de la Riva Agüero, a prominent aristocrat, as the first president of Peru. Congress and the president were soon at odds. Despite having agreed to strengthen the executive branch, the congress still insisted on legislative dominance. It clashed with the president over a variety of matters ranging from military appointments to expenditures.[112]

The new president vigorously set about restoring order and reorganizing the armed forces. The fortunate beneficiary of British loans negotiated by San Martín's envoy, García del Río, Riva Agüero restructured the navy and formed a new expeditionary force of 5,000 men. Because the republicans faced larger and better-organized royalist armies, he also sought support from Colombia. Despite congressional misgivings, Riva Agüero invited Bolívar to come to Peru or to send a division to aid his country. The Colom-

111 Vargas Ugarte, *Historia General,* 6:240. There is a vast literature on the Guayaquil meeting in which partisans of each of the two liberators argue the merits of their hero and denigrate his opponent. Gerhard Masur offers a balanced analysis in his "The Conference of Guayaquil," *HAHR,* 31:2 (May 1951), 189–229.

112 Vargas Ugarte, *Historia General,* 6:241–55.

bian president declined the invitation to lead Peruvian forces, but he dispatched a 4,000-man army under the command of General Sucre.

The arrival of Colombian forces coincided with a military and political crisis in Peru. Politics and nationality divided the troops that remained to defend the capital after the second Intermedios expedition departed. Peruvians no longer trusted *rioplatenses* and Chileans and disliked the Colombians sent to aid them. When the royalists advanced on Lima, the government proved unable to mount a coordinated defense. As a result, the royalist army of General Canterac recaptured Lima in June. The civil authorities, leading citizens, and General Sucre and his army withdrew to the fortress of Callao. After forcing the inhabitants of the capital to contribute 300,000 pesos to royalist coffers and plundering the city, Canterac's army withdrew a month later.[113]

The royalist occupation of Lima created a schism in the Peruvian government. Congress deposed President Riva Agüero, appointed the Marqués Torre Tagle chief executive, and named General Sucre commander of the armed forces. Riva Agüero and his supporters in congress and the army escaped to Trujillo, where they established a government. Bolívar, who finally had decided to intervene in Peru, arrived in September. The portion of congress that remained in Lima named him dictator and charged him with destroying the royalists. Thus, late in 1823, Peru was governed by a congress, two presidents and a dictator along the coast, and royalists in the sierra. The country's economy had been destroyed, and there was no resolution to its grave political and military crisis. As John Lynch has noted:

Peru in 1823 was the problem child of the American revolution, repugnant to liberators and royalists alike. . . . Incapable of liberating itself, Peru was loath to accept liberation from others. Indeed this prospect caused greater resentment than the Spanish presence had ever done, and Peruvian nationalism first expressed itself not against Spaniards but against Americans.[114]

Bolívar had no intention of allowing petty local disputes to undermine his power. When Riva Agüero attempted to negotiate with the royalists to retain control of Peru, the dictator accused him of being a "usurper, rebel, and traitor."[115] Many Peruvians, however, questioned Bolívar's intentions and interpreted Riva Agüero's actions differently. The prominent Indian

113 Ibid., 257–84; Jorge Basadre, *Historia de la República del Perú, 1822–1933*, 5th ed., 10 vols. (Lima: Ediciones Historia, 1961–1968), 1:27–39.
114 Lynch, *The Spanish American Revolutions*, 267–8; Vargas Ugarte, *Historia General*, 6:257–88; John Fisher, "La formación del Estado peruano (1808–1824) y Simón Bolívar," in *Problemas de la formación del Estado y la nación en Hispanoamérica*, ed. Inge Buisson et al. (Cologne: Bühlau Verlag, 1984), 465–80.
115 Bolívar, *Proclamas y discursos del Libertador*, 298.

leader Ignacio Quispe Ninavilca, for example, expressed these attitudes when he declared:

Colombia has come to invade our homes and to satiate its ambition with the fruit of our labor. How is it possible that this adventurous race is permitted to subjugate us and to annihilate our blood? . . . That monster [Bolívar], countrymen, who seeks to take us as slaves to his towns in Colombia and to bring Colombians here . . . has the backing in Lima of only four adulators who support his cruelty. . . . Riva Agüera alone can save us from the claws of these wild beasts.[116]

Nevertheless, Bolívar's men deposed Riva Agüero, sending him to prison in Guayaquil. The political situation in Lima did not improve, however. The government remained short of funds and filled with intrigue. At the end of the year, ill with tuberculosis and discouraged, Bolívar traveled north to Pativilca. In a moment of despondency, on January 12, 1824, he declared that unless his army received funds and supplies, he would resign and return to Colombia. It was the wrong message to send to the beleaguered government in Lima.

In the capital, President Torre Tagle decided to negotiate with the royalists. To Bolívar, the Peruvian leader appeared to be forging an alliance with the royalists against the Colombians. From his sickbed, he ordered Torre Tagle arrested as the royalist General Canterac advanced upon Lima. *Ríoplatense* and Chilean troops further complicated matters when they mutinied in Callao on February 5, demanding back pay. In the midst of the confusion, on February 29 the royalists occupied Lima, where they remained until December 1824. Exhausted by the conflict, Torre Tagle and many other prominent Peruvians joined the royalist cause. As the Peruvian historian Jorge Basadre has indicated, their actions are understandable. At the time, the Peruvian elite, who had lost control of their country to foreigners, perceived the war as a struggle between Spaniards and Colombians. They knew the Spaniards well and had reason to trust them; the Colombians appeared to them as ruthless conquerors unconcerned about Peru and interested only in power. It was only natural that they should favor the Europeans.[117]

116 Quoted in Bonilla, "Bolívar y las guerrillas indígenas en el Perú," 80. Bolívar feared and detested Ninavilca; he later referred to him as "a stupid and wicked Indian." Simón Bolívar to Pedro Briceño Méndez, Lima, August 2, 1826, in Bolívar, *Cartas del Libertador,* 5:209. Bolívar remained convinced that Indians, as a whole, retained their loyalty to the Crown. At the end of 1826, he asserted: "[The] people remain as *godo* [pro-Spanish] as before. . . . I believe that if the Spaniards reach these coasts, they could raise 4 or 5,000 Indian [troops] in this province alone." Bolívar to Rafael Urdaneta, Coro, December 24, 1826, ibid., 329. On Bolívar's low regard for and hostility to the Indians, see Henri Favre, "Bolívar y los indios," *Histórica,* X:1 (July 1986), 1–18.

117 Basadre, *Historia de la República del Perú,* 1:53–5; Anna, *The Fall of Royal Government in Peru,* 221–8.

The royalists lost the opportunity to destroy the divided republicans because they also fought among themselves. Captain General and Superior Political Chief La Serna was ably supported by the *liberal* generals José de Canterac and Jerónimo Valdés. From their capital in Cuzco, they controlled the Peruvian sierra. General Pedro Antonio de Olañeta, an absolutist, commanded Upper Peru. During the constitutional period, he had no alternative but to obey his superior, La Serna. But toward the end of 1823, he learned that Fernando VII had been restored to his absolutist throne and that the loathsome Constitution of 1812 had been abolished. Freed of the hated constitutional restraints, Olañeta rejected La Serna's authority and began a war against the constitutionalists. As a result, General Valdés was forced to use his army to fight Olañeta rather than the republicans on the coast. During the next year, constitutionalist and absolutist royalist armies waged war against one another while the republicans regrouped.[118]

Torre Tagle's "betrayal" in Lima proved to be fortuitous for Bolívar. He established his base of operations in Trujillo in the north rather than in the chaotic capital. There he amassed men, money, and equipment from the occupied Department of Quito to organize slowly the army of liberation.[119] In May the army marched into the sierra. There 6,000 Colombians, most of them from Quito, 2,000 Peruvians, and 1,000 *ríoplatenses* and Chileans advanced south through the Cordillera de los Andes. On August 6, 1824, they engaged the royalist army commanded by General Canterac at Junín. The republican cavalry won the day. After several hours of combat, the royalists retreated. Bolívar had won a great victory at a particularly fortuitous moment. The day before, the absolutist Olañeta had fought a major battle in Upper Peru with General Valdés, preventing the constitutionalist's highly disciplined army from attacking the republicans at Junín.[120]

---

118 Charles W. Arnade, *The Emergence of the Republic of Bolivia* (Gainesville: University of Florida Press, 1957), 103–33; Enrique de Gandia, "Las guerras de los absolutistas y liberales en América," *Revista de Indias,* 24 (July–December 1954), 407–30; Jorge Siles Salinas, *La independencia de Bolivia* (Madrid: Editorial Mapfre 1992), 315–24.

119 As Bolívar acknowledged: "Everything has been violence upon violence. The countryside, the cities have been left deserted in order to take 3,000 men and to extract 200,000 pesos. I know better than anyone how far one can go with violence and I have employed everything. In Quito and Guayaquil all the men have been taken in the temples and in the streets to draft recruits [to take to Peru]. Money has been taken at the point of a bayonet." Bolívar to Santander, Guayaquil, April 15, 1823, in Bolívar, *Cartas del Libertador,* III, 373. On the Ecuadorian contribution to the war, see also Luis A. Rodríguez S., *Ayacucho, la batalla de la libertad Americana* (Quito: Casa de la Cultura Ecuatoriana, 1975); and Alfredo Luna Tobar, *El Ecuador en la Independencia del Perú,* 3 vols. (Quito: Banco Central del Ecuador, 1986).

120 Lecuna, *Crónica razonada,* 3:406–20. According to Arnade, "General Valdés and his army of the south were supposed to have been north with Canterac. Bolívar would have never dared attack a united Spanish army." *The Emergence of the Republic of Bolivia,* 133–4.

Shortly thereafter, Bolívar began the descent to Lima with a portion of the republican army. In the highlands, Sucre stalked the royalist forces. Indians, who continually harassed the republicans, protected the royalists. In November, after uniting the royalist constitutionalist armies, General La Serna marched to destroy Sucre's forces. He engaged the republican general at Ayacucho on the morning of December 9, 1824. The royalist line broke after hours of fierce fighting. General La Serna was captured and Canterac surrendered.[121]

Bolívar occupied Lima in early December 1824. To many residents of the capital, it was another conquest. Nearly 4,000 civilians, among them President Torre Tagle, members of congress, high-ranking members of the republican government, nobles, merchants, and their families sought refuge in the fortress of Callao. In war-torn Lima, nearly 10 percent of the population fled from the liberators. Although General La Serna had agreed to the surrender of Callao in the capitulation of Ayacucho, the fortress commander, General José Ramón Rodil, refused. After a bitter year-long siege, Callao fell on January 22, 1826. More than half of the nearly 7,000 soldiers and civilians inside the fortress died during the siege, among them President Torre Tagle, the first prominent Peruvian to have declared independence formally in 1820.[122]

Bolívar reconvened the remnants of congress on February 10, 1825. Flushed with victory and in command of virtually the entire country, he declared: "Peruvians: The day that your congress meets shall be the day of my glory; the day in which the most vehement desire of my ambition shall be fulfilled. Not to command any more!" Surrounded by armed men, congress realized that this was only rhetoric. Since Bolívar also stated that "I will not abandon Peru, however; I will serve it with my sword," the legislators understood their task. They confirmed his dictatorship for another year and adjourned.[123] Bolívar named a council of government composed of General José de La Mar, José Sánchez Carrión, and Hipólito Unánue to help him administer the internal affairs of Peru. The most pressing problem, however, was the liberation of Upper Peru.

General Olañeta had abolished the constitutional government of the Kingdom of Charcas on February 11, 1824, and restored absolutism. The elite, who feared the earlier social conflict of the *republiquetas* and their guerrilla armies, initially supported the general. But after the royalist defeat at Ayacucho, many realized that the rule of the Spanish Monarchy in America might be doomed. The difficulty lay in selecting the right moment to

121 Lecuna, *Crónica razonada*, 3:431–74; Vargas Ugarte, *Historia General del Perú*, 6:344–68.
122 Vargas Ugarte, *Historia General del Perú*, 6:361–89; Anna, *The Fall of Royal Government in Peru*, 234–7.
123 Bolívar, *Proclamas y discursos*, 299, 306.

embrace independence. The situation was particularly delicate since it appeared possible that Olañeta might retain control of an independent Kingdom of Charcas. After all, Bolívar had attempted to woo the absolutist general by granting Olañeta the title of "liberator." But Olañeta remained loyal to the king. As a result, Sucre – elevated to the rank of marshal for his victory at Ayacucho – carefully advanced against the royalist in Upper Peru.

Political intrigue brought the conflict to an end. After Sucre won a few battles, the elite of Charcas, realizing that the Spanish Monarchy had lost, opted to protect their interests. The cities outside the control of Olañeta's army declared independence when the republican forces approached. Finally, conspirators assassinated Olañeta on April 1, 1825, during the battle of Tumusla. With his death, the royalist army changed sides, accepting Sucre's offer of amnesty. Since the vast majority of Olañeta's army was American, most officers retained their rank in the new republican army. Only a few Spaniards returned home.[124]

The future of Upper Peru remained unclear. Bolívar insisted on the principle of *uti possidetis:* that the new nations inherited the territorial jurisdiction of the independent viceroyalties and captaincy generals. In the case of Colombia, he had maintained that the Captaincy General of Venezuela and the Audiencia of Quito were part of the Viceroyalty of New Granada and therefore a single nation. The Audiencia of Charcas had been part of the Viceroyalty of Peru until 1776 and then of the Viceroyalty of the Río de la Plata. If the principle were applied strictly, Upper Peru should become part of the United Provinces in South America. But that region had failed to remain united and had alienated the people of Upper Peru during its three invasions in the previous decade. (And, of course, Bolívar did not dominate the Río de la Plata.) After 1810, the Viceroy of Peru had essentially annexed Charcas and many Peruvians believed Upper Peru should form part of their nation. Sucre, however, maintained that the region should become an independent country because its people desired it. Bolívar eventually agreed.

The constituent assembly, convened by Sucre, met at Chuquisaca on July 10, 1825. Although only thirty-nine deputies were present at the inauguration, ultimately forty-eight were seated. Because of property and literacy qualifications, the elite dominated the congress. Most were well educated; thirty were graduates of the University of San Francisco in Chuquisaca. Only two from the province of La Paz had fought for independence. After extensive debate, on August 6, 1825, the assembly decided, by a vote of forty-five to two, to declare Upper Peru independent of all nations in the

---

124 Arnade, *The Emergence of the Republic of Bolivia,* 150–82; Gandia, "Las guerras de los absolutistas y liberales," 413.

Old World and the New. The assembly adopted Bolívar's name for the new country, calling it Bolivia, and requested that he write its constitution.[125]

In his public utterances, Bolívar generally insisted that he favored a liberal civilian representative government, but his actions demonstrate that he really preferred autocratic rule. The draft of the constitution he had presented to the Congress of Angostura in 1819 included a powerful lifetime president with the ability to suspend civil liberties, a weak legislature, and a clear distinction between active and passive citizens. During the Congress of Cúcuta, he had declared that only those who served in the army should have the rights of active citizens. In those instances, he had presented his preferences to congresses that had convened to write constitutions. Now he had the opportunity to write a charter that reflected only his views.

The assembly adopted Bolívar's constitution on July 11, 1826. The Bolivarian charter declared that the government "is popular representative." But it established a lifetime president with vast power, including the right to designate his successor, a clear indication of Bolívar's distrust of democratic institutions and his preference for enlightened despotism. As he insisted: "A lifetime president, with the right to elect his successor, is the most sublime inspiration of republican ideas. . . . This measure avoids elections which are the greatest scourge of republics and produce only anarchy, which . . . is the most immediate and most terrible danger of popular governments." The legislature, with three chambers composed of tribunes, senators, and censors, was subservient to the executive. The constitution disenfranchised the vast majority of Bolivians when it divided the people into *citizens,* who possessed the right to vote and to hold office, and *Bolivians,* who enjoyed civil but not political rights. Citizens had to "know how to read and write, possess some employment or industry, or profess some science or art without being subject to another in the category of domestic service."[126]

At Bolívar's recommendation, the assembly elected Sucre president for life. The new executive devoted himself to restoring order and prosperity to the new nation. His government was a model of enlightened reform. But, unlike Bolívar, Sucre did not desire a lifetime appointment. He resigned at the end of 1828, after a revolt erupted in the country, and returned to his family in Quito. Thereafter, Bolivia charted its own independent path.[127]

Determined to consolidate his power, Bolívar decided to impose his constitution upon Peru. On August 16, 1826, he convened a constituent assembly in Lima that adopted the Bolivarian charter and elected him life-

125 Arnade, *The Emergence of the Republic of Bolivia,* 165–204; Siles Salinas, *La independencia de Bolivia,* 332–54.

126 Bolívar's address and the constitution are reproduced in Pombo and Guerra, *Constituciones de Colombia,* 3:115–54.

127 William F. Lofstron, *The Promise of and the Problem of Reform: Attempted Economic and Social Change in the First Years of Bolivian Independence* (Ithaca: Cornell University, 1972).

time president of Peru. Although initially acceptable to Bolivians, the document shocked the politically active population in Peru and Colombia. As Manuel Quijano Otero observed, "when studying this constitution, many will ask if the blood shed and the sacrifices made to shake off the yoke of the king of Spain were worth it."[128] Opposition soon emerged among *liberales* in Peru. Undeterred, Bolívar remained convinced that his charter was appropriate and hoped that Colombia would adopt it so that an Andean confederation might be formed uniting Bolivia, Peru, and Colombia. Bolívar's dream of an enlightened despot governing nearly half of South America was shattered by regional rivalries and by insistence on representative government by the politically active populations of the cities.

The regionalism that would destroy Colombia had begun to undermine the Santander administration. Venezuelan leaders like Páez challenged the authority of Bogotá. The situation had grown so tense by September 1826 that Bolívar returned to Colombia, leaving General Andrés de Santa Cruz in charge of Peru. His departure provided Peruvian *liberales* an opportunity to transform the government. In January 1827 they instigated a rebellion of the Colombian troops in Peru, which gave them the excuse to abolish the Bolivarian constitution. Santa Cruz accepted their decision and skillfully arranged for the withdrawal of Colombian soldiers from the country. On June 4 he convened a congress that elected General José de La Mar president of Peru.[129] The country faced an uncertain future, but it would be one shaped by Peruvians.

Bolívar returned to Colombia determined to resolve the nation's conflicts by imposing his Bolivarian constitution. But first he solved the country's immediate crisis, General Páez's rebellion against the national government in Bogotá, by granting him a pardon in return for the latter's support. The action, in effect, undermined the national government, which, in Bolívar's absence, had been administered by Vice President Santander. The President's subsequent efforts to impose his constitution on the country resulted in a break with the vice president and his *liberal* supporters.[130]

Unwilling to accept the Bolivarian charter, congress summoned a *gran*

128 Pombo and Guerra, *Constituciones de Colombia,* 3:115.

129 Basadre, *Historia de la república,* 1:113–60

130 After years of unquestioned military command, Bolívar was not used to the rough and tumble of civilian politics in Colombia. The liberal press's hostility to his constitution apparently distressed him and caused him to suspect that Santander was responsible for the attacks. Therefore, he ended their friendship. As he explained to Carlos Soublette: "Unable to support Santander's perfidious ingratitude any longer, I have written him today not to write me any more because I don't want to reply or grant him the title of friend." Bolívar to Carlos Soublette, Caracas, March 16, 1827, Lecuna, *Cartas del Libertador,* V, 414. A saddened Santander replied to Bolívar: "My vote will always be for your health and your prosperity; my heart always will love you with gratitude; my hand will never write a line that might harm you; and even though, all your life, you may not call me or believe me your friend, I will always be yours with sentiments of profound respect and just

convención, which met in April 1828 to resolve the nation's constitutional crisis. But after two months of bitter debates between *liberales* and bolivarians, the partisans of the president withdrew, leaving the convention without a quorum. On August 27, Bolívar established a dictatorship until a new constituent congress met in 1830, as stipulated by the Constitution of Cúcuta. Early the following month, he abolished the vice presidency and dismissed Santander. Many in central Colombia opposed the dictatorship. On September 25, 1828, a failed attempt to assassinate Bolívar resulted in the execution of several political and military leaders, among them the *mulato* admiral José Padilla. Although Santander also was accused of being a conspirator and sentenced to death, Bolívar was forced to commute the sentence to exile because of widespread public protest.

Colombia would experience little peace in the months that followed. The new Peruvian leaders had dispatched forces to assert territorial claims to lands in the possession of the northern republic. The two countries went to war in July 1828. A Colombian army led by Marshal Sucre won a major battle at Tarqui on February 27, 1829, which ended, for a time, the boundary conflict. The victory strengthened Bolívar's government, convincing some members of his cabinet to propose the establishment of a constitutional monarchy. Bolívar would remain president as long as he lived or wanted; thereafter a European prince would be elevated to the crown. Although Bolívar, apparently, had not suggested or supported the proposal, he was blamed by many who opposed it. Páez and the Venezuelans once again rebelled. This time they forbade Bolívar to set foot in the land of his birth. Other opposition movements erupted throughout central Colombia.[131]

In 1830, a constituent congress, known as *el Congreso Admirable,* failed to resolve the issues that divided the nation. On May 6 an assembly in Venezuela declared its independence and seceded from the union. A week later Quito, now called Ecuador, followed suit. Bolívar's most trusted lieutenant, Marshal Sucre, who had served as president of the Congreso Admirable, was murdered on June 4, 1830, as he returned home to Quito. In an abyss of despair as he prepared to go into exile, Bolívar concluded: "America is ungovernable . . ., [and] he who serves a revolution plows the sea. . . ."[132] He died of his lingering tuberculosis while still on Colombian soil on December 17, 1830.

consideration." Francisco de Paula Santander to Bolívar, Bogotá, April 29, 1827, in Roberto Cortázar, *Cartas y mensajes del General Francisco de Paula Santander,* 10 vols. (Bogotá: Librería Voluntad, 1953–1956) 8:138.

131 There are many partisan accounts of this controversial period of Colombian history and of Bolívar's life. For a recent evaluation, see David Bushnell, "The Last Dictatorship: Betrayal or Consummation?," *HAHR,* 63:1 (February 1983), 65–105.

132 Simón Bolívar to Juan José Flores, Barranquilla, November 9, 1830, in *Correspondencia del Libertador con el General Juan José Flores, 1825–1830* (Quito: Banco Central del Ecuador, 1977), 283–7.

Although the power of the Spanish Monarchy in America had finally ended, many members of the urban middle and upper classes remained ambivalent about independence. Despite its inequities, the old political order had provided opportunity as well as stability. The future seemed uncertain and very threatening. As the Peruvian jurist Manuel Lorenzo de Vidaurre declared in his *Cartas americanas:*

I love the Spanish nation like my grandmother and America like my mother. I weep to see these beloved persons destroyed. One, old but inexperienced and with bad habits that impel her, according to her inclination, to dominate and conquer. The other, young, weak, without resources, going from desperation to pusillanimity, from heroism to barbarity, with signs of virtue and with many vices.

He also voiced the Americans' anger at the Monarchy's failure to reach an accommodation with them. "There was time during which conciliation was possible. But it is impossible for Spain to extricate herself from her prejudices. Her pride exceeds her debility and shapes her character."[133]

133 Basadre, *Historia de la República,* 1:206.

Conclusion

During the second half of the eighteenth century and the early nineteenth century, the Spanish world underwent a major transformation. The reigns of Carlos III and Carlos IV (1759–1808) witnessed the development of modern political thought – which emphasized liberty, equality, civil rights, the rule of law, representative constitutional government, and laissez-faire economics – among a small but significant group of Spaniards and Americans. As long as the Crown governed effectively, these ideas remained largely intellectual pursuits. But the French invasion of Spain and the collapse of the Monarchy in 1808 provided the liberal minority with an unprecedented opportunity to implement its goals.

The disintegration of the Crown triggered a series of events that culminated in the establishment of representative government in the Spanish world. The initial step in that process was the formation of local governing juntas in Spain and America that invoked the Hispanic legal principle that sovereignty, in the absence of the king, reverted to the people. Although the Peninsular provinces made that transition easily, the American kingdoms faced the opposition of royal officials, resident Europeans, and their New World allies. The creation of the Junta Suprema Central Gubernativa del Reino appeared to provide a solution to the crisis of the Monarchy. That body not only recognized the rights of Spanish provinces but also acknowledged that the American kingdoms constituted integral and equal parts of the Monarchy and possessed the right to representation in the government.

The decisive French victories of 1809, however, destroyed the fragile balance established by the Junta Central. When the body dissolved itself in January 1810, appointing a Council of Regency in its place, some provinces of Spain and several kingdoms of America refused to recognize the legitimacy of the new government. The convening of the Cortes resolved the concerns of the provinces of Spain and many parts of the New World. The Spanish parliament provided American autonomists with a peaceful means of obtaining home rule. Moreover, the extensive debates in that congress, which were widely disseminated by the press during the 1810–1812 period, significantly influenced both the Spanish Americans who supported as well as those who opposed the new government in Spain.

The deputies of Spain and America, who enacted the Constitution of the Spanish Monarchy in 1812, transformed the Hispanic world. The Constitution of Cádiz was not a Spanish document; it was as much an American charter as a Spanish one. Indeed, it is unlikely that the Constitution of 1812 would have taken the form it did without the participation of representatives from the New World. The American deputies to the Cortes played a central role in drafting the constitution. Their arguments and proposals convinced some Spaniards to embrace substantial change in America as well as in the Peninsula. Some of the important *liberal* reforms that characterized the Spanish Constitution of 1812, such as the provincial deputation, are directly attributable to New World deputies. Similarly, some transformations that Spaniards sought for their region, such as *ayuntamientos* for small towns, had a profound effect in the New World, where *ayuntamientos* had been restricted to mayor urban centers.

The Constitution of Cádiz abolished seigniorial institutions, the Inquisition, Indian tribute, and forced labor – such as the *mita* in South America and personal service in the Peninsula – and asserted the state's control of the Church. It created a unitary state with equal laws for all parts of the Spanish Monarchy, substantially restricted the authority of the king, and entrusted the Cortes with decisive power. When it enfranchised all men, except those of African ancestry, without requiring either literacy or property qualifications, the Constitution of 1812 surpassed all existing representative governments, such as those of Great Britain, the United States, and France, in providing political rights to the vast majority of the male population.

The Constitution of the Spanish Monarchy expanded the electorate and dramatically increased the scope of political activity. The new charter established representative government at three levels: the municipality, the province, and the Monarchy. It allowed cities and towns with 1,000 or more inhabitants to form *ayuntamientos.* Political power was transferred from the center to the localities as vast numbers of people were incorporated into the political process. Although the elite clearly dominated politics, hundreds of thousands of middle- and lower-class men, including Indians, mestizos, and *castas,* became involved in politics in a meaningful way and made their presence felt.

Despite the unparalleled democratization of the political system, civil war erupted in America because some groups, which refused to accept the government in Spain, insisted upon forming local juntas, whereas others, which recognized the Regency and the Cortes, opposed them. Political divisions among the elites combined with regional antipathy and social tensions to exacerbate the conflict in the New World.

The American movements of 1810, like those in Spain, arose from a desire to remain independent of French domination. Some kingdoms of the New World, as well as some provinces of the Peninsula, questioned the legitimacy of the Council of Regency and its right to speak for the Nación Española. The great difference between the Peninsula and America was that the regions of Spain fought an external enemy, whereas the New World realms grappled with internal disputes. The conflict in America waxed and waned during the first constitutional period, 1810–14. At times, when the royal authorities acted with restraint, accommodation seemed possible. The situation changed with Fernando VII's return in 1814. He abolished the Cortes and the Constitution, restoring absolutism. Unfettered by that charter, the royal authorities in the New World crushed most autonomy movements. Only the isolated Río de la Plata remained beyond the reach of a weakened Spanish Monarchy.

Fernando VII's return provided an opportunity to restore the unity of the Spanish world. Virtually every act that had occurred since 1808 – the struggle against the French, the political revolution enacted by the Cortes, and the autonomy movements in America – had been taken in his name. Initially it appeared that he might accept moderate reforms, but ultimately the king opted to rely on force to restore royal order in the New World.

The Crown's repression prompted the minority of America's politically active population that favored independence to act decisively. Republicans renewed the struggle in Venezuela in 1817, and by 1819 the tide had turned against the Monarchy when a combined force of *neogranadinos* and Venezuelans defeated the royalists at Boyacá, forcing the viceroy and other officials to flee from Bogotá. In the south, José de San Martín won a decisive victory in Chile in April 1818.

The renewed conflict in South America enhanced the power of military men. Self-proclaimed generals like Simón Bolívar and former professional soldiers such as José de San Martín gained immense power and prestige as the leaders of the bloody struggles to win independence. Although civilian and clerical institutions – *ayuntamientos,* courts, parishes, cathedral chapters – continued to function, and although new governments were formed and congresses elected, military power predominated. Colombia provides the clearest example of that phenomenon.

Convened by Bolívar in February 1819, the Congress of Angostura legitimized his power and in December created the Republic of Colombia, incorporating Venezuela, New Granada, and Quito. Although Venezuela and New Granada possessed some representation at Angostura, Quito had none. Later in 1821, the Congress of Cúcuta, pressured by President Bolívar and intimidated by the army, ratified the formation of the Republic of Colombia, again without any representation from Quito. In contrast to the Spanish Constitution of 1812, written by a Cortes composed of elected representatives from all parts of the Monarchy – which granted considerable autonomy to the regions via the constitutional *ayuntamientos* and the provincial deputations, restricted the power of the king, and bestowed sovereignty on the legislature – the new Colombian constitution created a highly centralized government that granted vast authority to the president.

The military did not gain such power in the southern cone, even though the structures and processes of the Spanish Constitution of 1812 did not significantly influence either the Río de la Plata or Chile. Because the autonomists in those regions gained control early, neither area participated either in the formation of constitutional *ayuntamientos* and provincial deputations or in the popular elections established by the Constitution of Cádiz. Although Buenos Aires and Santiago experienced partisan conflicts and civil wars during the early years, the region escaped the brutal campaigns waged in northern South America. The Río de la Plata obtained its autonomy and ultimately its independence by default; the area experienced little armed conflict with the royal authorities. Similarly, Chile endured only limited warfare in its struggle for emancipation. After 1818 large military contingents left those regions to secure the independence of Peru, even though some royalist forces remained in the south. As a result, civilians dominated the governments of those regions.

By 1819 it was clear that Fernando VII would have to send more troops if he wished to retain control of America. But raising yet another expeditionary force to reconquer the New World only increased discontent in the Peninsula. The *liberales* in Spain exploited the army's disenchantment with the war in America, eventually forcing the king to restore the Constitution in March 1820. The return of constitutional order transformed the Hispanic political system for the third time in a decade.

The restoration of constitutional government elicited disparate responses from the American regions. When the news arrived in April, the people of New Spain and Guatemala enthusiastically reestablished the constitutional system. In the months that followed, they conducted elections for countless constitutional *ayuntamientos,* provincial deputations, and the Cortes. Political instability in the Peninsula during the previous dozen years, however, had convinced many *novohispanos* that it was prudent to establish an autonomous government within the Spanish Monarchy. The autonomists, the members of the national elite who ultimately gained power after independence, opted for a constitutional monarchy. They pursued two courses of action. New Spain's deputies to the Cortes proposed a project for New World autonomy that would create three American kingdoms governed by Spanish princes and allied with the Peninsula. The Spanish majority, however, rejected the proposal that would have granted Americans the home rule they had been seeking since 1808. At the same time, New Spain's autonomists encouraged and supported the royalist Colonel

Agustín de Iturbide, who accepted their plan for autonomy, which resembled the proposal presented to the Cortes. Independence was assured when Iturbide and his supporters won the backing of the majority of the royal army. Mexico achieved its independence not because the royal authorities were defeated militarily but because *novohispanos* no longer supported the Crown politically. Central America also declared independence and joined the new Mexican Empire. It seceded peacefully in 1823, after the empire was abolished, and formed a separate nation.

The newly independent Mexicans carefully followed the precedents of the Spanish constitutional system. Although they initially established an empire, they eventually formed a federal republic in 1824. They modeled their new constitution on the Spanish charter because it had been part of their recent political experience. After all, distinguished *novohispano* statesmen like José Guridi y Alcocer and Miguel Ramos Arizpe, who had participated in writing the Constitution of 1812, also served in the Mexican Constituent Congress. To many Mexicans, it was as much their Constitution as Spain's. In keeping with Hispanic constitutional practices, they also formed a government with a powerful legislature and a weak executive branch. Similarly, federalism in Mexico arose naturally from the earlier political experience; the provincial deputations simply converted themselves into states. Like Mexico, the new Central American republic established a federation based on Hispanic constitutional practices.

In South America the restoration of the Spanish Constitution provided those favoring independence the opportunity to press their campaign to liberate the continent. In contrast to New Spain, the South American insurgents defeated the royal authorities militarily. Two pincer movements, one from the south and the other from the north, eventually converged on Peru.

In 1820 the republicans began systematically to liberate Venezuela and New Granada. On October 9, 1820, Guayaquil declared independence, formed a republic, and attempted without success to free the highland provinces of the Kingdom of Quito. A mixed force consisting mainly of local troops, Colombians, and men from San Martín's army, under the command of General Antonio José de Sucre finally defeated the Spanish forces in Quito on May 24, 1822, at the Battle of Pichincha. Bolívar, who arrived from the north in June with more Colombian troops, incorporated the region into the Republic of Colombia despite opposition from both Quito and Guayaquil. Subsequently, Bolívar imposed martial law in the former Kingdom of Quito to impress men as well as to requisition money and supplies for the struggle against the royalists in Peru, the last bastion of royal power in America.

The southern forces led by San Martín landed in Lima in August 1820 with a liberating army composed of Chileans and *rioplatenses*. Although he controlled the coast, San Martín could not overcome the royalists in the highlands. In an effort to win the loyalty of the population, Spanish *liberales* forced Viceroy Joaquín de la Pezuela to abdicate on January 29, 1821, named General José de la Serna captain general and superior political chief, and implemented the Constitution of 1812. The Spanish constitutionalists reorganized the army and nearly drove San Martín's forces from the coast. But divisions within the royalist ranks prevented them from defeating the forces of independence.

Unable to obtain the support he needed in Peru and abroad, San Martín ceded the honor of final victory to Bolívar. Although the Colombians arrived in force in 1823, they made little progress. Divisions among Peruvians, shortage of supplies, and strong royalist armies kept them pinned down on the coast. However, the royalists were also divided. In Upper Peru the absolutist general Pedro Antonio Olañeta opposed La Serna and the Spanish *liberales*. After the Spanish Constitution was once again abolished, General Olañeta took up arms against the Spanish *liberales* on December 25, 1823. Internecine warfare contributed to the royalists' defeat. For nearly a year, while Bolívar and his men recovered, royalist constitutional and absolutist armies waged war in the highlands. Ultimately, General Sucre defeated the royalist constitutional army in the decisive battle of Ayacucho on December 9, 1824. Olañeta's absolutist forces, however, retained control of Upper Peru. Political intrigue finally ended the struggle: Olañeta was assassinated in April 1825. The death of the absolutist officer marked the end of royal power in Upper Peru. Subsequently, General Sucre formed the new republic of Bolivia. By 1826, when the last royal forces surrendered, Bolívar dominated South America as president of Colombia, dictator of Peru, and ruler of Bolivia.

Two competing political traditions emerged during the independence period: One, forged in more than a decade of war, emphasized strong executive power; the other, based on the civilian parliamentary experience, insisted upon legislative dominance. They epitomized a fundamental conflict about the nature of government. New Spain, which achieved independence through political compromise rather than by force of arms, is representative of the civil tradition. There the Spanish constitutional system triumphed and continued to evolve. Despite subsequent *golpes* by military men, civilian politicians dominated Mexican politics.

In contrast, military force ultimately liberated northern South America. Unlike Mexico, in Colombia, Peru, and Bolivia, the men of arms dominated the men of law. The Hispanic constitutional experience exerted little influence in the region. The three newly independent South American nations established strong centralist governments with powerful chief executives and weak legislatures. In 1830, Colombia – sometimes called *Gran Colombia* – splintered into three countries: Venezuela, New Granada, and Ecuador. The preponderance of the men of arms, however, was harder to eradicate.

The southern cone, which also had won independence by force, did not fall under the control of military men. The region endured only limited warfare with royalist forces. Most of the armed conflicts occurred between and among provinces. Although Santiago and Buenos Aires toyed with federalism, Chile eventually established a highly centralized oligarchical republic, whereas in the Río de la Plata, the various provinces formed a loose confederation. Despite vast differences in the nature of their regimes, civilians dominated both nations.

By 1826 the overseas possessions of the Spanish Monarchy, one of the world's most imposing political structures at the end of the eighteenth century, consisted only of Cuba, Puerto Rico, the Philippines, and a few other Pacific islands. Having achieved independence, the countries of the American continent would henceforth chart their own future. Most, however, entered a prolonged period of economic decline and political instability. Military strongmen – *caudillos* but not institutional militarists – dominated many nations, whose shattered institutions no longer functioned. The stable, more developed, and stronger countries of the North Atlantic – such as Britain, France, and the United States – flooded Spanish America with their exports, dominated their credit, and sometimes imposed their will upon the new American nations by force of arms.

Spain's and America's nineteenth-century experience provides stark proof of the cost of independence. Like its American offspring, the former metropolis suffered political chaos, economic decline, economic imperialism, and foreign intervention. Both the Peninsula and the nations of the New World endured civil wars and military *pronunciamientos.* In their efforts to resolve their political and economic crises, Spain and America experimented with monarchism and republicanism, centralism and federalism, and representative government and dictatorship. Unfortunately, there was no simple solution for nations whose economies had been destroyed by war and whose political systems had been shattered by revolution. Political order and economic growth would not begin to be restored in both regions until the 1870s.

Why did Spain and Spanish America decline politically and economically during the nineteenth century? Why did they not, like Britain and the United States after the latter's emancipation, enjoy political stability and continued economic growth? The answer lies in the nature of the Spanish Monarchy and the timing of Spanish American independence.

The emancipation of Spanish America did not merely consist of separation from the mother country, as in the case of the United States; it also destroyed a vast and responsive social, political, and economic system that functioned well despite its many imperfections. The worldwide Spanish

Monarchy had proven to be flexible and able to accommodate social tensions and conflicting political and economic interests for nearly 300 years. The American upper class formed an integral part of the Monarchy's elite and was tied to its European counterpart through marriage and, frequently, economic associations. Tangled family and business relationships linked American autonomists to Spanish royalists and constitutionalists to absolutists. These networks, which arose as a result of the interlocking bureaucracy that anchored the Monarchy, grew as the population and economy expanded. They provided the social, political, and economic space required to resolve conflicts and maintain the system in operation. Despite inefficiencies and inequities, the Spanish Monarchy functioned as an economic system and, as a unit, possessed the strength to participate effectively in the world economy. In the postindependence era it became apparent that, individually, the former Spanish Monarchy's separate parts were at a competitive disadvantage. In that regard, nineteenth-century Spain, like its American offspring, was just one more newly independent nation groping for a place in an uncertain and difficult world.

In contrast to the United States, which obtained its independence in 1783, just in time to benefit from the insatiable demand for its products generated by the twenty years of war in Europe that followed the French Revolution of 1789, the Spanish world achieved emancipation *after* the end of the European wars. Not only did the new nations have to rebuild their shattered economies, but they also faced a lack of demand for their products. Instead, Europe and the United States were eager to flood Spanish America with their own goods. The new countries did not enjoy prosperity during their formative years, as the United States had. Rather, the Spanish American states had to face grave internal and external problems with diminishing resources.

After independence, Spanish and American *liberales* advanced similar solutions to the fundamental socioeconomic problems their nations faced. They proposed abolishing privileges, primarily the clerical and military *fueros*. They also stripped the Church of its landed wealth and forced communal villages to establish private landholding. *Liberales* in all countries perceived these actions as necessary to creating the vibrant economies and modern societies they desired. Conservatives, who also favored economic growth, viewed the reforms as attempts to destroy religion, order, and morality. Similarly, most former Indian communities and many other *campesinos* did not consider beneficial the *liberal* efforts to modernize the countryside. These conflicts were not easily resolved; *liberal* – conservative, Church – state, and urban – rural struggles consumed Spain and America during the nineteenth century.

Only in the last third of the nineteenth century did the nations of America and Spain begin to consolidate their states. By the 1870s and 1880s,

Spain, and most Spanish American countries had established stable governments and undertaken the difficult process of economic rehabilitation. Unfortunately, the former Spanish Monarchy had languished during fifty crucial years in which Britain, France, Germany, and the United States had advanced to a different stage of economic development. In the period since the great political revolution had dissolved the Spanish Monarchy, the North Atlantic world had changed dramatically. Western European and U.S. industrial corporations and financial institutions had achieved such size and strength that the emerging economies of Spanish America and Spain simply could not compete. Consequently, the members of the former Spanish Monarchy were forced to accept a secondary role in the new world order. The failure of either Spanish absolutists or *liberales* to reach an accommodation with America had indeed proven costly to both sides.

As a result of the great political revolution that led to the dissolution of the Spanish Monarchy, however, Spain and the new nations of America developed a unique political culture based not on foreign models but on their own traditions and experience. After independence in America and after Fernando VII's death in the Peninsula, the old absolute Monarchy disappeared. The people of the Spanish-speaking world ceased being subjects of the Crown and became citizens of their nations. During the nineteenth century, the new political systems of Spain and Spanish America were consolidated on the basis of the liberal tradition of constitutional government and political representation that had emerged in the Cortes of Cádiz and its rival regimes in America. Despite power struggles, such as those between monarchists and republicans, centralists and federalists, and parliamentarians and *caudillos,* a liberal, representative, constitutional government remained the political ideal of the Spanish-speaking nations. Indeed, even *caudillos* and dictators have been forced to acknowledge, at least in principle, the supremacy of the rule of law and the ultimate desirability of civilian, representative, constitutional government.

Bibliography

Archives

Ecuador

Archivo Histórico del Banco Central (Quito)
Archivo Municipal de Quito (Quito)
Archivo Nacional de Historia (Quito)

Mexico

Archivo General de la Nación (Mexico, D.F.)
Archivo del Ayuntamiento de Jalapa (Jalapa)

Spain

Archivo del Congreso de Diputados (Madrid)
Archivo Histórico Nacional (Madrid)
Archivo General de Indias (Seville)

Periodicals

El Censor, 1816
El Despertador Americano, 1810
Diario de México, 1806, 1809, 1810
Gazeta de Buenos Ayres, 1810, 1811
Gazeta de Caracas, 1810, 1811, 1817
Gazeta de México, 1810
Mercurio Peruano, 1791

Other Printed Sources

Actas del Congreso de Cúcuta, 1821. 3 vols. Bogotá: Biblioteca de la Presidencia de la República, 1989.
Addy, George M. *The Enlightenment in the University of Salamanca.* Durham: Duke University Press, 1966.
Aguirre Abad, Francisco. *Bosquejo histórico de la República del Ecuador.* Guayaquil: Corporación de Estudios y Publicaciones, 1972.
Alamán, Lucas. *Historia de Méjico desde los primeros movimientos que prepararon su independencia en el año de 1808 hast la época presente.* 5 vols. Mexico Imprenta de Lara, 1849–1852.

Alcalá Galiano, Antonio. *Recuerdos de un Anciano*. Madrid: Ediciones Atlas, 1955.

Alemparte, Julio. *Carrera y Freire, Fundadores de la República*. Santiago: Editorial Nacimiento, 1963.

Alva Ixtlilxóchitl, Fernando de. *Obras históricas*, edited by Edmundo O'Gorman. 2 vols. Mexico: Universidad Nacional Autónoma de México, 1975–1977.

Álvarez, José María. *Instituciones de derecho real de Castilla y de Indias*, edited by Mario García Laguardia and María del Refugio González. 2 vols. Mexico: Universidad Nacional Autónoma de México, 1982.

Alzate y Ramírez, José Antonio de. *Periódicos*, vol. 1 of *Obras*, edited by Roberto Moreno. Mexico: Universidad Nacional Autónoma de México, 1980.

Anderson, Woodrow. "Reform as a Means to Quell Revolution." In *Mexico and the Spanish Cortes, 1810–1822*, edited by Nettie Lee Benson, 185–207. Austin: University of Texas Press, 1966.

Andrien, Kenneth J. "Economic Crisis, Taxes and the Quito Insurrection of 1765." *Past and Present* 129 (November 1990): 104–31.

    The Kingdom of Quito, 1690–1830: The State and Regional Development. Cambridge: Cambridge University Press, 1995.

    "The Sale of Fiscal Offices and the Decline of Royal Authority in the Viceroyalty of Peru, 1633–1700." *Hispanic American Historical Review* 62, no. 1 (February 1982): 49–71.

Anna, Timothy E. "Economic Causes of San Martín's Failure in Lima." *Hispanic American Historical Review* 54, no. 4 (November 1975):657–81.

    The Fall of Royal Government in Peru. Lincoln: University of Nebraska Press, 1979.

    "The Peruvian Declaration of Independence: Freedom by Coercion." *Journal of Latin American Studies* 7, no. 2 (November 1975):221–48.

    Spain and the Loss the America. Lincoln: University of Nebraska Press, 1983.

Annino, Antonio. "Prácticas criollas y liberalismo en la crisis del espacio urbano colonial. El 29 de noviembre de 1812 en la ciudad de México." *Secuencia* 24 (September–December 1992): 121–58.

Archer, Christon I. *The Army in Bourbon Mexico, 1760–1810*. Albuquerque: University of New Mexico Press, 1977.

    "Bite of the Hydra: The Rebellion of Cura Miguel Hidalgo, 1810–1811." In *Patterns of Contention in Mexican History*, edited by Jaime E. Rodríguez O., 69–93. Wilmington: Scholarly Resources, 1992.

    "Insurrection–Reaction–Revolution–Fragmentation: Reconstructing the Choreography of Meltdown in New Spain during the Independence Era." *Mexican Studies/Estudios Mexicanos* 10, no. 1 (Winter 1994): 63–98.

    "What Goes Around Comes Around. Political Change and Continuity in Mexico, 1750–1850." In *Mexico in the Age of Democratic Revolutions, 1750–1850*, edited by Jaime E. Rodríguez O., 261–80. Boulder: Lynne Rienner, 1994.

Argentina, Senate. *Biblioteca de mayo*. 10 vols. Buenos Aires: Imprenta del Congreso de la Nación, 1969.

Arnade, Charles W. *The Emergence of the Republic of Bolivia*. Gainesville: University of Florida Press, 1957.

Artola, Miguel. *Los afrancesados*. Madrid: Instituto de Estudios Políticos, 1953.

    "Campillo y las reformas de Carlos III." *Revista de Indias* 12 (October–December 1952):685–714.

    La España de Fernando VII. Madrid: Espasa-Calpe, 1968.

    Los orígenes de la España contemporánea. 2 vols. Madrid: Instituto de Estudios Políticos, 1959.

Arze Aguirre, Rene Danilo. *Participatión popular en la independencia de Bolivia.* La Paz: Organización de los Estados Americanos, 1979.

Avendaño Rojas, Xiomara. "La independencia y la autonomía provincial en el Reino de Guatemala, 1821–1823." Paper presented at the seminar La Independencia y la formación de las autonomías territoriales mexicanas, Instituto de Investigaciones doctor José María Luis Mora, August 24–5, 1994.

"Procesos electorales y clase política en la Federación de Centroamérica (1810–1840). Ph.D. diss., El Colegio de México, 1995.

Barbier, Jacques A. "Elites and Cadres in Bourbon Chile." *Hispanic American Historical Review* 52, no. 3 (August 1972):416–35.

Barbier, Jacques A. and Mark A. Burkholder. "Critique of Stanley J. Stein's 'Bureaucracy . . .'." *Hispanic American Historical Review* 62, no. 3 (August 1982):460–9.

Bartolache, José Ignacio. *Mercurio Volante.* Edited by Roberto Moreno. Mexico: Universidad Nacional Autónoma de México, 1979.

Basadre, Jorge. *Historia de la República del Perú, 1822–1933,* 5th ed. 10 vols. Lima: Ediciones Historia, 1961–1968.

Baskes, Jeremy. "Coerced or Voluntary? The *Repartimiento* and Market Participation of Peasants in Late Colonial Oaxaca." *Journal of Latin American Studies* 28, no. 1 (February 1996):1–28.

Benson, Nettie Lee. "The Contested Mexican Election of 1812." *Hispanic American Historical Review* 26, no. 3 (August 1946):336–50.

La Diputación Provincial y el federalismo mexicano. Mexico: El Colegio de México, 1955.

"The Election of 1809 in New Spain." Unpublished. Nettie Lee Benson Latin American Collection, University of Texas Library, Austin, June 1989.

"Texas' Failure to Send a Deputy to the Spanish Cortes, 1810–1812." *Southwestern Historical Quarterly* 54 (July 1960):1–22.

Benson, Nettie Lee, ed. *Mexico and the Spanish Cortes.* Austin: University of Texas Press, 1966.

Benson, Nettie Lee, and Charles Berry. "The Central American Delegation to the First Constituent Congress of Mexico, 1822–1823." *Hispanic American Historical Review* 49, no. 4 (November 1969):679–702.

Berruezo, María Teresa. *La participación americana en las Cortes de Cádiz (1810–1814).* Madrid: Centro de Estudios Constitucionales, 1986.

Berry, Charles R. "The Election of Mexican Deputies to the Spanish Cortes, 1810–1822." In *Mexico and the Spanish Cortes,* edited by Nettie Lee Benson, 10–42. Austin: University of Texas Press, 1966.

Blanco Acevedo, Pablo. *El federalismo de Artigas y la independencia nacional.* 2d ed. Montevideo: Impresora uruguaya, 1950.

Blanco Fombona, Rufino. *Bolívar y la guerra a muerte.* Caracas: Impresoras Unidas, 1969.

Blossom, Thomas. *Nariño: Hero of Colombian Independence.* Tucson: University of Arizona Press, 1967.

Bolívar, Simón. "Carta de Jamaica." In *Pensamiento político de la emancipación, 1790–1825,* 2 vols., compiled by José Luis Romero and Luis Alberto Romero, 2:83–99. Caracas: Biblioteca de Ayacucho, 1977.

Cartas del Libertador. 8 vols. Caracas: Fundación Vicente Lecuna, 1964–1970.

Correspondencia del Libertador con el General Juan José Flores, 1825–1830. Quito: Banco Central del Ecuador, 1977.

Obras completas. 2 vols. Havana: Editorial Lex, 1947.

Proclamas y discursos del Libertador. Caracas: Litografía del Comercio, 1939.

Bonilla, Heraclio. "Bolívar y las guerrillas indígenas en el Perú." *Cultura: Revista del Banco Central del Ecuador* 6, no. 16 (May–August 1983):81–95.

Borja, Luis F. "Para la historia del 10 de agosto de 1809." *Boletín de la Sociedad Ecuatoriana de Estudios Históricos Americanos* 2, no. 6 (May–June 1919):431–43.

Borja y Borja, Ramiro. *Derecho constitutional ecuatoriano.* 3 vols. Madrid: Ediciones de Cultura Hispánica, 1950.

Borrero, Manuel María. *La Revolución quiteña, 1809–1812.* Quito: Editorial Espejo, 1962.

Bracamonte y Susa, Pedro. "La ruptura del pacto social colonial y el reforzamiento de la identidad indígena en Yucatán, 1789–1847." In *Indio, nación y comunidad el el México del siglo XIX,* edited by Antonio Escobar O., 38–48. Mexico: Centro de Estudios Mexicanos y de Centroamérica and Centro de Investigaciones y Estudios Superiores en Antropología Social, 1993.

Brackenridge, Henry M. *Voyage to South America Performed by Order of the American Government in the Years 1817 and 1818.* 2 vols. London: J. Miller, 1820.

Brading, David. *The First America: The Spanish Monarchy, Creole Patriots, and the Liberal State, 1492–1867.* Cambridge: Cambridge University Press, 1991.

_____. *Miners and Merchants in Bourbon Mexico, 1763–1810.* Cambridge: Cambridge University Press, 1971.

Brito Figueroa, Federico. *Historia económica y social de Venezuela.* 2 vols. Caracas: Universidad Central de Venezuela, 1966.

_____. "Venezuela colonial: Las rebeliones de esclavos y la Revolución francesa." *CARAVELLE: Cahiers du Monde Hispanique et Luso-Bresilien* 54 (1990):263–89.

Brown, W. Kendall. *Bourbons and Brandy: Imperial Reform in Eighteenth-Century Arequipa.* Albuquerque: University of New Mexico Press, 1986.

Burgin, Miron. *The Economic Aspects of Argentine Federalism.* Cambridge: Harvard University Press, 1940.

Burkholder, Mark A. "From Creole to Peninsular: The Transformation of the Audiencia of Lima." *Hispanic American Historical Review,* 52, no. 3 (August 1972):395–415.

Burkholder, Mark A., and D. S. Chandler. *From Impotence to Authority: The Spanish Crown and the American Audiencias, 1687–1808.* Columbia: University of Missouri Press, 1977.

Bushnell, David. "The Last Dictatorship: Betrayal or Consummation?" *Hispanic American Historical Review* 63:1 (February 1983):65–105.

_____. *The Santander Regime in Gran Colombia.* Westport: Greenwood Press, 1970.

Bustamante, Carlos María de. *Cuadro Histórico de la revolución mexicana.* 3d ed. 3 vols. Comisión Nacional para la Celebración del Sesquicentenario de la Proclamación de la Independencia Nacional y del Cincuentenario de la Revolución Mexicana, 1961.

Byron, George Gordon Byron, Baron. *Childe Harold's Pilgrimage.* London: John Murray, 1859.

Caillet-Bois, Ricardo R. "El directorio, las provincias de la unión y el Congreso de Tucumán (1816–1819)." In *Historia de la Nación Argentina,* 2d ed., 10 vols., edited by Ricardo Lavene, 6:605–16. Buenos Aires: Editorial El Ateneo, 1941.

_____. "La revolución en el virreynato." In *Historia de la Nación Argentina,* 2d ed., 10 vols., edited by Ricardo Levene, 5:116–20. Buenos Aires: Editorial El Ateneo, 1941.

Campbell, Leon G. "A Colonial Establishment: Creole Domination of the Audiencia of Lima during the Late Eighteenth Century." *Hispanic American Historical Review* 52, no. 1 (February 1972):1–25.

_____. "Ideology and Federalism during the Great Rebellion." In *Resistance, Rebellion, and Consciousness in the Andean Peasant World, 18th to 20th Centuries,* edited by Steve J. Stern, 110–39. Madison: University of Wisconsin Press, 1989.

_____. *Military and Society in Colonial Peru, 1750–1810.* Philadelphia: American Philosophical Society, 1978.

Campos Harriet, Fernando. *Historia constitutional de Chile.* Santiago: Editorial Jurídica de Chile, 1956.

Cañedo, Juan de Dios. *Manifiesto a la nación española, sobre la representación de las provincias de ultramar en las próximas Cortes.* Madrid: Imprenta de Vega, 1820.

Canter, Juan "El año xii, las asambleas generales y la revolución del 8 de octubre." In *Historia de la Nación Argentina,* 2d ed., 10 vols, edited by Ricardo Levene, 5:403–510. Buenos Aires: Editorial El Ateneo, 1941.

"La Asamblea General Constituyente." In *Historia de la Nación Argentina,* 2d ed., 10 vols., edited by Ricardo Levene, 6:29–249. Buenos Aires: Editorial El Ateneo, 1941.

"La revolución de abril de 1815 y la organización del nuevo directorio." In *Historia de la Nación Argentina,* 2d ed., 10 vols., edited by Ricardo Levene, 6:252–98. Buenos Aires: Editorial El Ateneo, 1941.

Carrera Damas, Germán. *Boves: Aspectos socioeconómicos de la guerra independencia.* 2d ed. Caracas Universidad Central de Venezuela, 1968.

Carroll, Patrick J. *Blacks in Colonial Veracruz: Race, Ethnicity, and Regional Development.* Austin: University of Texas Press, 1991.

Carta escrita a un americano sobre la forma de gobierno que para hacer practicable la Constitución y las leyes, conviene establecer en Nueva España atendida su actual situación. Madrid: Ibarra, Impresor de Cámara de S.M., 1821.

Castel, Jorge. *La Junta Central Suprema y Gubernativa de España e Indias.* Madrid: Imprenta Marte, 1950.

Castro Gutiérrez, Felipe. *Movimientos populares en Nueva España: Michoacán, 1766–1767.* Mexico: Universidad Nacional Autónoma de México, 1990.

Nueva ley y nuevo rey: Reformas bórbonicas y rebelión popular en Nueva España. Zamora and Mexico: El Colegio de Michoacán and Universidad Nacional Autonoma de México, 1996.

"Orígenes sociales de la rebelión de San Luis Potosí, 1767." In *Patterns of Contention in Mexican History,* edited by Jaime E. Rodríguez O., 37–47. Wilmington: Scholarly Resources, 1992.

"La rebelión del indio Mariano (Nayarit, 1808)." *Estudios de Historia Novohispana* 10 (1991):347–67.

"El rey indio de la máscara de oro: La Historia y el mito en la ideología plebeya." *Históricas* 21 (February 1987):12–20.

Cespedes del Castillo, Guillermo. *Lima y Buenos Aires: Repercusiones económicas y políticas de la creación del virreynato del Río de la Plata.* Seville: Escuela de Estudios Hispanoamericanos, 1949.

Chavarri Sidera, Pilar. *Las elecciones de diputados a las Cortes Generales y Extraordinarias (1810–1813).* Madrid: Centro de Estudios Constitucionales, 1988.

Chávez, Julio César. *La revolución del 14 y 15.* Asunción: Librería Nizza, 1957.

Chust Calero, Manuel. "América y el problema federal en las Cortes de Cádiz." In *Republicanos y repúblicas en España,* edited by José A. Piquera and Manuel Chust, 45–75. Madrid: Siglo Veintiuno de España, 1996.

"De esclavos, encomenderos y mitayos. El anticolonialismo en las Cortes de Cádiz." *Mexican Studies/Estudios Mexicanos* 11, no. 2 (Summer 1995):179–202.

"La vía autonomista novohispana. Una propuesta federal en las Cortes de Cádiz." *Estudios de Historia Novohispana* 15 (1995):159–87.

Clément, Jean Pierre. "La Révolution française dans le *Mercurio Peruano.*" *CARAVELLE: Cahiers du Monde Hispanique et Luso-Bresilien* 54 (1990):137–51.

Cobban, Alfred. *In Search of Humanity: The Role of the Enlightenment in Modern History.* London: Cape, 1960.

Collier, Simon. *Ideas and Politics of Chilean Independence, 1808–1833*. Cambridge: Cambridge University Press, 1967.

Coll y Prat, Narciso. *Memoriales sobre la Independencia de Venezuela*. Caracas: Academia Nacional de Historia, 1960.

Colmenares, Germán. *Las haciendas de los Jesuitas en el Nuevo Reino de Granada*. Bogotá: Universidad Nacional de Colombia, 1969.

Comellas, José Luis. *Los primeros pronunciamientos en España, 1814–1820*. Madrid: Consejo Superior de Investigaciones Científicas, 1958.

El trienio constitucional. Madrid: Ediciones Rialp, 1963.

"Constitución de las Provincias Unidas en Sud-América." In *Estatutos, reglamentos y constituciones argentinas (1811–1898)*, 117–52. Buenos Aires: Universidad de Buenos Aires, 1956.

Corbiere, Emilio P. *El terrorismo en la Revolución de Mayo*. Buenos Aires: Editorial "La Facultad," Bernabé y Cía, 1937.

Cortázar, Roberto. *Cartas y mensajes del general Francisco de Paula Santander*. 10 vols. Bogotá: Librería Voluntad, 1953–1956.

Costeloe, Michael P. *Response to Revolution: Imperial Spain and the Spanish American Revolutions, 1810–1840*. Cambridge: Cambridge University Press, 1986.

"Spain and the Latin American Wars of Independence: The Free Trade Controversy, 1810–1820." *Hispanic American Historical Review* 61, no. 2 (May 1981):209–34.

Covarruvias, José de. *Memorias históricas de la última guerra con la Gran Bretaña desde el año de 1774: Estados Unidos de América, año 1774 y 1775*. Madrid: Imprenta de Antonio Ramírez, 1783.

Cubitt, David J. "La anexión de la Provincia de Guayaquil. Estudio del estilo político boliviano." *Revista del Archivo Histórico del Guayas* 13 (1978):5–27.

"Guerra y diplomacia en la República de Guayaquil, 1820–1822." *Revista de historia de América* 72 (January–June 1971):391–411.

Cunniff, Roger L. "Mexican Municipal Electoral Reform, 1810–1822." In *Mexico and the Spanish Cortes, 1810–1822*, edited by Nettie Lee Benson, 59–86. Austin: University of Texas Press, 1966.

Cushner, Nicolas P. *Farm and Factory: The Jesuits and the Development of Agrarian Capitalism in Colonial Quito, 1600–1767*. Albany: State University of New York Press, 1982.

Jesuit Ranches and the Agrarian Development of Colonial Argentina, 1650–1767. Albany: State University of New York Press, 1983.

Lords of the Land: Sugar, Wine, and Jesuit Estates of Coastal Peru, 1600–1767. Albany: State University of New York Press, 1980.

Cutter, Charles. *The Legal Culture of Northern New Spain, 1700–1810*. Albuquerque: University of New Mexico Press, 1995.

Davis, Roger P. "Ecuador under Gran Colombia: Regionalism, Localism, and Legitimacy in the Emergence of an Andean Republic." Ph.D. diss., University of Arizona, 1983.

Deans-Smith, Susan. *Bureaucrats, Planters, and Workers: The Making of the Tobacco Monopoly in Bourbon Mexico*. Austin: University of Texas Press, 1992.

Delgado, Jaime. *España y México en el siglo XIX*. 3 vols. Madrid: Consejo Superior de Investigaciones Científicas, 1950.

Del Río, Ignacio, *La aplicación regional de las reformas borbónicas en Nueva España: Sonora y Sinaloa, 1768–1787*. Mexico: Universidad Nacional Autónoma de México, 1995.

Demerson, Paula de. *María Francisca de Sales Portocarrero, Condesa de Montijo: Una figura de la Ilustración*. Madrid: Editora Nacional, 1975.

Destruje, Camilo. *Historia de la Revolución de Octubre y la campaña libertadora*. 2d ed. Guayaquil: Banco Central del Ecuador, 1982.

Díaz Díaz, Oswaldo. *La reconquista española*. 2 vols. Bogotá: Ediciones Lerner, 1964.

Diz-Lois, María Cristina. *El Manifiesto de 1814.* Pamplona: Estudio General de Navarra, 1967.

D.U.L.A. *Idea general de la conducta política de D. Miguel Ramos Arizpe, natural de la provincia de Coahuila, como diputado que ha sido por esta provincia en las Cortes generales y extraordinarias de la monarchía {sic} española desde al año de 1810 hasta el de 1821.* Madrid: Imprenta de Herculana de Villa, 1822.

Durand Flores, Guillermo. *El Perú en las Cortes de Cádiz.* 2 vols. Lima: Comisión Nacional del Sesquicentenario de la Independencia del Perú, 1974.

Eguía Ruiz, Constancio. *Los jesuitas y el motín de Esquilache.* Madrid: Consejo Superior de Investigaciones Científicas, 1947.

Engstrand, Iris H. W. *Spanish Scientists in the New World: The Eighteenth-Century Expeditions.* Seattle: University of Washington Press, 1981.

Escobar Ohmstede, Antonio. "Del gobierno indígena al Ayuntamiento constitucional en las Huastecas hidalguense y veracruzana, 1780–1853." *Mexican Studies/Estudios Mexicanos* 12, no. 1 (Winter 1996):1–26.

Estévez, Alfredo, and Oscar H. Elía. *Aspectos económico-financieros de la campaña sanmartiniana.* 2d ed. Buenos Aires: Editorial El Coloquio, 1976.

Estrada Ycaza, Julio. *La lucha de Guayaquil por el Estado de Quito.* 2 vols. Guayaquil: Banco Central del Ecuador, 1984.

Eyzaguirre, Jaime. *Ideario y ruta de la emancipación chilena.* Santiago: Editorial Universitaria, 1957.

———. *O'Higgins.* Santiago: Editorial Zig-Zag, 1946.

Ezquerra, Ramón. "La crítica española de la situación de América en el siglo XVIII." *Revista de Indias* 87–8 (1962):158–286.

Farriss, Nancy M. *Crown and Clergy in Colonial Mexico, 1759–1821: The Crisis of Ecclesiastical Privilege.* London: Athlone Press, 1968.

Favre, Henri. "Bolívar y los indios." *Histórica* 10, no. 1 (July 1986):1–18.

Fazio Fernández, Mariano. *Ideología de la Emancipación guayaquileña.* Guayaquil: Banco Central del Ecuador, 1987.

Fehrenbach, Charles W. "Moderados and Exaltados: The Liberal Opposition to Ferdinand VII, 1814–1823." *Hispanic American Historical Review* 50, no. 1 (February 1970):52–69.

———. "A Study of Spanish Liberalism: The Revolution of 1820." Ph.D. diss., University of Texas, Austin, 1961.

Felstiner, Mary Lowenthal. "Kinship Politics in the Chilean Independence Movement. *Hispanic American Historical Review* 56, no. 1 (February 1976):58–80.

Ferrer Benimeli, José A. *Masonería española contemporánea.* 2 vols. Madrid: Siglo Veintiuno, 1980.

Fisher, John R. *Commercial Relations between Spain and Spanish America in the Era of Free Trade, 1778–1796.* Liverpool: University of Liverpool, 1985.

———. "La formación del Estado peruano (1808–1824) y Simón Bolívar." In *Problemas de la formación del Estado y la nación en Hispanoamérica,* edited by Inge Buisson et al., 465–80. Cologne: Böhlau Verlag, 1984.

———. *Government and Society in Colonial Peru: The Intendant System, 1784–1814.* London: Athlone Press, 1970.

———. "Royalism, Regionalism, and Rebellion in Colonial Peru." *Hispanic American Historical Review* 59, no. 2 (May 1979):232–57.

———. *Trade, War, and Revolution: Exports from Spain to Spanish America, 1797–1820.* Liverpool: University of Liverpool Press, 1992.

Fisher, Lillian E. *The Intendant System in Spanish America.* Berkeley: University of California Press, 1929.

Flinter, George. *A History of the Revolution in Caracas: Comprising an Impartial Narrative of the Atrocities Committed by the Contending Parties.* London: T. and J. Allman, 1819.

Flores Caballero, Romeo. *La contrarrevolución en la independencia: Los españoles en la vida política, social y económica de México, 1804–1838.* Mexico: El Colegio de México, 1969.

Flores Galindo, Alberto. *Aristocracia y Plebe: Lima, 1760–1830.* Lima: Instituto Nacional de Cultura, 1984.

Florescano, Enrique. *Memoria mexicana. Ensayo sobre la reconstrucción del pasado: Epoca prehispánica–1821.* Mexico: Joaquín Mortiz, 1987.

Precios del maíz y crisis agrícolas en México, 1708–1810. Mexico: El Colegio de México, 1976.

Fontana Lazaro, Josep. *La quiebra de la monarquía absoluta, 1814–1820.* Barcelona: Ediciones Ariel, 1971.

Forero Benavides, Abelardo. *El 20 de Julio tiene 300 días.* Bogotá: Ediciones Universidad de los Andes, 1967.

Galatoire, Adolfo José. *Cuales fueron las enfermedades de San Martín.* Buenos Aires: Editorial Plus Ultra, 1973.

Gandia, Enrique de. "Las guerras de los absolutistas y liberales en América." *Revista de Indias* 24 (July–December 1954): 407–30.

Historia del 25 de mayo: Nacimiento de la libertad y la independencia argentina. Buenos Aires: Editorial Claridad, 1960.

Garavaglia, Juan Carlos, and Juan Carlos Grosso. "Estado borbónico y presión fiscal en la Nueva España, 1750–1821." In *América Latina: Dallo stato coloniale allo stato nazionalle (1750–1940),* 2 vols, 1:78–97. Milan: Franco Angeli, 1987.

García, Genaro, ed. *Documentos históricos mexicanos.* 7 vols. Mexico: Museo Nacional de Arquelogía, Historia y Etnología, 1910.

García-Baquero, Antonio. *Comercio colonial y las guerras revolucionarias.* Seville: Escuela de Estudios Hispanoamericanos, 1972.

García Melero, Luis Angel. *La independencia de los Estados Unidos de Norteamérica a través de la prensa española.* Madrid: Ministerio de Asuntos Exteriores, 1977.

Garner, Richard, with Spiro E. Stefanou. *Economic Growth and Change in Bourbon Mexico.* Gainesville: University Press of Florida, 1993.

Garrido, Margarita. *Reclamos y representaciones. Variaciones sobre la política en el Nuevo Reino de Granada, 1770–1815.* Bogotá: Banco de la República, 1993.

Garritz, Amaya, Virginia Guedea, and Teresa Lozano, eds. *Impresos novohispanos, 1808–1821.* 2 vols. Mexico: Universidad Nacional Autónoma de México, 1990.

Gay, Peter. *The Enlightenment: An Interpretation.* 2 vols. New York: Knopf, 1966–1969.

Gerbi, Antonello. *The Dispute of the New World: The History of a Polemic, 1750–1900.* Rev. ed. Pittsburgh: University of Pittsburgh Press, 1973.

Gianello, Leoncio. *Historia del Congreso de Tucumán.* Buenos Aires: Academia Nacional de Historia, 1966.

Gil Fortoul, José. *Historia consitutional de Venezuela.* 5th ed. 2 vols. Caracas: Librería Piñango, 1967.

Gilmore, Robert L. "The Imperial Crisis, Rebellion, and the Viceroy: Nueva Granada in 1809." *Hispanic American Historical Review* 40, no. 1 (February 1960):1–24.

Gil Novales, Alberto. *Las Sociedades Patrióticas (1820–1823).* 2 vols. Madrid: Editorial Tecnos, 1975.

Glick, Thomas F. "Science and Independence in Latin America (with Special Reference to New Granada)." *Hispanic American Historical Review* 71, no. 2 (May 1991): 307–34.

Godechot, Jacques. *La Grande Nation: L'expansion revolutionnaire de la France dans le monde de 1789 à 1799.* 2 vols. Paris: Aubier, 1956.

Gómez Hoyos, Rafael. *La independencia de Colombia.* Madrid: Editorial Mapfre, 1992.

Gómez Vizuete, Antonio. "Los primeros ayuntamientos liberales en Puerto Rico (1812–1814 y 1820–1823)." *Anuario de Estudios Americanos* 47 (1990):581–615.

González, Julio V. *Filiación histórica del gobierno representativo argentino.* 2 vols. Buenos Aires: Editorial "La Vanguardia,"1937–1938.

González, María del Refugio. "El Ilustre y Real Colegio de Abogados de México frente a la Revolución francesa (1808–1827)." In *La Revolución francesa en México* edited by Solange Alberro, Alicia Hernández Chávez, and Elías Trabulse, 111–35. Mexico: El Colegio de México, 1992.

"El Real e Ilustre Colegio de Abogados de México durante la transición al México independiente." In *Five Centuries of Mexican History/Cinco siglos de historia de México,* 2 vols., edited by Virginia Guedea and Jaime E. Rodríguez O., 1:267–84. Mexico: Instituto Dr. José María Luis Mora, 1992.

González Obregón, Luis. *La vida en México en 1810.* Viuda de C. Bouret, 1911.

Gortari Rabiela, Hira de. "Julio-agosto de 1808: 'La lealtad mexicana'." *Historia Mexicana* 39, no. 1 (July–September 1989): 181–203.

Graham, Gerald S., and R. A. Humphreys, eds. *The Navy and South America, 1807–1823: Correspondence of the Commanders-in-Chief on the South American Station.* London: Navy Records Society, 1962.

Grases, Pedro, ed. *Actas del Congreso de Angostura.* Caracas: Universidad Central de Venezuela, 1969.

Gray, William H. "Bolívar's Conquest of Guayaquil." *Hispanic American Historical Review* 27, no. 4 (November 1947):603–22.

Guardino, Peter. "Las guerrillas y la independencia peruana: Un ensayo de interpretación." *Pasado y Presente* 2, no. 3 (1989):101–17.

"Identity and Nationalism in Mexico: Guerrero, 1780–1840." *Journal of Historical Sociology* 7, no. 3 (September 1994):314–42.

Peasants, Politics, and the Formation of Mexico's National State: Guerrero, 1800–1857. Stanford: Stanford University Press, 1996.

Guedea, Virginia. "The Conspiracies of 1811 or How the Criollos Learned to Organize in Secret." Paper presented at the conference: Mexican Wars of Independence, the Empire, and the Early Republic, University of Calgary, April 4–5, 1991.

"Criollos y peninsulares en 1808. Dos puntos de vista sobre lo español." Licenciatura tesis, Universidad Iberoamericana, 1964.

"De la fidelidad a la infidencia: Los gobernadores de la parcialidad de San Juan." In *Patterns of Contention in Mexican History,* edited by Jaime E. Rodríguez O., 95–123. Wilmington: Scholarly Resources, 1992.

En busca de un gobierno alterno. Los Guadalupes de México. Mexico: Universidad Nacional Autónoma de México, 1992.

"The First Popular Elections in Mexico City, 1812–1813." In *The Evolution of the Mexican Political System,* edited by Jaime E. Rodríguez O., 45–69. Wilmington: Scholarly Resources, 1993.

"Ignacio Adalid, un *equilibrista* novohispano." In *Mexico in the Age of Democratic Revolutions, 1750–1850,* edited by Jaime E. Rodríguez O., 71–96. Boulder: Lynne Rienner, 1994.

"Los indios voluntarios de Fernando VII." *Estudios de Historia Moderna y Contemporánea de México* 10 (1986):11–83.

La insurgencia en el Departamento del Norte: Los Llanos de Apan y la Sierra de Puebla, 1810–1816. Mexico: Universidad Nacional Autónoma de Mexico, 1996.

"La medicina en las gacetas de México." *Mexican Studies/Estudios Mexicanos* 5, no. 2 (Summer 1989):175–99.

"México en 1812: Control político y bebidas prohibidas." *Estudios de Historia, Moderna y Contemporánea de México* 8 (1980):23–65.

"Una nueva forma de organización política: La sociedad secreta de Jalapa, 1812." In *Un hombre entre Europa y América: Homenaje a Juan Antonio Ortega y Medina,* edited by Amaya Garritz, 185–208. Universidad Nacional Autónoma de México, 1993.

"Los procesos electorales insurgentes." *Estudios de Historia Novohispana* 11 (1991): 201–49.

"El pueblo de México y 12 política capitalina, 1818–1812." *Mexican Studies/Estudios Mexicanos* 10, no. 1 (Winter 1994):27–61.

Güémez Pineda, Arturo. *Liberalismo en tierras del caminante Yucatán, 1812–1840.* Zamora: El Colegio de Michoacán, 1994.

Guerra, François-Xavier. *Modernidad e independencias: Ensayos sobre las revoluciones hispánicas.* Madrid: Editorial Mapfre, 1992.

Haigh, Samuel. *Sketches of Buenos Ayres, Chile, and Peru.* London: Effingham Wilson, 1831.

Halperín-Donghi, Tulio. *Politics, Economics, and Society in Argentina in the Revolutionary Period.* Cambridge: Cambridge University Press, 1975.

"Revolutionary Militarization in Buenos Aires, 1806–1815." *Past and Present* 40 (July 1968):84–107.

Hamerly, Michael T. *Historia social y económica de la antigua provincia de Guayaquil, 1763–1842.* Guayaquil: Archivo Histórico del Guayas, 1973.

Hamill, Hugh M., Jr. *The Hidalgo Revolt.* Gainesville: University of Florida Press, 1966.

Hamnett, Brian R. *La política española en una época revolucionaria, 1790–1820.* Mexico: Fondo de Cultura Económica, 1985.

Hanisch Espindola, Walter. *El Catecismo Político Cristiano. Las ideas y la época: 1810.* Santiago: Editorial Andrés Bello, 1970.

Hann, John H. "The Role of Mexican Deputies in the Proposal and Enactment of Measures of Economic Reform Applicable to Mexico." In *Mexico and the Spanish Cortes,* edited by Nettie Lee Benson, 153–68. Austin: University of Texas Press, 1966.

Hasbrouck, Alfred. *Foreign Legionaries in the Liberation of Spanish South America.* New York: Octagon Books, 1969.

Heredia, José Francisco. *Memorias del Regente Heredia.* Caracas: Academia Nacional de la Historia, 1960.

Hernández Chávez, Alicia. *La tradición republicana del buen gobierno.* Mexico: Fondo de Cultura Económica, 1993.

Hernández y Dávalos, Juan E. *Colección de documentos para la historia de la guerra de independencia de 1808 a 1821.* 6 vols. José María Sandoval Impresor, 1877–1882.

Herr, Richard. *The Eighteenth-Century Revolution in Spain.* Princeton: Princeton University Press, 1958.

"Hacia el derrumbe del antiguo régimen: Crisis fiscal y desamortización bajo Carlos VI." *Moneda y Crédito* 118 (September 1971):37–100.

Herrejón Peredo, Carlos, "México: Luces de Hidalgo y de Abad y Queipo," *CARAVELLE: Cahiers du Monde Hispanique et Luso-Bresilien* 54 (1990):107–35.

Hoffman, Fritz C. "The Financing of San Martín's Expeditions." *Hispanic American Historical Review* 32, no. 4 (November 1952):634–8.

Humboldt, Alexander Von. *Personal Narrative of Travels to the Equinoctial Regions of the New Continent during the Years 1799–1804.* 3d ed. 4 vols. London: Longman, Hurst, Rees, and Brown, 1822.

Political Essay on the Kingdom of New Spain. 4 vols. London: Longman, Hurst, Rees, and Brown, 1811.

Instituto de Historia Argentina "Doctor Emilio Ravignani." "Constitución de las Provincials Unidas en Sud-América." In *Estatutos, reglamentos y constituciones argentinas (1811–1898),* 117–52. Buenos Aires: Universidad de Buenos Aires, 1956.

Izard, Miguel. *El miedo de la revolución: La lucha por la libertad en Venezuela (1777–1830).* Madrid: Editorial Tecnos, 1979.

Izquierdo, José Joaquín. *Montaña y los orígenes del movimiento social y científico de México.* Mexico: Ediciones Ciencia, 1955.

Jáuregui Fríaz, Luis Antonio, "La anatomía del fisco colonial: La estructura administrativa de la real hacienda novohispana, 1786–1821." Ph.D. diss., El Colegio de México, 1994.

Jiménez Codinach, Guadalupe. *La Gran Bretaña y la Independencia de México, 1808–1821.* Fondo de Cultura Económica, 1991.

Jiménez Molinares, Gabriel. *Los mártires de Cartagena de 1816.* 2 vols. Cartagena: Imprenta Departamental, 1948–1950.

Jocelyn-Holt Letelier, Alfredo. *La independencia de Chile.* Madrid: Editorial Mapfre, 1992.

Johnson, Lyman L. "The Military as Catalyst of Change in Late Colonial Buenos Aires." In *Revolution and Restoration: The Arrangement of Power in Argentina, 1776–1860,* edited by Mark D. Szuchman and Jonathan C. Brown, 27–53. Lincoln: University of Nebraska Press, 1994.

Juárez Nieto, Carlos. *La oligarquía y el poder político en Valladolid de Michoacán, 1785–1810.* Morelia: Congreso del Estado, CNCA, INAH, Instituto Michoacano de Cultura, 1994.

Kagan, Richard L. *Lawsuits and Litigants in Castile, 1500–1700.* Chapel Hill: University of North Carolina Press, 1981.

Keeding, Ekkehard. *Das Zeitalter de Aufklärung in der Provinz Quito.* Cologne: Böhlau Verlag, 1983.

King, James. "The Colored Castes and American Representation in the Cortes of Cádiz." *Hispanic American Historical Review* 33, no. 1 (February 1953):33–64.

Kinsbruner, Jay. *Bernardo O'Higgins.* New York: Twayne, 1968.

Konrad, Herman K. *A Jesuit Hacienda in Colonial Mexico: Santa Lucía, 1576–1767.* Stanford: Stanford University Press, 1980.

Kuethe, Allan J. *Cuba, 1753–1815: Crown, Military, and Society.* Knoxville: University of Tennessee Press, 1986.

Military Reform and Society in New Granada, 1773–1808. Gainesville: University of Florida Press, 1978.

Lafuente Ferrari, Enrique. *El virrey Iturrigaray y los orígenes de la independencia de México.* Madrid: Instituto Gonzalo Fernández de Oviedo, 1941.

Lanning, John Tate. *Academic Culture in the Spanish Colonies.* London: Oxford University Press, 1940.

The Eighteenth-Century Enlightenment in the University of San Carlos de Guatemala. Ithaca: Cornell University Press, 1956.

Lasa Iraola, Ignacio. "El primer proceso de los liberales." *Hispania* 30, no. 115 (1970):327–83.

Laviana Cuetos, María Luisa. *Guayaquil en el siglo XVIII: Recursos naturales y desarrollo económico.* Seville: Escuela de Estudios Hispanoamericanos, 1987.

Lavrin, Asunción. "The Execution of the Law of Consolidation in New Spain." *Hispanic American Historical Review* 53, no. 1 (February 1973):27–49.

Leal Curiel, Carole. *El discurso de la fidelidad: Construcción social del espacio como símbolo del poder regio.* Caracas: Biblioteca de la Academia Nacional de Historia, 1990.

Lecuna, Vicente. *Catalogo de errores y calumnias en la historia de Bolívar.* 3 vols. New York: Colonial Press, 1956

Crónica razonada de las guerras de Bolívar. 3 vols. New York: Colonial Press, 1950.

Lemoine, Ernesto. *Morelos y la revolución de 1810.* 3d ed. Mexico: Universidad Nacional Autónoma de México, 1990.

Letelier, Valentín, ed. *Sesiones de los cuerpos lejislativos de la república de Chile, 1811 a 1845.* 37 vols. Santiago: Talleres Gráficos Nacionales, 1887–1908.

Levene, Ricardo, "La anarquía de 1820 en Buenos Aires." In *Historia de la Nación Argentina,*

2d ed., 10 vols., edited by Ricardo Levene, 6:287–342. Buenos Aires: Editorial El Ateneo, 1941.

Ensayo histórico sobre la Revolución de Mayo y Mariano Moreno. 4th ed. 3 vols. Buenos Aires: Ediciones Peuser, 1960.

"Formación del triunvirato." In *Historia de la Nación Argentina,* 2d ed., 10 vols., edited by Ricardo Levene, 5:371–401. Buenos Aires: Editorial El Ateneo, 1941.

"Las juntas provinciales creadas por el reglamento de 10 de febrero de 1811 y los origenes del federalismo." In *Historia de la Nación Argentina,* 2d ed., 10 vols., edited by Ricardo Levene, 5:325–40. Buenos Aires: Editorial El Ateneo, 1941.

Lista de los señores diputados nombrados para las Cortes del año 1820 y 1821. Mexico: Reimpresa en la oficina de J. B. Arizpe, 1820.

Llorens, Vicente. *Liberales y románticos: Una emigración española en Inglaterra, 1823–1824.* 2d ed. Madrid: Editorial Castalla, 1968.

Lofstron, William F. *The Promise of and the Problem of Reform: Attempted Economic and Social Change in the First Years of Bolivian Independence.* Ithaca: Cornell University Press, 1972.

Lombardi, John V. *Venezuela: The Search for Order, the Dream of Progress.* New York: Oxford University Press, 1982.

López Rozas, José. *Entre la monarquía y la república.* Buenos Aires: La Bastilla, 1976.

Lovett, Gabriel. *Napoleon and the Birth of Modern Spain.* 2 vols. New York: New York University Press, 1965.

Lucena Salmoral, Manuel. "El colapso económico de la Primera República de Venezuela." In *América Latina: Dallo stato coloniale allo stato nazionale (1750–1940),* 2 vols., 1:161–86. Milan: Franco Angeli, 1987.

Luna Tobar, Alfredo. *El Ecuador en la Independencia del Peru.* 3 vols. Quito: Banco Central del Ecuador, 1986.

Lynch, John. *Bourbon Spain, 1700–1808.* Oxford: Basil Blackwell, 1989.

The Spanish American Revolutions, 1808–1821. 2d ed. New York: W. W. Norton, 1986.

Spanish Colonial Administration, 1772–1810. London: Athlone Press, 1958.

Macías, Ana. *Génesis del gobierno constitucional en México, 1808–1820.* Mexico: Secretaría de Educación Pública, 1973.

MacLachlan, Colin M. *Spain's Empire in the New World: The Role of Ideas in Institutional and Social Change.* Berkeley: University of California Press, 1988.

Madariaga, Salvador de. *Bolívar.* 2 vols. Editorial Hermes, 1951.

Marchena Fernández, Juan. *Oficiales y soldados en el ejército de América.* Seville: Escuela de Estudios Hispanoamericanos, 1983.

Marfany, Roberto, *El Cabildo de Mayo.* Buenos Aires: Ediciones Theoría, 1961.

"La primera junta de gobierno de Buenos Aires (1810)." *Estudios Americanos* 19 (1960):223–34.

Marichal, Carlos. "Las guerras imperiales y los préstamos novohispanos, 1781–1804." *Historia Mexicana* 39, no. 4 (April–June 1990):881–907.

Marichal, Juan. "From Pistoia to Cádiz: A Generation's Itinerary, 1786–1812." In *The Ibero-American Enlightenment,* edited by A. Owen Aldridge, 97–110. Urbana: University of Illinois Press, 1971.

Martin, Cheryl English, *Governance and Society in Colonial Mexico: Chihuahua in the Eighteenth Century.* Stanford: Stanford University Press, 1996.

Martínez de Velasco, Angel. *La formación de la Junta Central.* Pamplona: Eunsa, 1972.

Martínez Marina, Francisco. Introduction to *Siete Partidas.* Biblioteca de Autores Españoles, vol. 194. Madrid: Ediciones Atlas, 1966.

Teoría de las cortes. Biblioteca de Autores Españoles, 2 vols. Madrid: Ediciones Atlas, 1969.

Masur, Gerhard. "The Conference of Guayaquil." *Hispanic American Historical Review* 31, no. 2 (May 1951):189–229.

Simón Bolívar. Albuquerque: University of New Mexico Press, 1969.

McFarlane, Anthony. *Colombia before Independence: Economy, Society, and Politics under Bourbon Rule.* Cambridge: Cambridge University Press, 1993.

"The 'Rebellion of the Barrios': Urban Insurrection in Bourbon Quito." *Hispanic American Historical Review* 69, no. 2 (May 1989):283–330.

McKinley, P. Michael. *Pre-Revolutionary Caracas: Politics, Economy, and Society 1777–1811.* Cambridge: Cambridge University Press, 1985.

Meléndez, Carlos. *La independencia de Centroamérica.* Madrid: Editorial Mapfre, 1993.

Méndez, Cecilia. "Los campesinos, la independencia y la iniciación de la República. El caso de los inquichanos realistas: Ayacucho, 1825–1828." In *Poder y violencia en los Andes,* edited by Henrique Urbano, 165–88. Cuzco: Centro de Estudios Regionales Andinos Bartolomé de Las Casas, 1991.

"Rebellion without Resistance: Huanta's Monarchist Peasants in the Making of the Peruvian State, Ayacucho 1825–1850" Ph.D. diss., State University of New York at Stony Brook, 1996.

Menegus Bornemann, Margarita. "Economía y comunidades indígenas: El efecto de la supresión del sistema de reparto de mercancías en la intendencia de México, 1786–1810." *Mexican Studies/Estudios Mexicanos* 5, no. 2 (Summer 1989):201–19.

Mesa Oliver, Rocío, and Luis Olivera López, eds. *Catálogo de la Colección La Fragua de la Biblioteca Nacional de México, 1800–1810.* Mexico: Universidad Nacional Autónoma de México, 1993.

Catálogo de la Colección La Fragua de la Biblioteca Nacional de México, 1811–1821. Mexico: Universidad Nacional Autónoma de México, 1996.

Mesonero Romanos, Ramón. *Memorias de un setentón.* Madrid: Ediciones Atlas, 1957.

Michelena, José Mariano. "Verdadero origen de la revolución de 1809 en el Departamento de Michoacán." In *Documentos históricos mexicanos,* 7 vols., edited by Genaro García, 1:467–71. Mexico: Museo Nacional de Arguelogía, Historia y Etnología, 1910.

Mier, Servando Teresa de. "Carta de despedida a los mexicanos." In *La formación de un republicano,* vol. 4 of *Obras completas de Servando Teresa de Mier,* edited by Jaime E. Rodríguez O., 107–14. Mexico: Universidad Nacional Autónoma de México, 1988.

Escritos inéditos de Fray Servando Teresa de Mier, edited by José María Miguel y Verges and Hugo Díaz-Thomé. Mexico: El Colegio de México, 1944.

"Idea de la Constitución dada a las Américas por los reyes de España antes de la invasión del antiguo despotismo." In *La formación de un republicano,* vol. 4 of *Obras Completas de Servando Teresa de Mier,* edited by Jaime E. Rodríguez O., 33–80. Mexico: Universidad Nacional Autónoma de México, 1988.

"Manifiesto Apologético." In *Escritos inéditos de Fray Servando Teresa de Mier,* edited by José María Miguel y Verges and Hugo Díaz-Thomé, 39–168. Mexico: El Colegio de México, 1944.

Miño Grijalva, Manuel. *Obrajes y tejedores de Nueva España (1700–1810).* Madrid: Instituto de Estudios Fiscales, 1990.

Mirafuentes Galván, José Luis. "Identidad india, legitimidad y emancipación política en el noroeste de México (Copala, 1771)." In *Patterns of Contention in Mexican History,* edited by Jaime E. Rodríguez O., 49–67. Wilmington: Scholarly Resources, 1992.

Miranda, José. *Humboldt y México.* Mexico: Universidad Nacional Autónoma de México, 1962.

Las ideas y las instituciones políticas mexicanas, primera parte, 1521–1820. 2d ed. Mexico: Universidad Nacional Autónoma de México, 1978.

Mitre, Bartolomé. *Historia de Belgrano y de la independencia argentina.* 3 vols. Buenos Aires: Librería de Mayo, 1876.
   Historia de Belgrano y de la independencia argentina. 6th ed. Buenos Aires: J. Roldán, 1927.
   Historia de San Martín y de la emancipación sud-americana. 3 vols. Buenos Aires: Imprenta de "La Nación," 1887.
Monsalve, José D. *Antonio de Villavicencio y la Revolución de la Independencia.* 2 vols. Bogotá: Imprenta Nacional, 1920.
Moore, John Preston. *The Cabildo in Peru under the Bourbons.* Durham: Duke University Press, 1966.
Morán Orti, Manuel. *Poder y gobierno en las Cortes de Cádiz, 1810–1813.* Pamplona: Ediciones Universidad de Navarra, 1986.
Moreno Cebrían, Alfredo. "Venta y beneficios de los corregimientos peruanos." *Revista de Indias* 36, no. 143–4 (January–June 1976):213–46.
Moreno Yáñes, Segundo E. *Sublevaciones indígenas en la Audiencia de Quito.* 3d ed. Quito: Universidad Católica del Ecuador, 1985.
Mörner, Magnus. *The Expulsion of the Jesuits from Latin America.* New York: Knopf, 1965.
   The Political and Economic Activities of the Jesuits in the La Plata Region. Stockholm: Victor Pettersons Bokindustri Aktiebolag, 1953.
Muñoz Ora, Carlos E. "Prognóstico de la Independencia de América y un proyecto de Monarquías en 1781." *Revista de Historia de América* 50 (December 1960):439–73.
Muro, Fernando. "El 'beneficio' de oficios públicos en Indias." *Anuario de Estudios Americanos* 35 (1978):1–67.
Nader, Helen. *Liberty in Absolutist Spain: The Habsburg Sale of Towns, 1516–1700.* Baltimore: Johns Hopkins University Press, 1990.
Narancio, E. M. *La independencia de Uruguay.* Madrid: Editorial Mapfre, 1992.
   El origen del Estado Oriental. Montevideo: Anales de la Universidad, 1948.
Navarro, José Gabriel. *La Revolución de Quito del 10 de agosto de 1809.* Quito: Editorial "Fray Jodoco Ricke," 1962.
Navarro García, Luis. *Intendencias en Indias.* Seville: Escuela de Estudios Hispanoamericanos, 1956.
Nebel, Richard, *Santa María Tonantzin, Virgen de Guadalupe: Continuidad y transformación religiosa en México.* Mexico: Fondo de Cultura Económica, 1995.
Noboa, Aurelio, ed. *Colección de tratados.* 2 vols. Guayaquil: Imprenta de Noboa, 1901.
O'Gorman, Edmundo. *Destierro de Sombras. Luz en el origen de la imagen y culto de Nuestra Señora de Guadalupe del Tepeyac.* Mexico: Universidad Nacional Autónoma de México, 1986.
O'Leary, Daniel Florencio. *Memorias.* 3 vols. Caracas: Imprenta de "El Monitor," 1883.
Olmedo, José Joaquín de. *José Joaquín de Olmedo. Epistolario.* Biblioteca Mínima Ecuatoriana. Puebla: Editorial J. M. Cajica, 1960.
Olmos Sánchez, Isabel. *La sociedad mexicana en vísperas de la independencia (1787–1821).* Murcia: Universidad de Murcia, 1989.
O'Phelan Godoy, Scarlett. "Por el Rey, religión y la patria: Las juntas de gobierno de 1809 en La Paz y Quito." *Bulletin de L'Institut Français d'Etudes Andines* 17, no. 2 (1988):61–80.
   Rebellions and Revolts in Eighteenth-Century Peru and Upper Peru. Cologne: Bühlau Verlag, 1985.
Ortíz, Sergio Elías. *Génesis de la revolución del 20 de Julio de 1810.* Bogotá: Editorial Kelly, 1960.
Ortiz de la Tabla, Javier. *Comercio exterior de Veracruz, 1778–1821.* Seville: Escuela de Estudios Hispanoamericanos, 1978.

Ortiz Escamilla, Juan. *Guerra y gobierno: Los pueblos y la independencia de México.* Mexico: Instituto de Investigaciones José María Luis Mora, 1997.

Osorio Romero, Ignacio. *Colegios y profesores Jesuitas que enseñaron latín en Nueva España, 1572–1767.* Mexico: Universidad Nacional Autónoma de México, 1979.

Otero, José P. *Historia del Libertador don José de San Martín.* 4 vols. Buenos Aires: Cabaut y Cía, 1932.

Ouweneel, Arij. *Shadows over Anáhuac: An Ecological Interpretation of Crisis and Development in Central Mexico, 1730–1800.* Albuquerque: University of New Mexico Press, 1996.

Palmer, Robert R. *The Age of Democratic Revolutions: Political History of Europe and America, 1760–1800.* 2 vols. Princeton: Princeton University Press, 1959–1964.

Parra Pérez, Caracciolo. *Historia de la Primera República de Venezuela.* 2 vols. Madrid: Ediciones Guadarrama, 1959.

Parry, John H. *The Sale of Public Office in the Spanish Indies under the Habsburgs.* Berkeley: University of California Press, 1963.

Peñalver, Fernando. "Memoria presentada al Supremo Congreso de Venezuela en que manifiesta sus opiniones sobre la necesidad de dividir la Provincia de Caracas para hacer la Constitución Federal permanente." In Academia Nacional de Historia, *Pensamiento constitucional hispanoamericano,* 5 vols, 5:25–39. Caracas: Academia Nacional de Historia, 1961.

Pérez Guilhou, Dardo. *Las ideas monárquicas en el Congreso de Tucumán.* Buenos Aires: Editorial Depalma, 1966.

Pérez Sánchez, Alfonso E., and Eleanor A. Sayre. *Goya and the Spirit of the Enlightenment.* Boston: Little, Brown, 1989.

Peset, José Luis. *Ciencia y libertad: El papel del científico ante la Independencia americana.* Madrid: Consejo Superior de Investigaciones Científicas, 1987.

Phelan, John L. "El auge y caída de los criollos en la audiencia de Nueva Granada." *Boletín de Historia y Antigüedades* 59 (1972):597–618.

  The Kingdom of Quito in the Seventeenth Century: Bureaucratic Politics in the Spanish Empire. Madison: University of Wisconsin Press, 1967.

  The People and the King: The Comunero Revolution in Colombia, 1781. Madison: University of Wisconsin Press, 1978.

Piccirilli, Ricardo. *Rivadavia y su tiempo.* 2d ed. 3 vols. Buenos Aires: Ediciones Peuser, 1960.

  San Martín y la política de los pueblos. Buenos Aires: Ediciones Gure, 1957.

Piel, Jean. "The Place of the Peasantry in the National Life of Peru in the Nineteenth Century." *Past and Present* 46 (February 1970):108–33.

Pietschmann, Horst. *Las reformas borbónicas y el sistema de intendentes en Nueva España.* Mexico: Fondo de Cultura Económica, 1996.

Pinto, Manuel M. *La revolución de la Intendencia de La Paz en el virreinato del Río de la Plata.* La Paz: Alcaldía Municipal, 1953.

Pintos Vieites, María del Carmen. *La política de Fernando VII entre 1814 y 1820.* Pamplona: Studio General de Navarra, 1958.

Poinsett, Joel R. *Notes on Mexico made in the Autumn of 1822.* Philadelphia: H. C. Carey & Lea, 1824.

Pombo, Manuel Antonio, and José Joaquín Guerra. *Constituciones de Colombia.* 3 vols. Bogotá: Biblioteca Banco Popular, 1986.

Ponce Ribadeneira, Alfredo. *Quito, 1809–1812.* Madrid: Imprenta Juan Bravo, 1960.

Poole, Stafford. *Our Lady of Guadalupe. The Origins and Sources of a Mexican National Symbol, 1531–1797.* Tucson: University of Arizona Press, 1995.

Pradeau, Alberto Francisco. *La expulsión de los Jesuitas de las Provincias de Sonora, Ostimuri y Sinaloa en 1767.* Mexico: Antigua Librería Robredo de Porrúa, 1959.

Priestley, Herbert. *José de Gálvez, Visitor-General of New Spain, 1765–1771.* Berkeley: University of California Press, 1916.

Puente Candamo, José A. de la. *La independencia de Perú.* Madrid: Editorial Mapfre, 1992.

Quirós, José María. *Guía de negociantes. Compendio de la legislación mercantil de España e Indias.* Mexico: Universidad Nacional Autónoma de Mexico, 1986.

Quiroz-Martínez, Olga Victoria. *La Introducción de la filosofía moderna en España.* Mexico: El Colegio de México, 1949.

Quito. "Manifiesto del Pueblo de Quito." *Boletín de la Sociedad Ecuatoriana de Estudios Históricos Americanos* 2, no. 6 (May–June 1919): 429–30.

Ramos-Pérez, Demetrio. *Entre el Plata y Bogotá: Cuatro claves de la emancipación ecuatoriana.* Madrid: Ediciones de Cultura Hispánica, 1987.

"Sobre un aspecto de las 'tácticas' de Boves." *Boletín de la Academia Nacional de Historia* 51 (1968):69–73.

"Wagram y sus consecuencias, como determinantes del clima público de la revolución de 19 de abril de 1810 en Caracas." In *Estudios sobre la emancipaón de Hispanoamérica, 33–85.* Madrid: Instituto Gonzalo Fernández de Oviedo, 1963.

Rees Jones, Ricardo. *El despotismo ilustrado y los intendentes de la Nueva España.* Mexico: Universidad Nacional Autónoma de México, 1979.

Resnick, Enoch F. "The Council of State and Spanish America, 1814–1820." Ph.D. diss., American University, 1970.

Restrepo, José Manuel. *Historia de la Revolución de la República de Colombia.* 4 vols. Bensazon: Imprenta de José Jacquin, 1858.

Rieu-Millan, Marie Laure. *Los Diputados americanos en las Cortes de Cádiz.* Madrid: Consejo Superior de Investigaciones Científicas, 1990.

Ringrose, David. *Spain, Europe and the "Spanish Miracle," 1700–1900.* Cambridge: Cambridge University Press, 1996.

Rivera Serna, Raúl. *Los guerrilleros del Centro en la emancipación peruana.* Lima: Talleres Gráficos P. L. Villanueva, 1958.

Robertson, William Spence. *The Life of Miranda.* 2 vols. New York: Cooper Square, 1969.

Rocafuerte, Vicente. *Bosquejo ligerísimo de la Revolución de Mégico* [sic] *desde el grito de Iguala hasta la proclamación imperial de Iturbide.* Philadelphia: Imprenta de Teracrouef y Naroajeb, 1822.

Rodríguez, Laura. "The Riots of 1766 in Madrid." *European Studies Review* 3, no. 3 (May 1973):223–42.

"The Spanish Riots of 1766." *Past and Present* 59 (May 1973):117–46.

Rodríguez, Mario. "The 'American Question' at the Cortes of Madrid." *The Americas* 38, no. 3 (January 1982):293–314.

The Cádiz Experiment in Central America, 1808 to 1826. Berkeley: University of California Press, 1978.

La revolución americana de 1776 y el mundo hispánico: Ensayos y documentos. Madrid: Editorial Tecnos, 1976.

Rodríguez Casado, Vicente. *La política y los políticos en el reinado de Carlos III.* Madrid: Ediciones Rialp, 1962.

Rodríguez O., Jaime E. "The Constitution of 1824 and the Formation of the Mexican State." In *The Evolution of the Mexican Political System,* edited by Jaime E. Rodríguez O., 71–90. Wilmington: Scholarly Resources, 1993.

The Emergence of Spanish America: Vicente Rocafuerte and Spanish Americanism, 1808–1832. Berkeley: University of California Press, 1975.

"The Struggle for the Nation: The First Centralist–Federalist Conflict in Mexico." *The Americas* 49, no. 1 (July 1992):1–22.

"The Transition from Colony to Nation: New Spain, 1820–1821." In *Mexico in the Age of*

Democratic Revolutions, 1750–1850, edited by Jaime E. Rodríguez O., 97–132. Boulder: Lynne Rienner, 1994.

"Two Revolutions: France 1798 and Mexico 1810." *The Americas* 47, no. 2 (October 1990):161–76.

Rodríguez O., Jaime E., ed. *Estudios sobre Vicente Rocafuerte.* Guayaquil: Archivo Histórico del Guayas, 1975.

Rodríguez Plata, Horacio. *La Antigua Provincia de Socorro y la Independencia.* Bogotá: Editorial Bogotá, 1963.

Rodríguez S., Luis A. *Ayacucho, la batalla de la libertad Americana.* Quito: Casa de la Cultura Ecuatoriana, 1975.

Rugeley, Terry. *Yucatán's Maya Peasantry & the Origins of the Caste War.* Austin: University of Texas Press, 1996.

Salvucci, Richard J. *Textiles and Capitalism in Mexico: An Economic History of the Obrajes, 1539–40.* Princeton: Princeton University Press, 1987.

San Miguel, Evaristo. *Vida de D. Agustín Argüelles.* 4 vols. Madrid: Imprenta de Colegio de Sordo-Mudos, 1851–1852.

Seed, Patricia. "'Are These Not Also Men?': The Indians' Humanity and Capacity for Spanish Civilization." *Journal of Latin American Studies* 25, no. 3 (October 1993): 629–52.

Shafer, Robert J. *The Economic Societies in the Spanish World, 1763–1821.* Syracuse: Syracuse University Press, 1958.

Siebzehner, Batia. *La universidad americana y la Illustración: Autoridad y conocimiento en Nueva España y el Río de la Plata Madrid:* Editorial Mapfre, 1992.

Sierra, Catalina. *El nacimiento de México.* 2d ed. Mexico: Miguel Angel Porrúa, 1984.

Siles Salinas, Jorge. *La independencia de Bolivia.* Madrid: Editorial Mapfre, 1992.

Silva, Renan. "La revolución francesa en el 'Papel Periódico de Santafé de Bogotá.'" *CARAVELLE: Cahiers du Monde Hispanique et Luso-Bresilien* 54 (1990):165–78.

Silva Castro, Raúl. *Egaña y la Patria Vieja, 1810–1814.* Santiago: Editorial Andrés Bello, 1959.

Solís, Ramón. *El Cádiz de las Cortes. Vida en la ciudad en los años 1810 a 1813.* Madrid: Editorial Alianza, 1969.

Spain, Cortes. *Colección de decretos y orderes de las Cortes Cádiz.* 2 vols. Madrid: Cortes Generales, 1987.

Diario de las sesiones de Cortes: Legislatura de 1821. 3 vols. Madrid: Imprenta de J. A. García, 1871–1873.

Steele, Arthur R. *Flowers for the King: The Expeditions of Ruiz and Pavón and the Flora of Peru.* Durham: Duke University Press, 1964.

Stein, Stanley, "Bureaucracy and Business in the Spanish Empire, 1759–1804: Failure of a Bourbon Reform in Mexico and Peru." *Hispanic American Historical Review* 61, no. 1 (February 1981):2–28.

"Reply." *Hispanic American Historical Review* 62, no 3 (August 1982):469–77.

Stevenson, William B. *Historical and Descriptive Narrative of Twenty Years Residence in South America.* 3 vols. London: Hurst, Robinson, and Co., 1825.

Stoan, Stephen K. *Pablo Morillo and Venezuela, 1815–1820.* Columbus: Ohio State University Press, 1974.

Street, John. *Artigas and the Emancipation of Uruguay.* Cambridge: Cambridge University Press, 1959.

Suárez, Federico. *Cortes de Cádiz.* 2 vols. Pamplona: Ediciones Universidad de Navarra, 1967–1968.

La crisis política del antiguo régimen en España, 1800–1840. 2d ed. Madrid: Ediciones Rialp, 1958.

Suárez, Francisco. *Tratado de las leyes y de Dios legislador,* translated by Jaime Torrubiano Ripoll. Madrid: Reus, 1918.

Super, John. *La vida en Querétaro durante la colonia, 1531–1810.* Mexico: Fondo de Cultura Económica, 1983.

Tandrón, Humberto. *El Real Consulado de Caracas y el comercio exterior de Venezuela.* Caracas: Universidad Central de Venezuela, 1976.

Taylor, William. *Magistrates of the Sacred: Priests and Parishioners in Eighteenth-Century Mexico.* Stanford: Stanford University Press, 1996.

Tena Ramírez, Felipe, ed. *Leyes fundamentales de México, 1808–1991.* 16th ed. Mexico: Editorial Porrúa, 1991.

TePaske, John J. "The Financial Disintegration of the Royal Government in Mexico during the Epoch of Independence." In *The Independence of Mexico and the Creation of the New Nation,* edited by Jaime E. Rodríguez O., 63–83. Los Angeles: University of California, Los Angeles, Latin American Center, 1989.

Terán Najas, Rosemarie. *Los proyectos del Imperio borbónico en la Real Audiencia de Quito.* Quito: Abya-Yala, 1988.

Thompson, Lawrence S. *Printing in Colonial Spanish America.* Hamden: Anchor, 1962.

Tjarks, Germán O. E. *El Consulado de Buenos Aires y sus proyecciones en la historia del Río de la Plata.* 2 vols. Buenos Aires: Universidad de Buenos Aires, 1962.

Torquemada, Juan de. *Monarquía indiana,* edited by Miguel León-Portilla. 7 vols. Mexico: Universidad Nacional Autónoma de México, 1975–1983.

Torre Reyes, Carlos de la. *La Revolución de Quito del 10 de Agosto de 1809.* Quito: Ministerio de Educación, 1961.

Torre Villar, Ernesto de la, ed. *Los Guadalupes y la independencia.* 2d ed. Mexico: Editorial Jus, 1985.

Torres, Camilo. "Memorial de agravios." In *Pensamiento político de la emancipación,* edited by José Luis Romero and Luis Alberto Romero, 34–5. Caracas: Biblioteca de Ayacucho, 1977.

Tutino, John. *From Insurrection to Revolution in Mexico: Social Bases of Agrarian Violence, 1750–1940.* Princeton: Princeton University Press, 1986.

Tyrer, Robson. *Historia demográfica y económica de la Audiencia de Quito.* Quito: Banco Central del Ecuador, 1988.

Uribe Uran, Victor Manuel. "Kill All the Lawyers!: Lawyers and the Independence Movement in New Granada, 1809–1820." *The Americas* 52, no. 2 (October 1995):175–210.

———. "Rebellion of the Young Mandarins: Lawyers, Political Parties, and the State in Colombia, 1780–1850." Ph.D. diss., University of Pittsburgh, 1993.

Uslar Pietri, Juan. *Historia de la rebelión popular de 1814.* Paris: Ediciones Soberbia, 1954.

Valdes, Dennis Nodín. "The Decline of the Sociedad de Castas in Mexico City." Ph.D. diss., University of Michigan, Ann Arbor, 1978.

Valencia Avarla, Luis, ed. *Anales de la República.* 2 vols. Santiago: Imprenta Universitaria, 1951.

Valencia Llano, Alonso. "Elites, burocracia, clero y sectores populares en la Independencia Quiteña (1809–1812)." *Procesos: Revista ecuatoriana de historia* 3 (1992):55–101.

Van Young, Eric. "Millennium in the Northern Marches: The Mad Messiah of Durango and Popular Rebellion in Mexico, 1800–1815." *Comparative Studies in History and Society* 28, no. 3 (July 1986):385–413.

———. "Quetzalcóatl, King Ferdinand, and Ignacio Allende Go to the Seashore: Or Messianism and Mystical Kingship in Mexico, 1800–1821." In *The Independence of Mexico and the Creation of the New Nation,* edited by Jaime E. Rodríguez O., 109–27. Los Angeles: University of California, Los Angeles, Latin American Center, 1989.

Varela, Luis V. *Historia constitucional de la República Argentina.* 4 vols. Buenos Aires: Taller de Impresiones Oficiales, 1910.

Varela Tortajada, Javier. "La élite ilustrada ante las nuevas ideas: Actitudes y contradicciones." In *España y la Revolución francesa,* edited by Enrique Moral Saldoval, 55–72. Madrid: Editorial Pablo Iglesias, 1989.

Vargas Ugarte, Rubén. *Historia General del Perú.* 6 vols. Lima: Carlos Milla Batres, 1966.

Vega, Josefa. "Los primeros préstamos de la guerra de independencia." *Historia Mexicana* 39, no. 4 (April–June 1990):919–31.

Velasco, Juan de. *Historia del Reino de Quito en la América meridional.* In *Padre Juan de Velasco S.I.* Biblioteca Ecuadoriana Mínima, 2 vols. Puebla: Editorial Cajica, 1961.

Venezuela. Academia Nacional de Historia. *La Constitución Federal de Venezuela de 1811.* Caracas: Academia Nacional de Historia, 1959.

Textos oficiales de la Primera República. 2 vols. Caracas: Academia Nacional de Historia, 1959.

Ventura Beleño, Eusebio. *Recopilación sumaria de los autos acordados de la Real Audiencia y Sala del Crimen de esta Nueva España,* edited by María del Refugio González. 2 vols. Mexico: Universidad Nacional Autónoma de México, 1981.

Vergara Arias, Gustavo. *Montoneras y guerrillas indígenas en la etapa de la emancipación del Perú.* Lima: Editorial Salesiana, 1973.

Vidaurre, Manuel de. *Manifiesto sobre la nulidad de las elecciones que a nombre de los países ultramarinos se practicaron en Madrid por algunos americanos el día de 28 y 29 de mayo del año de 1820.* Madrid: Imprenta de Vega, 1820.

Villalobos R., Sergio. *El comercio y contrabando en el Río de la Plata y Chile.* Buenos Aires: Universidad de Buenos Aires, 1965.

Tradición y reforma en 1810. Santiago: Universidad de Chile, 1961.

Warren, Harris G. "The Origin of General Mina's Invasion of Mexico." *Southwestern Historical Quarterly* 52 (July 1938):1–20.

"Xavier Mina's Invasion of Mexico." *Hispanic American Historical Review* 23 (February 1943):52–76.

Warren, Richard A. "Vagrants and Citizens: Politics and the Poor in Mexico City, 1808–1836." Ph.D. diss., University of Chicago, 1994.

Washburn, Douglas A. "The Bourbon Reforms: A Social and Economic History of the Audiencia of Quito, 1760–1810." Ph.D. diss., University of Texas, Austin, 1984.

Webster, C. K., ed. *Britain and the Independence of Latin America, 1812–1830.* 2 vols. London: Oxford University Press, 1968.

Whitaker, Arthur P. "Changing and Unchanging Interpretations of the Enlightenment in Spanish America." In *The Ibero-American Enlightenment,* edited by A. Owen Aldridge, 21–57. Urbana: University of Illinois Press, 1971.

White, Richard Alan. *Paraguay's Autonomous Revolution, 1810–1840.* Albuquerque: University of New Mexico Press, 1978.

Williams, John Hoyt. "Governor Velasco, the Portuguese and the Paraguayan Revolution of 1811." *The Americas* 28, no. 4 (April 1972):441–9.

The Rise and Fall of the Paraguayan Republic, 1810–1870. Austin: University of Texas Press, 1979.

Wold, Ruth. *Diario de México: Primer cotidiado de Nueva España.* Madrid: Editorial Gredos, 1970.

Zúniga, Neptalí. *Juan Pío Montúfar y Larrea.* Quito: Talleres Gráficos Nacionales, 1945.

Index

Absolutism, 169–74, 180, 192–4, 232–4

Abascal, José Fernando de, 66, 142,143,144, 147,168, 180

Abasolo, Mariano, 160

African: origin population, 82, 86, 91–2, 239

Alausí, Kingdom of Quito, 148, 223

Alamán, Lucas, 200, 203

Alberti, Manuel, 124

Alegre, Javier, 17

Allende, Ignacio, 160, 163

Alvarez, Manuel Bernardo, 151

Alvarez Jonte, Antonio, 129

Alvear, Carlos María de, 129, 176

Alzaga, Martín de, 57, 58, 129

Alzate, José Antonio, 18, 45

Amar y Borbón, Antonio, 69–70, 71, 150–2

Ambato, Kingdom of Quito,148

América Meridional (South America), 1, 79, 196, 213, 242

América Septentrional (North America), 78–9, 166, 196, 213

American deputies to the Cortes, 3, 82–92, 103, 149, 152, 164, 195–6, 199–200, 202–4

American Question, 83–92, 200–4

Americans, 2, 20, 63; autonomy of, 107–9; conflicts of, 108–9; Consulado de México's view of, 85; demand equality, 61, 83–8; loyalty of, 52, 58–9; sense of identity, 13–19, 48, social structure of, 11–12.

Andes, 181, 190

Andrien, Kenneth, 33

Angostura, Congress of, 187, 219, 220, 240

Antioquia, New Granada, 155, 156

Aranda, Conde de, 49

Archer, Christon I., 159, 175

Areche, Antonio de, 23–4

Aréchega, Tomás, 69, 144

Arismendi, Juan Bautista, 171, 191

Argüelles, Agustín, 87, 88, 105

Army of the Andes, 180, 181. *See also* Army of the West

Army of the North, 177, 178, 179, 180. *See also* Army of Peru

Army of Peru, 179. *See also* Army of the North

Army of the Three Guarantees, 208, 209

Army of the West, 177, 178, 180. *See also* Army of the Andes

Arredondo, Manuel, 144

Artigas, José Gervasio, 129, 130, 134–6, 178

Artola, Miguel, 59

Asunción, Paraguay, 133

audiencias, 7, 21, 22, 87

autonomists, 174; in Chile, 179–81; and Constitution of 1812, 196–7; and monarchies, 174–5; in South America, 174, 179

autonomy, 2, 64, 77–8, 94–5, 163, 164, 168, 172, 173

Aymerich, Melchor, 197–8, 224

ayuntamiento, 21, 96, 174, 194, 239–40; constitutional, 87, 89, 92; elections by,

267